PENGUIN REFERENCE BOOKS

THE PENGUIN DICTIONARY
OF CIVIL ENGINEERING

12.9.88

John S. Scott, who was born in 1915, is a chartered structural and mining engineer, a certified colliery manager, and a qualified linguist. He has worked in Austria, France, Saudi Arabia and the UK and has spent ten years in civil engineering, but now writes books all the time. He is married, has six children and lives in London.

Brock

THE PENGUIN DICTIONARY OF
CIVIL ENGINEERING

JOHN S. SCOTT

Illustrated by
Clifford Bayliss

Cross-referenced to *A Dictionary of Building*
(Penguin Reference Book 1979)

Third Edition

PENGUIN BOOKS

Penguin Books Ltd, 27 Wrights Lane, London W8 5TZ (Publishing and Editorial)
and Harmondsworth, Middlesex, England (Distribution and Warehouse)
Viking Penguin Inc., 40 West 23rd Street, New York, New York 10010, USA
Penguin Books Australia Ltd, Ringwood, Victoria, Australia
Penguin Books Canada Ltd, 2801 John Street, Markham, Ontario, Canada L3R 1B4
Penguin Books (NZ) Ltd, 182–190 Wairau Road, Auckland 10, New Zealand

First published 1958
Second edition 1965
Reprinted 1967
Third edition 1980
Reprinted 1981, 1984, 1985, 1987

Copyright © John S. Scott, 1958, 1965, 1980
All rights reserved

Made and printed in Great Britain by
Hazell Watson & Viney Limited,
Member of the BPCC Group,
Aylesbury, Bucks
Set in Monotype Times

PREFACE TO THIRD EDITION

At the time of this revision in 1979, metrication, which had started with the building industry and its corresponding government departments in 1970, was half completed in the UK. The BSI had metricated, so had several large nationalized industries including the National Coal Board and British Steel, but others had not. Feet, inches, yards, pounds, acres and miles have therefore occasionally been left in, but new emphasis has been given to kilograms, kilometres, metres, centimetres and millimetres. Newtons (N), newtons per square metre (N/m^2), pascals (Pa) and bars have been introduced to the text.

There is a bewildering variety of choice and little authoritative guidance, even from the continent of Europe where the Système International (SI) originated. In practice, for stress in metals the N/mm^2 is widely used, since it is conveniently large (1 N/mm^2 = 145 psi) though the meganewton per square metre or megapascal might serve equally well (1 N/mm^2 = 1 MN/m^2 = 1 MPa). For modulus of elasticity, a unit 1000 times larger is convenient and the GN/m^2 has been used, though the kN/mm^2 might be more logical. For soil stresses, which are much smaller than metal stresses, common units are kN/m^2 (1 kN/m^2 = 0·145 psi).

The bar had legal status on the continent of Europe and is still widely used there (10 bars = 1 N/mm^2 = 145 psi), being roughly one atmosphere. The standard atmosphere is slightly different: 760 mm mercury = 0·101 N/mm^2.

Another unit widely used on the European continent is the 'technical' atmosphere of 1 kg/cm^2 or 1 kilopond/cm^2 (kp/cm^2). Roughly equivalent to 1 bar and to 10 metres of water, it is almost exactly 0·098 N/mm^2.

When in doubt refer to BS 350 'Conversion Factors'.

J. S. S.

ACKNOWLEDGEMENTS

The publications of the British Standards Institution and of the American Society for Testing and Materials are recommended to readers, so are those of the engineering institutions. The author is grateful to J. H. G. Cook, Douglas Day, Jack Senior and other engineers who have told him of mistakes. He would be happy to insert other corrections in the next edition.

Although the pronoun 'he' is used for convenience when referring to those employed in civil engineering, this should now read 'he' or 'she' as women are entering the field in increasing numbers.

ABBREVIATIONS

See also Units and Conversion Factors, p. 9

(1) *Abbreviations indicating the branch of engineering for each entry (given in square brackets at the beginning of the entry)*

air sur.	photogrammetry	sewage	sewage treatment and
d.o.	drawing office practice		sewerage
elec.	electrical engineering	s.m.	soil mechanics
hyd.	hydraulics and hydrology	stat.	statistics
mech.	mechanical engineering	stru.	structural design
min.	mining	sur.	topographical or mine
rly	railways		surveying
r.m.	rock mechanics		

Most of these headings are briefly described in the text.

(2) *Abbreviations of units (in singular or plural)*

AC	alternating current	kg	kilogram
bhp	brake horsepower	kJ	kilojoule
BThU or Btu	British thermal unit	km	kilometre
cc	cubic centimetre (millilitre)	kN	kilonewton
cm	centimetre	kN/m²	kilonewtons per square
cu. ft	cubic foot		metre
cu. m or m³	cubic metre	kph	kilometres per hour
cu. yd or yd³	cubic yard	lb	pound
DC	direct current	m	metre
dia.	diameter	m³	cubic metre
E	modulus of elasticity	mg	milligram
fpm	feet per minute	MN/m²	meganewtons per square
ft	feet		metre
g	gram or gravity	mPa	megapascal
	(acceleration)	mm	millimetre
gpm	gallons per minute	Pa	pascal
I	moment of inertia	psi	pounds per square inch
in.	inch	rpm	revolutions per minute
J	joule	sec.	second

(3) *Abbreviations of authorities*

AASHO	American Association of State Highway Officials
ACI	American Concrete Institute
ASCE	American Society of Civil Engineers (ASCE MEP refers to this Society's Manuals of Engineering Practice, of which 55 had been published by 1979)
ASTM	American Society for Testing and Materials
BS (or BSS)	British Standard (Specification)
BSI	British Standards Institution
Inst. C.E. or I.C.E.	Institution of Civil Engineers, London
Inst. Struct. E.	Institution of Structural Engineers, London

CROSS-REFERENCES

Cross-references in text are indicated by italic type, those to the *Dictionary of Building* by the letter (*B*).

The great bulk of the terms used in building and civil engineering has forced the publisher to divide the material into two volumes, a *Dictionary of Building* and a *Dictionary of Civil Engineering*. Since many terms have two or more senses, these senses are likely to be listed separately in the two volumes. It will help the reader if he will first study the list of subject abbreviations at the beginning of each book, which is a rough guide to its contents. Some other subjects, less easily allocated to one of the books, are in the list below.

Dictionary of Civil Engineering

concrete, reinforced concrete, prestressed concrete, cast iron, wrought iron, and steels

welding

underpinning, bridges, space frames, timber preservation, concrete formwork

scientific terms such as dewpoint, electro-osmosis, geomorphology

lightweight concretes

Dictionary of Building

building trades, their tools and materials including plastics

brazing, soldering, capillary joints, silver brazing

carpentry, timber houses, shoring of buildings, air houses

contracts, bills of quantities, quantity surveying

heating and ventilation, insulating materials and techniques, degree-days

UNITS AND CONVERSION FACTORS

See also BS 350, Conversion Factors

Lengths

25·4 millimetres = 1 inch
39·37 inches = 3·281 ft = 1 metre
5280 ft = 1760 yd = 1 mile = 1·609 kilometre = 1609 metres
1 international sea mile = 1852 metres
1 fathom = 6 ft = 1·829 metres

Areas

645 sq. mm = 6·45 sq. cm = 1 sq. inch
10·76 sq. ft = 1 sq. metre = 1·196 sq. yd
100 sq. metres = 1 are = 119·6 sq. yd
10,000 sq. metres = 100 ares = 1 hectare = 2·47 acres
1,000,000 sq. m = 100 hectares = 1 sq. kilometre (km)
4840 sq. yd = 1 acre = 0·4047 hectare
1 sq. (Gunter's) chain = 484 sq. yd = 0·1 acre
640 acres = 1 sq. mile = 2·59 sq. km

Volumes

There are three different gallons in use in the English-speaking world. The imperial gallon of Britain is so called to distinguish it from the two others, one wet and one dry, in use in the USA. Generally the wet US gallon, 0·833 of the imperial gallon, is the only one that concerns engineers.

1 imperial gallon of water weighs 10 lb (4·546 kg)
62·4 lb of water occupy 1 cubic ft = 6·24 imperial gallons
1 US wet gallon = 0·833 imperial gallon = 3·785 litres
1 US dry gallon = 0·967 imperial gallon = 4·404 litres
1 imperial gallon = 4·546 litres
1 litre of water weighs 1 kg and occupies 0·22 of an imperial gallon
1 US barrel (bbl.) contains 5·62 cu. ft (or 4 cu. ft or 376 lb)
35·28 cu. ft = 1 cu. metre
1 acre foot = 43,560 cu. ft = 1235 cu. metres

Weights

16 ounces = 1 pound (lb) = 454 grams (g)
112 lb = 1 hundredweight (cwt)
20 cwt = 2240 lb = 1 long ton = 1016 kilograms (kg)
1 US cental = 100 lb
20 centals = 1 short ton = 2000 lb = 2 kilopounds (kips)
50 kg = 1 $\left\{ \begin{array}{l} \text{Zentner} \\ \text{quintal} \end{array} \right\}$ = 110 lb = 0·98 cwt
But 100 kg = 1 quintal métrique
1000 kg = 1 tonne = 2200 lb
1 US sack (or bag) of cement weighs 94 lb = ¼ barrel
112 lb of cement is taken as occupying 1·25 cu. ft

1 Canadian bag of cement weighs 87·5 lb
1 UK bag of cement weighs 50 kg
1 tonne = 1000 kilograms (kg)
1 kg force (kilopond (kp)) = 9·81 newton

Pressure, stress, force per unit area

1 pascal (Pa) = 1 newton per sq. metre (N/m^2) = 0·000,145 psi
1,000,000 Pa = 1 megapascal (MPa) = 1 N/mm^2 = 1,000,000 N/m^2 = 1 MN/m^2
        = 10 bar = 10,000 millibar = 145 psi = 0·065 ton/in^2
1 'technical' atmosphere = 1 kg/cm^2 = 14·2 psi = about 1 bar (and 10 m water pressure)
1 'standard' atmosphere = 760 mm mercury = 101·325 kPa
1 psi = 6895 Pa = 6895 N/m^2 = 0·06895 bar

Energy, work and power

SI units: 1 joule = 1 newton-metre = 1 watt-second = 1 pascal-cubic metre
1 kilogram-metre = 7·233 foot-pounds = 9·81 N-m = 9·81 joules
1 horsepower USA (and British) = 746 watts = 76 kg-m/sec. = 550 ft-lb/sec.
But 1 metric horsepower = 75 kg-m/sec.
Thus 1 USA (and British) horsepower = 1·014 metric horsepower

Heat and insulation

273 kelvin = 0 degree Celsius (formerly 0 degree Centigrade) but the interval between degrees Kelvin and degrees C is the same, so 373 K = 100°C
1 British thermal unit = 0·252 kilogram-calorie = 1055 joules = 1·055 kJ
1 Btu/lb = 2·326 kilojoule/kilogram

Thermal conductivity, k-value
1 Btu/in. sq. ft hour degree F = 0·144 watt/metre degree C
Therefore to translate k imperial to k metric, divide by 7

Thermal transmittance, U-value
(for a particular wall or roof of known thickness)
1 Btu/sq. ft hour degree F = 5·68 watt/m^2 degree C
To translate U-value imperial to U-value metric, multiply by 5·7

USE AND MISUSE OF SI UNITS

There are at least two ways of using dimensions:

1. As on the engineer's working drawing, where everything is precisely dimensioned to the nearest millimetre or less, and precision is the main aim.

2. The conversational mode, in which one speaks of a 50-gallon drum, a 100-yard race, a saw with 22 teeth per inch or a file with 3 cuts per centimetre.

For the first mode, SI units are appropriate. For the second, they may be unsuitable though often the convenience of the metric system is a help. This text makes wide use of centimetres for this reason. Centimetres are used where millimetres are unwieldy because of their implied precision or because they are simply too small. A file with 3 cuts per cm has 0·33 of a cut per mm. This would not be a good way of describing a file from any viewpoint.

A

AASHO The American Association of State Highway Officials.

abaca *See* fibre rope.

Abney level [sur.] *A hand level* used for taking levels up steep slopes and as a *clinometer*.

Abrams' law A law discovered by Duff Abrams in USA and earlier (1892) in France by Féret. It states that the strength of a concrete or mortar depends inversely on the weight of water divided by the weight of cement in the mix. The lowest *water/cement ratio* which can be handled without *vibration* is about 0·45. The minimum amount of water necessary for the chemical action of the setting of cement is about 0·25 but more than this is needed in order to wet the sand and stone. Therefore even *vibrated concrete* or *vacuum concrete* must not be reduced to a water/cement ratio below about 0·35.

abscissa *See* graph.

absolute humidity *See* humidity of air.

absorbing well or **well drain** A *well* to drain away water. *See also* **vertical sand drain**.

absorption loss [hyd.] Losses of water which occur during the first filling of a reservoir in the wetting of rocks and soil. *Compare* seepage.

absorption pit A *soakaway*. *Compare* **disposal well**.

abutment A support of an arch or bridge, which usually resists a horizontal force from an arch, as well as its weight. *See* **arch dam, prestressed concrete**, *and* (*B*).

abutment wall *See* **wing wall**.

Abyssinian well A pointed, perforated tube driven into the ground by sledge hammer or by ramming with a light *pile hammer*. Water can be extracted from it by pumping. It is the ancestor of the *wellpoint*.

accelerated curing The use of an artifici-ally heated, moist environment to cure concrete and so increase its early and mature strengths. *Steam curing* is a common method. The temperature rise of the concrete should not exceed 15°C per hour for the first three hours and 35°C per hour thereafter, otherwise the ultimate strength of the concrete may be reduced. Accelerated curing cannot be used with *high-alumina cement*, nor should it be used with concrete containing *calcium chloride*.

accelerator A substance such as calcium chloride, $CaCl_2$, added in small quantities (max 0·03% of the cement) to plain concrete to hasten its hardening rate, or its set, or both. *Compare* **retarder**. *See* **admixture**, *also* (*B*).

accidental error [sur.] *Compensating error.*

accuracy [sur.] Accuracy is nearness to truth and is measured by the *deviation* of a measurement from the *average*. Absolute accuracy is unobtainable. The practical limits of accuracy in building are about 3 mm for the placing of walls and floors, and about 20 mm for long tunnels meeting in the centre of mountains. *Compare* **precision**.

acid steel Steel made by a process in which the furnace is lined with *silica* refractory, or in which the flux is silica. *Compare* **basic steel**.

acoustic strain gauge A *strain gauge* for measuring the extension or shortening of parts of a structure by tight wires fixed into them. If plucked, these wires emit a note which becomes higher when they are stretched and lower when they are shortened. An instrument, which was developed by the *Building Research Establishment* (*B*), can record a strain of one-millionth.

acre foot [hyd.] A unit of measure for the capacity of a reservoir, the volume contained in 1 acre of water 1 foot deep. *See* conversion factors, p. 9.

Ac system *See* **airfield soil classification.**

activated sludge process [sewage] Treatment of the *effluent* from *primary treatment* (sedimentation) by blowing air through it in an aeration tank for several hours, followed by settlement in a *secondary sedimentation* tank. Of the *sludge* that settles out, a proportion (activated sludge) is returned to the inlet of the aeration tank, the remainder (waste sludge) flows away for *de-watering* and disposal. The returned sludge, that has been activated by several hours' aeration and has separated in the sedimentation tank, inoculates the incoming effluent (or influent) with its flourishing microbial population. The process is much more efficient than a *trickling filter*, in that it needs only one seventh of the land area for the same volume of sewage but it also needs expensive, skilled, careful supervision to operate the compressors and other mechanical plant. Consequently it is almost universally used for the large treatment plants of cities.

active earth pressure [s.m.] The horizontal push from earth on to a wall. The active earth force from sand on to a *free retaining wall* is equivalent to that from a fluid of density ·25 to ·30 times that of the sand. The force from sand on to a *fixed retaining wall* is very much more. For clays the force is more complicated and even for sand it is not safe to assume that the centre of gravity of the force is at one third of the height of the wall. The centre of gravity may often be higher than this. *See* **earth pressure, passive earth pressure, Rankine's theory, yield.**

active layer [s.m.] The layer at the surface of the ground, which moves seasonally as the soil-volume changes, expanding when frozen in winter, and shrinking when it thaws and dries in summer. *Foundations* should be laid below the active layer. *See* **permafrost.**

additive *See* **admixture.**

additive constant [sur.] In *stadia work*, a length added to the product of the *intercept* on the staff and the *multiplying constant* to give the true distance between telescope centre and staff. It is often less than 0·3 m. *See* **anallatic telescope.**

adhesion or **bond** The sticking together of structural parts by mechanical or chemical bonding using a *cement* or glue. Timber parts are stuck with glue, bricks are bonded in mortar, and steel is bonded to concrete by its adhesion with the cement. *See also* **specific adhesion, mechanical bond.**

adit [min.] or **drift** A nearly level tunnel driven to underground workings. Adits usually have a slight slope for water to drain towards the entrance. *See* **khanat.**

adjusting screw [sur.] A finely threaded screw on a surveying instrument to give it the final adjustment for level, focus, or position. *See* **clip screws.**

adjustment [sur.] (1) or **balancing** When a series of survey observations is inconsistent within itself, an adjustment is made to each observation so that it becomes consistent with the others. For instance if the 3 angles of a triangle do not add up to 180° but to 180°+03 minutes, one minute of arc is subtracted from each angle. *See* **Bowditch's rule.**

(2) An operation carried out on the *bubbles*, *foot screws*, centring device, etc., of a surveying instrument to make the instrument truly level, the bubble truly parallel with the line of sight, etc. An adjustment may be *permanent* or *temporary*.

admixture or **additive** In *concrete*, plaster, etc., a substance other than *aggregate*, *cement*, or water, added in small quantities to the *mix* to alter its properties or those of the hard concrete. The most important admixtures for concrete are *accelerators*, *air-entraining agents*, *plasticizers* and *retarders* but there are many others including anti-frost, bonding, colouring, corrosion-inhibiting, damp-proofing, expanding, fungicidal, gas-forming, germicidal, grouting, insecticidal, and non-shrinking agents. *See* BS 5075.

adopted street *See* **dedicated street.**

adsorption Condensation of a film of gas or liquid on the surface of a solid. *See* **held water.**

advanced waste water treatment [sewage] Removal of the nutrients – nitrates, ammonia, phosphates and other soluble matter – from an effluent, enabling it to be used directly as a *raw water* for domestic or industrial purposes. De-nitrification often takes place as part of secondary treatment but if an additional stage is needed, this is called 'advanced treatment'.

aeolian [s.m.] Wind-blown, a description often applied to *loess*.

aerated concrete Aerated concrete is in reality foamed calcium silicate, but the names aerated concrete, gas concrete, and foamed concrete are probably too well established to be changed. It has only three essential constituents, since it does not need the sand and stone which are essential to concrete. It needs only binder (cement or lime or a mixture of the two), water, and gas bubbles (which later fill with air). The bubbles are usually made by aluminium powder reacting with the lime of the binder. Air bubbles may also be made, by whisking with an *air-entraining* agent or similar *admixture*. Commercial practice includes a number of other admixtures which improve foaming or reduce the cost of binder (*fly-ash* instead of cement). The two main sorts of aerated concrete are the *autoclaved* factory-made variety, subjected to curing under high steam-pressure for some 10–20 hours, and the site-cast variety, which is much weaker than the autoclaved concrete but is nevertheless useful for insulating steam pipes, etc. In countries where high insulation in walls and roofs is essential (Sweden, Canada) the lightweight autoclaved reinforced floor beams and wall panels, about 0·4 m wide and up to 6 m long, have

become extremely popular. In fact 70% of new factory roofing is made with them in Sweden, where they originated. Aerated concretes are made at any density from 0·4 to 1 g/cc (occasionally up to 1·44). At the lowest density the k-value is about 0·1 watt per metre degree C and the wet cube strength about 1·4 N/mm², whereas at 0·8 g/cc, k = 0·23 watt per metre degree C and the cube strength is 4·8 N/mm². The other autoclaved materials used in building are *sandlime bricks* (*B*). Cellular concrete is the US term for this material, which in Britain is called by its various makers Celcon, Durox, Siporex, and Thermalite. *See* **lightweight concretes.**

aeration tank [sewage] *See* **activated sludge process.**

aerial ropeway (In USA called **aerial tramway**) A line of towers carrying steel ropes which serve as tracks for buckets (called carriers) for coal, ore, or building material in mountainous regions or into the sea where a road, railway, bridge, or tunnel would be cumbersome or costly or slow to build. It differs from a *cableway* in that it has more than 2 towers. Loads vary up to 1 ton and speeds may be up to 150 m/min. For different types *see* **bi-cable/continuous/jig back/monocable/twin-cable ropeways.**

aerial surveying *Photogrammetry*.

aerial tramway American term for an *aerial ropeway*.

aerodynamic instability [stru.] Flutter during wind, which is so large as to endanger a structure, a term used to describe the failure of the *Tacoma Narrows bridge*. *See* **Golden Gate bridge.**

A-frame [stru.] A *frame* which may or may not be symmetrical but consists generally of two sloping legs joined at the top and braced farther down by a horizontal or diagonal brace. An A-pole is a wooden A-frame.

aftercooler [mech.] A cooler inserted in the compressed-air circuit between the compressors and the mine (or other consumer of air) to cool and dehumidify the air and reduce its volume, and thus effectively increase the capacity of the pipeline. *See* **intercooler**.

ageing (aging in USA) An alteration in the strength properties of a material with time, usually a strengthening or hardening, such as with duralumin after heat treatment, mild steel after cold working, concrete throughout its life, or plywood a few days after it has been glued. Age-hardening implies embrittlement because of age.

agent In a civil engineering *contract (B)*, the person who legally represents the contractor and acts for him on all occasions. He is often a civil engineer.

aggregate Broken stone, slag, gravel, sand, or similar inert material which forms a substantial part of *concretes*, *asphalts* or *roads* including *macadam*. Aggregate is described as coarse if it stays on a screen with holes 5 mm square, and as sand or fine aggregate if it passes through them.

aggregate/cement ratio The weight of aggregate divided by the weight of cement in a concrete.

aging *See* **ageing**.

agitating truck or **lorry** A *truck mixer*.

Aglite A UK *lightweight aggregate* made from *expanded clay (B)*.

agonic line [sur.] A line on a map of the earth along which the magnetic *declination* is zero.

agricultural drain A *field drain*.

A-horizon [s.m.] The uppermost of the three layers (A-, B-, C-) of soil science. Its upper part accumulates organic matter from plant roots while its lower part is *leached* of its soluble constituents and fine grains into the *B-horizon. See* **podzol**.

air base [air sur.] The distance between the exposure stations of adjacent, overlapping aerial photographs. *See* **timing**.

air compressor *See* **compressor**.

air content of fresh concrete The air content of fresh concrete is measured, under BS 1881:1970, by applying air pressure to an enclosed sample of known volume and measuring the reduction in volume.

air embolism *Caisson disease*.

air-entrained concrete A concrete used for making roads. It has about 5% air and is therefore less dense than ordinary good concrete, but it has excellent frost resistance. The strength loss is roughly 5% for each 1% of air entrained.

air-entraining agent An *admixture* to concrete or cement, that drags small bubbles of air, about 1 mm or smaller in diameter, into the mix. The bubbles increase the workability, allowing both sand and water contents to be reduced. One agent used is vinsol resin, a residue from the distillation of pine tree stumps. The frost resistance of the concrete or mortar is improved both during setting and after hardening. *See* BS CP 110.

airfield soil classification [s.m.] or **Ac system** A soil *classification* published by Arthur Casagrande in USA in 1948. It is based on sieve analyses and on the *consistency limits. Cohesive* soils are divided into those with a *liquid limit* below or above 50%, the former being generally *silts* and the latter *clays*.

air-flush drilling Exploratory drilling using compressed air instead of water to cool the drilling bit and to clear the chippings. Developed in deserts where water was scarce, it is used also to drill water wells, etc., in the UK.

air-lift pump A pump consisting of two pipes hanging vertically in a well or sump (one may be within the other). Compressed air is injected into the larger pipe at its base from the smaller one. This air, as it expands and rises, reduces the density of the water in the larger pipe. The pressure of the water around the large pipe forces more water into it. The large pipe must be submerged to a considerable depth, but if this can be done, large volumes of very dirty water or mud can be pumped, at a high expense in compressed air. *See* **compound air lift, hydraulic ejector, mammoth pump.**

air lock [min.] A compartment with two airtight doors, one to a tunnel, caisson, etc., under excess air pressure, the other to an area at lower pressure. The air lock can thus give access between these two areas, but the two doors must never be open simultaneously. Similar air doors exist in mines to ensure that the ventilation is not short-circuited. *See* **man-lock, materials lock.**

airplane mapping *Photogrammetry.*

air pump *See* **vacuum pump.**

air survey A survey made by *photogrammetry.*

air valve [hyd.] A valve in a water pipe at a summit. It allows air but not water to pass out automatically.

air vessel [mech.] In the pipeline on the discharge side of a *reciprocating pump*, a small tank containing air, provided to even out the pulsations of the pump.

Akashi-Kaikyo Bridge A *suspension bridge* with a main span of 1780 m and two side spans of 890 m. This road bridge joining the Japanese islands of Honshu and Shikoku will probably be by far the world's largest single span when it is completed in 1988.

Alclad Trade name for aluminium alloy coated with pure aluminium to give high corrosion resistance. *See* **clad steel.**

alidade [sur.] or **sight rule** An instrument used in *plane-tabling*, placed on the table, used as a straight edge. It carries, above it, sights by which the straight edge can be aligned with the object. In USA the term is also applied to the telescope and its attachments on a *theodolite.*

align [sur.] To arrange in line; also spelt 'aline', mainly in USA.

alignment [sur.] (1) The fixing of points on the ground in the correct lines for setting out a road, railway, wall, transmission line, canal, etc.

(2) A ground plan showing a route, as opposed to a profile or section, which shows levels and elevations.

alignment chart A *nomogram.*

aline *See* **align.**

alloy A mixture of two or more metals made usually with the intention of combining their qualities.

alloy steel or **special steel** A *steel* which contains elements not in *carbon steel* or present in smaller amount. Carbon steels generally contain less than 5% all added together of the following metals, alloy steels contain much more: nickel, chromium, manganese, molybdenum, vanadium.

altar A step back in the wall of a dry dock, used for holding the feet of the wooden shores which steady the vessel when the dock is empty.

alternator [elec.] A machine which generates alternating current by the rotation of its rotor, driven usually by a steam or water *turbine* or other *prime mover.*

altitude [sur.] (1) The height of a place above sea level.

(2) The angular height of an object such as a star above the horizon.

altitude level [sur.] A precise *level tube* on the vernier of the vertical circle of a theodolite. It helps to measure vertical angles accurately.

alumina or **aluminium oxide** Al_2O_3 An important constituent of ordinary *clays* (in chemical combination), as well as of *corundum.*

aluminium (in USA **aluminum**) Chemical symbol Al. The most important element in *light alloys* (except magnesium alloys). A metal which has the low *specific gravity* of 2·70 and the low *ultimate tensile strength* (for a metal) of 93 N/mm^2. For this reason when used to carry load it is always *alloyed* to form stronger metals called light alloys. Its *reduction* is performed by *electrolysis* of *bauxite.*

aluminium oxide *Alumina.*

alumino-thermic reaction The chemical reaction which takes place when powdered aluminium is ignited with the oxides of other metals. The aluminium takes the oxygen from the other metals, burning fiercely, usually melting them. It is used for welding steel in the *thermit* process.

aluminous cement *See* **high-alumina cement.**

aluminum *See* **aluminium.**

American caisson *See* **box caisson.**

American Ephemeris and Nautical Almanac [sur.] An annual publication containing astronomical data for several years ahead, published by the Government Printing Office, Washington. *See* **Nautical Almanac.**

American Society for Testing and Materials or **ASTM** The main organization in USA that corresponds to the *British Standards Institution* in publishing standards.

American wire gage or **Brown and Sharp wire gage** Thicknesses of non-ferrous wire and sheet, some 25% different from *Standard wire gauge* (*B*).

amplitude The depth of a wave measured from the level of calm water. The word is used for every sort of wave. The double amplitude is twice the amplitude.

anallatic lens [sur.] The additional lens used in a telescope to make it internally focusing. When used for *stadia work* the *additive constant* is zero.

anallatic telescope [sur.] One in which for *stadia work* the *additive constant* is zero.

analogy A comparison between two effects, of which one is the better known. This comparison makes easier the understanding of the less well-known effect. The alternating current analogy is used in investigating tides, other electrical analogies in the *seepage* of water through sands, the *column analogy* and the *membrane analogy* in *structural analysis*. They often correspond to a similarity between the mathematical relationships.

analysis *See* **mechanical analysis, dimensional analysis, structural analysis.**

anchor A tie rod holding back a *sheet pile* retaining wall to a *dead man* buried in the ground behind it, or the whole assembly of tie and dead man.

See also **anchor bolt, dead man,** *and below.*

anchorage (1) or **anchor wall** A *dead man*. *See also* **cantilever bridge,** *and* **anchor,** etc. (*B*). (2) [stru.] An essential piece of *post-tensioning* equipment cast into the concrete at the end of a *tendon*. It grips the tendon and transfers load from the steel to the concrete with the minimum of slip.

anchorage distance The distance behind a quay wall at which the *dead man* must be placed so as to ensure that it will not slip with the quay wall, and that it anchors it effectively.

anchor and collar A heavy metal hinge for lock gates. It is built into the lock masonry and carries a projecting plate with a hole into which the *pintle* (*B*) of the gate drops.

anchor block A *dead man*.

anchor bolt or **foundation bolt** or **holding-down bolt** A bolt with its threaded part projecting from masonry or concrete and secured into it so as to hold down a steel building-frame against wind loads, or machinery against its own vibration. *See* **Lewis bolt, expansion bolt, Rawlbolt.**

anchor gate A gate like a canal lock gate, held in position at the top by the pintle of an *anchor and collar* or similar hinge.

anchor ice [hyd.] Ice on the bed of a stream.

anchoring spud *See* **spud.**

anchor pile A *pile* to take tension or sideways pull.

anchor plate A plate at the foot of an *anchor bolt*, buried in the concrete.

anchor tower A tower to which the leg of a *derrick* crane is anchored, when the crane is so high that it must be built on towers. There are two anchor towers and one *crane tower*.

anchor wall *See* **anchorage.**

aneroid barometer [sur.] A small barometer working on the principle of a sealed box which expands with a drop in air pressure and contracts with an increase in pressure. It is used in altimeters for aircraft and by surveyors in approximate measurements of altitude. *See* **barometric pressure.**

angle [stru.] or **angle bar** *See* **angle section.**

angle cleat A small bracket of *angle section* fixed in a horizontal position, normally to a wall or stanchion, to support or to locate a structural member.

angledozer A *bulldozer* with the mouldboard set at an angle so that it pushes earth partly sideways and partly ahead.

angle iron An *angle section.*

angle-iron smith [mech.] A skilled man who shapes and welds *angle sections*, directing the *strikers* who hammer the hot metal to shape round the pegs of a *template* (*B*).

angle of friction [mech.] In the study of bodies sliding on plane surfaces, the angle between the perpendicular to the surface and the resultant force (between the body and surface) when the body begins to slide.

angle of internal friction [s.m.] For quite dry or quite submerged soils without *cohesion* such as clean sands, the angle of internal friction is approximately the *angle of repose.* More precisely it is the angle ϕ in the equation: Shearing resistance of soil = Normal force on surface of sliding $\times \tan \phi$ where $\tan \phi$ is determined by experiment. ϕ is not related to absolute grain size but to the roughness and relative sizes of the particles, and is larger for angular, dense, well-graded sands than for loose, uniform, rounded sands. *See* **angle of shearing resistance.**

angle of repose [s.m.] For any given granular material the steepest angle to the horizontal at which a heaped surface will stand in stated conditions. *See* **angle of internal friction.**

angle of shearing resistance [s.m.] The value of ϕ in *Coulomb's equation* for cohesive soils, $s = c + p \tan \phi$. ϕ is determined by experiment. It is 0 for a saturated clay sheared without change of water content, but for most silts or clays in other conditions ϕ is not 0. *See* **angle of internal friction.**

angle section or **angle** or **angle bar** A *rolled steel* or other metal section shaped like an L, made in sizes up to about 0·2 m leg length. It may be equal or unequal in leg lengths.

anion An *ion* which moves to the *anode* in *electrolysis. See* **cation.**

anisotropic [stru.] Not *isotropic.*

annealed wire or **binding wire** Soft steel wire (usually called iron wire), used for binding *reinforcement.*

annealing Softening a metal (originally steel, now copper and other metals, as well as glass) by heating it to a suitable temperature and, for steel, holding it there for several hours, ending this treatment with gradual cooling. Annealing may remove stresses and weakness caused during casting, or brittleness, or it may produce machinability, softness, or cold-working properties. For copper, *see* **dead-soft temper** (*B*).

annual variation [sur.] The change each year in the magnetic *declination* of a place.

anode [elec.] The opposite *pole* from the *cathode* in *electrolysis.* The pole at which the basic chemical part of the salt (radical) collects or at which oxidation occurs. DC enters at the anode: to remember this, the *mnemonic* is: the anode is the in-ode.

anodizing or **anodic oxidation** A protective durable film of oxide formed by making a magnesium or aluminium alloy object the *anode* in a bath of chromic or sulphuric acid through which an electric current is passed. This oxide film can generally take any of a number of varied and brilliant dyes.

anticlastic or **saddleback shell** [stru.] A horse's saddle is curved up in front and behind to hold the rider in place. A saddleback shell is similarly curved, convex upwards in one direction and concave upwards at right angles to it. The shape occurs naturally in awnings or in tents with two or more tentpoles, in soap bubbles or in rubber sheet or other pure-tension materials, and is useful to structural engineers building shells in compressible materials, because of its stiffness and strength.

anti-crack reinforcement A close mesh of light steel rods or chicken-wire placed just below the surface of concrete to reduce surface cracking.

antidune [hyd.] A sandhill like a *dune* but formed at higher flow rates and with the steep face upstream.

anti-flood and tidal valve A *check valve* in a drain which is below flood level or high-tide level.

anti-friction metal *See* **white metal.**

anti-sag bar [stru.] or **sag bar** A vertical *tie rod* from the ridge of a truss down to the horizontal tie beam. It may also connect horizontal steel rails in wall framing or purlins in roofing, for the same reason, to reduce their deflection.

apparent horizon *See* **sensible horizon.**

apron (1) A *hard standing* in an airfield.

(2) [hyd.] A hard surface to the sea bed or to the bed or banks of a stream or canal to prevent *scour*. An apron may be of *bagwork*, *mass concrete*, *reinforced concrete*, timber or *rip-rap*, or a *mattress*. *See also* (*B*).

aquaplaning Skidding of motor vehicles on wet roads, or of aircraft on wet runways, a defect that can be avoided on concrete surfaces by roughening the surface texture during casting or by grooving the slab transversely afterwards.

aqueduct A conduit (which may include tunnel and bridge) for carrying water over long distances. The term is usually confined to water-carrying bridges. *Compare* **viaduct.**

aquiclude [hyd.] An *aquitard.*

aquifer [hyd.] Rock or soil that not only contains quantities of water but also yields it easily to a pipe or well that enters it. It must consequently be both porous and of high *permeability*, like uniformly sized gravel or fissured sandstone or limestone.

aquifuge [hyd.] Ground that neither contains nor transmits water in useful quantities. *Compare* **aquifer.**

aquitard, aquiclude [hyd.] A geological

formation of low *permeability*, that delays the flow of water from an *aquifer*. It may itself contain a large quantity of water, but gives it up too slowly to be considered an aquifer.

arbor [mech.] In USA a *mandrel* or a drive shaft.

arch [stru.] A *beam* curved usually in a vertical plane, for carrying heavy loads such as bridges or long-span roofs. Arches are made of any solid material but usually of *light alloy*, *prestressed concrete*, *steel* or *reinforced concrete*, stone, *mass concrete*, timber, or brick.

arch dam A *dam* which is held up by horizontal thrust from the sides of the valley (*abutments*). It must therefore be built on rock, as yielding ground would cause the dam to fail. It may be of concrete, stone, or brick, concrete being the commonest. In dams the *arch* is curved in a horizontal plane. *See* **gravity-arch dam.**

Archimedean screw [hyd.] An ancient water-lifting device. An inclined spirally-threaded pipe (or screw in a pipe) which turns and lifts water from its submerged lower end.

Archimedes, principle of *See* **principle of Archimedes.**

arch rib [stru.] A main load-bearing member of a ribbed *arch*, a local deepening of an arch.

arch ring (1) [stru.] The load-bearing part of an *arch*.

(2) *See* **ring.**

arc welding Many electric *fusion welding* processes for steel and other metals in which a hot electric arc (6000°C) is struck between the parent metal and an *electrode*. A filler rod provides the weld metal and may also be the electrode. Because the metal can melt completely, and usually does, strong joins can be made and these methods are among those most used for heavy or light structural work. *See* **atomic hydrogen, automatic, carbon-arc, electrogas, electroslag, manual metal-arc welding,** *also* B S 499.

are [sur.] The metric unit of area, 100

sq. metres. One hectare is 100 ares.

argon-arc welding [mech.] *See* **shielded-arc welding.**

arm [stru.] or **lever arm** (1) *See* **bending moment.**

(2) The arm of an *eccentricity* is the distance by which a force is out of centre, eccentric.

armour Permanent protection to a structure in water, provided by *tetrapods*, *rip-rap*, etc.

armoured cable [elec.] Electrical power cable used in mines, or buried under streets, with two layers of hard-steel wire wound in opposite directions round the cable (double wire armoured). *See also* (*B*).

armoured pipe [hyd.] Pipe made of plastics protected by steel wire. The first underwater armoured water supply pipe in Britain was laid in October 1973 between the Ayrshire coast and the Isle of Bute, 150 mm bore and 2 km long, in 8 hours.

Armstrong scale [d.o.] An *open-divided scale*, so arranged that eight different *scale* relationships are obtained. The eight scales are arranged in pairs on each edge thus: On one side are 3 in. and $1\frac{1}{2}$ in. to 1 ft; $\frac{3}{4}$ in. and $\frac{3}{8}$ in. to 1 ft. On the other side are 1 in. and $\frac{1}{2}$ in. to 1 ft; $\frac{1}{4}$ in. and $\frac{1}{8}$ in. to 1 ft. Armstrong scales are usually divided at the ends into inches but may be obtained divided instead into tenths of a foot.

arrest point [mech.] A *critical point.*

arrissing tool A tool like a *float* used in road-making to round off the edge of a concrete slab.

arrow [sur.] A short piece of stiff galvanized wire used for marking points on the ground temporarily.

arterial road A main *road*, *street*, or *avenue*, with tributary roads, etc., joining it. *Compare* **freeway, parkway.**

artesian well [hyd.] A well, nowadays usually a borehole, from which water flows without pumping. Because too much water is drawn from them, many artesian wells have become pumped wells. The first known to history were dug in Flanders, near Béthune, after 1100 A.D., into a fractured chalk bed that extended underground up into the hills of Artois and so provided ample water under pressure. Early North American artesian wells gushed to a height of 45 m, or so. Modern hydrologists have shown that some artesian pressure may be caused by sinking of the ground surface.

artificial cementing or **grouting** The permanent or temporary strengthening or waterproofing of rocks or loose soils through holes drilled or *jetted* into them. Three general methods in use for soils are each suitable for certain grain sizes: above 2 mm *cementation*; from 2 mm to 0·2 mm *injection* of either silicate (*Joosten process*) or bituminous emulsion; from 0·2 mm down to silt size, 0·002 mm, *freezing* is generally used but is of course only temporary, though ice is as strong and watertight as a moderately strong concrete. Stiff-fissured clays can also be cement grouted, other clays can be *electro-chemically* hardened. Where the range of void sizes is wide, it is usually economical to seal the large voids first with coarse grout, then to inject thin grout to seal the small voids. The four traditional procedures for grouting are: open-ended pipe, stage grouting, sleeve grouting, and claquage grouting. The open-ended pipe is the simplest technique, and suitable for coarse material like an open gravel. Stage grouting can be used in rock, drilling and grouting by stages of 1·5 to 3 m of hole at a time, re-drilling through each grouted length as the hole is deepened. Sleeve grouting involves the use of the *tube à manchette*. In claquage grouting, fine-grained soils can be penetrated by tongues of grout injected at high pressure, that compact the soil and reduce its permeability. The high pressure can lift the ground and may affect nearby structures. The finest solutions can be injected with solutions of water-soluble acrylamide or phenoplasts or polysaccharides, sometimes with a metal salt to give an insoluble precipitate. *See* base exchange.

artificial harbour A harbour formed by building one or more *breakwaters* round an area of sea.

artificial horizon [sur.] A saucer of mercury used for giving by reflection a truly horizontal direction when measuring *altitudes* with a *sextant*. *See* horizon.

artificial islands In the Arctic conditions of the Beaufort Sea, north of Canada, with ice floes endangering ships even in the summer, exploration wells for oil or gas are best drilled from land. The first artificial island there was built by *suction dredger* in August 1975 in 7 m of water behind a breakwater, built first 180 m long and 60–90 m wide. In less than 800 hours' dredging, 1·75 million cu. m of sand were placed using a 500 m long *floating pipeline*, achieving an island 97 m across and 5 m above sea level. Later a further island was built in 12 m of water, followed by another in 20 m depth. Other artificial islands have been built in easier seas.

artificial recharge [hyd.] Replenishment of ground water artificially through shafts, wells, pits or trenches, with water that has been used and sometimes treated either chemically or treated by sand filtration. The *recharge* water may also be from a lake or river. A great improvement in water quality can be achieved underground because the water may filter many hundreds of metres through air-filled ground. A beach that has been scoured can be artificially recharged by dumping on it sand or rock – often called beach replenishment.

asbestos [min.] A mineral silicate, consisting of fibrous crystals found in veins in rocks. The crystals are thin, tough fibres like textile, which can withstand very high temperatures without change when pure. *See* (*B*).

ASCE The American Society of Civil Engineers.

asphalt Black mineral hydrocarbons containing bituminous substances, which are decomposition products of petroleum, found at the surface of the ground near petroleum deposits. Waterproof surfacing material can also be made by distilling petroleum. It is applied in two main ways, first as *mastic asphalt* in *tanking* (*B*) or roofing, secondly as *rolled asphalt*. The distinction between asphalt and bitumen is mainly chemical. To the layman they are similar except that asphalt is reserved for solid surfacings, the term bitumen being used for liquids suitable for coating aggregates.

asphalt cement An American term for asphalt or bitumen being used as a binder.

asphaltic concrete American term for a road surfacing of *rolled asphalt*. *Compare* asphalt cement.

ASTM The *American Society for Testing and Materials*.

astronomical eyepiece [sur.] or **inverting eyepiece** The eyepiece of a telescope designed for the minimum light-loss. An erecting eyepiece has 4 lenses, an inverting eyepiece 2 lenses. The latter therefore loses much less light than the erecting eyepiece.

astronomy [sur.] The study of the sun and other stars and their movements. Observations of stars are made to obtain precisely the latitude, longitude, time, or a true geographical *bearing*.

atomic-hydrogen welding [mech.] *Arc welding* by a single-phase AC arc struck between tungsten *electrodes* each encircled with a jacket from which hydrogen flows out. The hydrogen is dissociated into atoms by the arc and recombines and burns outside it, forming a *shielded* weld at a very high temperature. *Automatic welding* is possible.

Atterberg limits [s.m.] The *consistency limits* of a clay.

auger [s.m.] Two main types of earth auger exist: (a) the percussion type, used in *shell and auger* boring (b) the helical screw type, of which many varieties exist from 4 to 60 cm dia., some of the smaller ones being hand operated by one or two men (*post-hole auger*). *Truck-mounted drilling rigs* are power operated and make vertical holes. Other types can make horizontal holes but some of this work has been superseded by *pipe-pushing* techniques. The auger can, if need be, run in a tube with welded joints that acts as a permanent steel support to the hole, but this support may not be needed in small holes.

autoclaving or **high-pressure steam-curing.** Treatment of freshly-cast concrete or *aerated concrete* or sand-lime bricks for 10–20 hours at about 10 atmospheres of steam pressure (190°C). From the viewpoint of strength this is an excellent method of curing, since the material acquires the same eventual strength as with air-curing, in a day instead of a month. Low-pressure steam-curing does not allow the concrete to achieve such a high eventual strength, but with either high or low pressure, a 28-day strength is achieved in about 24 hours. The method was first used in the USA (and possibly in the world) in 1939 at the Boettcher School, Denver, Colorado, and achieved cube strengths of 90 N/mm^2 using a long cycle of 24 hours' pre-steaming, 8 hours' heating, 24 hours' curing and 16 hours' cooling and blowdown.

autocollimation, optical compensation, automatic compensation [sur.] A pendulum-operated device in an *automatic level* that keeps the line of sight horizontal.

autogenous healing The closing up and disappearance of breaks or cracks in concrete when the concrete parts are kept damp and in contact. In *pre-stressed concrete*, cracks heal without damping provided that the overload is released sufficiently for the cracks to close.

autogenous welding [mech.] The joining of pieces of metal to other pieces of

the same metal by fusion usually in a gas flame, sometimes without flux, but usually with a filler rod of the same metal. Particularly used for *fusion welding* of copper.

automatic level, autoset level, self-aligning level, self-levelling level [sur.] Different names of different makers for levelling instruments that, unlike the *dumpy level*, maintain a horizontal line of sight regardless of a slight displacement of the vertical axis. They use *autocollimation*.

automatic siphon spillway [hyd.] *See* siphon spillway.

automatic welding Many efficient, highly productive methods of making welds of first-class quality, by *arc welding* or *resistance welding*. They are not used on building sites, only in shop fabrication. The methods may be fully automatic, semi-automatic or machine welding. The last is the commonest type but involves the attendance of an operator. With their currents of 2000 amp per welding head, much higher rates of metal deposition are possible than with manual methods (max. 600 amp). Multiple welding heads also are sometimes possible. Some methods are: *atomic-hydrogen, electroslag, electrogas, MIG, seam, spot, submerged-arc*, and *TIG welding*.

automation The automatic operation of production processes, made possible by such devices as the *bi-metal strip*, the *float switch*, the *photo-electric cell*, *remote control*, the steam governor and microprocessors.

autopatrol or **motor grader** A self-powered blade *grader* for preparing road *sub-grades*.

avenue A road which in USA usually runs north–south, the word *street* being reserved mainly for east–west directions. Both streets and avenues are numbered in a logical way from which the position of each number can be closely estimated.

average [stat.] The average of *n* values is the sum of the values divided by *n*.

This idea is used in surveying as well as in sampling and the calculation of batting averages in cricket. In a series of n survey measurements, the average of the n values is likely to have $\sqrt{n}$ times less error than any one measurement, other things being equal. *See* **mean, personal equation.**

axial-flow fan [min.] *A propeller fan.*

axman [sur.] American term for *chainman*, a man who carries an axe for cutting and driving survey pegs.

axonometric projection [d.o.] A way of showing a plan and a part elevation on the same drawing. The plan is turned through 30° or 45° and vertical lines are drawn from the corners to show the part elevations. *See* **projection.**

azimuth [sur.] The horizontal bearing of a line measured clockwise from the meridian.

azimuthal projection [sur.] A map on which from one point, usually the centre, all points are on their true *bearings.*

B

Bacillus coli [hyd.] An old name for *Escherichia coli*.

backacter or **drag shovel** or **trench hoe** A *face shovel* acting in reverse, that is digging towards the machine. It can easily dig down to a depth of about 4 m below the tracks. It does not make such a clean-walled trench as the *trencher*, therefore the walls must be trimmed by hand if they are likely to stand for long enough to need timbering.

back cutting Additional excavation required to make up an embankment (or railway, road, or canal) where the original amount of cut was insufficient.

back gauge [stru.] or **back mark** The distance from the back edge of an *angle* or other *rolled-steel section* to the centre line of the rivet or bolt hole through it.

back-inlet gulley A water-sealed branch entry to a drain, covered by a grating but otherwise open to the air. Rainwater or waste pipes discharge into it under the grating but above the water seal. It is of cast iron or *stoneware* (*B*).

back mark *See* **back gauge**.

back observation [sur.] or **back sight** Any sight taken towards the last station passed. *Compare* **fore sight**.

back prop A raking strut which transfers the weight of the timbering of deep trenches to the ground. Back props are inserted under every second or third *frame*.

back sight [sur.] A *back observation*. Back sight refers particularly to readings of a levelling staff, for which the ASCE prefers the newer term *plus sight*.

back water [hyd.] Water held back by an obstruction.

backwater curve [hyd.] The curve of the surface of the water measured along an open channel after inserting a weir or dam in the channel and thus raising the water level. The curve is concave upwards.

bacteria bed [sewage] A *trickling filter*.

baffle [hyd.] or **baffle plate** or **baffler** A plate used for deflecting the flow of any fluid such as air, water, or flue gas.

baffle pier [hyd.] A *groyne*.

bagwork [hyd.] A *revetment* to protect sea walls or river banks from *scour*, consisting of dry concrete sewn in bags and tamped against the river bank. Occasionally the material in the bags is gravel. Sea-wall bagwork is usually held together by steel dowel rods driven through the bags like skewers.

bail [min.] A steel half hoop over a sinking *kibble* by which it hangs from the hoisting rope.

bailer (1) [s.m.] A *sand pump*.

(2) A length of 3 to 12 m of pipe with a foot valve. It passes down an oil-well casing and is used for raising oil which contains sand or for any other reason will not flow or cannot be pumped.

Bailey bridge [stru.] A military bridge developed in Britain about 1942, the first British welded lattice bridge. It is built in panels, which are connected at the four corners by steel pins to the next panels. To build bridges of higher strength, panels can be connected together in two or three storeys with 1, 2, or 3 panels in each storey.

Baker bell dolphin *See* **bell dolphin**.

balance bar or **beam** [hyd.] A large, usually wooden beam projecting from a lock gate. By pushing on this beam when the water level is the same on each side, the lock gate is opened.

balance box A loaded box at the far side of a crane from the *jib* and the load, to counterbalance them.

balance bridge A *bascule bridge*.

balanced earthworks An excavation scheme designed so that the cuts equal the fills. There will be theoretically no earth left over and no *back cutting* to complete the last fill.

balance point An intersection between a *mass-haul curve* and the datum line. At this point all excavated material has been used up in fill.

balancing [sur.] *Adjustment* (1).

balata Rubber latex from the South American bullet tree for making conveyor belts and belts for power transmission.

balk or **baulk** Earth between excavations, a *dumpling. See also* (*B*).

ballast Coarse stone or hard clinker or slag used as a bed for railway *sleepers* in the *permanent way. See also* (*B*).

ball mill [min.] A cylindrical or conical mill for grinding mineral. It is charged with steel balls which are about 13 cm dia. when new and gradually wear down to nothing.

band chain [sur.] or **band** or **steel band** A strong steel or *invar* accurate *tape* that may be either bare metal etched, or coated with plastics to protect the steel and carry the figures and graduations. According to BS 4484:1969 'Measuring Instruments', etched or coated tapes are 10, 20 or 30 m long, etched bands are 30 or 50 m long. A band is of thicker steel than a tape.

banderolle [sur.] A *range pole*.

band screen [hyd.] An endless moving belt of wire mesh for removing solids from water at the intake to a power station or water works.

bank (1) An *embankment*.

(2) Inclined rail track.

banking *Superelevation*.

bank of transformers [elec.] A set of power *transformers* installed together.

bank protection [hyd.] Devices for reducing scour by sea or river. *Groynes, mattresses*, the *turfing* of banks, covering with pegged-down brushwood, *revetments*, or planting with grass or withies.

banksman A crane-driver's helper. He signals to the driver when to raise, lower, swing his jib, etc., and the crane driver obeys no one else.

bank storage [hyd.] Water absorbed by the banks of a stream and returned to it as the stream level falls. It helps to reduce flood peaks.

banquette (1) A *berm*.

(2) A bridge footway above road level.

bar (1) A hot-rolled piece of steel or iron, usually round, rectangular, or hexagonal in cross section. Steel bars may also be forged. Light alloy bars are usually *extruded*.

(2) Silt, sand, or gravel dropped at the mouth of a river where its stream velocity falls and its carrying capacity also falls. Such bars are always moving. *See* **ebb channel, flood channel**.

bar bender or **iron fighter** or **steel bender** or **steel fixer** (1) A *skilled man* who cuts and bends steel *reinforcement* and binds it in position ready for the concrete to be poured round it. A bar bender usually also attends while the concrete is being poured, to correct any bars which fall out of place.

(2) A machine for bending *reinforcement*.

Barber Greene tamping levelling finisher A 3 m wide road-making machine which weighs unladen 10 tons and can tamp, level, and finish 80 tons hourly of bituminous aggregate. It can lay the material in thicknesses from 6 to 150 mm and at speeds which vary with the thickness up to 13 m/min. Naturally, a considerable fleet of lorries is needed to feed such a machine.

barge A craft of 4·3 m width or more, carrying in Britain 70 to 150 tons, on the continent of Europe previously up to 300 tons and now 500 tons.

barge bed A mud bottom near the bank of a river where barges can moor and sit on the mud at low tide. The bank is often protected by a *double-wall cofferdam. See illustration opposite.*

Barnes's formula for flow in slimy sewers A more accurate formula than *Crimp and Bruges*. It states: velocity in metres

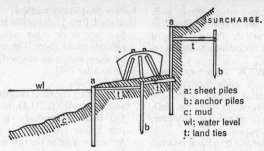

a: sheet piles
b: anchor piles
c: mud
wl: water level
t: land ties

Barge bed

per second equals $46·5m^{0·7}\sqrt{i}$ where *m* is the *hydraulic mean depth* in metres and *i* the slope.

barometer An instrument which shows the atmospheric pressure. It may be an *aneroid* or a more cumbersome but accurate instrument, the mercury barometer.

barometric pressure The pressure of the atmosphere. Air pressure as measured by the *aneroid barometer* can be used by surveyors to estimate *altitude* to an accuracy of about 3 m. Two barometers must be used, one being left at the base, where it is read frequently during the time that the other is taken to the point whose altitude is required. The temperatures and times of the readings at the two points should also be noted.

barrage A low dam, gated across its entire width, placed across a river to raise its level, normally for irrigation or navigation. There are several across the Nile as well as other large rivers.

barrel vault or **cylindrical vault** or **tunnel vault** or **wagon vault** A continuous plain arch or vault of semi-circular shape, usually considerably longer than its diameter; often of brickwork or masonry. The *reinforced* or *pre-stressed-concrete* barrel-vault *shell* is now being used more and more to roof factories or other areas which must not be obstructed with closely spaced columns.

bascule bridge or **balance bridge** or **counterpoise bridge** A bridge which is

hinged at the bank to allow ships to pass under it by raising the part over the river and lowering the part over the bank behind the hinge. Modern bascule bridges are being made of *light alloy*. Tower Bridge, London, is an old bascule bridge. *See* **drawbridge.**

base The *base course* of a road.

base course In a road the *surfacing* layers other than the *wearing course*, but particularly in the *California bearing ratio* method of designing *flexible pavements*, a layer of chosen and compacted soil which is covered with a thin layer of asphalt.

base exchange [s.m.] A reversible chemical process. A chemical exchange of bases (metals, cations) in solution. It is a type of *ion exchange* used especially for water softening and for *de-mineralization* of water. Another type of base exchange is used in the *electro-chemical hardening* of clays.

base flow [hyd.] That part of the flow of a stream that comes from the *ground-water* or long-term lake storage or snow melt.

base line (1) [sur.] A line measured very accurately so as to form the starting lengths for the calculations of a survey, usually a *triangulation*. The base line forms one side of a triangle (or several triangles) whose other sides are calculated from the base line and the measured angles of the triangle.

(2) [air sur.] An *air base*.

base plate [sur.] The part of a *theodolite* which carries the lower ends of the

27

three *foot screws* whose upper ends are fixed to the *tribrach*. The base plate is screwed to the tripod head whenever the theodolite is *set up* on the tripod.

basic refractory A *refractory lining* material low in silica content, used for metallurgical furnace linings. It contains metal oxides like lime CaO, magnesia MgO, or calcined dolomite, a mixture of the two.

basic steel Steel made by a basic process, that is a process in which the furnace is lined with *basic refractory*. The lining combines with the phosphorus in the ore, the two being floated off in the *slag*. The steel is thus freed from this impurity. *See* **cold shortness.**

bastard cut [mech.] A file type of intermediate coarseness. *See* **cut** [mech.].

batching plant The mechanical equipment for measuring, by weight or by volume, the quantities of different ingredients required to make the correct mix of concrete.

batch mixer A *concrete mixer* which mixes batches of concrete, as opposed to a *continuous mixer*.

bat faggot A *fascine* about 1·5 m long and 0·9 m girth made of chestnut, hazel, or oak sticks about 8 cm girth from which the branches have been stripped. *See* **faggoting.**

bathotonic reagent *See* **depressant.**

batten plate [stru.] In composite stanchions built up from pairs of rolled sections such as *channels*, *angles*, or *joists*, a batten plate is a horizontal rectangular plate connected square across the pairs of sections by riveting or welding. *Compare* **lacing.**

batter or **rake** (1) An artificial, uniform steep slope.

(2) Its inclination, expressed as 1 metre horizontally for so many metres vertically. *See* **retaining wall** *illustration.*

batter level A *clinometer* for measuring the slope of earth cuts and fills.

batter pile or **raking pile** A *pile* (usually driven not bored) at an angle to the vertical.

battery *See* **blasting machine.**

battledeck [stru.] Steel plates stiffened by flats, angles or other *rolled sections* welded under them. Originally used on ships, they were adapted for bridge decks after 1945.

baulk *See* **balk.**

bauxite [min.] The most important ore of *aluminium* $Al_2O_3.2H_2O$, named after Les Baux in Provence. It does not fuse below 1600°C. It is used as a *refractory*, and as the raw material for *high-alumina cement*.

beaching [hyd.] Loose-graded stones from 7 to 20 cm in size used in a layer 0·3 to 0·6 m thick for revetting reservoirs and embankments below the level of the *pitching*.

beach replenishment [hyd.] *See* **artificial recharge.**

beacon [sur.] *See* **monument.**

beaded section [stru.] A *light alloy* angle section or channel section *extruded* with beads or bulbs at the extremities like a *bulb angle*. These beads are an advantage of *extrusion*, since they cannot be easily formed by rolling and they increase the bending strength of the section in a metal-saving way.

beam [stru.] A structural member designed to resist loads which bend it. The bending effect at any point in a beam is found by calculating the *bending moment*. Beams are usually of wood, steel, light alloy, or reinforced or prestressed concrete.

beam and slab floor A reinforced-concrete floor in which the *slab* is carried on reinforced-concrete beams. This is the oldest reinforced-concrete floor for large spans but is superseded for offices by the *plate floor* and *hollow-tile floor*, because of its inflexible internal plan, with beams projecting beneath. It is still used for heavy construction, bridge decks, factories, etc.

Beaman stadia arc [sur.] A *direct-reading tacheometer*.

beam bender [mech.] A machine for straightening or bending rolled-steel joists.

beam compasses [d.o.] A light wooden beam fitted with adjustable heads to take a point and a pen or a pencil and thus to draw arcs of larger radius than is possible with a pair of compasses.

beam engine [mech.] An early *steam engine* with vertical cylinder. It operated the Cornish pump.

beamless floor [stru.] A *plate floor*.

beam test The determination of the *modulus of rupture* of a concrete or mortar by casting from it a standard beam without reinforcement, supported and loaded in a standard way. The *bending moment* at failure is recorded and from it the maximum tensile stress (assumed equal to the maximum compressive stress) is calculated. In this way an estimate of the strength of the concrete or mortar or cement can be obtained without the expense of a laboratory testing machine.

bearing (1) [stru.] The support of a *beam*, or the length (or area) of the beam which rests on its support.

(2) [stru.] The compressive stress between a beam and its support (bearing pressure), particularly on foundations.

(3) [sur.] The horizontal angle turned between a datum direction such as true north and a given line. *See* azimuth, magnetic bearing, true bearing.

bearing capacity [s.m.] The load per unit area which the ground can safely carry.

bearing pile A *pile* which carries weight, as opposed to a *sheet pile* which takes earth pressure or a raker which takes thrust. It may be either an *end-bearing pile* or a *friction pile*.

bearing pressure [stru.] or **bearing stress** The load on a *bearing* surface divided by its area.

bearing stratum [stru.] The stratum (or formation or bed) which has been chosen as the most economical or suitable to carry the load in question.

bearing test *See* plate bearing test.

Beaufort scale An ancient scale of wind speeds used by sailors, that varies from 0 for a mirror-smooth calm (less than 1 kph) to 12 for a hurricane of 120 kph or more. The wind force in Newtons, according to BSCP 3, ch. 5, part 2, 'Wind loads', is 0.6 cv^2A where $v =$ wind speed, m/sec, $A =$ projected area, m^2, and the coefficient, c, is 1.5 for flat surfaces and 1 for cylinders. Many other values of c exist. It can even be negative for wind suction on the lee side of a roof.

bed load [hyd.] The weight or volume of silt, sand, gravel, or other material rolled along a stream bed in unit time. *See* sediment.

bed plate [mech.] or **bedplate** A cast-iron plate or steel frame on which a machine sits. It is usually held down to the concrete floor by *anchor bolts*.

bedrock (1) [min.] (USA **ledge** or **ledge rock**) In alluvial mining the hard rock (which may itself be cemented alluvium) at the bottom of the gold-bearing gravel. It is specially important for the miner because much of the gold drops through and is concentrated near to the bedrock.

(2) A loose term meaning hard rock underlying gravel or other loose surface soil.

beetle head A *drop hammer*.

Belanger's critical velocity *See* critical velocity.

Belgian truss A *Fink truss*.

bell dolphin or **Baker bell dolphin** A large bell-shaped steel or concrete fender, suspended on a cluster of piles in the open sea for the mooring of vessels, first used at Heysham jetty. *See illustration overleaf.*

bellmouth overflow [hyd.] An overflow from a reservoir through a tower built up from the bed to the overflow level. The water is led out usually through a tunnel.

belly rod *See* camber rod.

belt conveyor [min.] An endless belt of rubber-covered textile from 0.45 to 1.5 m wide used for carrying coal, gravel, or similar loose material. It must be straight in plan but can pass through limited *vertical curves* which

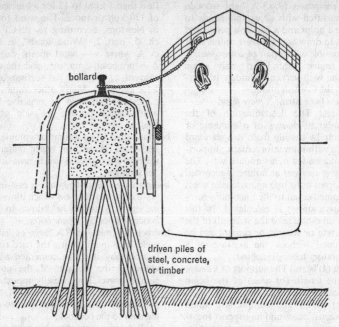

bollard

driven piles of
steel, concrete,
or timber

Baker bell dolphin for mooring at sea. The dotted line shows allowable movement of bell

are concave above and unlimited curves which are convex above. Coal cannot be carried at an angle steeper than 18° on a smooth belt because it slips back. Belt speeds vary from 15 m/min. in a movable to 150 m/min. in a permanent conveyor. All *conveyors* now being installed in UK coal mines are made of synthetic material which does not burn, such as PVC which even prevents the textile burning.

bench (1) A *berm*.

(2) [min.] An artificial long horizontal step from which mineral or stone is quarried, usually by blasting from vertical holes.

benched foundation or **stepped foundation** A foundation on a sloping *bearing stratum*, cut in steps to ensure that it shall not slide when concreted and loaded up, as a sloping foundation could.

benching (1) A *berm* above a ditch.

(2) [min.] Quarrying with benches about 3 m deep or more.

benching iron [sur.] A triangular steel plate with points at the corners. The points are driven into the ground and the plate is used as a temporary *bench mark* or *change point* in levelling.

bench mark [sur.] A relatively fixed point whose level is known and used as a *datum* for levelling.

bending formula [stru.] The formula for bending, in beams of any homogeneous material, is

Bending moment = stress × *modulus of section*

usually written $M = fz$ or $M = \dfrac{fI}{y}$.

bending moment [stru.] The total bending effect at any section of a beam is called the bending moment. It is equal to the algebraic sum of all the moments to the right of the section (or to the left of the section, which amounts to the same thing) and is called M for short. Every bending moment can be expressed as a force times a distance called the *arm*. The units are pound-inches, ton-inches, kg-m, newton-metres, tonne-m, etc. *See* Navier's hypothesis.

bending-moment diagram [stru.] A diagram which shows for one loading the amount of the *bending moment* at any point along a beam. From this diagram, the position and amount of the maximum bending moment can be immediately seen.

bending-moment envelope [stru.] Several bending-moment diagrams (one for each loading carried by the beam), laid on top of each other to show the worst bending moment at any point for all possible loadings.

bending schedule A list of reinforcement which accompanies a reinforcement detail drawing, prepared by a reinforced-concrete designer. It shows the dimensioned shapes of all the bars and the number of bars required. The *bar bender* bends his reinforcement according to the schedule and places it according to the drawing. *See* cutting list, BS 4466.

bends The bends is slang for *caisson disease*.

bend test A test of a weld or of the steel in a flat bar, in which the bar is bent cold through 180° to verify its *ductility*. If there is no cracking the piece is considered *ductile*.

bent [stru.] A two-dimensional *frame* which is self-supporting, but only within these dimensions. It has at least two legs and is usually placed at right angles to the length of the structure which it carries such as a bridge, pipeline, aqueduct, etc. *See* trestle.

bentonite A *clay* composed, like fuller's earth, mainly of the same clay mineral montmorillonite. Found in Wyoming, USA, where it is known for its remarkable accordion-like expansion when its water content increases. It is used for making *refractories* and rubber compounds, as a filler for *synthetic resins* (B) and for making oilwell *drilling fluids*, in which its *thixotropy* in small concentrations is very useful.

bentonite mud A thixotropic suspension of *bentonite* in water, used for holding up the sides of deep trenches excavated by machine. Bentonite slurry is often used as a lubricant to reduce skin friction in *pipe-pushing* or in *pile*-driving or in the sinking of a *caisson*. *See* diaphragm wall.

berm A horizontal ledge in an earth bank or cutting to ensure the stability of a steep slope.

Bernoulli's assumption [stru.] In any bent beam, sections which were plane before bending are plane after bending. *See* Navier's hypothesis.

Bernoulli's theorem [hyd.] The *energy* per unit mass of a stream at one point is equal to that at another point upstream (or downstream) plus (or minus) the friction losses. Stated differently: Pressure energy + *potential energy* + *kinetic energy* + losses = a constant.

berth A place where a ship can tie up and load or unload.

berthing impact The forces on piers, jetties, etc., during the berthing of vessels. The forces are usually estimated from the *kinetic energy* of a large vessel berthing at about 15 cm/sec.

bevelled washer or tapered washer A *washer* made from a wedge-shaped piece of steel plate. It is thinner at one edge than the other so as to fit under a nut on the flange of a *rolled-steel joist* or other section with tapered flanges.

B-horizon [s.m.] In soil science, the horizon between the *A-horizon* and *C-horizon*. It contains the metal oxides and other soluble materials leached from the A-horizon above it. It is the lower part of the *topsoil*.

bi-cable ropeway An *aerial ropeway* in which one or more *track cables* carry

31

the loads and a *traction rope* moves them along. *See* **monocable.**

billet An intermediate product made by *cogging* a steel *ingot*. It is usually less than 160 sq. cm in cross-section. *See* **bloom.**

bi-metal strip A strip of two metals with different *coefficients of expansion*, one metal forming each side of the strip. As the temperature changes, the strip curves one way or the other by a calculated amount. Bi-metal strips are used in *thermostats* (*B*), gas heaters for water, thermal *relays*, etc.

binder (1) *Cement*, *tar*, *bitumen*, *gypsum plaster* (*B*), *lime* (*B*) or similar material used for joining masonry.

(2) [s.m.] The clay or silt in *hoggin* or the *cement* in rock.

(3) or *stirrup* A small diameter steel rod usually about 6 to 10 mm dia. used for holding together the main steel in a *reinforced-concrete* beam or column.

binding wire *Annealed wire.*

bio-chemical oxygen demand [sewage] or **BOD** The oxygen absorbed by a sewage sample in 5 days at 20°C. *See* **Royal Commission Standard.**

biological filter [sewage] A **trickling filter.**

biological shield A thick wall surrounding a nuclear reactor, which protects workers from radiation. The shield may be of concrete, sheet lead, or other heavy material, and the concrete can be made denser than usual by replacing the stone with iron or lead shot or barytes (specific gravity 4·5) or other heavy mineral.

birdseye view [air sur.] An *oblique* aerial photograph.

Birmingham (or **Stub's**) **wire gauge, BWG** Numbers that describe thicknesses of wire and sheet steel, close to but different from the *Standard Wire Gauge* (*B*). A further complication is that another slightly different gauge is the Birmingham gauge (BG).

bit *See* (*B*), *also* **detachable bit.**

bitumen A black sticky mixture of hydrocarbons completely soluble in carbon disulphide. It can be obtained from natural deposits (usually of oxidized petroleum) or by distilling petroleum. *See* **asphalt.**

bituminous carpet A wearing course containing a tar or bitumen binder and having a thickness not greater than 38 mm (BS 892).

bituminous emulsion or **bitumen road emulsion** A liquid mixture of water and tar or *bitumen* which has the advantage that it can be applied to roads in cold damp weather. *See* **emulsion.**

black [mech.] A description of steel as it comes from the forge or rolling mill, covered with *mill scale*, which is not removed except when the steel is prepared for a protective paint or *metal coating* (*B*).

black bolts [mech.] Bolts covered with *black* iron oxide (*scale*), of less uniform shape than bright *turned bolts*. *See* **clearing hole.**

black diamond [min.] or **carbon** or **carbonado** *Diamond* which is not used as a gem because of its grey or black colour but forms a valuable cutting point for many tools. It comes from Brazil mainly and is preferred to *bort* because it does not have the crystalline cleavage of bort.

blade grader A *grader.*

blading back [s.m.] Pushing soil in a *windrow* back with a *grader* to the position from which it came.

Blake breaker *See* **jaw breaker.**

blank carburizing [mech.] A *carburizing* carried out without the carbon. It is a *heat treatment.*

blank flange [mech.] An undrilled *flange.*

blank nitriding [mech.] A *nitriding* without ammonia or nitrogen.

blast furnace A smelting furnace in which heated air is blown in at the bottom, for reducing iron, copper, or other metals from their ores. The charge is fed in at the top, the metal and slag tapped off at convenient holes at the foot.

blast-furnace cement *See* **Portland blast-furnace cement.**

blasting (1) [min.] or **shot firing** The

breaking of rock by boring in it a hole which is filled with *explosive* and detonated or otherwise fired.

(2) *See* sand blast.

blasting fuse [min.] *Safety fuse*.

blasting machine [min.] (or **battery** or **exploder** in Britain) American term for a portable electric generator worked by a *rack* and pinion or by a turning handle, the whole weighing about 5 kg. The most powerful exploder available in Britain generates 1200 volts and will fire 500 shots simultaneously, but most exploders are designed for only a small number of shots.

bleeding Separation of clear water from the cement paste of mortar or concrete. Two types are known, the first beneficial, the second harmful to concrete strength, but they may co-exist. During compaction, water can flow out of concrete, lie on its surface, and thus encourage good curing for the first few hours during hot weather. Some *admixtures* are said to encourage this sort of bleeding. The other sort of bleeding occurs after compaction. Water segregates beside or under the steel or larger stones, weakening the bond between them and the body of the concrete. A *plasticizer* should enable the *water/cement ratio* to be lowered, reducing this sort of bleeding. A second vibration, some hours after the first one, is sometimes used to expel this excess water.

blind drain A *rubble drain*.

blinding (1) or **mat** or **mattress** or **sealing coat** A layer of lean concrete usually 5 to 10 cm thick, put down on soil such as clay to seal it and provide a clean bed for reinforcement to be laid on.

(2) The spreading of grit or sand to fill the voids in a road *wearing course*.

bloated clay *See* lightweight aggregate.

block (1) [mech.] The frame holding the pulley or pulleys of *lifting tackle*.

(2) *See below and* (*B*).

block-in-course Large blocks of hard stone with worked beds and ham-

mered faces laid in courses in dock walls, of variable length but constant depth, not deeper than 0·3 m.

block pavement A road *wearing course* made of rectangular blocks of stone or wood, as opposed to *sheet pavement*.

blockwork Masonry in *breakwaters* and other marine structures built of pre-cast concrete (or stone) blocks weighing from 10 to 50 tons to resist movement by waves. *See* coursed blockwork, sliced blockwork, and (*B*).

blockyard or **casting yard** A space where precast concrete pieces are poured and allowed to harden before use.

Blondin After Blondin the tightrope-walker; the French word for a *cableway*.

bloom A half-finished rolled or forged piece of steel or wrought iron with a cross-sectional area greater than 160 sq. cm (*compare* billet). If used as a stanchion base, the top surface is machined.

blow *See* boil.

blow down (1) [mech.] or **blowing down** (**blow off** in USA) Opening a valve in a steam *boiler* mud drum or other place where boiler sediment collects, so as to eject it. This may be done periodically by hand or continuously by an automatic arrangement.

(2) A *pneumatic caisson* is blown down when it refuses to move downwards, by merely reducing the air pressure. The men are withdrawn and the air pressure is reduced, but by not more than one quarter of the gauge reading. If this does not move the caisson, more *kentledge* must be added.

blow off (1) An outlet on a pipeline for discharging sediment or water or for emptying a low sewer.

(2) *See* blow down (1).

blow out (1) In compressed air work a sudden loss of compressed air from the tunnel or *caisson*, which increases rapidly and may become disastrous.

(2) [min.] An oilwell from which oil and gas may flow out uncontrollably because the *drilling fluid* was not dense enough.

blueprint [d.o.] A *contact print* on *ferro-prussiate paper* of a drawing made on transparent paper or linen. It is developed either in water or in a special solution. It has white lines on a blue ground. Because of the dark ground, blueprints are now obsolescent, although the print from a faint pencil drawing is much better than from a *dyeline*.

Board of Trade unit *See* **kilowatt hour.**

BOD *See* **bio-chemical oxygen demand.**

bog blasting *See* **peat blasting.**

boil or **blow** A flow of soil, usually fine sand or *silt*, into the bottom of an excavation, forced in by water or water and air under pressure. It starts as a small spring and like *piping* may increase rapidly. Therefore boils should be stopped immediately, before they bring disaster. They can be prevented by reducing the pressure difference. This can be done in one of several ways. (*a*) By *wellpoints* or other relatively slow processes of *groundwater lowering* outside the excavation. (*b*) The sinking of *relief wells* inside the excavation, deep below the final excavation level, if filled with gravel or drain pipes provide a safe path for water under pressure to flow up. (*c*) The sinking of pumped wells below final excavation level inside the cofferdam may be possible only combined with *groundwater lowering* outside. (*d*) The pressure inside the excavation can be increased by flooding it or filling it with gravel. Flooding or refilling are the only possible courses in an emergency. A spring is a boil with very little sand in the flow. *See* **graded filter, quicksand.**

boiler [mech.] or **steam boiler** A plant for raising steam. Large boilers evaporate about 400 kg of water per second and are usually coal or oil fired. Such boilers are used in power stations, the power plants of mines, rolling mills, and similar heavy industry. *See* **pulverized coal,** *also* (*B*).

boiler-house foundations *See* **refrigerator foundations.**

boiler rating [mech.] The heating capacity of a boiler expressed in *British Thermal Units* (*See* p. 10) per hour, kilowatts, kg of steam/second, etc.

bollard (1) A cast-iron post anchored deeply into the masonry of a quay wall, used for mooring vessels. *See* **bell dolphin.**

(2) A post anchored in a road to protect a kerb, wall, or street *refuge* or to divert traffic.

bolster (1) A support for a bridge truss on an abutment.

(2) Padding or lagging generally; in particular that used round the edge of a *limpet dam* to make a watertight joint with a dock wall.

bolt [mech.] A cylindrical bar which is screwed at one end for a nut and forged with a square or hexagonal head at the other end. The oldest (except forge welding) and commonest way of fixing steel parts together. Part of the bar next the head has no screw thread. *Compare* **screw.** *See* **black bolts.**

bolt sleeve A cardboard, asbestos cement, or steel tube round a bolt in a concrete wall. It prevents the concrete sticking to the bolt and also acts as a *distance piece* to keep the shutters at the correct distance apart.

bond (1) [stru.] or **grip** or **interface strength** *Adhesion.*

(2) [mech.] or **whip** A short length of wire rope by which loads are fixed to a crane hook. *See* **sling.**

(3) [elec.] A short conductor between the ends of rails at a rail joint, or between the parts of an earthing system or lightning protective system or other metal work. The ends of rails even when welded together are also electrically bonded to reduce the electrical resistance of the joint. *See also* (*B*).

bond breaker A *release agent*, or for *lift-slabs* a *sealant* (3).

bond length The *grip length* of a reinforcing bar.

bond stress A shear stress at the surface of a reinforcing bar, which prevents relative movement between bar and concrete. It is helped by *mechanical bond*. *See* **adhesion**. The allowable bond stress is about one-tenth of the concrete compressive stress.

boning [sur.] (1) or **boning in** Setting out a slope by *boning rods*. Two rods are held on pegs which have been previously set on the slope at correct levels and a third rod is lined in as it is moved about between them.

(2) Checking the amount of twist or winding of a timber or stone surface. *See* **boning pegs** (*B*), **winding strips** (*B*).

boning rod [sur.] A T-shaped staff about 1·2 m long made of two pieces of 50 × 12 mm board nailed together. The short T-piece, which is held uppermost, is used for sighting and lining up with the other boning rods. *See* **boning, sight rail, traveller**.

boogie box *See* **boojee pump**.

boojee pump or **boogie box** or **grouting machine** or **grout pan** A container for pressure *grouting* with cement *slurry* behind tunnel linings or into fissures in rock. It is usually stirred by a compressed-air engine and forced out by air pressure, but for mining work in which very high pressures may be needed pumps often provide the high pressure.

booking [sur.] The recording of field observations in a legible and understandable way for later use in the field or drawing office, often by another person.

boom (1) Any beam used in *lifting tackle*, such as the *jib* of a *crane*.

(2) A *chord*. The horizontal member, top or bottom, of any built-up *girder* or *truss*.

(3) A barrier across a stretch of water that may be designed to stop submarines, or be a *floating boom* to hold oil slicks, etc.

booster [mech.] A pump or compressor inserted into a water or compressed-air pipeline near the consumer, so as to increase his pressure.

boot (1) The lower end of a bucket elevator, from which the buckets lift material.

(2) A projection from a concrete beam to carry facing brick, stone, or other *cladding* (*B*).

boot man A labourer wearing the company's boots, for standing in fresh concrete or mud. He is paid extra while wearing the boots (boot money).

Bordeaux connection [mech.] A *thimble* for the end of a steel wire rope with a link fitted permanently into it. It is a convenient way of joining wire rope to short-link crane chain.

border stone A *kerb* stone.

bore (1) [mech.] The internal diameter of a pipe or other cylinder.

(2) [min.] A borehole, or to make a borehole.

(3) [hyd.] A wave advancing with a nearly vertical front upstream during the flowing tide in an estuary, as in the Severn estuary. Occasionally, in a flood, a bore may travel downstream.

bored pile or **bored cast-in-place/cast-in-situ pile** A *pile* formed by pouring concrete into a hole formed in the ground, usually containing some light reinforcement. They can now be made 1·25 m dia., 60 m deep, and 12° off vertical, apart from *under-reaming*. These piles were first made in about 1905 and are now a favourite method of taking foundations through soft surface soil on to a *bearing stratum* in London. *Compare* **driven cast-in-place pile**. *See* **reamer** (2).

borehole A hole driven into the ground to get information about the strata, or to release water pressure by *vertical sand drains* or to obtain water, oil, gas, salt, or sulphur. Occasionally boreholes are sunk from the surface to shallow mines to admit water pipes, hydraulic fill, power cables, or fresh air. *See* **bored pile, cable drill, diamond drilling, Magic Mole, pipe-pushing, rotary drilling**.

borehole log [s.m.] A record of the findings at a borehole, including details of the groundwater level (and gain of water in *air-flush drilling*) with descriptions of the cores, percentage core recovery, etc. *Well logging* is a specialized activity developed for the deep holes of oilwell drilling but can also be applied in shallow holes.

borehole pump [min.] A centrifugal pump, electrically driven through rods from a motor on the surface, or (for deep well *submersible pumps*) by an electric motor at the foot of the pump casing. These pumps are used for dewatering mine shafts or for pumping drinking water and are therefore obtainable in capacities from 50 to 50,000 litres/min.

borehole samples [min.] Samples obtained from boreholes, namely *diamond drill* or shot-drill cores, or sludge or chippings from other drilling methods. For an investigation into the strength of a *clay*, an *undisturbed sample* must be obtained.

borehole surveying [min.] The measurement of the *deviation* of a borehole from the straight.

boring [min.] (1) Making a hole in rock for blasting, using a rotative or percussive drill.

(2) Driving a borehole. *See above*; *also* **auger, bort, jetting, wash boring.**

borrow Material dug to provide *fill* elsewhere.

borrow pit An excavation dug to provide *fill*.

bort [min.] or **boart** A crystalline *diamond* which lacks the brilliance and purity of colour which would make it a gem but is nevertheless very valuable as a cutting agent in *diamond drills*.

Bosporus Bridge The longest span (1074 m) suspension bridge in Europe; a road bridge completed in 1973 for $36 million, a capital cost which was recovered by mid 1976. Built like the *Severn bridge* to Freeman Fox's design, it aroused interest with its economical aerofoil deck design and the off-vertical, continuous suspender ropes each side of the deck, carrying its weight up to the main cables above them. It was built in $3\frac{1}{2}$ years instead of the normal $5\frac{1}{2}$.

Boston caisson A *Gow caisson*.

bottom cut [min.] or **draw cut** In small tunnels in rock, a *cut* consisting of two converging rows of holes. One row is horizontal and near the floor, the other is placed about the middle of the tunnel. The two rows are fired together and a wedge of rock is blasted out. Where more space is available, the *wedge cut* is preferred.

bottoming (1) Large stones in a road laid on the *formation*.

(2) [rly] The ballast in a *permanent way*.

(3) The last few centimetres of excavation usually removed by spade to ensure that the bottom is to the correct level and smooth.

bottom-opening skip A *drop bottom bucket*.

bottom sampler [hyd.] A *sounding lead* with adhesive on the underside, or a coring device for picking material up from the sea bed.

boulder clay [min.] (**till** or **tillite** in USA) Material consisting of rocks crushed by moving glaciers and containing scratched stones of boulder-size down to sand-size, with some clay, all unstratified.

boulevard In USA a wide road which in cities is usually planted with shade trees, sometimes also on the central strip. *See* **street.**

Bourdon pressure gauge [mech.] A tube of oval cross-section which tends to straighten as the pressure inside it increases. It is a very simple, robust, and useful gauge for boilers, *pore-water pressure* measurements, and so on.

Boussinesq equation [s.m.] In 1885 Boussinesq published his analysis of the stresses in the soil beneath a loaded foundation assuming the soil to be a semi-infinite elastic solid. Although most soil is not strictly elastic, Boussinesq's rigorous mathematical work was proved broadly correct 50 years later by workers in *soil mechanics* who showed that the lines of equal vertical stress under a loaded point are roughly circular. *See* **bulb of pressure.**

Bowditch's rule [sur.] An *adjustment* for

a *closed traverse* which has been made by compass. Angles and sides are assumed equally liable to error. The correction to apply to any line for an error in *latitude* is

$$\frac{\text{length of line}}{\text{perimeter of traverse}} \times \text{total error in latitude.}$$

The correction for errors in departure is made in the same way.

bowk [min.] A *kibble*.

bowl scraper or **scraper** or **wheel scraper** A towed steel box or bowl hung in a frame with 2 or 4 rubber-tyred wheels. The bottom edge digs into the ground when required and fills the bowl as it is towed or pushed forward. The soil is ejected at the dump by tilting or by a 'tail gate' or ejector which sweeps the soil from the back of the bowl to the opening. Scrapers vary from 5 to 40 cu. m capacity. A 100 hp tractor is needed to pull a 9 cu. m scraper at top speed in bad weather, and it may need a *pusher tractor* for help in digging. Towed scrapers not only transport earth, they also spread and level it. Scrapers give their highest outputs for hauls of less than 100 m but the most economical haul varies from 130 m for 2 cu. m scrapers to 500 m for 14 cu. m scrapers. *See* **wheeled tractor**.

bowstring girder A *girder* shaped like a bow with the string downwards. It may be of concrete, steel, or timber. Modern laminated timber girders are made up to 50 m span, and can be delivered ready made in spans up to 24 m. They are developed from the *Belfast truss* (B).

box beam A *box girder*.

box caisson or **American caisson** or **stranded caisson** A large open-topped box (closed at the bottom) built on shore, floated out, and sunk over the ground chosen for a foundation. The box forms part of the final structure. It is commonly used for bridge piers, as it enables construction to be done in the dry. It is usually built of reinforced concrete. *See* **caisson**.

box culvert A culvert of rectangular or square cross-section.

box dam A *cofferdam* completely surrounding an area.

box drain A small rectangular *drain* of brick or concrete.

box frame construction [stru.] A method of building a long thin block of flats, offices, etc., with concrete slab floors carried on load-bearing walls across the thickness of the building. The walls may be of brick or concrete but for flats of up to six storeys are usually of brick. When both walls and slabs are seen on the elevation, it looks like an egg box. This construction is of simple design and economical in steel, particularly with the relatively deep slabs of *hollow-tile* construction.

box girder [stru.] or **box beam** A hollow, square or rectangular girder made of steel or light alloy, or reinforced or prestressed concrete, or timber. Steel box girders caused alarm in the early 1970s because two bridges which were being built then collapsed, causing 40 deaths – one bridge was over the river Cleddau at Milford Haven, Wales, the other over the river Yarra at Melbourne, Australia. The Merrison committee reported optimistically on box girders in 1973, emphasizing that responsibilities must be clearly allocated: the consulting engineer should design the permanent structure and the contractor should build the bridge, as well as designing and building any temporary structures.

box heading A *heading* close-timbered both in roof and sides.

boxing [rly] A bed of *ballast* between rail sleepers.

boxing up [rly] Packing ballast under sleepers to raise sagging track.

box pile A steel *pile* made from two *steel sheet piles* or *channels* or *angle sections* or joists, welded along their contact lines.

box sextant [sur.] A compact *sextant* suitable for rapid land surveys. Like the nautical sextant it has a small telescope but can read angles with a vernier only to the nearest minute of arc. The telescope is removable and may be not always needed. The size may be up to 10 cm dia.

box shear test [s.m.] A simple standard method of measuring the *shear strength* of soil in a box split in two, to which pressure is applied at the same time as a shearing force.

brace (1) [stru.] A member, usually diagonal, which takes tension or compression or stiffens a structure, generally against wind.

(2) American term for a *strut* in trench timbering.

bracing [stru.] (1) A stiffening member in a structure; a brace.

(2) The act of inserting braces into a structure.

Braithwaite piles *See* **screw pile.**

branding iron An *indenting roller.*

brass [mech.] An alloy generally of copper and zinc, mainly copper. *See* (*B*).

braze welding Welding with a filler wire or strip that has a lower melting point than the parent metal. *Bronze welding*, one type, uses copper alloys.

brazing spelter *See* **hard solder** (*B*).

breakdown or **breaking of an emulsion** The separation of an *emulsion* into two or more of its constituents; for *bituminous emulsions*, their separation into bitumen and water.

breaker [min.] A machine for breaking rock, that is a *gyratory* or *jaw breaker*. Between breakers and crushers there is no sharp distinction, but crushing implies a smaller product than breaking.

breaking ground [min.] The transformation of a hard rock face into a pile of shattered stones. This is usually done by *blasting* in drilled holes for hard ground, by *pneumatic pick* in medium ground, and by hand pick in soft ground. Other methods are *broaching*, *channellers*, driving in *gads*, *jet drilling*, and *plug and feathers*.

breaking point [mech.] or **breaking piece** Ore *breakers* are provided with parts which break and thus unload the machine when an unbreakable piece sticks in them. In a *jaw breaker* a *toggle* usually breaks and is quickly replaced. Without this provision serious damage would be done to the breaker or motor. The idea is comparable to the fusing of electric circuits.

breaking strength *See* **ultimate strength** *and below.*

breaking stress [stru.] The *crushing strength* of a concrete, brick, or stone or the *ultimate tensile strength* of a metal *tensile test* piece.

break-pressure tank [hyd.] Small open tanks placed at the level of the *hydraulic gradient* of a *gravity main* in hilly country to reduce the maximum pressure on the main. The main discharges into each tank in turn, and a new section of main takes off from each tank. Large savings in the cost of the main can thus be made, since it is under very much smaller pressure than is a continuous main.

breakwater or **mole** A wall built out into the sea to protect a harbour (natural or *artificial*) from the waves. The two main types of construction are *rubble mound* and *blockwork*. See **tetrapod**, **floating breakwater.**

breast The *mouldboard* of a plough or *dozer.*

bridge A structure which covers a gap. Generally bridges carry a road or railway across a river, canal, or another railway. For the longest spans (600 m or more) only steel *suspension bridges* are used. From 300 to 600 m the suspension bridge, the steel arch bridge, and the cantilever bridge are equally suitable. For spans under 240 m the concrete arch can be used as well as the above three. *See* **long span.**

bridge bearing The support at the bridge pier, which carries the weight of a bridge. Bridge bearings may be fixed or seated on *expansion rollers*. The surfaces of contact between bridge and bearing are usually spherical or cylindrical.

bridge cap or **bridge pier cap** The highest part of a bridge pier, on which the *bridge bearings* or rollers are seated. It may be of stone, brick, or plain or reinforced concrete, usually the last for heavy loads.

bridge deck The load-bearing floor of a bridge, that which carries and spreads the loads to the main beams. It is either of reinforced concrete, *prestressed concrete*, welded steel or (rarely) *light alloy*. *See* **bascule bridge, jack arch, troughing.**

bridge pier A support for a bridge. It may be of masonry, timber, concrete or steel, but in any case is founded on firm ground below the river mud.

bridge pier cap A *bridge cap.*

bridges *See* **Akashi-Kaikyo/Bosporus/ cable-stayed/Forth/Forth Road/Golden Gate/Humber/Kill Van Kull/Parramatta / Plougastel / Quebec / Severn / Sydney Harbour/Tacoma Narrows/ Träneberg/Verrazano Narrows bridge.**

bridge thrust A horizontal force in an arch bridge caused by the arch shape. It is resisted at the abutment by a horizontal reaction from the ground, or, as in the *bowstring* girder, by a pull in a tie beam (the bowstring).

bridge truss A *truss* suitable for carrying bridge loads, such as a *Warren* or *Vierendeel girder* or *Pratt truss.*

bright bolt *See* **turned bolt.**

Brinell hardness test [mech.] A hard steel ball 1, 2, 5 or 10 mm dia. is loaded with a weight for 15 sec., and the diameter of the indentation is then measured. The Brinell hardness number (BHN) is worked out from

$$\frac{\text{load in kilograms}}{\text{spherical area of impression in sq. mm}}$$

From this figure can be obtained corresponding numbers for the *diamond pyramid hardness* test and the *Rockwell hardness test*, which are more suitable for case-hardened material. The Brinell method is suitable for soft metal and mild steel, and even for tough steel which is not case-hardened. For a steel that has not been hardened by cold work, the ultimate tensile strength in tons/sq. cm is roughly 0·034 times the Brinell hardness number (BHN). Thus the BHN for mild steel is between 120 and 140; both hardened tool-steel and white cast-iron have a BHN between 400 and 600. *See* BS 240.

briquette (1) [min.] A lump of fuel or ore (green pellet) made from dust by compression or sintering at high temperature, enabling dust to be used that would otherwise wastefully pollute the air.

(2) Specimens of cement cast in the shape of an hour-glass with a thick waist, used in the tensile testing of cement.

Britannia Bridge A bridge built in 1850 over the Menai Strait between Wales and Anglesey, a long *plate girder* bridge, remarkable for its high (for 1850) temperature movement of 10 cm at each end.

British Standard or **British Standard Specification** or **BS** A numbered publication of the *British Standards Institution* describing the quality of a material or the dimensions of a manufacture such as pipes or bricks. Frequently the dimensions and the quality are described in two different standards. The use by architects or engineers of British Standards in their *specifications* can reduce the bulk of the description to a reference (for steel frames, for example, to BS 449).

British Standards Institution or **BSI** The British organization for standardizing, by agreement between maker and user, the methods of test and dimensions of materials as well as *codes of practice* and nomenclature. Corresponding abbreviations in other countries are: France AFNOR (Association Française de Normalisation), Germany DIN (Deutsche Industrie Normal), USA ASTM (American Society for Testing and Materials) and ASA (American Standards Association), Soviet Union GOST.

British Thermal Unit *See* (*B*).

brittle fracture [mech.] *Cleavage fracture.* Brittle fracture became widely known first because of startling failures of welded 'Liberty ships' in the cold weather of the North Atlantic from 1942 onwards. These failures, unsuspected in mild steel, were eventually attributed, at least in part, to low temperatures causing failures at stresses lower than expected.

broaching or **broach channelling** or **line drilling** A rock excavation method used where the rock left in place must not be shattered by explosive. A line of holes is drilled close together along the break line. The rock between them is knocked out with a chisel called a broach and the block is finally moved with wedges. If the holes are as far as 10 cm apart, light charges may be fired or the *plug and feathers* used. *See* **channeller.**

broad gauge [rly] A gauge wider than the 1·435 m used generally in Europe, for example Brunel's gauge of 2·13 m used for the original Great Western Railway, later reduced to *standard gauge.*

broad irrigation The disposal of sewage by allowing it to flow over and soak into carefully levelled farmland, without pipe drains. *Compare* **intermittent filtration.**

bronze welding Gas welding of copper, steel, or other metals with a silicon brass *filler rod.* It is easier than fusion welding because the temperature is lower, but it is nevertheless above 850°C.

brooming The crushing and spreading of the top of a wooden pile with no *driving band* when driven into hard ground.

brothers A sling of chain or rope, the term may mean either a *two-leg* or *four-leg* sling.

Brown and Sharp wire gauge [mech.] Another name for *American wire gauge.*

brushwood *See* **fascine.**

BS *British Standard.*

BSCP British Standard *code of practice.*

BSI *British Standards Institution.*

BThU *British Thermal Unit. See* Conversion factors, p. 9.

bubble [sur.] The air bubble within a *level tube,* or the level tube itself.

bubble trier [sur.] A *level trier.*

bubble tube [sur.] A *level tube.*

bucket [hyd.] (1) A cup on the perimeter of a *Pelton wheel.*

(2) A reversed curve in the profile of a *spillway,* designed to deflect the water horizontally at its foot from the steep overflow face on to the *apron* below the dam (USA).

(3) A container of a *bucket elevator, bucket-ladder dredger,* etc.

(4) A *kibble.*

bucket elevator An endless chain (or two linked) with buckets attached for raising loose material such as *slurry,* coal, or stone at slopes varying from 45° to vertical.

bucket-ladder dredger A *dredger* whose main equipment is a *bucket elevator* reaching below its keel into the mud to be dredged. The buckets dig mud as well as lift it. They discharge at the top into a chute which leads to a *dumb* barge or to a hold for mud in the dredger.

bucket-ladder excavator A *trench excavator.*

bucket-wheel excavator [min.] *See* **rotary excavator** (2).

buckle [stru.] To load a *strut* by *eccentric loading* or too heavy loading until it bends sharply and thus approaches failure or fails. *See* **crippling load.**

buckling load [stru.] The *crippling load* of a *long column.*

buffer stop [rly] A fixture bolted to track-rails, consisting of a sleeper set at 1·05 m above them to take the *impact* of wagons moving into it.

buggy or **concrete cart** (USA) A two-wheeled or motor-driven cart, usually rubber-tyred, which carries up to 170 litres of concrete from a mixer or a concrete hopper to the forms (ACI).

building code In USA, local building laws, which correspond to by-laws in Britain.

building owner The owner of the works to be built on a site: an individual, an organization, a government, etc. *See* **client**.

building paper *See* (*B*).

built up [stru.] Description of a steel or light alloy or wooden beam, girder, or stanchion built of different sections riveted or welded or glued together.

bulb angle A steel *angle section* enlarged to a bulb at one end. *See* **beaded section**.

bulb of pressure [s.m.] The mass of compressed soil below a loaded foundation. The term is also used to describe the bulb-shaped lines of equal vertical stress below a footing, *see* **Boussinesq equation**.

bulk density [s.m.] The weight per unit volume of any material including voids and water contained in it. Normal, well-compacted concrete has a bulk density, air-dry, of $2 \cdot 3$ tonne/m^3. Normal aggregates (not lightweight nor dense) weigh from 1450 to 1750 kg/m^3. *See* **dry density, relative density**.

bulking [s.m.] (1) The increase in volume of excavated material above the volume of the excavation from which it came, often more than 100%.

(2) The increase in volume of dry sand when its moisture content increases. This may amount to 40% when 5% of water is added. This increase disappears entirely when the water content is raised to 20%.

bulk modulus *See* **elastic constants**.

bulk spreader [s.m.] or **powder spreader** A machine for carrying cement or other material in *soil stabilization*. It also spreads it on the prepared soil.

bulldog grip [mech.] A U-bolt threaded at both ends. The ends pass through a specially shaped washer. The grip is used as a rope clamp since it grips a length of steel rope doubled back on itself. The hold is effective provided that at least three grips are used and that the units all face in the same direction. *See* **rope fastenings**.

bulldozer (1) A caterpillar *tractor* with a wide blade, the *mouldboard*, mounted in front of it, at right angles to the track of the machine. The mouldboard can be raised or lowered and serves to move material by pushing. Bulldozers can also be mounted on *wheeled tractors*.

(2) The mouldboard and all its adjusting gear, which if fitted to a crawler tractor would make it a bulldozer. *See* **dozer**.

bullhead rail [rly] An old type of British rail rounded at top and bottom, carried in a *chair*.

bull wheel A large wheel at the base of a *derrick* mast, which rotates the mast during *slewing*.

bump [r.m.] A noise caused by breakage within the mass of rock, not at its surface as in a *rock burst*. Bumps occur in coal mines or other mines in soft rock and are rarely dangerous.

bump cutter A set of diamond saws fitted on to a machine that is sensitive to upward irregularities in the surface of a carriageway and cuts them off. Used on concrete or asphalt.

bunker A storage container for coal, ore, or stone, etc.

buoyancy [hyd.] The reduction in weight of a body immersed in a fluid. It is equal to the weight of the fluid displaced by the body. If the body floats, its weight is equal to the weight of fluid displaced. This is the *principle of Archimedes*.

buoyant foundation or **buoyant raft** A reinforced-concrete *raft foundation*, usually with walls round the edges, so designed that the total of its own weight and all loads which it carries is approximately equal to the weight of the soil or water displaced. It is used in river estuaries where no foundation is available except nearly fluid silt or mud. *See* **Vierendeel girder, flotation**.

burden [min.] The burden of the *toe* of a blasting hole is its distance from the nearest *free face* measured at right angles to the hole.

burn To cut metal with a gas flame.

burnt shale Carbonaceous shale (occasionally used as road-making material) which has been in a tip for some years and has been heated by spontaneous combustion or by destructive distillation of oil shale.

bush hammer A light, percussive originally hand tool, now a compressed-air or electric tool of about 3 kg weight, for removing the outer skin from stone or concrete to expose the lower layers and reveal a surface texture which is pleasantly rough.

bush hammering Dressing concrete with a *bush hammer* to remove the outer 1 to 6 mm skin.

butane A paraffin hydrocarbon gas C_4H_{10} usually obtained by refining petroleum, and used in *bottled gas* (*B*).

butterfly valve [hyd.] A circular disc inside a pipe, hinged at two pivots on a diameter. It is often used for controlling the flow in large pipes in hydroelectric schemes between *forebay* and power station. It is perfectly balanced and needs therefore very little power to open it.

buttress A concrete or masonry thickening pier at right angles to a wall, built to help the wall to resist earth thrust or water pressure or arch thrust. Unlike a *counterfort*, a buttress is visible, being placed on the opposite side of the wall from the thrust. *See also* flying buttress.

buttress drain [rly] *See* chevron drain.

buttress screw thread [mech.] A screw thread designed to carry a heavy axial load in one direction only. The front face of the thread, carrying the thrust, is perpendicular to the axis of the screw, the back face is at 45° to it. *See* square thread.

butt strap A steel plate which covers a butt joint and connects the two members by welding or riveting.

butt weld [mech.] A *weld* between two pieces without overlap, frequently a *resistance weld*, or a *flash-butt weld*.

butt-welded tube [mech.] Steel tube made by bending mild steel plate into a cylindrical shape and welding the joint.

byatt A horizontal timber, which supports decking, walkways, etc., in trench excavations.

bye channel or bye wash or diversion or diversion cut A ditch along a contour, dug to lead dirty water around, and not into, a reservoir.

by-pass A pipe or conduit or road for directing flow of traffic around, instead of through, another pipe or conduit or road.

C

cabinet projection [d.o.] A way of showing solid objects on a drawing. The object is drawn in plan or elevation. Faces perpendicular to the plan or to the wall elevated are drawn at an angle of 45°, and to half the proportional length of those in the plan. *See* **axonometric projection, planometric projection.**

cable (1) [elec.] A collection of insulated conductors protected if need be by armouring. *See* **armoured cable.**

(2) In a *cableway*, the stationary steel wire *rope* also called the *track cable.*

(3) In *prestressed concrete*, a *tendon* consisting of a number of wires or strands.

cable drill [min.] or **churn drill** or **percussion drill** A heavy drilling rig used in drilling 7 to 25 cm dia. vertical holes in prospecting, quarrying (and in oil-well drilling down to 1500 m in USA). The rig consists of a tower known as a *derrick* for handling the tools, a steel wire rope hung from the top of the derrick which raises and lowers the tools into the hole, and the tools themselves which are moved up and down at the bottom of the hole (during drilling) by the walking beam. Drilling speeds vary from 3 m per hour in clay or soapstone to 0·3 m per hour in hard limestone. Small units are used for *site investigation.*

cable duct A protective earthenware pipe or a hole cast in concrete, through which electric or *prestressing* cables are pulled. Prestressing cables, after stressing up, are grouted into the ducts, that is, the ducts are filled with cement *grout*, but BS 4975 disagrees with this practice. *See* **Ductube.**

cable-laid rope Rope twisted with an *ordinary lay*, not *Lang lay*.

cable railway An incline up which wagons are pulled by an endless steel wire rope, overhead or beneath the wagons.

cable-stayed bridge [stru.] A bridge type that closely resembles the *self-anchored suspension bridge* but differs from it mainly in that each cable is connected directed to deck girder without *suspenders*. There are therefore more than the usual two cables needed for a *suspension bridge*. Few, if any, were built before 1955. Most of them are in Germany but the longest span (457 m) is over the Hooghly at Calcutta. The next longest is in France at St Nazaire, over the river Loire.

cableway A *materials-handling* device used in bridging, dam building, ore transporting, and excavation, consisting of two towers carrying between them a heavy steel rope called a *track cable*. A carriage on grooved track wheels can be pulled along the track cable by the *traction rope*. A load may hang from the carriage by the hoisting or fall rope, which lowers or raises the load. Average travelling speeds are about 360 m/min., hoisting speeds up to 120 m/min., and loads 5 to 10 tons for spans of 100 to 1000 m. Cableways may have both towers stationary (fixed cableway), one tower stationary (radial cableway), or both towers movable on rails (full-travelling cableway). *Compare* **aerial ropeway** *and see* **Blondin, excavating cableway, slack-line cableway, luffing cableway mast.**

cableway excavator A *slack-line cableway.*

cableway transporter A crane like a *transporter crane* but much more lightly built and having as track for the carrier a steel rope hung between the ends of the girder. The girder is thus not loaded in bending, or only slightly, but mainly in compression, and can be much lighter than a transporter crane girder, since it acts more as a strut than as a girder.

cadastral mapping [sur.] Mapping land for the purpose of recording its ownership.

caisson (1) [hyd.] A *ship caisson*.

(2) A cylindrical or rectangular ring-wall for keeping water or soft ground from flowing into an excavation while digging for foundations down to good ground. It may be open or closed at the foot, and later forms part of the foundations. *See* **box/Chicago/Gow/open caisson, compressed air, drop shaft, monolith, pneumatic caisson**.

caisson disease A disease which affects workers in *compressed air* who come too quickly out of the *air lock*. It is caused by bubbles of nitrogen coming out of the blood. The only treatment is to take the sufferer to a *medical lock* or the nearest air lock immediately, for recompression and slow decompression. It is also called the bends, diver's palsy, diver's paralysis, air embolism, compressed-air disease, or screws. *See* **decanting, helium**.

caisson pile A *Gow caisson*.

calcine [min.] To heat ore or mineral for some time at a high temperature to drive off carbon dioxide and water.

calcite $CaCO_3$ Crystalline calcium carbonate found in marble and other limestones.

calcium aluminate The refractory part of *high-alumina cement* consists of various calcium aluminates, some of them being even more refractory than monocalcium aluminate, which is white and melts at 1608°C.

calcium chloride, $CaCl_2$ An *admixture* used sometimes in proportions up to 0·03% by weight of the cement to accelerate its hardening rate, and therefore added to concrete during frost to accelerate its heat release. It is now never used in contact with steel.

calcium silicate The basis of *aerated concrete* and of *calcium silicate bricks* (B). *See* BS 187.

calfdozer A small *bulldozer*.

calibrate To check the graduations of an *instrument* or machine and if necessary to graduate it correctly.

calibre (or **caliber** in USA) The bore (internal diameter) of a pipe, or the capacity of other plant.

California bearing ratio method or **CBR method** A method of designing *flexible pavements* on the basis of the CBR test (below).

California bearing ratio test [s.m.] or **CBR test** A standardized testing procedure begun by California State Highways Department in 1929 for comparing the strengths of *base courses* of roads or airstrips. The soil is first compacted in a mould and then soaked for four days with a load on its surface. The expansion due to moistening is then measured, a good figure being less than 3%, a bad figure 7 to 20%. Finally the resistance of the soil to a standard plunger of area 19·35 sq. cm which has penetrated 2·5 mm is measured. The ratio of this resistance to the corresponding resistance in crushed rock is then calculated. This ratio is the CBR. *Compare* **Proctor plasticity needle**.

calking *See* **caulking**.

calliper log A continuous record of the uncased diameter of a borehole, useful in *well logging* for many purposes. Loose sands or shales can cave into a hole and create a hole twice the diameter of the bit.

callipers [mech.] A pair of steel legs pivoted together like a draughtsman's dividers, used for measuring the bore of pipes or their outside diameter.

calorific value or **heating value** The amount of heat liberated by the complete burning of unit weight of a fuel, expressed in heat units per unit weight. Thus for solid or liquid fuels it is expressed in kilojoules/kg. In some countries the kg-calorie per kg is used. 1 kJ/kg = 0·43 Btu/lb; 1 kcal = 4·187 kilojoule.

camber [hyd.] A *gate chamber*. *See also* (B), *and* **hog**.

camber rod [stru.] or **belly rod** The tensioning rod below a *trussed beam*.

camel [hyd.] A large hollow steel float tied to a ship to raise it in the water and float it past a shallow place. *See* **saucer.**

camouflet [min.] A cavity underground, formed by an explosion that makes no crater. It is usually achieved by *chambering.*

camp sheathing or **camp shedding** or **camp sheeting** (1) A *retaining wall* often used to hold back the river bank at a *barge bed*. It consists of two connected rows of timber piles 1·5 to 3 m apart, the space between being filled with earth.

(2) A light *sheet pile* wall.

canal [hyd.] A channel dug or built up to carry water for navigation, water power, irrigation, or other purposes.

canalization [hyd.] The dividing of a river into *reaches* separated by locks and weirs to help navigation, prevent flooding, generate power, or for irrigation. The ships or barges pass the weirs through the *locks*. Outstanding recent examples are in the Tennessee Valley (USA) and the Rhône (France). On a smaller scale, in England, the Thames is canalized.

canal lift [hyd.] A tank drawn on wheels up or down an incline (or vertically) for passing barges through a *lock* with a lift larger than about 15 m.

cant [rly] or **banking** *Superelevation.*

cantilever [stru.] A beam which is built in and held down by weight or otherwise securely fixed at one end, and hangs freely at the other, an overhanging beam. In modern structural materials, metals and concrete, the cantilever corresponds to the old bracket of masonry or cast iron or timber.

cantilever arm [stru.] In a *cantilever bridge*, the part overhanging from the support into the central span, and carrying at its end one end of the *suspended span.*

cantilever bridge [stru.] Generally a symmetrical three-span bridge of which each of the outer spans is anchored down at the shore and overhangs into the central span about one third of the span. The suspended span, resting on the *cantilever arms*, occupies the remaining one third of the central span. The *Forth Bridge* (1890) has the unusual number of two main spans of 520 m clear, flanked by two side spans of 210 m each. The centre pier therefore carries a bridge element which overhangs on both sides. It has, however, a width at the base of 76 m. The *Quebec bridge* (1917) is a normal cantilever bridge with central span of 550 m, with 157 m side spans.

cantilever crane A *transporter crane* of which one or both ends overhang.

cantilever formwork *Climbing formwork.*

cantilever foundation [stru.] A foundation for a column or stanchion which for some reason does not have enough space for a truly central base. This frequently occurs on city sites where a large concentrated load from a stanchion comes down at the edge of the site. The base is therefore built well within the site and a concrete or steel beam is built upon the base to carry at its outer end the overhanging stanchion. The inner end of the beam

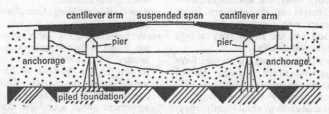

Cantilever bridge

must be counterweighted by a sufficient proportion of the weight of the rest of the building to prevent it lifting. The whole arrangement of base and cantilever beam is called a cantilever foundation.

cantilever wall (1) A reinforced-concrete *retaining wall* stabilized usually by the weight of the retained material on its heel.

(2) A *sheet pile* wall stabilized by its length of penetration below ground level on the free side. *Compare* **tied retaining wall.**

cantledge *See* **kentledge.**

cap (1) A *pilecap.*

(2) A *capping piece.*

(3) A *detonator.*

capacity curve [hyd.] A graph which shows the volume of a reservoir or tank at any given water level.

cape chisel *See* **crosscut chisel.**

capel [mech.] An eyed steel socket on the end of a steel wire rope, used for *capping* it.

capillarity [s.m.] The rising of fluid in tiny hair-like spaces (capillaries) above the level of the fluid in an open vessel. In soils, water rises between $\dfrac{1}{eD}$ and $\dfrac{5}{eD}$ cm, where e = *voids ratio*, D = *effective size* of the soil. The maximum rise (within 24 hours) occurs with soils of D about 0·02 mm but much larger rises may occur with finer soils in several years.

capillary fringe [s.m.] Ground above the *water table* that is continuously wetted with capillary water. Above it is more capillary water, but not continuously. The height of the capillary fringe increases with increasing fineness of the soil and the fringe rises or falls with the water table.

capillary pressure [s.m.] or **seepage force** In ground which is being drained from outside an excavation (*see* **wellpoint**), capillary pressures help the excavated earth to stand steeply. However, if the ground is being drained from inside and not from outside the excavation, the capillary pressures will help the earth face to collapse. In *silt* with pores from ·05 to ·005 mm in size, the capillary pressure varies from 6 to 60 kPa. In *clays* the pressure is theoretically more (but clay is very much harder to drain) and in sands the pressure is much less than in silts. *See* **electro-osmosis.**

capillary rise [s.m.] In a glass tube of 0·02 mm bore, water will rise about 1·5 m. *See* **capillarity.**

capillary water [s.m.] Water maintained above the *water table* by capillarity.

capping [min.] American term for *overburden.*

capping piece A horizontal timber placed over the ends of two *walings* butted together. It takes the thrust of a *strut* and transfers it to the walings.

capstan [mech.] A *winch* used in railway sidings for moving wagons or on quaysides for moving ships. It differs from hoists or other haulage engines in having a drum with a vertical shaft, the engine usually hidden below ground.

carbon, carbonado *See* **black diamond.**

carbon-arc welding [mech.] *Welding* in an electric arc of which one electrode is a carbon rod, the other the piece being welded. Extra metal is supplied by a *filler rod* held in the arc. This method is used for building up metal and filling in holes but the *metal-arc* is usual for joining edges.

carbon-dioxide recorder An instrument which records on a chart the CO_2 content of a *flue gas* and therefore keeps a record of the efficiency of a *boiler* at any instant.

carbon-dioxide welding One form of *MIG welding.*

carbon monoxide CO A highly poisonous gas which is particularly dangerous because it has neither taste nor smell, formed by the burning of fuels in insufficient air, for example, when car engines are idling. There is little agreement about acceptable concentrations. For the second Mersey

Tunnel, the cost of ventilation to achieve 130 parts per million of CO was estimated at £4.20 per hour, and to achieve 83 ppm of CO, £14.50/hr.

carbon silicide *See* **silicon carbide.**

carbon steel [mech.] A *steel* whose properties are determined by the amount of carbon present. It contains no chromium, nickel, or molybdenum which are typical elements in *alloy steels*. Its maximum manganese content is about $1\frac{1}{2}\%$, that of silicon and copper about $\frac{1}{2}\%$ each. It generally means a *high-carbon steel*, since *mild steels* are *low-carbon* steels.

Carborundum A trade name for silicon carbide, a *refractory* and abrasive which is harder than *quartz*. It can be used at temperatures up to 2500°C.

carburizing [mech.] The introduction of carbon into the surface of steel by holding it at a suitable temperature, above the *critical point*, in contact with a source of carbon and nitrogen (often hoof and horn). Carburizing is usually followed either by direct quenching from the carburizing operation or by other suitable heat treatment to produce a hard case of *cementite* and a ductile tough *core*. *See* **case-hardening, cementation, gas carburizing.**

carpet *See* **bituminous carpet, wearing course.**

carriageway The part of a highway which carries vehicles (BS 892).

carriers Containers or buckets which travel on the *track rope* of a *cableway* or *aerial ropeway*, hung from grooved wheels.

Cartesian coordinates or **rectangular co-ordinates** *Coordinates* measured perpendicularly from fixed axes of reference which are at right angles to each other. The distances east or west are also called eastings, westings, abscissae, or departures. The distances north or south are called northings, southings, ordinates, or latitudes.

cartographer [d.o.] One who prepares charts or maps from data supplied by a hydrographical or *land surveyor*. He may be a draughtsman who has never worked outside a drawing office, or a qualified surveyor.

cartridge paper [d.o.] A hard opaque white *drawing paper* used for pencil or ink drawing.

cascade A series of vertical steps in a stream, sewer, etc., separating lengths in which the fall is normal. This arrangement avoids very steep slopes which may *scour* the bed with high flows or cause blockages with very small flows.

case [mech.] The surface of steel which has been hardened by *case-hardening*, leaving a relatively ductile *core* within the case.

cased pile A concrete pile cast into a steel casing in the ground.

case-hardening [mech.] Surface hardening of steel by *carburizing*, *cyaniding*, or *nitriding* followed sometimes by further heatings and *quenching*.

casing (1) *Formwork* for concrete.

(2) [min.] Steel pipe lining to oil or water wells or other *boreholes*.

(3) [mech.] A steel plate enclosure to a *fan* which widens out to a final *volute*.

castellated beam [stru.] Trade name for a steel beam formed by cutting a *rolled-steel joist* along the web in a zig-zag shape. After cutting in two, the two halves are rearranged with the crests of the cuts meeting, and are then welded together at these crests. The resulting beam is 50% deeper and has a moment of resistance about 100% larger.

casting yard A *blockyard*.

cast-in-place A more easily understood but less usual term than *cast-in-situ*.

cast-in-situ Concrete or plaster poured in place. The term is particularly applied to *piles* and lintels since these are often *precast*. *See* **bored pile.**

cast iron [mech.] Alloys of iron and carbon containing more than 1·7% and usually 2·4 to 4% of carbon. Cast-iron articles are made by casting from remelted *pig* iron with cast iron and steel scrap. It has a low melting point, flows well, and is easier to pour into intricate shapes than steel or wrought iron (which never melts). *See* **malleable cast iron.**

cast steel [mech.] or **crucible steel** Steel which has not been *forged* or *rolled* since casting. All steel is cast during steel-making but most of it is subsequently so worked as to change its shape considerably. Steel castings are expensive because of the difficulty of getting the molten metal to flow properly at a reasonably low temperature. *See* ingot.

cast-welded rail joint A welded joint between two butted rails, usually cast by the *thermit process.*

catch basin [sewage] American term for a *catch pit.*

catch drain A *grip* (1).

catch feeder [hyd.] A ditch for *irrigation.*

catchment area or **drainage area** or **drainage basin** or **gathering ground** The area drained by a watercourse or providing water for a reservoir. *See* **watershed.**

catch pit A pit provided in a drainage system at an accessible point, to collect grit (which is dug out periodically) and prevent it from blocking inaccessible parts of the drains.

catch points [rly] On an upgrade, a cut made through the rails, so that a wagon which becomes unhitched and runs back is harmlessly derailed. *See* **points.**

catchwater (1) A *grip* (1).

(2) [hyd.] A channel cut along the edge of high ground to divert the streams running off it from the lowlying ground that might be flooded by them. In the UK, the Great Ouse Flood Protection Scheme has a catchwater leading the waters of the Lark, the Wissey and the Little Ouse away from the Cambridgeshire fens.

catenary [stru.] The curve into which a uniformly loaded rope falls when hung between two points. It is seen in *suspension bridges*, *cableways*, and *ropeways.*

catenary correction [sur.] *Sag correction.*

catenary suspension An overhead suspension of an electric power conductor by vertical links of different lengths which hang it from a steel wire rope stretched tightly above it. In this way a power conductor can be kept at constant height above the locomotive which it feeds.

caterpillar gate [hyd.] A massive steel gate for controlling the flow through a spillway. It is carried on *crawler tracks* with hardened steel rollers bearing on steeply sloping rails at each side of the opening. In England this is often called a caterpillar *penstock.* The name caterpillar gate, used in USA, is less confusing.

caterpillars [mech.] A popular name for *crawler track* for tractors.

cat-head sheave A *sheave* high up on a pile frame.

cathode [elec.] or **kathode** The plate (*electrode*) in *electrolysis* at which metals or hydrogen are released or at which chemical reduction occurs. *Compare* **anode.**

cathodic protection Electrical protection of underground or underwater structures such as pipelines from corrosion. The structure is made the *cathode* in a direct current circuit which has a higher voltage than (and an opposite direction from) the estimated corrosion voltage. The *anode* is designed to be worn away and is more easily and cheaply replaced than the pipeline. Another method working on a similar principle used for many years is *galvanizing.* In the presence of an *electrolyte* a current flows from the zinc to the steel, dissolving the zinc and protecting bare parts of the steel. This is *sacrificial protection. See* BSCP 1021 Cathodic Protection.

cation [elec.] An electrically charged atom which migrates naturally to the cathode in an *electrolyte.* Most metals and hydrogen produce cations. Cations can exist outside of electrolysis, for instance in clays. *See* **base exchange, anion.**

caulking (1) The blocking of a seam or joint to make it air-tight, water-tight, or steam-tight by driving in tow, lead, oakum, or *dry pack*.

(2) [mech.] Making boiler plates tight by deforming the exposed edges of plates with a *caulking tool* struck by a hammer, thus driving each exposed edge into contact with its neighbour.

caulking tool [mech.] A blunt *cold chisel* often with an offset shape for *caulking* boiler plates and driving in caulking materials.

causeway (1) A road carried over marsh or water by an earth bank or wall.

(2) Scots. A road surfaced with *setts*.

caving [r.m.] A common mining method, involving the removal of mineral without leaving support in the void from which it was taken. The rock breaks and increases in volume because of air spaces between the rock pieces. The broken rock in the *goaf* can thus provide some support for the rock above, and delays the appearance of subsidence at the surface.

cavitation [mech.] In pumping at excessive speeds certain parts of the pump may move faster than the water. This occurs with *centrifugal pumps* or turbine *runners* near the *draft tube*. The result is corrosion of metal parts due to the liberation of oxygen from the water.

cavity tanking *Tanking* (*B*), waterproofing of a basement that is achieved by air gaps rather than by waterproof materials. Inside the retaining wall, which holds back the earth outside the building, is an air gap which can be drained to a sump from which the water can be pumped (if it is below the level of the drains). If the floor also leaks, it can be similarly drained. The wet floor must be covered by *paving flags*, on which nibs about 2 cm deep are cast below at the corners, allowing ample drainage space under them. A *damp-proof course* (*B*) is laid on the flags and the *topping* (2) over this. Cavity tanking is

absolutely reliable. From the ancient builders, until about 1900, it was the only known method. But it wastes space – sometimes, the whole cellar.

CBR *See* **California bearing ratio.**

celerity [hyd.] The overall speed of a wave.

cellular cofferdam A *double-wall cofferdam* used in very large projects in water. The double wall consists of a succession of cells in contact, each cell being, for example, an 18 m dia. steel *sheet-pile* ring filled with sand. The width of the cell is usually about equal to its unsupported height. The junctions between the 18 m dia. rings are made, in one type of cellular cofferdam, by arcs of steel sheet piling. Another type is the 'diaphragm cell' in which all cells are similar and are joined along a straight line, with circular arcs only on the outer walls. The straight line, or diaphragm, acts as a tie or strut between the outer walls.

cellular concrete US term for *aerated concrete*.

cellulose nitrate *Nitrocellulose*.

cement (1) The bond or matrix between the particles in a rock, particularly that binding the sand grains in a sandstone or a quartzite or a conglomerate.

(2) A powder that, mixed with water, binds a stone-sand mixture into a strong concrete within a few days. Most cements, except *high-alumina cement*, contain at least some *Portland cement*. Nearly all set well under water. Non-Portland cements include *supersulphated* and *high-alumina cements*. *See also* **Perspex** (*B*).

cementation (1) Injecting cement *grout* under pressure into fissured rocks to strengthen them and make them water-tight. It is a form of *artificial cementing* used in shaft sinking and tunnelling, and is also called the *grouting method of shaft sinking*. *See* **oil-well cement.**

(2) Impregnating wrought-iron bars

49

with carbon by packing them with charcoal and heating them for several days. This was the old method of steel-making, but the term is also often applied to *carburizing* and sometimes to *sherardizing* (*B*), or similar processes in which steel or iron is packed and heated with a metal to acquire a protective coating.

cemented carbides [mech.] or **sintered carbides** Materials used for the tips of very-high-speed tools. Tungsten and molybdenum carbides are the main constituents with some tantalum, cobalt, and titanium. *See* **hard facing, sintering, Stellite.**

cement grout *See* **grout.**

cement gun A compressed-air operated ejector for making *pneumatic mortar* or *gunite.*

cementite [mech.] The very hard but brittle constituent of white cast iron, Fe_3C, an iron carbide also present in the *case* made during *carburizing* or *cementation.*

cement joggle A method of preventing relative movement between concrete blocks in *blockwork* structures by leaving an indentation for the height of each block opposite a corresponding notch in the next block. When the blocks are set, this cavity (in two blocks) is filled with concrete or mortar, poured in. *See* **joggle.**

cement mortar *Mortar* composed of 4 (or fewer) parts of sand to 1 of cement, with a suitable amount of water.

centesimal measure [sur.] Division of a circle into 400 grads or grades, each with 100 minutes, each minute having 100 seconds. A full circle less one second is written 399^g $99'$ $99''$, and a full circle *sexagesimal* less one second is written $359°$ $59'$ $59''$.

centi- A prefix meaning 'one hundredth part of'.

centimetre or **cm** One hundredth part of the *metric* unit of length the *metre.* 2·54 cm are equivalent to 1 in.

central reservation or **reserve** A *median strip.*

centre (or in USA **on center**) *See* **centres.**

centre cut [min.] *See* **wedge cut.**

centre of gravity [stru.] or **centre of mass** or **mass centre** That point in a body at which it will balance if supported. It is the point at which the weight acts, and its location is important for all engineers. Structural engineers are interested in the centre of gravity of a number of forces since they try to place all columns with their *centroids* at the centre of gravity of the forces carried.

centre of pressure [hyd.] The point on an area subjected to fluid pressure, over which the whole force due to the pressures on the area may be taken to act.

centre punch [mech.] A small hard-steel bar with a blunt central point. The point is placed over the centre mark of a hole to be drilled in metal and the other end of the bar is struck with a hammer. The small dent thus made ensures that the bit starts drilling in the correct place. A centre punch looks like a *nail punch* (*B*), except for its point.

centres [d.o.] or **centre to centre** (In USA **on center**) A description of a dimension, for example 2 m centres (or 2 m crs) means 2 m between the centres of the pieces in question.

centre to centre *Centres.*

centrifugal blower [mech.] A small low-pressure, high-volume fan with a rotating impeller.

centrifugal brake [mech.] A safety mechanism on hoist drums which throws the brake shoes outwards on to the fixed brake drum when the load begins to run away.

centrifugal compressor [mech.] An air compressor which is not *reciprocating* and usually is made of several *centrifugal blowers* in series.

centrifugal force [mech.] A body carried round in a circle must (by Newton's Laws of Motion) tend at every instant to continue in a straight line, that is at a tangent to the circle. This tendency, its centrifugal force, is equal to its mass × its acceleration, that is the acceleration diverting it from straight-line motion. It is this force which requires railway and road curves to have *superelevation*. The centrifugal force of a train is considered to act at 1·8 m above rail level.

centrifugal pump A pump with a high-speed rotating *impeller*. Water enters near the centre of the impeller and is thrown outwards by the blades. These pumps take up less space than *reciprocating pumps*, are often suitable for direct electric drive, and are therefore often preferred, particularly in large plants pumping clean water. *See* **specific speed**.

centrifuge [mech.] A rapidly turning machine, rotating at several 1000 rpm, used in *soil mechanics* (*see* **centrifuge moisture equivalent**), and for dewatering sewage sludge.

centrifuge moisture equivalent [s.m.] or **CME** The percentage of water retained by a soil which has been first saturated with water and then subjected to a force equal to 1000 times the force of gravity for one hour (ASCE MEP 22). It is a way of comparing road soils which is generally less used than the *consistency limits*.

centroid [stru.] The centre of area of a section, that point about which the *static moment* of all the elements of area is equal to zero. For a homogeneous beam the *neutral axis* passes through the centroid. *See* **eccentricity**.

cess [rly] The flat area at formation level, adjoining the ballast of a rail track.

cesspit or **cesspool** A tank, usually underground, of brick or concrete, for collecting sewage where no sewage treatment is available. It is pumped out periodically by the *water authority* for a fee. A cesspool may be overflowing, pervious (leaching), or impervious, but these points are settled by the authority. *See also* (*B*).

cesspool A *cesspit*.

chain or **land chain** [sur.] A land surveyor's measure, 20 m long (formerly 66 ft and 100 ft) made up of 100 steel links with *tallies* to mark each metre (BS 4484:1969). The *Gunter's chain*, 66 ft long with 100 links of 7·92 in., was long used because of its convenience in land area measurements – 10 square chains = 1 acre. The chain is more convenient and less easily damaged than the band and is often quite accurate enough for the long chainages needed in land area measurement.

chainage [sur.] A length measured by *chain* or steel *tape*.

chain block [mech.] A *differential pulley block*.

chain book [sur.] A *field book* in which the surveyor records his lengths measured on the ground.

chain-bucket dredger [hyd.] A *bucket-ladder dredger*.

chainman [sur.] A junior member of a survey team who carries the chain. *Axman* in USA.

chain of locks [hyd.] A series of interconnected locks in which the *head gate* of each lower lock is the *tail gate* for the lock above it. Each *chamber* is followed immediately by another.

chain pump [mech.] A way of raising water by discs passing up a pipe on a chain. For short lifts it is less inefficient than it appears to be on paper.

chain saw A power saw used for cutting timber in the forest.

chain sling [mech.] A *sling* of *wrought iron* or 1½% *manganese steel*.

chain survey A survey in which no angles are measured, only lengths. It may be a *triangulation*; if so the angles can be deduced from the triangles.

chair (1) [rly] or **rail chair** A cast-iron support 20 × 37 cm in plan screwed to a *sleeper* in British practice. It holds a *bullhead rail* wedged into it with a steel spring or hardwood *key*. *See* **rail fastening**.

(2) A bar bent in such a way that it holds up the top steel of a reinforced-concrete slab by resting on the bottom steel.

chair bolt [rly] A bolt which passes up

through a *sleeper* and chair from below and holds the *chair* down by a nut screwed on to it.

chalk line A length of bricklayer's line well rubbed with chalk, held tight and plucked against a wall, floor, or other surface to mark a straight line on it. It is also used by plasterers, miners, mural painters, and others.

chamber [hyd.] or **lock bay** In a canal *lock* the space enclosed between the upper and lower gates.

chambered-level tube [sur.] A *level tube* with an air chamber at one end from which air can be added to the bubble by tilting. Temperature modifications to the bubble length can thus be corrected.

chambering [min.] or **springing** or **squibbing** The firing of successively larger charges of explosive with little *stemming* until the bottom of the hole is sufficiently enlarged (chambered) to take the final charge (which is properly stemmed). The method is much used for heavy blasts in quarrying. *See* **camouflet, jet drilling, torpedo.**

change face [sur.] or **reverse face** To *transit* a *theodolite*, that is to rotate the telescope through 180° vertically and 180° horizontally, so that the vertical circle is at the opposite side from before, when viewing the same object. *See* **face left, face right.**

change point (1) [sur.] or **turning point** In levelling, a point on which two readings of the staff are taken, a *foresight* and a *backsight*.

(2) [mech.] A *critical point*.

channel or **channel iron** or **channel section** A rolled-steel section of ⌷-shape.

channeller (or **channeler** in USA) A powerful quarrying machine with a row of chisels which cuts a slot in stone at any angle, and without explosive.

Channel Tunnel A project for which 3 km of tunnel were bored in 1882, 1·5 km near Dover and 1·5 km near Sangatte, France. Both were driven by the tunnelling machine invented by Col. Beaumont. Proposals made in 1960 by the Channel Tunnel Study Group and accepted with minor amendments by the two governments in 1964 included two single-track railway tunnels 7·3 m dia. with a 3·8 m dia. pilot tunnel between them for drainage and maintenance, to have tracks electrified at 25,000 volts DC. Only a few metres were driven in 1975 before the funds ran out.

characteristic strength [stru.] A design concept introduced by BSCP 110: 1972, that clarifies the process of structural design. It is the mean strength of the material less 1·64 times the standard deviation of the strengths. This value is used for steel and concrete but it does not allow for overloads, nor for mistakes in design or building. Consequently a partial safety factor must be applied to a characteristic strength, so as to show the safe working stress.

charging hopper The part of a *concrete mixer* resting on the ground. The cement, sand, and gravel are placed in it. The hopper is then raised and shoots them into the drum.

Charpy test [mech.] An *impact test* in which a notched test-piece supported at both ends is broken by a blow from a striker on the face opposite to and immediately behind the notch.

chartered civil/structural/municipal, etc., engineer Someone who has been admitted to full (corporate) membership of one of these institutions, usually by examination; he is either a full member or an associate member, but not a graduate member nor a student member. Membership of other engineering institutions is very similar.

check (1) Generally, a verification of a survey, a calculation, etc.

(2) [hyd.] A structure which controls the water level in an irrigation canal or ditch.

(3) [hyd.] An area of land between ridges which confine the irrigation water.

checker [d.o.] An engineer *section leader* who is usually fully qualified and checks structural drawings.

check rail or **guard rail, safety rail, side rail** On railway curves, a third rail fixed close outside the inner rail to reduce the wear on the outer rail caused by centrifugal thrust and to keep the inner wheel on the rail.

check valve [mech.] or **clack** or **non-return valve** or **reflux valve** A valve which allows flow in a pipe one way only. A check valve is always placed on the delivery side of a mine pump or other *force pump*. It protects the pump from the considerable weight of water in the shaft pipes which could otherwise flow back, reverse the pump, or damage it. The usual type is a *flap valve*.

chemical gauging [hyd.] or **chemi-hydrometry** Measuring the quantity of flowing water by determining the dilution of a chemical solution introduced upstream at a known rate and concentration.

chemical precipitation [sewage] Chemical settlement of sewage.

chemi-hydrometry *See* **chemical gauging**.

chemise A wall which *revets* an earth bank.

chequer plate or **chequered plate** Steel or cast-iron plate, perforated or patterned to make a non-slip floor in power stations, factories, fire escapes, etc.

chert Non-crystalline silica which is found in limestones. *Flint* is a form of chert.

chevron drain [rly] or **herringbone drain** Diagonal, stone-filled trenches in railway cuttings laid out in herringbone pattern to drain into buttress drains which are laid out along the line of steepest slope.

Chicago caisson or **Chicago well** A small *cofferdam* used in medium stiff clays, about 1·2 m dia. lined with planks added in 1·5 m lengths and sunk to hard ground for pier *foundations*. The vertical plank supports are held in place by steel rings wedged against the sides. *See* **cylinder, Gow caisson**.

Chicago well A *Chicago caisson*.

chief draughtsman [stru.] The chief of a structural drawing office (unless a chief designer is over him). He is generally a *designer* with high qualifications and much experience.

chilled cast iron [mech.] Iron cast in a metal mould so as to harden the surface of the casting to about 2 cm depth. Railway wheels are sometimes of chilled iron.

Chinaman chute A structure like a *gantry* with a ramp up to it, on to which earth or other material is pushed by a *bulldozer* or dragged by a scraper for loading into a lorry below.

chipping [mech.] Removing surface defects from steel or iron by *cold chisel* or *chipping chisel* (BS 2094).

chipping chisel [mech.] A *cold chisel* or *chipping hammer*.

chipping hammer or **chipping chisel** A welder's compressed-air tool for cleaning steel after welding. It weighs from 3 to 6 kg.

chippings Crushed stone from 3 to 25 mm. *See* **coated chippings**.

chlorination A *disinfection* process in *water treatment*. It is the most popular one in most English-speaking countries. Usually 0·1 to 0·2 mg/litre of free residual chlorine are left in the water as it flows from the waterworks. Chlorine is a strong oxidizing agent and for this reason an excellent disinfectant, but a poisonous gas. Some authorities (New York) have therefore ceased to buy gaseous chlorine and use calcium hypochlorite ($CaOCl_2$) or other compounds of chlorine instead (hypochlorination). Hazardous cylinders of chlorine gas are not needed at such waterworks. In USA chlorine is regularly used in *sewage treatment* to reduce smell and for other reasons, but not in Britain.

chord [stru.] or **boom** or **flange** The top or bottom, generally horizontal part of a metal, timber, or concrete *girder* or *truss*.

C-horizon [s.m.] The parent material, without humus, below the topsoil of the *A-horizon* and *B-horizon*, from which these are derived by leaching and deposition respectively. *See* **subsoil.**

chuck [mech.] A rotating part on a lathe for holding the work or on a drill for holding the drilling-bit. Every sort of drill, from the rock drill to the carpenter's brace, has a chuck.

churn drill [min.] A *cable drill.*

chute [hyd.] A steep channel usually for leading water on to a water wheel.

Ciment Fondu *High-alumina cement.*

Cipolletti weir [hyd.] A *measuring weir* with a trapezoidal opening widest at the top, having the sides sloping at 1 horizontal to 4 vertical. It is convenient to use, since a vertical stick can be graduated in such a way as to read discharge directly.

circuit breaker [elec.] A device which automatically breaks a circuit when the current exceeds a certain value. It is a *cutout* for currents which are larger than can safely be interrupted by a fuse. It can also be opened like a switch, but can usually not be reclosed unless the circuit is working correctly without overload.

circular-arc method [s.m.] or **cylindrical-surface method** or **slip-circle method** A simple method of determining the stability of an earth slope in *clay* soil. Failure is assumed to occur by *shear* along a circular arc of the length of the earth mass. The resistance to failure is the area of the cylindrical surface of failure times the *shear strength* of the clay. *See also* **rotational slide.**

circular level [sur.] A *level tube* in which the upper surface of the glass has a spherical curve.

circular mil [elec.] The area of a circle with a dia. of 1 mil ($\cdot 001$ in.). One circular mil therefore has an area of $\cdot 7854 \times 10^{-6}$ sq. in. Mainly used in USA.

circulating water The water which circulates in a coal washery or ore concentration plant, etc. To reduce pollution, it has been found possible to completely avoid its release into nearby rivers, streams or sewers.

circumpolar stars [sur.] Stars which never set at certain latitudes on the earth. At the pole, all visible stars are circumpolar, at the equator none are. At intermediate points only those stars are circumpolar which have a declination more than 90° minus the latitude of the place. *See* **culmination.**

civil engineer A person qualified for *civil engineering* work by a university degree or, in Britain, by membership of the Institution of Civil Engineers (AMICE or MICE). Members of the Institutions of Municipal Engineers, of Highway Engineers, of Public Health Engineers, or of Structural Engineers would generally also be regarded as civil engineers.

civil engineering Originally the whole of non-military engineering at the time of the founding of the Institution of Civil Engineers (about 1825), the sense has now become limited to that part which is neither mechanical nor electrical. It includes land drainage, water supply, rivers, canals, harbours, docks, marine construction, water power, *sewage disposal, sewerage, bridges, tunnels,* railways, *roads, traffic engineering, foundations,* airports, municipal engineering, *soil mechanics, structural design,* town planning, and transportation engineering. The field is so wide that it is difficult for any engineer to specialize in more than two of the subjects mentioned. The work of a civil engineer consists in preparing plans after surveying a site, letting contracts, supervising construction, and so on. In USA, the Massachusetts Institute of Technology recognizes 5 areas of specialization, namely structures, materials, hydrodynamics, soils, and systems (with special stress on systems which affect the other four, e.g. water-resources systems, transport systems, environmental-control systems, information systems).

civil engineering assistant One who does the work of a *civil engineer* on the site or in an office but is not in sole charge of his work. *See* below.

civil engineering draughtsman One who

prepares civil engineering drawings. Like a *civil engineering assistant*, he may or may not be qualified.

civil engineering technician *See* **technician engineer.**

clack *See* **check valve.**

clad steel [mech.] *Carbon* or low *alloy steel* with a layer of some other metal or alloy firmly bonded to one or more surfaces (BS 2094). *Compare* **Alclad.**

clamp handle [sur.] A hand grip for tensioning a steel tape when less than a full tape length is being measured.

clamping screw [sur.] On *theodolites*, a screw for clamping a vernier so that the *tangent screw* can be used.

clamshell grab A *grab* shaped like a clamshell.

clapotis [hyd.] The lapping of waves on a wall that rises above the water level. It doubles the wave height and so raises the mean sea level and pressure on the wall.

clap sill [hyd.] A *lock sill.*

claquage grouting *See* **artificial cementing.**

clarification Removal of tiny suspended solids from *raw water* or *sewage*, in small concentrations, often as little as 100 mg/litre, usually by settlement in a circular tank called a clarifier. Sedimentation is removal of dirt that settles from relatively dirtier water.

In the USA, a clarifier is usually a sewage sedimentation tank, but never in the UK. *See* **waterworks.**

classification of soils [s.m.] Soil particles are described (after *mechanical analysis* of a soil sample) as sand, silt, or clay on the basis of the sizes in the table below. The BSI classification is often used in Europe by civil engineers. *Clays* are defined by their *consistency limits.*

classifier [s.m.] A separator for dividing sand or other pulp into two sizes, the overflow (or slime or undersize) and the underflow (or sand or *oversize*). Water is generally the medium but air is used with fine powders. *See* **cyclone.**

classify [s.m.] To divide a mixture of particles or lumps of various sizes into products of definite size limits.

clay [s.m.] Very fine-grained soil of *colloid* size, consisting mainly of hydrated silicate of aluminium. It is a plastic *cohesive soil* which shrinks on drying, expands on wetting, and when compressed gives up water. Under the electron microscope clay crystals have been seen to have a platy shape in which for Wyoming *bentonite* the ratio of length to thickness is about 250 to 1 (like mica). For other clays it is about 10 to 1. Clays are described

Soil description		British Standards Institution after BS 1377	American Society for Testing and Materials
		Size in millimetres	
frictional soils	coarse sand	2·0 to 0·6	2·0 to 0·25
	medium sand	0·6 to 0·2	—
	fine sand	0·2 to 0·06	0·25 to 0·05
		0·06 mm is the smallest practicable size for sieving.	
	coarse silt	0·06 to 0·02 ⎫	
	medium silt	0·02 to 0·006 ⎬	0·05 to 0·005
	fine silt	0·006 to 0·002 ⎭	
cohesive soils	clay	under 0·002	under 0·005

See also **airfield soil classification, grading curve, soil mechanics.**

for engineering purposes by their *consistency limits*. According to its *unconfined compressive strength*, a clay may be defined as very soft (less than 35 kN/m²), soft (35–70 kN/m²), medium or firm (70–140 kN/m²), stiff (140–280 kN/m²), hard or very stiff (280 kN/m²). Clays are further described as organic, intact, etc. *See* **classification of soils, sensitivity ratio.**

clay cutter (1) In *suction cutter dredgers*, a hydraulically or shaft-driven bit which may be a metre or more in diameter, fixed to the suction pipe and raised or lowered with it.

(2) A steel pipe used for sinking rapid holes with a *cable drill* in clay, particularly the shallow holes needed for *bored piles*. It is about 1·2 m long, of diameter equal to that of the hole required, and drops into the clay under its own weight with sufficient force to penetrate it. After each drop the pipe is hoisted out of the hole and the clay within it is removed by spade.

clay puddle or **puddle clay** or **pug** Plastic clay used for waterproofing. It is used for lining ponds or ditches, in coffering or in *cut-off walls* to dams. In Britain, clay puddle is a spadeable clay halfway between the *liquid* and the *plastic limits*. In USA it is a much wetter clay near the liquid limit and it cannot be spaded.

clay sampler [s.m.] A *soil sampler*.

clay spade A *grafting tool*.

cleaning Removing clay, etc., from sand or gravel.

clearance [mech.] The space between a moving object and a stationary object, particularly that between a rail wagon and a wall or tunnel.

clearance hole *See* **clearing hole.**

clearing or **clearing and grubbing** Removal of tree stumps and shrubs before excavation of a site. Graders and other earth-moving plant cannot work on soil containing roots.

clearing hole or **clearance hole** [mech.] A hole drilled slightly larger than the bolt which passes through it, generally 1·5 mm larger for *black bolts* or for *high-strength bolts*.

clear span [stru.] The horizontal distance, or clear unobstructed opening, between two supports of a beam. It is always less than the *effective span*.

clear-water reservoir [hyd.] A *service reservoir*.

cleat *See* **angle cleat**, also (*B*).

cleavage fracture [mech.] or **brittle fracture** or **crystalline fracture** Fracture of steel or iron along cleavage planes showing bright facets and characterized by a lack of visible *plastic deformation* (BS 2094). This is a type of breakage which is abnormal in *mild steel*. *See also* **cup-and-cone fracture, impact test.**

clevis [mech.] A U-shaped iron bar, drilled at the ends of the U. It is used as a *shackle* for connecting steel wire ropes to a load.

client The person or organization by whom an engineer or architect is employed, to whom he is responsible and from whom he draws his fees. He is usually the *building owner* in a building contract.

climbing formwork or **cantilever formwork** (1) Wall forms which are self-supporting, being held in place by hook bolts cast into the concrete or by through bolts which are later removed from it. Usually the bolts carry long vertical members (soldiers) which in cantilever can support consecutively several lifts of *formwork* and are therefore moved up less frequently than the forms. In some types there are two wall forms, an upper and a lower. The lower one is leap-frogged over the upper one, and the wall is thus never completely stripped until its full height is reached.

(2) *Sliding forms.* To avoid confusion, this sense should perhaps be avoided.

clinograph (1) [min.] A *borehole surveying* instrument which records the angle of slope of the *borehole* at any point. Several types exist, many being electrically operated, some with an internal camera and gyroscopic orientation.

(2) [d.o.] An adjustable *set square*, not graduated to show angles.

clinometer [sur.] A hand-held instrument used for sighting down or up inclined planes to measure the angle of dip.

clip In *ropeways* a V-shaped steel bar bolted on to the traction rope.

clip screws [sur.] or **adjusting/clipping screws** The screws on the verniers of the vertical circle of a *theodolite* by which the verniers may be adjusted to eliminate error.

close boarding *See* **close timbering.**

closed traverse [sur.] A *traverse* which finishes at its starting point. A convenient way of checking the accuracy of a traverse is to close it, since the sum of the angles turned is 360°, the sum of the *eastings* is 0 and the sum of the *latitudes* is 0. *See* **closing error.**

closer A sheet pile cut or made to close a *cofferdam* when a standard pile will not fill the gap. *See* **creep,** *also* (*B*).

close timbering or **close boarding** Planks placed touching each other against the ground, used in *running ground*.

closing error [sur.] or **error of closure** In a *closed traverse*, the discrepancy between the starting point and the finishing point calculated from the recorded angles and distances. The error is usually distributed proportionately among the angles and distances, by *adjustment*.

clough [hyd.] A *sluice gate* in a *culvert*.

clutch or **interlock** (1) In *steel sheet piling*, the hook shape at the edge of each pile which grips a corresponding hook on the next pile.

(2) When rolled-steel joists are used as piles, a special section which grips the joists each side of it for their full length.

CME *See* **centrifuge moisture equivalent.**

coagulation A water- or sewage-treatment process in which a chemical, added to the water or sewage, precipitates something, usually a metal hydroxide *floc* that catches the tiny particles which cause turbidity in

water, enabling them to be removed relatively easily by settlement. Coagulation precedes *clarification* and is often used for treating drinking waters, rarely for sewage. Alum is the commonest coagulant for drinking water in the UK. *Compare* **flocculation.** *See* **waterworks.**

coarse aggregate or **stone** (1) For concrete, *aggregate* which stays on a sieve of 5 mm square opening. *See* **fine aggregate.**

(2) For bituminous material, coarse aggregate which stays on a 3 mm sieve.

coat *See* **sealing coat, tack coat, covered electrode,** *and* (*B*).

coated chippings/grit Chippings or grit which have been coated thinly with bituminous material for scattering over a wearing course.

coated macadam *See* **tarmacadam.**

cobbles Rounded stones used for paving. *Compare* **sett.**

code of practice A publication issued sometimes by the BSI, to describe what is considered to be good practice in the work in question. Codes of practice do not generally have the force of law, but supplement building by-laws. American *building codes* generally have the force of law.

coefficient of compressibility [s.m.] The change in *voids ratio* per unit increase of pressure. *Compare* **modulus of volume change.**

coefficient of consolidation [s.m.] In the *consolidation* of soils a value expressed in sq. cm per minute, if the permeability is in cm per minute. It is equal to:

$$\frac{\text{coefficient of permeability} \times (1 + \text{initial voids ratio})}{\text{coefficient of compressibility} \times \text{density of water.}}$$

coefficient of contraction [hyd.] The ratio of the smallest cross-sectional area of a jet discharged under pressure from an orifice, to the area of the orifice.

coefficient of discharge [hyd.] The ratio of the observed to the theoretical discharge of a liquid through an orifice, weir, or pipe. *See* **effective area of an orifice.**

coefficient of expansion or **coefficient of thermal expansion** The expansion of a material per unit length for each degree rise in temperature. For steel and concrete and brickwork the value is roughly 0·00001 per degree C, though for some brickwork it can be as low as half this. The ordinary value involves a change in length of 1 cm in a 30 m long member, when the temperature changes by 33°C. If this change were prevented by complete restraint, it would cause a stress of 7 N/mm² in unreinforced concrete with a modulus of elasticity of 20 kN/mm², and of course a higher stress in concretes with higher E values. Such high stresses explain why *movement joints* are built into concrete.

coefficient of friction [mech.] The ratio between the force causing a body to slide along a plane and the force normal to the plane.

coefficient of imperviousness American term for *impermeability factor.*

coefficient of internal friction [s.m.] The tangent of the angle ϕ, the *angle of internal friction.*

coefficient of permeability [s.m.] The imaginary average velocity of flow through the total (voids and solids) area of soil under a *hydraulic gradient* of 1. *See* **permeability.**

coefficient of traction [mech.] *See* **tractive resistance.**

coefficient of uniformity [s.m.] The ratio between the grain diameter which is larger than 60% by weight of the particles in a soil sample, to that diameter, the *effective size*, which is larger than 10% by weight of the particles. It is more briefly expressed as $\frac{D_{60}}{D_{10}}$. Uniform soils have uniformity coefficient less than 3. Non-uniform soils have a relatively flat *grading curve*, uniform soils a steep one.

coefficient of variation In statistics an estimate of the variability of, for instance, the *crushing strength* of a brick from a certain kiln. It is the ratio of the *standard deviation* of a series of values to its mean. A simpler figure is used in the British Standard for sand-lime bricks (BS 187). It is the ratio of the strength of the seven weakest to the average strength of the sample of twelve. This ratio is never allowed to be lower than 0·8, and for the best bricks a minimum figure of 0·9 is required.

coefficient of velocity [hyd.] Of an opening through which fluid is flowing; the ratio of the measured discharge velocity to the theoretical discharge velocity.

coefficient of volume change [s.m.] The *modulus of volume change.*

coffer A canal lock *chamber.*

cofferdam A temporary *dam*, either *sheet piling* driven into the ground or a dam built above the ground to exclude water and thus give access to an area which is ordinarily submerged or waterlogged. Cofferdams are used down to 10 m below water level in deep foundation work. For greater depths a *caisson* or *cellular cofferdam* is needed. *See* **half-tide cofferdam.**

cogging [mech.] The start of the *hot rolling* of steel from *ingot* to *billet*, the purpose being to reduce the cross-sectional area of the ingot as fast as possible to a bar which can be rolled in a finishing mill to a *rolled-steel section* or forged to the final product.

cohesionless soil [s.m.] Sand, gravel, and similar soils, also known as *frictional soils* since their properties are defined more by their *angle of internal friction* than by *cohesion.*

cohesion of soil [s.m.] The stickiness of *clay* or *silt*, absent from sands, characteristic of clays. It is the *shear strength* of clay, which generally equals about half its *unconfined compressive strength*. *See* **Coulomb's equation.**

cohesive soil [s.m.] A sticky soil like *clay* or clayey silt. Some authorities define it as a soil with a *shear strength* equal to half its *unconfined compressive strength*. *See* **cohesionless soil, Coulomb's equation.**

Colcrete Trade name for a method of concreting roads or large foundations, which consists of laying the coarse aggregate on the ground, passing the cement, sand, and water through a special mixer, and pumping (or pouring) it into position. Since only about one-third of the concrete thus passes into the mixer the method is suitable, and can be economical, for pouring very large volumes at one time, as in dams. It is also suitable for underwater work, since the *Colgrout* enters the stone through a pipe. *Compare* **trémie.**

cold bend test [mech.] The *bend test*.

cold chisel [mech.] A fitter's chisel used for cold-cutting mild steel (or similar soft metals) when struck with a hammer.

cold drawing [mech.] or **wire drawing** Making steel wire by drawing it through successively smaller round holes in steel blocks called *dies*. This *hardens* the steel, raises its *ultimate tensile strength*, and reduces its diameter. By this means steel wire for *prestressing* and for mine winding ropes and haulage ropes is made. The strongest metal is that which has passed through the largest number of dies and is therefore of the smallest diameter. Wire of 2300 MN/m^2 ultimate strength is obtainable, of dia. 2·03 mm. Thick wire of 7·01 mm is worth about 1500 MN/m^2. *See* **Standard Wire Gauge** (*B*), **extrusion.**

cold rolling [stru.] Cold bending of steel sheet from 1·5 to 5 mm thick to make very light structural sections (channels and angles). They are widely used for building. *See* **Lally column, Stransteel.**

cold sett [mech.] A smith's chisel with a steel-bar handle held by one man while the *striker* hits the back of the sett with his sledge-hammer.

cold shortness [mech.] Brittleness at room temperatures. In iron or steel

this is due to too much phosphorus.

cold working [mech.] The shaping of metals at room temperature by *cold drawing*, *cold rolling* or pressing or stamping. It results in work *hardening* for such metals as iron, copper and aluminium. This involves generally an increase in strength but if carried too far may make the metal brittle. Since they have no yield point, cold-worked steel bars are specified by their 0·2% proof stress, as in BS 4461. *See* **hot working.**

Colgrout A cement-sand grout very well mixed with water, used in *Colcrete*. It is poured or pumped through pipes 75 mm dia. previously set deep into gravel or broken stone packed in *formwork*.

collapse design [stru.] *Plastic design* of steel structures based on the research initiated by Prof. Sir John Baker at Cambridge, England, from 1935 onwards.

collecting system [sewage] Every drain or sewer in a sewerage system between the house and the outfall or sewage disposal works.

collimation error [sur.] Error in surveying instruments caused by the line of sight not being horizontal or being otherwise out of line.

collimation line [sur.] The line of sight of a surveying instrument. It passes through the intersection of the *cross hairs* in the *reticule*.

collimation mark or **fiducial mark** [air sur.] A mark on the register glass of an air survey camera, usually at each corner of the glass. Images of the marks appear on each air photo. The diagonals between these marks meet at the principal point (plumb or nadir point), P, on the photo. For a *vertical photo* the point P on the ground was vertically below the camera at the instant of exposure. P in the camera is on its vertical axis or centre.

collimation method [sur.] In levelling, also known as the 'height of instrument' method as opposed to the '*rise*

59

and fall' method. Throughout the fieldwork the instrument height is always known by taking the first sight on a point of known level. At any time, therefore, the level of a point can be quickly worked out by subtracting its staff reading from the level of the instrument (instrument height). The main difference from 'rise and fall' is that the calculations of level are usually made during the survey. The method is convenient for obtaining the levels of many points from one set-up.

colloidal grout *See* **Colgrout.**

colloids [s.m.] Particles smaller than 0·002 mm (the European definition of the largest size of *clay* particles) and larger than ·000001 mm, ten times the diameter of an atom. Particles smaller than ·0002 mm do not settle in water and those between ·002 and ·0002 mm settle only very slowly. *Mechanical analysis* of clays is thus not fruitful and X-ray studies are often more useful than microscopic examination, since with the microscope an object of ·002 mm size can only just be seen. Colloids make up most of living matter.

column [stru.] A vertical post (*strut*) carrying load. *See* **long column, stanchion, etc.**

column analogy [stru.] An *analogy* due to *Hardy Cross* between the equations for slope and deflection of a bent beam and those for load and moment in a short eccentrically loaded column. It cannot be so widely used as *moment distribution* but the particular cases of fixed-base *portals* and arches can be rapidly analysed by it.

column head In reinforced-concrete *mushroom construction* an enlargement (thickening) of the column where it meets the slab.

combined stresses [stru.] Bending or twisting stresses combined with direct tension or compression.

combined system [sewage] A system of drainage by which *soil* and surface water are carried in the same *drains*

and *sewers*. In the combined or *partially separate system*, rainwater may be connected through a trap to a foul drain. But in the *separate system*, sewage must not flow into a purely rainwater drain.

comminutor [sewage] In the *preliminary treatment* of sewage, this is a device with a screen that catches the solids and shreds them small enough to pass through. It eliminates the need for handling the solids.

compacting factor test A test of the *workability* of freshly mixed concrete made by weighing the concrete which will fill a container of standard size and shape when allowed to fall into it under standard conditions of test (BS 1881). This test is more precise and sensitive than the *slump test* but requires slightly more elaborate apparatus and is therefore more often used in the laboratory than on the site.

compaction [s.m.] Artificial increase of the *dry density* of a granular soil by mechanical means such as rolling the surface layers, or for deep compaction driving *sand piles*, *vibroflotation*, or impact methods. The AASHO recommends for embankments less than 15 m high that a dry density of at least 1450 kg per cu. m should be obtained. For embankments over this height at least 1900 kg per cu. m is required. Apart from the method of running earth-moving plant over the area to be compacted, there are many methods and six main types of compacting plant: (a) *pneumatic-tyred rollers*, in which the rear wheels cover the gaps left by the front wheels (b) *tamping rollers* (c) *sheepsfoot rollers* (d) *vibrating rollers* (e) *frog rammers* (trench compactors) and (f) *vibrating plates*. The last two, for confined spaces, are operated by one man. *See also* **optimum moisture content,** and *compare* **consolidation.**

compact material Material which can be dug with a pick. *See* **loose ground.** It is usually a granular soil with a *relative compaction* of 90% or more.

comparator [mech.] An instrument for accurately measuring short lengths. A reading telescope is arranged to travel along a scale and to observe in turn the points whose distance apart is to be measured. It is used in *photogrammetry* for measuring the two rectangular coordinates of a point on a photograph.

comparator base [sur.] A carefully measured horizontal distance, usually one tape-length long, used as a means of checking and comparing the tapes used in the field (ASCE MEP 15). This term is used little if at all in Britain, the term standardization length being more usual.

compass [sur.] or magnetic compass An instrument carrying a steel magnetized needle pivoted so as to be free to turn in a horizontal plane. The needle automatically orients itself in the magnetic north–south direction, and thus gives a reference line from which any *bearing* can be measured. The bearings can be accurate to within 1° of arc.

compasses [d.o.] A pair of compasses is an instrument for drawing circles.

compass traverse [sur.] A *traverse* in which the magnetic bearings of all the lines are measured.

compensating diaphragm [sur.] A fitting to a telescope in *stadia work* which alters the interval between *stadia hairs* when a sloping sight is made. In this way the horizontal distance of the staff from the surveyor can be directly calculated from the staff *intercept*.

compensating error [sur.] or accidental error. One of the three kinds of *error* in measurement, the others being *gross* and *systematic errors*. Compensating errors are small and equally likely to be + or − in sign. *See* probable error.

compensation water The water which must be allowed to pass a *dam* so as to satisfy those people who used the water before the dam was built.

composite construction *See* (B), *also* BSCP 117.

composites [stru.] New materials such as cement or gypsum or concrete reinforced with glassfibre, *fibre-reinforced concrete*, etc.

compound air lift An *air-lift pump* modified for use where the available depth of immersion is not enough. Two air-lift pipes are used. The first pipe is made only as high as it can pump, and discharges into a second pipe which acts as the *sump* for the second air-lift pipe within it. With this large submergence the second pipe pumps twice the height of the first.

compound curve [sur.] A *curve* consisting of two or more arcs of different radii curving in the same direction and having a common tangent or transition curve at their point of junction (BS 892).

compound dredger A *bucket-ladder dredger* which is also provided with a claycutter like a *suction-cutter dredger*.

compound engine [mech.] A steam or compressed-air engine in which the working fluid expands in two stages in series from the small high-pressure cylinder to the larger low-pressure cylinder. A compound engine uses steam more efficiently than a simple engine but it is more complicated. Both types were used for winding, pumping, air compression, and other duties about mines. *See* compounding.

compound girder or plated beam A *rolled-steel joist* with plates fixed to the flanges by welding or riveting.

compounding [mech.] The expansion of steam or compressed air in two or more cylinders in series. If the working fluid is compressed air it is often passed through a reheater, but this is not usual with steam. *See* multiple-expansion engine.

compound pipe [hyd.] A pipe consisting of several lengths of different diameter in series.

compound pump [mech.] A pump driven by a steam *compound engine*.

compressed air (1) [mech.] A source of power for drills and motors; like steam it must be raised to a high pressure.

This is done in *reciprocating* or turbo-compressors in several stages with *intercoolers* and *aftercoolers*. Compressed air power, although important in *civil engineering*, is indispensable in mining where for certain very deep mines it is the only practicable source of power, since it both improves the ventilation and cools the air at the working face. It is also completely safe in gassy mines.

(2) Compressed air excludes water from tunnels, shafts, or *pneumatic caissons* while they are being driven, provided that the air pressure is equal to the water pressure at the face of the excavation. Pneumatic caissons can be carried down to 30 m of water, involving an air pressure of about 0·35 N/mm² above atmospheric. A man working in this pressure needs 2·5 hours' decompression and may consequently work for only about 5 hours per day. The requirements are similar to those in the *diving bell*. The risks of *caisson disease* are not severe for pressures smaller than 0·1 N/mm² (1 bar) above atmospheric pressure, but for pressures above this, great care must be taken and a *medical lock* may be needed. *See* **decanting.**

(3) In *diamond drilling*, *air-flush drilling* is used as a substitute for water in caving ground which would soften and cave even more with water. The rock cuttings are brought up by the air, and the cutting-bit cooled by it. Although consumption of diamonds may be slightly increased, the costs per metre drilled are not necessarily higher.

(4) *See* **air-lift pump.**

compressed-air disease *Caisson disease.*

compression [mech.] A force which tends to shorten a member; a push; the opposite of a tension.

compression boom or **chord** A *compression flange.*

compression failure [stru.] *See* **long column, short column.**

compression flange [stru.] or **compression boom** or **chord** That part of a beam or girder which is compressed. It is the upper part at the mid-span and the lower part at the support of a continuous beam.

compression testing (1) [s.m.] For clays the compression test is an important laboratory measure of strength. *See* **unconfined compression test, triaxial compression test.**

(2) The crushing of bricks, stone, concrete, etc., to determine their *ultimate compressive strengths. See* **cube test.**

compressive strength [stru.] The resistance expressed in force per unit area of a structural material at failure in a compression test, expressed in USA as psi, and in Britain as newton/mm² or meganewton/m² (1 N/mm² = 1 MN/m²).

compressor [mech.] or **air compressor** A machine for compressing air to about 7 bars for rock drilling. Compressors are reciprocating, centrifugal, or *free-piston compressors.*

concentrated load [stru.] or **point load** A load which is not spread over a large area, the contrary of a *distributed load.* A knife-edge load is a particular concentrated load.

conchoidal [min.] Description of a type of fracture which is shell-shaped like that of pitch, *glass*, and resins. This fracture shows that the structure is not crystalline.

concrete A mixture of water, sand, stone, and a binder (nowadays usually *Portland cement*) which hardens to a stonelike mass. Lime and other concretes were used by the ancient Romans and in Britain for foundations in the nineteenth century, but the production of strong, cheap, uniform Portland cement has enormously increased its use. *See* **aerated/air-entrained concrete, lightweight concretes, prestressed/reinforced/vacuum/vibrated concrete, creep, cube test, water/cement ratio, workability.**

concrete breaker or **ripper** or **road breaker** A compressed-air tool like a heavy rock drill, fitted with a point for breaking roads and masonry. It weighs about 50 kg.

concrete cart *See* **buggy.**

concrete cutting Concrete can be cut by many methods, the oldest being the compressed-air-driven rock drill or concrete breaker or pneumatic pick, which are noisy and slow. *Diamond saws* are fast and effective and are in regular use for sawing concrete up to 1·2 m thick. But there is no depth limitation for *diamond drills*, however heavily the concrete is reinforced. *Thermic boring* is effective but has the disadvantage of fire hazard. A safer, recent introduction is jet blasting with high-pressure water containing sand, the Hydrojet, but it does not cut reinforcement.

concrete-finishing machine A machine for making roads or runways, usually carried on *road forms* or rails parallel to them, which smooths compacted concrete to the required shape.

concrete mixer A machine, usually with a rotating drum, in which aggregates, cement and water are mixed for 2 to 3 minutes to make concrete. Mixers are now described (BS 1305:1974) by stating only the volume of wet concrete produced, either in litres, for those smaller than 1 m³, or in m³, for those larger than 1 m³. *See* **batch / continuous / non-tilting / tilting / truck mixer, concrete paver.**

concrete paver A road-making *concrete mixer* which moves on crawler tracks or rails and carries a *concreting boom* to help place the concrete.

concrete pile (1) or **driven pile** A reinforced-concrete precast *pile* driven into the ground by a *pile driver* or crane.

(2) A reinforced-concrete *pile* cast in a hole bored in the ground (*in situ* or *cast-in-situ* pile). This type is common in central London. *See also* **driven cast-in-place pile.**

concrete pipe Pipe made of concrete, varying in bore from 100 mm to several metres, porous for use as *subsoil drains* or capable of withstanding considerable water pressure.

Diameters under 0·4 m usually have no reinforcement. *See* **tube.**

concrete placer A device for pushing concrete along a pipe by compressed air. It can be a much smaller piece of plant than the *concrete pump*, and it is therefore convenient for tunnelling. *See also* **placing plant.**

concrete properties Concrete properties are measured under the six parts of BS 1881:1970 and 1971 which cover *slump*, compaction, *V.-B. consistometer* test for workability, air content of air-entrained concrete, *cube test*, *beam test* and other strength tests including tensile tests, saturated and dry densities, dynamic and static *moduli of elasticity*, length changes on wetting and drying, water absorption, also the analysis of fresh or hardened concrete for cement content and type, aggregate content and grading and original water content.

concrete pump Usually a lorry-mounted unit, hydraulically driven and fed with concrete from a hopper on the lorry. The main restriction on pumped concrete is that it must be fluid or the pipes block up, but in good conditions very high rates of flow are reached, 40 cu. m/hour being normal, pumping to 500 m distance and to 50 m height. Sometimes a *placing boom* is used with a concrete pump.

concrete roofs Concrete can be used for building many sorts of roof. The simplest roofs, solid reinforced-concrete slabs, are suitable for spans up to about 6 m. For spans from 4·5 to 10 m, *hollow-tile floor* construction is lighter, cheaper, and sometimes also thinner. Precast beams can be laid dry very rapidly to form a floor, and precast, *prestressed* beams can be used for large spans and low construction depths. The main difficulty with prestressed floor beams is that it is difficult to obtain them bent upwards by an equal amount and the ceiling may therefore be uneven. For large spans of about 30 m the concrete dome or *shell* is completely smooth underneath. The flat *Diagrid floor* is popular now though expensive, and spans 15 m without difficulty. Prestressed or *reinforced-concrete* girders often cover large spans.

concrete spreader A road-making machine carried usually on the *road forms* or rails parallel to them. It spreads concrete uniformly, either from a heap dumped in front of it or from concrete dumped on to itself. *Compare* **slip-form paver.**

concrete-vibrating machine A machine which travels like the *concrete-finishing machine* or *spreader* and vibrates up to 30 cu. m of concrete per hour. *See* **vibrated concrete, vibrator, slip-form paver.**

concreting boom A light metal *truss* supported at one end on a frame near a *concrete mixer* and at the other end on another frame on wheels. On its underside is a rail along which a concreting bucket can travel, carried by a pair of overhead wheels. A 200 litre capacity bucket can be carried on a 12 m long boom weighing 180 kg. A *placing boom* is much more elaborate.

condensate Water which condenses from air, flue gas, etc., cooled below the *dewpoint.*

conduit [hyd.] Any *open channel*, pipe, etc., for flowing fluid.

cone penetration test [s.m.] or **deep penetration test** The testing of soils by pressing a standard cone into the ground under a known load and measuring the penetration. These methods are used in Scandinavia and Holland. In the Dutch deep-sounding test, which is used in Holland to deeper than 30 m, an inner mandrel is driven separately from the outer casing. This enables the toe resistance to be measured separately from the skin friction of the casing. This method is used for forecasting the resistance to driving of *bearing piles*, and can supply rapidly and cheaply the information for a preliminary site exploration. The cone diameter is 36 mm, so the force required to push it in is not very great. The method is not suitable for clays, for which the *vane test* is preferred, nor for stony soils. *Compare* **dynamic penetration test.**

confined compression test See **triaxial compression test.**

confined water [hyd.] *Groundwater* that is overlain by impermeable ground. It can be under a pressure higher than atmospheric, like a flowing *artesian well*. When a pipe is driven into it, the water can then rise above the bottom of the impermeable bed that confines it. Certain types of confined groundwater are not annually renewable. *See also* **unconfined water.**

conglomerate [min.] or **pudding stone** A cemented rock containing rounded stones.

consistence Of concrete, its ease of flow or *workability*, measured by the old *slump test* or the newer *compacting factor test*. Although the terms *consistency index* and *consistency limits* are established, the word 'consistency' should where possible be kept for the sense of continuity or reliability, and 'consistence' for degree of density or stiffness.

consistency index [s.m.] A figure for comparing the stiffness of *clays* in their natural state. It is calculated as follows:

$$\frac{(liquid\ limit) - (\text{water content of sample}) \times 100\%}{(\text{liquid limit}) - (plastic\ limit).}$$

It may rise above 100% but such values indicate a stiff clay.

consistency limits [s.m.] or **Atterberg limits** The *liquid limit*, *plastic limit*, *shrinkage limit*, and sometimes also the sticky limit of a clay. These are all water contents of a clay, each in a certain condition defined in Britain by BS 1377. They are the standard way of describing clays and correspond to *mechanical analysis* for sands.

consistometer *See* **V.-B. consistometer.**

consolidated quick test [s.m.] A test of the shear strength of a *cohesive soil* made in the laboratory after full consolidation under load. The *triaxial* or *shear test* is carried out quickly without drainage or further consolidation. *See also* **drained shear/quick/unconfined compression test.**

consolidation [s.m.] The gradual, slow compression of a *cohesive soil* due to weight acting on it, which occurs as water, or water and air are driven out of the voids in the soil. Consolidation only occurs with *clays* or other soils of low *permeability*. It is not the same as *compaction*, which is a mechanical, immediate process and only occurs in soils with at least some sand. The theory of consolidation of clays under increased pressure was first published about 1925 by Terzaghi. With this paper Terzaghi founded the new science of Erdbaumechanik which became *soil mechanics* in English. *See also* **consolidation settlement, effective/pore-water pressure.**

consolidation press [s.m.] or **consolidometer** or **oedometer** A laboratory apparatus for obtaining the data necessary for plotting the curve of pressure to *voids ratio* of a clay sample. In this way the *coefficient* of *consolidation* of the clay can be determined and sometimes its variation in *permeability* with increasing *consolidation*.

consolidation settlement [s.m.] The settlement of loaded clay which takes place over a period of years, but can sometimes be accelerated by *vertical sand drains*. The Leaning Tower of Pisa is an example of unequal consolidation settlement. *See* above.

consolidometer A *consolidation press*.

constructional engineer A fabricator or contractor working on steel frames. *Compare* **structural engineer.**

constructional fitter and erector *See* **steel erector.**

construction joint A surface in *reinforced concrete* along which concreting was stopped one day and completed later. The concrete each side of the joint is usually united by reinforcement cross-ing the joint. *See* **dry joint, starter bar, stunt end.**

construction spanner A *podger*.

construction way [rly] Temporary track for building the *permanent way*.

consultant A registered architect, *chartered engineer* or specialist who acts for a *client*. His functions often go much further than consultation and he, with his staff, provides the complete design and supervision of the construction until completion.

consulting engineer A *chartered engineer* who is approached by an architect or client or another engineer for the purpose of designing a dam, railway, sewage-treatment plant, building, etc. The engineer advises his client on the choice of project. Once the project is agreed on, the engineer ceases to advise and begins to draw out a scheme which he expands in detail after the client's approval, and supervises to completion.

consumptive use [hyd.] The quantity of water lost by transpiration and evaporation from fields.

contact aerator A tank in which sewage is aerated by compressed-air injection.

contact bed [sewage] A forerunner to the *trickling filter*. It worked intermittently.

contactor [elec.] An electrically operated switch, used for controlling the motors of coalcutters or other powerful machines. The main switch is opened or closed by the operation of the *pilot circuit*.

contact pressure under foundations [s.m.] Although foundation slabs are usually calculated on the assumption that their load is uniformly spread over their area of contact, this is rarely so in reality. In footings on sand, the actual contact pressure decreases from centre to rim, while on clay, the contact pressure at the centre is less than at the rim. This means that on clay the real bending moments are greater than those calculated, while on sand they are less.

contact print [d.o.] A print on light-sensitive paper, made by placing a drawing in opaque ink or pencil on transparent paper in contact with the light-sensitive paper and exposing it to light for a period. *See* **blueprint, dyeline.**

continuity [stru.] or **fixity** The joining of floors to beams, of beams to other beams and columns so effectively that they bend together under load and so strengthen each other. This is easily done in concrete or welded metal, less so in other materials. *See* **continuous beam,** *also* (*B*).

continuous beam [stru.] A beam of several spans in the same straight line joined together so effectively that a known load on one span will produce an effect on the others which can be calculated. A continuous beam generally has at least three supports. This sort of *continuity* is economical and safe where the supports are unlikely to settle. *See* **end span.**

continuous filter [sewage] A *trickling filter*.

continuous gabion or **Reno mattress** A steel wire-mesh basket about 6 m by 2 m, by 30 cm deep, containing 70 kg stones, linked to others each side of it and thus protecting a silt bank from erosion. The mouth of the River Witham in East Anglia was protected in this way in 1973 – it was underlain by 0·8 mm thick plastics sheet, woven from 95% polypropylene to hold the silt in and let water through.

continuous grading *See* **gap-graded aggregate.**

continuously welded track [rly] A main line railway in which the rails are joined by welding rather than by *fishplates*. Most of the welding is done in a depot. The few site joints are made with *thermit*, except in Russia where *flash-butt welding* machines are used at the site of the weld. Everywhere else these machines are used at the depot. In Europe, welded rails are not normally laid in curves with a radius less than 600 m. Welded track increases the life of rails by about a third, halves track maintenance, dramatically reduces breakages of rails, raises running speeds and passenger comfort, reduces damage to the formation and to sleepers, but is expensive and needs excellent organization. By 1975 a quarter of UK tracks had been continuously welded and a further 1000 km a year were being welded.

continuous mixer A *concrete mixer* into which stones, sand, cement and water are continuously poured and from which concrete flows in an uninterrupted stream.

continuous rating [elec.] *See* **rating** (3).

continuous ropeway An *aerial ropeway* in which the loaded *carriers* travel one way and the empty carriers return on the ropes the other side of the ropeway towers.

contour *See* **contour line.**

contour check [hyd.] Compartments of a field made by borders following the contours, a form of terracing (ASCE MEP 11). *See* **contour ploughing.**

contour gradient [sur.] A line set out on the ground at a certain constant slope. (A contour line is set out at zero slope.)

contour interval [sur.] or **vertical interval** Contour lines are drawn at a vertical distance apart which is called the vertical interval. For British Ordnance Survey maps to a scale of 1:50 000, formerly 1 in. to 1 mile, it is 15 m, formerly 50 ft. Contours are drawn at Ordnance Datum and every 15 m or 50 ft above.

contour line [sur.] or **contour** A line on a *map* drawn between all points at the same level, as for instance the high-water line.

contour ploughing or **terracing** Soil conservation on slopes by ploughing horizontally or with furrows at very gentle slopes along which water can scour only very slightly.

contracted weir [hyd.] A *measuring weir* which is shorter than the width of the channel, and is therefore said to have side or *end contractions*. *Compare* suppressed weir.

contraction in area [mech.] or **necking** In the *tensile testing* of metals, the reduction from the original area of the bar to the cross-section at the point of fracture. For ductile metal like rivet steel the contraction may be more than 50%, and is accompanied by *elongation*.

contraction joint or **shrinkage joint** In concrete work, a break in a structure made to allow for the drying and temperature shrinkages (of concrete or masonry) and thus to prevent cracks forming at undesirable places. Since all materials containing cement shrink appreciably on drying, contraction joints are needed in every long structure. *See* **movement joint.**

contract manager An experienced foreman, timekeeper, civil engineer, or quantity surveyor working for a building or civil engineering contractor. He calculates costs of work and may hold the City and Guilds Certificate (A and B) in Building Quantities and Estimating.

contractor A person who signs a *contract* (*B*) to do certain specified work at certain rates of payment, generally within a stated time.

contractor's agent *See* **agent.**

contraflexure [stru.] Contrary flexure, a change of direction of bending. A point of contraflexure is called in USA a point of inflexion. It is a point at which the *bending moment* is zero, changing from hogging on one side of the point to sagging on the other side.

control [hyd.] A part of a channel where bed and bank conditions make the water level a good indication of the flow, for example a weir or a waterfall or a hard bed to the stream. *See* **Venturi flume.**

control point [sur.] A point on the ground of accurately known position (and usually altitude) which is a starting point or check on a *plane table* survey, *traverse*, or *photogrammetry*. *See* vertical, horizontal control.

control valve [mech.] A *discharge valve*.

conversion factor [d.o.] *See* p. 9.

conveyor [mech.] Equipment for moving sand, stone, ore, coal, etc., continuously over relatively short distances. *See* belt/helical/pneumatic conveyor, elevator.

coordinates [d.o.] Coordinates are distances measured in a certain way from fixed straight lines called axes of reference which intersect at the *origin*. The purpose of coordinates is to locate a point. The system invented by Descartes, using *Cartesian* coordinates, is the most commonly used and convenient system. *See* **graph.**

copper-bearing steel *Weather-resisting steel.*

copper welding *Fusion welding* of copper. *Compare* bronze welding.

cordage rope *Fibre rope.*

Cordtex [min.] or **Cordeau** *Detonating fuse.*

corduroy road A road built of 7 cm dia. saplings, equal in length to the width of the road, wired tightly together at the ends. This is an excellent temporary road, very quickly laid, which will float in liquid mud, but it is expensive in timber. It can, however, be picked up and re-used elsewhere.

core (1) A *cut-off wall* of clay or concrete or other material.

(2) A piece inserted into a mould for concrete before pouring the concrete, so as to form a hollow in it for a bolt, *prestressing* cable, etc. Cores for prestressing cables are laid in the cable path, wired to the reinforcement. They may be tubes which are inflated before the concrete is poured and a few hours later deflated and withdrawn. Another type, also of rubber, contains a steel cable withdrawn after pouring the concrete. In both cases the rubber core when pulled reduces in diameter and detaches itself from the concrete.

(3) [stru.] or **kern** The middle part of a wall or column. The limits of the

core are the limits of the area through which the resultant compression on the whole section must pass if there is to be no tension anywhere in the section. For a wall, the core is the *middle third*.

(4) [stru.] In a spirally reinforced *column*, the concrete within the centre line of the spiral reinforcement.

(5) The cylinder of rock or soil or concrete cut out by a *diamond drill* or *soil sampler*, etc.

(6) [mech.] The softer steel within a *carburized* steel *case*.

(7) [elec.] A conductor within a cable including its insulation.

core barrel [min.] Next to the cutting bit of a *core drill* is a length of pipe known as the core barrel which contains the core. In very soft rock it may be double so that the inner lining does not rotate nor damage the core. *See* **Sprague and Henwood core barrel, wire-line core barrel**.

core box [min.] A large wooden box, divided up into narrow strips by partitions. It contains the *cores* from a borehole in the order in which they were extracted from the ground.

core catcher [s.m.] A steel spring used for keeping samples of sand from dropping out of a *soil sampler*.

core cutter (1) [min.] or **core lifter** An attachment at the foot of the *core barrel* which grips the core and breaks it at the root when the core is withdrawn for examination.

(2) [s.m.] A *soil sampler*.

(3) A rotary drill for cutting a cylinder from a road for test purposes.

cored hole A hole cast by leaving a *core* in a concrete (or metal or plastics) piece. When the core is removed shortly after the concrete is poured, it leaves a neat hole. The contrary of a drilled hole.

core drill [min.] A power-driven tool for extracting a continuous core of rock for inspection, usually a *diamond drill* or shot drill. Water is pumped down the hollow drilling rods and returns outside them with the rock cuttings to the surface.

cored slab A *voided slab*.

core lifter A *core cutter*.

corers [min.] or **coring tools** In *rotary drilling* for oil wells, cores are not usually made, since speed of drilling is the aim and the debris of drilling is brought up by the drilling fluid. Corers are the special tools used for extracting cores when an oil horizon or other important bed is being approached.

core wall (1) A *cut-off wall*.

(2) or **shear wall** Interconnected reinforced-concrete walls running the full height of a block of flats or offices, and centrally located in the block, usually surrounding the plumbing services, particularly the hot and cold water and the drainage, also the stairs and the lift shafts. The core walls stiffen a tall building against earthquake or wind forces and can be designed to be built very rapidly by *sliding forms*.

coring tools *Corers*.

corporate member *See* **chartered civil/ structural engineer**.

correction [sur.] *See* **adjustment, tape corrections**.

corrosion The gradual removal or weakening of metal from its surface by chemical attack. It can be of two types – the high-temperature types that occur in fires will not be discussed here. The low-temperature type, very much more widespread, requires the presence of water and oxygen and is helped by sulphur dioxide and carbon dioxide, and probably by other materials in small quantities in the water or air. It is always electrolytic, an oxidation, rusting for iron or steel. In Britain the loss of thickness of steel sheet piles submerged in fresh water on both faces is about 0.1 mm yearly. In salt water, the loss is about 50% more. But below groundwater level, submerged in the calm conditions of undisturbed soil, steel will suffer so little corrosion that no protection is needed. Above groundwater level or in disturbed soil (thus in the presence of both air and water) some protection is needed, whether metal or paint or concrete coating or *cathodic protection*. Copper, lead, zinc and aluminium when not in contact with other metals form a thin film of oxide, the *patina* (*B*), which protects them from further oxidation, but if they – especially zinc or aluminium – are in contact with iron through an electrolyte (which may be merely an invisible film of dirty water on the surface of the metal) they will dissolve in sacrificial protection of the iron. They are therefore used in *metal coating* (*B*) to protect iron and steel. *Weather-resisting steel* has good corrosion resistance in air. *See* BS 5493, 'Protection of iron and steel structures from corrosion'.

corrosion fatigue [mech.] A weakening of steel by small *fatigue* cracks which are entered and corroded by water during reversals of stress. Even relatively pure water like tap water lowers the *endurance limit* considerably.

corundum [min.] Al_2O_3, alumina, a very hard mineral used as an abrasive, since its *hardness* is only less than that of *diamond*.

Coulomb's equation [s.m.] A simplified statement of the *shear strength* of soils, given by the equation:

$$S = C + P \tan \phi$$

in which S = shear strength, C is the *cohesion*, P is the pressure at right angles to the plane of shear, and ϕ is the angle of shearing resistance of the soil. Coulomb thought this out in 1776 and it is therefore about 100 years older than any other equation used in *soil mechanics* today.

Council of Engineering Institutions *See* technician engineer.

counter-arched revetment A brickwork *revetment* to a *cutting* with arches between *counterforts* like a *multiple-arch dam*.

counter bore [mech.] To enlarge a hole by drilling.

counter bracing [stru.] or cross bracing Two *diagonal braces* provided in each *panel* of a *truss* to stabilize it and carry wind loads.

counter drain A drain running along the foot of a canal or dam bank to remove leakage and strengthen the bank.

counterfort (1) A strengthening pier at right angles to a *retaining wall* on the side of the retained material (therefore not visible) to stabilize it against overturning or to increase its bending strength. *Compare* buttress.

(2) A trench cut into the sloping earth face of a cutting so as to drain it. It is filled with large stones or gravel or faggots or other material that will drain freely and prevent the sides from collapsing.

counterpoise bridge A *bascule bridge*.

course [sur.] The direction and length of a survey line. *See also* (*B*).

coursed blockwork or coursed masonry In *breakwater* construction where precast concrete blocks of 10 to 50 tons are common, *blockwork* laid like masonry in horizontal, bonded courses. *Compare* sliced blockwork. *See* Titan crane.

coursed masonry *Coursed blockwork*.

cover The thickness of concrete between any bar and the nearest face of the concrete member. *See also* effective depth.

covered electrode [mech.] A metal *electrode* used in *arc welding*. It is coated with a material that protects or improves the weld metal and stabilizes the electric arc.

cover meter or electromagnetic cover meter A *non-destructive testing* intrument that can locate steel in concrete up to a distance of about 70 mm from the surface.

cover plate or cover strap. A *fishplate*.

crab The moving hoist of an *overhead travelling crane*, running on rails at the top of the gantry. It may be called a crab because it travels at right angles to the crane rails. *Compare* telpher. *See* Titan crane.

crack inducer A *dummy joint*.

cracking in concrete Cracking is always expected in *reinforced concrete*, since it has such a high *shrinkage* on hardening. Additional cracks will occur on the stretched side of a beam but reinforcement should be inserted sufficient in quantity and closeness to make the cracks invisible to the naked eye and very close together. If a contraction or expansion joint is inserted, this will also reduce cracking near it. *See* **autogenous healing, prestressed concrete.**

cradle (1) On a slipway the low framework running on rails which is sunk below a ship at high tide to take its weight and pull it up the slipway or for launching a ship after repair. *See* **sue load.**

(2) A temporary framework to carry something during construction.

craftsman *See* **tradesman** (*B*).

crane [mech.] Generally means power-operated *lifting tackle* with a *jib* which can move loads a considerable distance horizontally as well as lift and lower them. *See* **crab, crane driver, derrick, excavator, telpher** *and* **creeper/floating/Goliath/jib/level-luffing/mobile/portal, Titan/tower cranes,** *also* BSCP 3010 'Safe use of cranes', and BS 3810 'Glossary of materials handling'.

crane gantry *See* **gantry.**

crane post [mech.] The upright mast of a *jib crane*, which at its top end holds the upper end of the jib by a tie rod or ropes and at its lower end is pivoted on the ground with the lower end of the jib.

crane slinger *See* **slinger.**

crane tower or **king tower** Of the three towers supporting a *derrick* (6), that which carries the mast and the crane machinery. The other two are anchor towers.

crawler track [mech.] or **caterpillars** An endless chain of plates used instead of wheels by *tractors* which travel over soft ground. The ground pressure is only about 50 kN/m² instead of at least 140 kN/m² with tyres, therefore crawler-tracked vehicles can travel much more easily over soft ground than can rubber-tyred vehicles.

creep (1) [stru.] Gradually increasing permanent deformation of a material under stress, well known to mechanical engineers as high-temperature creep. In civil engineering, however, creep can be useful to the building owner because it tends to load the whole structure more uniformly. Hard-drawn steel at high stresses extends, whereas the concrete compresses, under creep. The numerical values of creep are important in *prestressed concrete* because they are responsible for part of the *losses of prestress*. According to BSCP 110:1972, concrete creep can be assumed proportional to the concrete stress for stresses up to one third of the cube strength at *transfer*. It varies from 36 to 48×10^{-6} per unit length, with transfer at a cube strength of 40 N/mm² or more. As for *shrinkage*, half the creep takes place in the first month and three-quarters in the first six months.

(2) The slow movement of a *free retaining wall* which holds up a bank of shrinkable clay. If the clay shrinks every year and the cracks between the clay and the wall are filled with debris during the drought, the wall may be forced forward every year in the wet season by the swelling of the clay. This may eventually overturn the wall.

(3) When *sheet piles* are driven singly they have a tendency to accumulate a forward leaning movement. This may be counteracted by driving the piles in panels of 12 or so at a time, driving each pile only slightly ahead of its neighbours at any one time. In closing a cofferdam a special *closer* is often needed even if there has been no creep, merely because the width available for the last pile is not as calculated.

(4) [hyd.] *See* **saltation.**

creeper cranes Heavy *cranes* used for building steel *cantilever bridges*. They usually travel along the top *chord* during construction.

creep slide *See* **detritus slide.**

creosote An oil distilled from coal tar between 240° and 270° C, used as a *preservative* for timber.

crest gate or **spillway gate** A gate to maintain or to lower the water level, built into the spillway of a dam. *See* **radial/roller/sector/sliding/tilting gate, stop log.**

crib or **grillage** One or more layers of timber or steel across each other to spread a load over a foundation and not to overload the ground.

crib dam or **crib wall** A *dam* or *retaining wall* built of rectangular interlocking timber or precast concrete members forming skeletons or cells laid on top of each other and filled with earth or rock. They are built to a *batter* of 1 in 6 to 1 in 8. *See* **gravity retaining wall.**

cribwork Large timber cells which are sunk full of concrete to make a bridge foundation.

Crimp and Bruges' formula [sewage] A formula connecting rate of flow (*v*), hydraulic mean depth (*m*), and the slope of sewer (*i*).

$$v = 56m^{0.67}\sqrt{i}.$$

The units are metres/sec. and metres. It is now believed that the value of *v* obtained from this formula is 20% lower than experiments on new pipes show. This is on the safe side. *Compare* **Barnes's formula.**

crimper An *indenting roller.*

crippling load [stru.] or **buckling load** The load at which a *long column* begins to bend noticeably. This load does not break the strut unless the deflection of the strut is allowed to increase. At this load *Hooke's law* no longer applies and a very small increase of load gives a very large increase of deflection. *See* **crushing test, Euler.**

critical density of sands [s.m.] *See* **critical voids ratio.**

critical height [s.m.] of vertical cuts in a *cohesive soil* is the height to which they will stand without timbering.

This height is proportional to the *cohesion* of the soil. The resistance of the cut to sliding is proportional to the height *h*, whereas the forces producing sliding are proportional to h^2. The critical height can be shown theoretically to be equal to twice the *unconfined compressive strength* of the soil divided by its density. Sands have no critical height, since they will stand safely to any height at their angle of repose.

critical hydraulic gradient [s.m.] The *hydraulic gradient* at which a sand becomes a *quicksand.* This can happen to any sand if the upward velocity of water flowing up through it is high enough to make it 'float'. *See also* **boil, piping.**

critical path scheduling *See* (*B*).

critical point [mech.] or **arrest point** or **critical temperature** A temperature at which, on heating or cooling a plain *carbon steel*, a change in its molecular structure is shown by a noticeable delay (arrest) in the heating or cooling. A steel warming up will darken and one cooling down will brighten in colour. Magnetized bars do not lose their magnetic properties until the critical point is passed, hence magnetic indicators can show blacksmiths the critical temperature. Drill steels must be forged at a temperature slightly above the critical, and *tempered* and *quenched* at a slightly lower temperature just above the critical point with rising temperature. The critical point on heating (decalescent point) is about 750°C, the critical point on cooling (recalescent point) is about 700°C. Both temperatures vary with the carbon content.

critical velocity [hyd.] (1) In an *open channel*, that velocity at which the *Froude number* is 1. In a pressure pipe, Reynolds's critical velocity is at the change point from laminar to turbulent or vice versa, where friction ceases to be proportional to the first power of the velocity and becomes proportional to a higher power, practically the square. Reynolds's number for this is about 2000 with water.

(2) Kennedy's critical velocity in open channels is that which will neither deposit nor pick up silt.

(3) Belanger's critical velocity is that condition in open channels for which the velocity head equals one half the mean depth (ASCE MEP 11).

critical voids ratio of sands [s.m.] During shear tests it has been noticed that dense sands expand and loosely packed sands contract. The intermediate state, at which, during the shear test, a sand will neither expand nor contract, is described as its critical *voids ratio*. The importance of this value is that there need be no fear of *flow slides* or sudden *liquefaction* of a sand which has a voids ratio less than the critical. (The *shaking test* proves this expansion and contraction of sands and silts.)

cropper A tool for cutting steel bars (bar cropper).

cross bracing See **counter bracing**.

crosscut chisel [mech.] (**cape chisel** in USA) A *cold chisel* of rectangular section with a cutting edge at a steep angle for hard cutting.

crosscut file [mech.] or **double-cut file** A file with two intersecting rows of cuts forming a repeating pattern of cutting points. See *cut* (4).

crossfrogs See **frog**.

cross hair [sur.] or **spider line** A straight vertical or horizontal line which fixes the line of sight in a surveying telescope. It is set in the *reticule*.

cross hatching [d.o.] *Hatching*.

crosshead (1) [mech.] A steel block which slides between steel guides in a steam engine and helps to convert the to-and-fro motion of the piston into rotary motion.

(2) [min.] A steel frame which slides between the guides in a sinking shaft. It is carried up and down by, but is not attached to, the bail of the *kibble*. It thus prevents the kibble from swaying during hoisting and is demanded by law in some states of USA.

crossings [rly] See **frog**.

crossover [rly] A track which joins two parallel tracks and is therefore S-shaped in plan. See **scissors crossover**.

cross poling In trench excavation, short *poling boards* placed horizontally to cover a gap between *runners*. They are inserted behind the runners next the earth where the runners cannot be driven.

cross-section (1) [d.o.] The shape of a body cut transversely to its length, sometimes called a transverse section. A cross-section of a pipe is therefore an O. Hence a scale drawing of a body cut across.

(2) A vertical *section* of the ground suitable for calculating earthwork quantities.

cross-sectional area [mech.] or **CSA** The area of a cross-section, often referring to the area of steel in sq. mm in a bar, joist, stanchion, etc.

cross staff [sur.] A brass box with slits in opposite faces forming sight lines perpendicular or at 45° to each other. See **optical square**.

crowbar or **bar** or **crow** A round or hexagonal steel bar 1 to 2 m long usually with a point at one end and a chisel shape or claw at the other end. When shorter than 1 m it becomes a *pinch bar* (*B*).

crowd shovel A *face shovel*.

crown or **soffit** or **vertex** The highest part of an arch shape, particularly of the inside of a drain or sewer. Compare **invert**.

crushing strength The load at which a material fails in compression, divided by its cross-sectional area, properly called its crushing *stress*. This figure is used for comparing the strengths of concretes, bricks, stones, mortars, and similar walling materials.

crushing test Any test in which a material is made to fail as a *short column*, such as the *cube test* or *dump test*.

crystalline fracture [mech.] All metal fractures are crystalline but this term is reserved for *cleavage fracture*.

cube strength The strength of a concrete cube when crushed. *See below.*

cube test (1) A test of the strength of a *Portland cement* made by testing to destruction, in standard conditions, a cube of mortar made with this cement and standard sand.

(2) A test of site concrete made similarly to (1) by casting a 150 mm or 100 mm cube, curing it in standard conditions, and crushing it either at 7 days or at 28 days. The allowable compressive stress in bending in Britain has been $0.25 \times$ the 28-day strength and the allowable direct compression was $0.19 \times$ the 28-day strength. The allowable shear stress without reinforcement is one tenth of the bending stress allowed. This is based on the assumption that the tensile strength of concrete is one tenth of its compressive strength, an assumption which is roughly true. *See* cylinder test, wet cube strength.

culmination [sur.] or meridian passage or transit The journey of a star or the sun across the *meridian*, used by surveyors for determining (*a*) the geographical meridian, (*b*) the longitude, calculated from the observed time of transit and astronomical tables. Each star crosses the meridian twice in 24 hours, once at its upper and once at its lower culmination. The two are only visible for *circumpolar* stars, for other stars only the upper culmination is seen.

culvert (1) A covered channel up to about 4 m width or a large pipe for carrying a watercourse under ground level, usually under a road or railway. It is usually laid by *cut and cover*.

(2) A tunnel through which water is pumped from, or flows into, a *dry dock*.

cumec [hyd.] One cubic metre per second, analogous with *cusec*.

cumulative errors [sur.] *Systematic errors.*

cup-and-cone fracture [mech.] A typical *plastic fracture* of a *ductile* material in tension. One side of the break is cup-shaped and the other cone-shaped, fitting into it. This is the normal *plastic fracture* of mild steel, accompanied by *necking*.

cuphead [mech.] The shape of the head of a rivet or bolt which is rounded like the inside of a shallow cup or deep saucer.

cupola [mech.] A vertical cylindrical furnace in which pig iron is melted to make iron castings.

curb *See* kerb.

curing or maturing Keeping concrete or mortar damp for the first week or month of its life so that the cement is always provided with enough water to harden. This improves the final strength of concrete, particularly at the surface, and should reduce surface cracking or *dusting*. The curing time is shorter for rapid hardening than for ordinary cement, and is longer for low-heat and supersulphated cements. Similarly it is shorter when accelerators are used and longer with retarders. *See* accelerated curing.

curing compound Usually a tar-based liquid that is sprayed over fresh concrete to prevent it drying out and to ensure high strength. When the compound has solidified it becomes a *curing membrane*.

curing membrane Polythene sheet, building paper or other sheet material laid over fresh concrete to prevent it drying out. *See above.*

curing period The amount of time for any given weather during which concrete members must be kept damp after casting. In Britain, usually a week is required.

current meter [hyd.] or rotary meter An instrument with a vane like a windmill which rotates when a fluid passes through it. The distance travelled by the flowing water is recorded on a revolution counter geared to the vane. The observer works out the velocity from the counter reading and the time of submergence. This instrument is used for measuring the current in wide rivers. The velocity is measured at a number of points and depths systematically spaced across it so that the mean velocity can be obtained. The mean velocity is the velocity which multiplied by the cross-sectional area of the water gives the quantity flowing. *See also* **float, flow meter, Pitot tube. rating, Venturi meter.**

curtain *See* **grout curtain.**

curtain wall *See* (*B*).

curve (1) A bend in a road or railway. Railway curves are set out usually to circular arcs, they may be *horizontal curves* or *vertical curves*, the usual sense being a horizontal curve. *See* **compound/reverse/transition curve.**

(2) [d.o.] A celluloid or pearwood shape used by draughtsmen for drawing curves.

curve ranging [sur.] Setting out points on a curve.

cusec [hyd.] One cubic foot per second, a unit of flow of water. 35·3 cu. secs. = 1 cumec.

cushion head A very descriptive American term for a *pile helmet*.

cut (1) *See* **cutting.**

(2) [hyd.] or **lock cut** A short canal beside a river which enables boats to by-pass a *weir* and go through a lock.

(3) [min.] Any pattern for drilling a round of shot holes in tunnelling or shaft sinking, such as the *bottom cut, pyramid cut, wedge cut. See* **cut holes.**

(4) [mech.] The shape of the cutting teeth of a file, whether made by one row of parallel incisions or by two rows of incisions which intersect at about 45°. The first is single cut or float cut, the second double cut or cross cut. Cut also refers to the coarseness or fineness of the teeth. Short files are more finely cut than long ones as the following table shows. The table gives the average number of teeth per linear centimetre (except for saw files which are much finer).

Description of file	10 cm long files	50 cm long files
Bastard	16	6
Second cut	17	7
Smooth	24	13
Dead smooth	35	22

(5) *Flame cutting.*

cut-and-cover A method used for excavating the New York subway as well as for the London District and Metropolitan underground railways. The excavation to *formation level* is made in the open and then filled in over the tunnel after the brick, concrete, or other lining has been built. *Compare* **tube railway.**

cut and fill Road or railway or canal construction which is partly embanked and partly below ground in cut.

cut holes [min.] American term for a set of holes fired first in tunnelling or shaft sinking so as to break out a wedge of rock and form a *free face* for the outer holes. *See* **cut, lifter/ relief/rib holes, sumpers.**

cut of a file *See* **cut** [mech.].

cut-off (1) A construction below ground level intended to reduce water seepage; for example, a *cut-off wall* or a *grout curtain* under a cut-off wall.

(2) The drainage of rainfall into the soil, as opposed to *run-off*, more often called *infiltration.*

cut-off depth The depth below excavation level to which *sheet piling* or a *cut-off trench* reaches.

cut-off trench In dams, a trench excavated well below the foundation to an impervious layer and then filled with clay or concrete to make a watertight barrier. *See below.*

cut-off wall or **core wall** A watertight wall of *clay puddle* or concrete which is built up from the *cut-off trench. See* **grout curtain.**

cutout [elec.] A circuit-breaking device such as an electric fuse or *circuit breaker.*

cutter-dredger A *suction cutter-dredger.*

cutting or **cut** An excavation for carrying a canal, railway, road, or pipeline below ground level in the open.

cutting curb [min.] or **drum curb** or **shoe** A steel ring on which a *drop shaft* is built. The sharp metal edge on its vertical blade cuts the ground.

cutting list or **summary of reinforcement** A list of steel bars showing diameters and lengths only, from which the reinforcement is ordered. This list is prepared by the contractor from the *bending schedules* issued by the reinforced-concrete designer with his detail drawings.

cutting-out piece A short timber in trench timbering which can be sawn out to ease the striking of the timbering.

cutwater The streamlined head of a bridge pier. *Compare* **starling**.

cyanide hardening [mech.] or **cyaniding** The introduction of carbon and nitrogen into the surface of low and medium *carbon steel* by holding it at about 800°C in contact with molten cyanides. Cyaniding is followed either by direct *quenching* from the cyaniding operation or by other suitable heat treatment to produce a hard case. It is a form of *case hardening*.

cyclone [min.] A cone-shaped air cleaner. It removes the dust from the air by centrifugal separation. It has been developed for use as an air classifier for particles small enough to be airborne, and has been successfully used, with water or heavy medium, for washing various minerals.

cyclopean Concrete aggregate larger than 15 cm used in mass concrete for dams and other thick structures.

cylinder (1) In USA, particularly New York, steel tubes 0·25 to 1·5 m dia., 3 mm or more thick, driven through bad ground to bedrock, excavated inside, filled with concrete and used as a pile foundation for skyscrapers and in underpinning. *See* **pile core**.

(2) *A monolith* of circular cross-section. Small cylinders resemble the *Chicago caisson*, and even smaller ones resemble *bored piles*. *See* **screw pile**.

cylinder caisson A *drop shaft*.

cylinder prestressed concrete pipe A *prestressed concrete cylinder pipe*.

cylinder test A concrete cylinder 152 mm dia. and 305 mm long is used in USA for testing site concrete. When tested in similar conditions to the 150 mm cube used in Britain, the cylinder, for geometrical reasons, gives only about 0·75 of the strength of the same concrete crushed as a cube. *See* **cube test**.

cylindrical slide [s.m.] A *rotational slide*.

cylindrical-surface method *See* **circular-arc method**.

cylindrical vault *See* **barrel vault**.

D

dam (1) A wall to hold back water. For some different types *see* **arch dam, earthen dam, gravity-arch dam, multiple-arch dam.**

(2) Cast-steel plates with fingers formed on them, built into the road surface of a bridge in meshing pairs over an expansion joint, so as to allow traffic to pass freely over the joint.

damping [stru.] A force which tends to reduce vibration as friction reduces ordinary motion. *See* **resonance.**

damp-proof membrane A vertical, horizontal or sloping waterproof skin, that may be of asphalt 20 mm thick, copper sheet, polythene film, etc., or many other materials such as blue brick or slate. *See* **damp-proof course** (*B*).

Darcy's law [s.m.] For the velocity of percolation of water in saturated soil; states that

Velocity = *coefficient of permeability* × *hydraulic gradient*.

datum [sur.] Any level taken as a reference point for levelling. The datum for any building site in Britain is usually the nearest *Ordnance bench mark*.

day joint A *stunt end.*

dead load [stru.] or **dead weight** The weight of a structure and any permanent loads fixed on it. *Compare* **live load.**

dead man, anchorage or **anchor block/wall** A buried plate, wall, or block, some distance from a *sheet pile* or other *retaining wall*, which serves to anchor back the wall through a tie between the two. The dead man is held in place by its own weight and by *passive pressure* from the soil. *See* **anchor, anchorage distance, cantilever bridge, suspension bridge, land tie, stay pile.**

dead-mild steel or **dead-soft steel** [mech.] Steel with ·07 to ·15% carbon, used for bending, drawing, pressing, and flangeing. *See* **mild steel, wrought iron.**

dead-smooth file [mech.] The finest grade of file *cut*.

debris dam [hyd.] A barrier built across a stream channel to store sand, gravel, and so on. *See* **drift barrier.**

deca- A prefix of the *decimal system* meaning ten times.

decalescent point [mech.] *Critical point.*

decanting In *pneumatic caisson* sinking where accommodation in airlocks, particularly *manlocks*, is very limited, the process of locking men through from high pressures (pressures much above 1·3 bar) in 10 to 15 minutes. Immediately the men leave the lock they go into a special, more spacious manlock, where they are recompressed to the full working pressure and decompressed at the correct rate (from 1 to 5 minutes for each 70 millibars above atmospheric pressure). *See* **caisson disease.**

deci- A prefix in the *decimal system* meaning one tenth.

decimal system Any system of counting or measuring in tens or tenths, hundreds or hundredths, and so on. The *metric system* of measurement is decimal, the feet and inches system *duodecimal* (*B*).

deck (1) or **decking** A flat roof or a quay, jetty, or bridge floor, generally a floor with no roof over.

(2) *Formwork* for a level surface.

deck bridge A bridge in which the top *chord* carries the deck. *Compare* **through bridge.**

declination [sur.] (1) The angular distance (or elevation) of a star from the celestial equator.

(2) The variation in degrees of the magnetic compass needle from true north at any point. The declination is variable from place to place and at each place from year to year. *See* **annual variation.**

dedicated street or **adopted street** American term for a street administered by a *local authority* (*B*).

deep blasting or **explosive compaction** [s.m.] A *ground improvement* method suitable for free-running soils, in which successive small explosive charges are detonated underground at or below the depth of the foundation which is to be loaded.

deep compaction [s.m.] *See* **compaction, sand piles, Vibroflot.**

deep foundation [stru.] A foundation usually on some type of *pile* or *caisson*, generally more than 3 m below ground. Deep foundations are often needed in conjunction with *ground engineering* work.

deep manhole An *inspection chamber* built with an access shaft above it. The access shaft is considerably smaller in plan than the manhole. *See* **shallow manhole, side-entrance manhole.**

deep-penetration electrodes In the *arc welding* of heavy steel members, a type of electrode which fuses the plates to about 0·8 mm from the surface.

deep-penetration test [s.m.] *Cone penetration test.*

deep well A well passing through shallow impermeable strata (which may yield water) but drawing its water only from beneath them.

deep well pump A centrifugal pump which is driven by a long shaft from a surface electric motor, the pump being at the foot of the borehole. The motor is easily accessible for maintenance, unlike the *submersible pump*.

deflection (or **deflexion**) (1) [stru.] The *elastic* movement of loaded parts of a structure. The word often refers to the sinking of the mid-span of a beam which in British housing generally is not allowed to exceed $\frac{1}{325}$ of the span. *See* **deformation.**

(2) [sur.] The angle between a line and the extension of the preceding line of a *traverse* is a deflection angle. It is used for setting out circular *curves*, the curve being marked out by points spaced equally apart, therefore at the same deflection angle from each other (intersection angle).

deflection curve *See* **elastic curve.**

deflectometer An instrument for measuring the deflections of structures, usually of beams under load. One type has an *invar* wire tightly strung between the loaded structure and a *dial gauge*.

deformation [stru.] A more general term than *deflection*, which includes the *plastic*, non-recoverable movement of a structure.

deformed bars Concrete reinforcement consisting of steel bars with projections or indentations, which increase the *mechanical bond* between the steel and the concrete.

deformeter [stru.] An instrument used in the *model analysis* of a structure to help in drawing out its influence line. A model of the structure is made and carefully cut at the required point. The deformeter applies shears or rotations at the cut and the resulting deflected shape of the structure is the *influence line* at the cut for shear or rotation, whichever is applied.

degree of a curve [sur.] American method of describing circular curves by the number of degrees subtended at the centre of a circle by a chord 100 ft long. As the radius increases, the number of degrees decreases. In Britain the radius of the curve is usually stated instead of the degree.

degree of compaction [s.m.] or **degree of density** The tightness of packing of a soil sample, estimated by the formula

$$\frac{\text{(voids ratio in loosest state) minus} \atop \text{(voids ratio of sample)}}{\text{(voids ratio in loosest state) minus} \atop \text{(voids ratio in densest state).}}$$

degree of saturation [s.m.] The percentage of the volume of water-filled voids to the total volume of voids between the soil grains. It gives a measure of the air in the voids, since the air content is 100 % minus the degree of saturation.

Dehottay process [s.m.] A refinement of the ground *freezing* process for shaft sinking or foundations. Instead of circulating brine in the pipes installed in the ground, liquid carbon dioxide is pumped in. An advantage of carbon dioxide is that when it passes out through a leak in the pipe into the freezing ground it has no effect on its freezability. If brine escapes, the freezing point of the ground is so much lowered that it may be impossible to freeze it again.

delay-action detonator [min.] A *detonator* which explodes at a suitable fraction of a second after the passing of the firing current from the exploder. In shaft sinking or tunnel driving this is very convenient, as the *cut holes* can be arranged to fire first without delay and delay-action detonators can be used for the *relief holes*. The complete round of shots can thus be fired once without the shot firer being obliged to return to the face after the cut holes have been fired, to connect up to the relief holes in the unpleasant, often poisonous fumes.

delivery [mech.] The volume of air or water delivered per minute or per second by a compressor or a pump.

de-mineralized water (usually the same as **de-ionized water**) Feedwater for high-pressure steam boilers – e.g. at a power station – has to be raised to such a purity that its total dissolved and suspended solids do not exceed one part per million. In the past this was done by distillation but now **ion exchange** is used.

de-nitrification [sewage] *See* **advanced treatment.**

dense concrete Concrete is regarded as dense (though not necessarily strong) if it weighs more than 1900 kg per cu. m. If its density is over 2250 kg per cu. m it is almost always strong. Generally strength is proportional to density.

densification [s.m.] Most methods of *ground improvement*.

density The weight per unit volume of a substance (at a certain temperature stated for solids and liquids only when great accuracy is required). The density of water is 62·4 lb per cu. ft or 1 kg per litre or 1 tonne per cubic metre. The density of dry air at 29·92 in. of mercury (760 mm) and 0°C is 1·23 kg per cu. m. The density of air falls as it becomes wetter.

density current, gravity current, turbidity current, also known as **internal, layered, subsurface or stratified flow** Currents of fluid of different density occur when colder or sediment-laden (dense) water enters a reservoir and creeps along the bottom. When salt water meets fresh water in an estuary, the fresh water generally stays separate and floats above, though eventually the two may mix together. The same occurs when other gases mix with air. In sewage *sedimentation* tanks a difference of only 0·2°C can thus disturb the settlement process.

density/moisture relationship [s.m.] *See* **dry-density/moisture-content relationship.**

dental [hyd.] A tooth-like projection on an *apron* or other surface to deflect or break the force of flowing water, a form of baffle (ASCE MEP 11).

dentated sill [hyd.] A notched sill to break the force of a stream and reduce *scour*.

departure [sur.] The distance of a point east or west of the north–south reference line. A point is completely located by its departure and its *latitude*, which are its *coordinates*.

depressant or **bathotonic reagent** or **surface-tension depressant** A flotation reagent which so lowers the *surface tension* that finely powdered worthless material can sink through floating bubbles covered with valuable mineral. Soap is a well-known depressant.

derrick A lifting device which may be hand-operated by one man or worked by several powerful motors. The main types are described below, starting with the simplest and smallest. Strictly, a derrick is a stationary crane, but

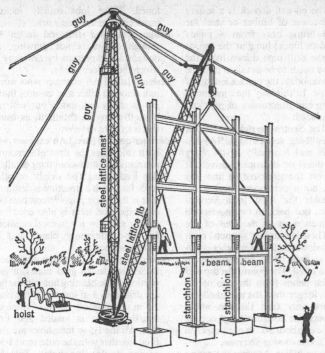

Guy derrick lowering into place one bent of a steel frame

some Scotch derricks move on two or more rails.

(1) The **pole** or **gin-pole** or **guyed-mast** or **standing derrick** is a pole held in a nearly vertical position by four or more guy ropes. A hoisting rope passes over a pulley at the top of the pole and raises the load by a winch fixed at the foot of the pole. Though generally hand-operated for small sizes the pole may be from 5 to 30 m long.

(2) The **shear legs** or **shears derrick** has two poles lashed together at the top, from which the hoisting tackle is hung. Two guy ropes only are needed but the shears are rather less manoeuvrable (and therefore more stable) than the pole, which can be moved towards any of its guy ropes.

(3) The **guy derrick** has a pole or

mast from which is suspended the upper end of a boom or lifting jib, pivoted at the foot of the mast. The boom is shorter than the mast and this enables it to turn a full circle, passing under all the guy ropes when it is in a vertical position. The mast is held up by guy ropes in the same way as type (1). Both the guy derrick and the simple pole are much used for erecting steel-framed buildings, because of their manoeuvrability, the small space they take up, and the relatively great heights which they can lift to.

(4) The **three-legged derrick** is a development of the shear legs, and having three legs needs no guy ropes. It is used for vertical lifting only, such as well sinking, *diamond drilling*, and sinking *bored piles*.

(5) The **oil-well derrick** is a square latticed tower of timber or steel for vertical lifting only from a pulley (the crown block) hung at the top. It stores the drill pipe drawn from the hole and needs to be as tall as possible to accommodate the biggest lengths of drill pipe. In this way the amount of screwing and unscrewing of pipe can be minimized.

(6) The **Scotch derrick** or **derrick crane** (**stiff-leg derrick** in USA) has no guys and is usually a stationary crane, diesel or electrically driven. It works on the principle of the guy derrick but a permanent steel structure holds the mast in a vertical position, tied back to two horizontal legs which meet at the foot of the mast. These legs (called sleepers) must be held down by heavy weights (*kentledge*) at their ends, proportional to the load lifted. The boom, the top end of which hangs from the top of the mast, is longer than the mast and can therefore only turn through about 240°, since the horizontal legs occupy an angle of about 90° to each other in plan. *Compare* **swing-jib crane**.

derricking or **luffing** Altering the radius of the hoisting rope, that is lowering or raising the jib of a crane or derrick. *See* **level-luffing crane**.

derricking jib crane *See* **luffing jib crane**.

derrick tower gantry Strong wooden or steel staging consisting of three towers, one *crane tower* for the mast and jib of the derrick, and two anchor towers for the legs and their *kentledge*. The towers are tied together at their upper ends by the derrick legs.

de-salination, de-salting Removal of dissolved salts from water, usually for making drinking water from seawater or brackish water. Drinking water should have less than 500 parts per million of dissolved salts, and seawater has $3 \cdot 5\%$ (35,000 ppm). There are two types of process: first employed were the distillation processes, which are still being used, and now the *membrane processes* are being deve-

loped. These jobs usually include much civil engineering work.

design [stru.] *See* **structural design** Although design is not drawing, all designs are expressed by *drawings* to which the builder works.

designer [stru.] An engineer who works in a drawing office and ensures that a job is safely calculated but will not himself draw the details if, as usual, this is left to a *detailer*.

designer-detailer [stru.] An engineer who both calculates the sizes of structural members and draws out their details.

design load [stru.] The weight or other force for which a structure is designed, that is the worst possible combination of loads. The term is also used in a similar sense by mechanical engineers for air-conditioning plant, and by other engineers.

de-stressing [r.m.] To reduce rockbursts in South African gold mines, a proportion of the blasting holes in the face are drilled to 3 m instead of the usual $1 \cdot 5$ m. The inmost $1 \cdot 5$ m of these de-stressing holes is loaded and fired first. All the $1 \cdot 5$ m long holes are then fired together with the outermost $1 \cdot 5$ m of the de-stressing holes. This has significantly reduced the accident rate, which has also been helped by the timing of the shotfiring. Shots are fired from the surface when no one is underground. Rockbursts often occur soon after shotfiring.

detachable bit [min.] A threaded piece of metal screwed to the end of a rock-drill steel, as a cutting point. The steel thus remains permanently at the working place and only the bits need to be sent to the smith's shop for retipping or resharpening. Its cutting edge is coated with *hard facing*.

detail or **detail drawing** or **working drawing** A drawing which has enough detail on it for the *contractor* to build his work correctly and for the site dimensions to be true to the drawing.

detailer A draughtsman of any sort (structural, architectural, mechanical, etc.) who works out and draws *details* of construction, sometimes under the supervision of a *designer*, sometimes on his own responsibility.

detail paper [d.o.] Lightweight, nearly transparent, cheap *drawing paper*, used for making a first rough drawing but not normally for printing purposes.

detonating fuse [min.] or **Cordeau, Cordtex** or **Primacord** Fuse used in quarrying in *well holes* and similar types of blasting where several distant charges must be fired simultaneously and surely. Its firing speed is 6000 m per sec. It consists of a textile wrapping round a detonating core such as *TNT* or *PETN*. No *primer* or *detonator* need be used, since the fuse detonates every cartridge which it touches.

detonation The rapid explosion of very *high explosives* such as are used in *detonating fuse* or *detonators*.

detonator [min.] or **cap** A small sealed copper or aluminium tube, at one end containing an explosive mixture, usually fired electrically by a *blasting machine*, but in small-scale work by a *safety fuse* inserted into the detonator, crimped on to it, and lit with a match or taper. If it is electrically fired, the detonator is sealed at the factory with two copper wires leading out of it which are connected to the exploder through the neighbouring detonators in series. Whether electrically fired or otherwise, every detonator is inserted into a *primer* which fires all the other cartridges in its hole. *See also* **delay-action detonator, detonating fuse.**

detritus chamber or **pit** *See* **detritus tank.**

detritus slide [s.m.] or **creep slide** The slow movement of detritus downhill on a shale or clay layer, a common sort of *landslip* generally not dangerous.

detritus tank or **detritus chamber, grit chamber** A tank in which grit is removed by settlement from sewage.

deviation (1) [stat.] The difference between one value of a set and the *average* of the set. It is a figure used in estimating the reliability or variability

of a test, such as a *crushing strength* of brick or of a *cube* of concrete. *See* **standard deviation.**

(2) [min.] or **drift** Any departure of a *borehole* from the straight, usually measured by the magnetic bearing and the dip value. All boreholes depart from the straight, particularly long ones drilled by rotary methods (diamond or shot drill). *See* **borehole surveying.**

devil (1) An iron firegrate (often wheeled) used for heating asphalting tools or for softening a small area of bituminous road.

(2) or **lifter** A stretcher carried by two men, for loading stone, in American quarrying.

dewatering (1) [min.] The pumping out of a drowned shaft or caisson with a *submersible pump* or an *air-lift pump* or by any other means.

(2) *Groundwater lowering*.

(3) [sewage] Reduction of the water content of *sludge*, always a difficult task. Although a reduction of the water content of a sludge from 98 % to 96 % water seems a minute improvement, it is in fact a real commercial success. It means there are now 4 %, instead of 2 %, dry solids and the solids/water ratio has been raised from 1 in 49 to 1 in 24. There is thus less than half as much water as before, and the bulk of the sludge for expensive disposal has been more than halved.

dewpoint The temperature at which air of a given absolute *humidity* begins to give up its water vapour as drops of dew. It is the temperature at which the *relative humidity* rises to 100 % and can be found from tables. It is important in buildings to keep the air temperature above the dewpoint, since *condensate* is formed at all points where the air is cooled below it.

diagonal brace [stru.] A sloping member which carries compression or tension forces or both at different times and is generally used to stabilize a frame against wind or other horizontal forces. *See* **counter bracing.**

diagonal eyepiece [sur.] The eyepiece of a *prismatic telescope*.

diagonal tension In reinforced or pre-stressed concrete the *principal* tensile stress due to horizontal tension and vertical shear.

Diagrid floor [stru.] A network of diagonally intersecting ribs spanning a rectangular space. The ribs may be of metal or concrete and are often *pre-stressed*. As a roof it can admit a large amount of light, is not heavy, and occupies a small depth. The span/depth ratio in concrete may be about 30.

dial gauge [mech.] An instrument which shows, by its needle indication on a graduated dial, displacements of its plunger equal to one hundredth of a millimetre or less. The plunger is accurately geared to the needle. It is used in conjunction with *deflectometers* and *proving rings*.

diamond [min.] One of the carbon minerals, a gem formed in volcanic necks. The hardest mineral, apart from its value as a gemstone, it is extremely useful as a cutting agent. (*See* **black diamond**.) The diamond fields of India, now exhausted, yielded every diamond known before 1725, when diamonds were discovered in Brazil. In 1867 the first diamonds were discovered in the Orange river, South Africa, followed a few years later by the discovery of the world's richest diamond fields in the same country. Production is now artificially limited (the limitation being helped by South African law) to keep up the price both of industrial and gem diamonds. Large deposits of heavy diamonds are worked in USSR.

diamond drilling [min.] Rotative boring in rock with a hollow cylindrical bit set with diamonds, usually in a tung-sten-carbide alloy crown, so as to obtain a *core* for geological or minera-logical examination. In spite of the cost of diamonds worn out or lost in the hole, diamond drilling is the only method for drilling small holes near to the horizontal or upwards. It is also the most popular drilling method for small downward holes. Diamond drilling speeds may be up to 3 m per hour; core diameters are up to 500 mm.

diamond pyramid hardness test [mech.] Testing the *hardness* of a metal surface by pressing a diamond pyramid point into it and measuring the area of the indentation. The figure obtained in this way is related to the *Brinell hardness* number. *See* **Vickers hardness test**.

diamond saw A diamond saw is a thin steel disc set with diamonds on the tungsten-carbide matrix of the rim so as to cut stone, concrete, steel or other hard material. Diamond saws cut like a *circular saw* (*B*), except that they must be cooled by a water spray. *Pretensioned* precast floor slabs or beams are cut to length by diamond saws. They will saw 8 cm thick granite at 8 cm per minute, and the sawn granite surface is smooth enough to be polished immediately without rough grinding. The rim of the wheel moves at about 15 m/sec. so that a 50 cm dia. saw rotates at about 1800 rpm, while a 75 cm dia. saw rotates more slowly, at about 1150 rpm, to provide the same rim speed. A reciprocating saw can cut 1·2 m deep.

diaphragm (1) [stru.] In a bridge a stiffening plate between main girders, or a stiffening web across a hollow building block.

(2) [sur.] A brass fitting in a surveying telescope which carries the *reticule*.

diaphragm pump A reciprocating pump with neither ram nor piston but a flexible rubber, canvas, or leather partition moved to and fro by a rod. It is used by contractors more than any other pump, since it can handle gritty water containing 15% solids, and even small stones, with little wear.

diaphragm wall (1) A concrete retaining wall underground, which may be as much as 24 m deep, built in a mech-anically excavated trench that has been filled with *bentonite*-loaded or ordinary mud to support it during excavation. Reinforcement is dropped into the mud and the concrete is lowered into the bottom of the trench by *trémie*. The method is relatively silent and vibrationless compared with driving sheet piles. In 1973 a French method of converting bentonite slurry to concrete by adding cement (Sepicos) was said to be economical, because there was no need to buy concrete nor to pay for the removal of waste mud. About 150 kg cement were added per cu. m of mud, with some lignosulphite retarder. The 28-day strength was very low, varying from 1 to 3 N/mm^2, but the material was impermeable and crack-free and sometimes this is all that is needed. *See* **masthead gear.**

(2) A usually windowless brick *cavity wall* (*B*) with an unusually wide cavity, some 45 cm wide. It is bridged, not by *wall ties* (*B*) but by periodical 11 cm thick brick walls, from one 11-cm leaf to the other, creating a series of box sections that stiffen the wall. It is suitable for swimming pools, sports halls, warehouses, etc., and is claimed to be cheaper and faster than other brick walls of the same height.

die A very hard metal block with a hole through which *ductile* metal is *cold drawn* to convert it to wire or pipe. *See* **wire gauge** (*B*). Another sort of die is used for forming a *screw thread* (*B*) on a bar by forcing it into and twisting it through the die.

die-formed strand [stru.] A *strand* for *prestressed concrete* which began to be commercially available in the UK about 1964. When strand is passed through a die, its bulk is reduced some 27 to 37 per cent, enabling more strands and thus more force to be packed into a given area of concrete.

Diesel engine [mech.] An *internal-combustion engine* which burns a relatively cheap oil of about the consistency of light lubricating oil. The oil fuel is pumped into the cylinder (solid injection or airless injection) by a pump, or in the original types of engine by a blast of compressed air. The fuel is ignited solely by the high compression in the cylinder, without electrical spark.

Diesel hammer *See* **pile hammer.**

differential pulley block [mech.] or **chain block** A builder's *lifting tackle* consisting of an endless chain threaded over two wheels of slightly different diameters turning together on the same shaft. The lifting power increases as the diameters become closer. The chain cannot run back and a man can safely lift 500 kg or more alone.

differential settlement [stru.] or **relative settlement** Uneven sinking of different parts of a building. The allowable difference between one column and the next is less for a building with marble facings and plastered interior walls than for a steel-framed single-storey factory with hardboard facings to its inside walls. The worst differential settlement is unlikely to exceed half the total settlement in a normal *settlement crater*. If the foundations are designed to limit the total settlement to 5 cm, the 2·5 cm maximum expected differential settlement is unlikely to damage even the most sensitive building seriously. Uniform settlements of several metres occur in some cities (Mexico City, Chicago), but they do not damage the buildings and may even not sever its connections with the outside world (pipes, drains, cables).

diffuser (1) [hyd.] In centrifugal pumps, compressors, fans or turbines, the gradually increasing cross-section at the inlet or outlet, which reduces the speed of the air or water and thus increases its pressure. *See* **draft tube.**

(2) [sewage] A porous plate or similar device through which air is blown to aerate sewage, or at an *outfall*, holes in the sewer wall that distribute the sewage uniformly.

diffusion (1) [min.] The movement of the molecules of gases in all directions which causes them to intermingle without ventilation current, in a way which is often contrary to gravity. *See* **Graham's law of diffusion.**

(2) Wood preservation by laying a stiff paste or a concentrated solution on to green timber, and allowing it to penetrate gradually.

digestion [sewage] A way of treating sewage *sludge* in the absence of air in closed, heated tanks. With effective treatment it gives off a gas that is mainly methane (CH_4), with one third carbon dioxide, but the process takes three weeks even with heating. Because of the expense and care needed, the process is not now favoured in the cold climate of the UK. Even after digestion, the bulk of the sludge still has to be disposed of.

dike *See* **dyke.**

dilatancy [s.m.] A property of *silt* which distinguishes it from *clays*. If a pat of wet silt is shaken in the hand it exudes water and becomes shiny. If the pat is then pressed, the water re-enters the silt, leaving a matt surface on the silt because of a dilation or increase in volume. *See* **shaking test.**

dimensional analysis [hyd.] In the *model analysis* of rivers, ports, ships, breakwaters, airplanes and other problems involving the flow of fluids, *dynamic* or *kinematic* or *geometric similarity* (components of dimensional similarity) help to simplify the study. These relationships enable the experimenter to see quickly the effect of variations in flow rate and size of model compared with similar variations in the full-size structure (prototype). *See* **Reynolds number.**

DIN Deutsche Industrie Normal, meaning German *Standard*.

dip [min.] The angle of maximum slope of the beds of rock measured from the horizontal at any point. The dip is shown at *outcrops* on geological maps by an arrow pointing downwards with a figure giving the dip in degrees. The dip is at right angles to the *strike*.

dip compass *See* **dip needle.**

dip needle [sur.] or **dip compass** or **dipping**

needle A magnetic needle with a horizontal pivot which allows the needle to swing only in a vertical plane. The needle is set in the magnetic meridian and the inclination to the horizontal of the needle is read off. This angle of dip is the dip of the earth's magnetic field at that point.

dipper dredger *See* **grab dredger.**

direct-acting pump [mech.] A compressed-air or steam-driven *reciprocating* pump having the power cylinder and water cylinder at opposite ends of the same piston rod. There are therefore no important rotating parts.

directional drilling The drilling of a hole with an intentional *deviation* (2). Single holes can now be drilled with several others branching off them all round so as to increase their gas or oil output. In offshore drilling, any hole has to be used to the maximum because of the high cost of the drilling-or production-platform built over it. The technique has been greatly helped by improved *turbodrills* and *borehole surveys*. The turbodrill, with stationary drill pipe behind it, can be turned to any desired angle by a short length of bent pipe between it and the main drill pipe. *Sidetracking* is more difficult with rotary drilling, and the accuracy possible with turbodrill sidetracking was previously unheard of. Holes have been drilled with 10 degrees of intentional curvature per 30 m of hole. On one occasion a 7·6 cm dia. hole was drilled for 200 m under a river and up to a target on the far bank, so as to provide a passage through which a service pipe could be pulled.

direct reading tacheometer [sur.] A *tacheometer* from which the plan length (from the staff *intercept*) and the difference in level between staff and instrument can be read directly without measuring the vertical angle.

direct stress [mech.] A *stress* which is wholly compression or tension and involves no bending or shear.

discharge The volume of fluid per unit

time flowing along a pipe or channel, or the output rate of plant such as a pump.

discharge coefficient [hyd.] *See* **coefficient of discharge.**

discharge curve [hyd.] A curve relating the water level (*stage*) of a stream to its discharge.

discharge head [mech.] The height between the intake of a pump and the point at which it discharges freely into the air. Strictly speaking this is the static discharge head, and the total discharge head is this height together with another height representing the friction in the pipe and pump, plus the *velocity head.*

discharge valve [hyd.] or **control valve** A valve for reducing or increasing the flow in a pipe, as opposed to a *stop valve.*

disease *See* **caisson disease.**

disinfection Destruction of micro-organisms that harm humans. Conventional *waterworks* treatment without disinfection eliminates 90% of the bacteria and viruses in water. The remaining 10% are removed usually by *chlorination* in the UK, in France by ozonizing, elsewhere also by other methods, e.g. ultra-violet radiation. Disinfection is always the last process in water treatment.

dispersing agent [s.m.] A deflocculating agent, usually sodium oxalate, used in the *wet analysis* to prevent particles joining together and thus settling more quickly than they should.

dispersion A suspension of very fine particles (often *colloids*) in a liquid medium. Most paints and some varnishes are dispersions. *See* **emulsion.**

displacement (1) [mech.] The volume displaced (swept) by a piston or ram moving from top to bottom of its stroke. For a pump this is equal to the theoretical amount of water delivered per stroke. For an engine (compressed air, steam, or internal combustion) the product of displacement and the mean pressure in the cylinder is equal to the work done per stroke. From this the engine power is calculated.

(2) [hyd.] The volume of water displaced by a floating vessel. By the *principle of Archimedes* it weighs the same as the vessel and its contents.

displacement pile Any solid or hollow driven *pile* that is closed at its lower end by a shoe or plug and displaces ground when it is driven can therefore be called a displacement pile. This displacement may weaken the ground or affect nearby structures unfavourably. It may even lift the ground or piles nearby, involving the need to re-drive those that were driven first. *Bored piles* do not displace ground, but replace it and may therefore be preferable in the neighbourhood of sensitive structures. Small-displacement piles include open-ended tubes, or box-sections, or H-sections and *screw piles.*

displacement pump Any ram-operated or piston-operated pump; but the term is generally kept for *diaphragm pumps,* or for *air-lift pumps* in which compressed air displaces the water. They can pump very dirty water or mud or corrosive liquids without excessive wear on their metal parts.

displacer A *plum* in concrete.

disposal well or **injection well** A well (usually drilled not dug) into which poisonous or corrosive liquid is poured and left. Checks should first be made that groundwater will not be poisoned nor earth movements caused (if the hole is in an arid area).

distance piece or **separator** A part used for maintaining the position and spacing of bars or rails and check rails, or built-in members or formwork during concreting, or permanently. *See* **bolt sleeve.**

distancing unit [sur.] An *electronic length-measuring unit.*

Distomat [sur.] An *electronic length-measuring instrument* made by Wild of Switzerland that is suitable for engineering work, being designed for rapid, accurate measurement of distances up to 1 km, to within 2 cm. One type measures distances up to 300 m and also calculates the difference in level between the two points. A display from the calculator in the control unit shows to 6 digits, the measured slope, the calculated plan length and vertical distance.

distributed load [stru.] A *design load* uniformly distributed along a beam. *See* **live load**.

distribution curve [stat.] A *frequency curve*.

distribution reservoir [hyd.] A *service reservoir*.

distribution steel In a reinforced-concrete slab, the subsidiary reinforcement placed at right angles to the main steel to hold it in place during concreting and to spread concentrated loads over a large area of slab.

distribution tile American term for clay *agricultural drains* which distribute the overflow from a septic tank to the soil.

ditch Either a drainage or an irrigation channel.

ditcher or **trencher** A *trench excavator*.

ditching by explosives Holes are punched or bored to about 15 cm from the bottom of the ditch along its centre line, and about one cartridge of explosive is charged per 0·6 m of hole. A line of holes along the ditch is fired simultaneously. The rubbish is thus scattered effectively and a rough ditch is made.

diver Most divers wear *SCUBA* or *standard diving gear*. In SCUBA, a diver is very mobile but also more vulnerable to the cold. An underwater current of 1 knot (0·5 m/sec.) has the same effect on the diver as an 80 kph wind on the surface would, and this is the strongest current that a diver can work in. Consequently most dives are made at slack water (high or low) not during running tides. Pneumatic tools used under water need compressed air at a pressure that is larger than would be needed on the surface by the amount of submergence. Thus at 30 m depth of water (3 atmospheres)

the compressors at the surface must provide air at 3 atm. higher pressure. Since breathing alone is hard work under water, it is inadvisable to expect divers to work hard, but theoretically they can do underwater cutting, welding, guniting, carpentry, steel plating and shipwright's work. Divers normally do not work below 60 m depth but 90% of dives are less deep than 10 m. When the diver comes up from 60 m, he must spend a large part of the shift decompressing in the air lock at the surface. *See* **caisson disease, decanting.**

diversion or **diversion cut** A *bye channel* excavated to cause a stream or river to by-pass civil engineering work either permanently or during construction only.

diversion cut *See* **diversion.**

diversion dam [hyd.] A barrier across a stream built to turn all or some of the water into a *diversion*.

diversion requirement *See* **gross duty of water.**

diver's paralysis *Caisson disease.*

divide American term for a *watershed.*

dividers [d.o.] An instrument used for transferring equal lengths from one point to another on a drawing. Like the compass it has two legs hinged together at one end, but unlike the compass it has both legs pointed.

diving Divers wearing *standard diving dress* are often needed for harbour maintenance and construction, or for the laying of pipelines or cables. A diving crew consists of the diver and his linesman, plus two air-pump operators, or one if the air is pumped by power-driven compressor to the diver. Other men are needed for taking tools down to the diver or for bringing material up from him. The absolute minimum crew is thus 3 or 4 men, so that diving work is necessarily expensive. It is therefore not surprising that *SCUBA* diving has become popular, since it involves one man only, at least to shallow depths.

diving bell A bell-shaped steel chamber

raised and lowered to the sea bed or river bottom by a powerful crane. It is open at the bottom and gives to the men within it access to the bed to prepare foundations, etc. In the simple diving bell the men are withdrawn within the bell at the end of the shift, with the rock they have excavated. A more advanced type has an *air lock* through which rock can be hoisted. *Divers* are more mobile and a diving suit is cheaper than a diving bell. For these reasons diving bells are now obsolescent. A modern diving bell, in which four men can work, measures 3·5 by 2 by 2 m high and weighs 15 tons in air. Clean cool air must be pumped into the bell at the pressure of the bell, at a rate of at least 0·3 m³ per man each minute. A standby compressor and its prime mover are also essential. In addition, if compressed-air tools are used, high-pressure compressed air must be supplied for these. Electric light with flameproof fittings is needed, at 50 volts maximum, and a telephone to the crane driver for the divers to tell him when to raise or lower the bell. A lifeline through a watertight joint in the roof enables emergency signals to be made to a linesman serving the bell on the barge or the dockside. The bell must be raised slowly to conform to the decompression rate laid down by law. Men working in a bell have to be passed as medically fit and must be supervised by a doctor, as for other work in compressed air. Smeaton used one of the first, if not the first, diving bell in the UK in 1784, with an air pump on the roof which was above water level. *See* **helium diving bell, limpet, compressed air** (2).

dock A basin for shipping which is cut off from the tides by dock gates (except for tidal docks). *See* **dry/floating/self-docking/wet dock.**

docking blocks Blocks which support the underside of the hull of a ship in *dry dock*. The centre row are called keel blocks; a row is also provided at

each side. They are made of oak or other hardwood, preferably with a softwood cap which does not damage the hull.

dog A square-section spike driven into a wooden sleeper to hold heavy timbering or a flat-bottomed rail. *See also* (*B*).

dolly A block of hardwood or other material placed over the *pile helmet* to receive the shock of the *pile hammer* and thus reduce the damage to the head of the pile from driving. *See* **grommet.**

dolomite [min.] $CaMgCO_3$, a source of basic *refractory* as well as of limes for *iointless flooring* (*B*).

dolphin A mooring in the open sea or a guide to help ships to come into a narrow harbour entrance. It is usually built of *raking piles* of steel or timber driven into the sea bed. *See* **bell dolphin.**

dome [min.] A locally spherical shape of the strata, which, if it contains open-textured sandstones beneath impervious shales or salt, may well be an excellent natural oil reservoir, as are the salt domes of Texas.

Doppler shift The tone of a railway engine whistle approaching a listener is higher in pitch than when it recedes from the listener. The difference in frequency in the two tones, known as the Doppler shift, could be used to calculate the speed of the railway engine and is used for measuring the speed of a river, in the *ultrasonic flow meter*.

dosing chamber A *dosing tank*.

dosing siphon [sewage] An automatic siphon that discharges the contents of a *dosing tank*.

dosing tank or **dosing chamber** A tank into which raw or partly treated sewage flows until the desired quantity has accumulated, after which it is discharged automatically for treatment. It ensures that the flow rate is never too small for the process to work properly.

double-acting [mech.] A description of

reciprocating pumps or compressed-air or steam engines, which means that both sides of the piston are working under pressure, so that every stroke of an engine is a power stroke and every stroke of a pump delivers fluid. A double-acting *pile hammer* forces its hammer down by steam or compressed air. *See* **single-acting.**

double-cut file *See* **crosscut file.**

double-drum hoist [min.] A mining haulage engine consisting of two drums which can be separately driven and connected or disconnected by a clutch.

double-headed nail (In USA **duplex-headed nail**) A round wire nail on which two heads are formed, so that although the nail can be driven home to fix concrete *formwork*, a second head 12 mm higher than the first enables the nail to be quickly withdrawn with a claw hammer.

double-layer grid [stru.] or **two-way grid** A space frame, often of steel tubes joined in square pyramids with their apices and bases interconnected by other tubes forming two grids, one above the other. Thus two horizontal layers of steel tubes are held apart by occasional diagonals to form pyramids. The first roof of this type was the 138 m span roof of the jumbo jet hangar at London Airport, erected in 1960 by jacking from the column heads with *lift-slab* techniques. All grids of this type have two layers, one above and one below, therefore the term two-way grid is easier to understand. Double-layer grids are occasionally curved. *See* **grid** (3).

double lock [hyd.] Two parallel canal-lock chambers with a sluice between them that halves the water loss.

double-rope tramway American term for an *aerial ropeway* with two *track cables* and one endless *traction rope*.

double-seal manhole cover Two manhole covers, one fitting over the other in the same cast-iron frame. To make the cover airtight, the grooves in the frame may be filled with grease. This also helps to preserve the metal of the manhole cover and to prevent it becoming difficult to remove.

double sling A *chain sling* or rope sling, also described as a *two-leg sling*, which is less confusing.

double-wall cofferdam A *cofferdam* consisting of two rows of sheet piling held at the right spacing by tie bars. The space between the rows is filled with gravel or other permeable material. This width should be not less than 0·8 to 1·0 times the retained height of water or soil. Such structures as the *cellular* or *Ohio cofferdams* are used in water when a single skin of sheet pile could not be strong enough to hold the depth of water required. Drainage holes need to be provided near the foot of the inner wall.

down-the-hole drill Drilling a deep vertical hole with a *rock drill* becomes slow when the length and weight of the drill rods are enough to absorb most of the energy of the blow. Down-the-hole rock drills have short drill rods because the machine enters the hole it is drilling, consequently saving power and drilling fast. The term is usually confined to air-driven drills, so *turbodrills* are not included.

dowsing Searching for water and ore deposits by the feeling of a branch or a pendulum held in the hand. Most engineers prefer the evidence of boreholes.

dozer A *calfdozer*, *angledozer*, etc.

Dracone A plastics 'sausage' that can be folded up when empty and carried on a lorry. It can be towed in the sea carrying hundreds of tons of fresh water, oil, etc., or may be used as a storage tank or as a *floating boom*. *See* **Fabridam.**

draft tube [mech.] The metal casing by which the water leaves a *turbine*. It corresponds to the *diffuser* of a centrifugal pump.

drafting machine [d.o.] *See* **draughting.**

drag (1) A simple towed implement with tines, blades, or chains for scraping or levelling a surface of loose material. *See also* (B).

drag (2) [hyd.] The drag on a particle in flowing water or air is the force of skin friction plus the 'form drag' from the pressure difference in front of and behind the particle. As in aerodynamics, it is accompanied by an upward lifting force at right angles, and opposed by the particle's submerged weight. In a channel, the drag of all the particles together is its *roughness*.

draghead or **trailing suction-cutter dredger** or **trailer dredger** A large and extremely powerful *suction dredger*, so called because it steams ahead while dredging and so trails the suction pipe behind it. They are thought to have been first developed by the US Army Corps of Engineers before 1900, but have since been much used in Europe. A typical 'trailer' has a hold (hopper) capacity of 18,000 tons, that it can fill in one hour with its two pumps of 22,000 m³ hourly capacity from 22 m depth. The total engine power is 21,500 hp, overall length 143 m, and it can dredge to 35 m depth. The suction pipes are both 40 m long and 1·2 m dia. Overflow pipes carry away surplus water. Dumping is through 26 bottom valves, 13 on each side, each 3·6 m dia., distributed along the 54·6 m length of the hopper, controlled from the bridge. The main disadvantage of these dredgers is that they must interrupt dredging when they move away to dump their load. This can be avoided by delivery into a hopper barge alongside, or a *floating pipeline*. A 6,000 hp hopper dredge made in USA in 1969 cost about $15 million, with swell compensators, air conditioning, helicopter landing pad, etc. Some 49 m long, it belonged to the US Army Corps of Engineers.

dragline or **dragline excavator** An *excavator* which works by pulling a bucket on ropes towards it. The bucket is hung on the end of a long jib and a skilful operator can throw the bucket considerably beyond the end of the jib. It is generally used for digging below the level of its tracks. *See* **walking dragline.**

dragline scraper Rope-controlled equipment for withdrawing piled material like coal, coke, sand, or broken stone from a stockyard and pulling it up on to a loading platform from which it drops into lorries or wagons. At the platform end is a double-drum haulage engine whose two drums in turn pull the two ropes which control the scraper bucket. The main rope pulls it full of material towards the loading platform. The return rope passes over a return sheave at the far side of the stockyard and pulls the empty scraper bucket back to the pile of material. The name is misleading, since in conception the dragline scraper is closer to the mining *scraper loader* than to the *dragline*. It is a stationary piece of plant, though sometimes both ends are built to travel a short distance on rails laid perpendicular to the direction of the ropes.

drag shovel A *backacter*.

drain A channel, pipe, or duct for conveying surface or subsoil water or sewage. *See also* **absorbing well, agricultural/box/French/rubble drain,** *and* **below.**

drainage The removal of water by flow or pumping from the ground or from its surface or from buildings. It may include *sewerage*.

drainage area, drainage basin A *catchment area*.

drainage tunnel [min.] A tunnel driven mainly for drainage. Its cost is justified by the reduction in the total head which the mine pumps must work against and their resulting lower first cost and working charges.

drained shear test [s.m.] or **slow test** A *shear test* or triaxial compression test, applied to a specimen of cohesive soil after completed *consolidation* under normal load, carried out in drained conditions slowly enough to allow further consolidation due to shear during the test. Drained tests give higher strengths than *quick* or *consolidated quick tests*.

drain pipes Pipes below ground that remove *sewage*, or rainwater. They may be of *pitch fibre* (*B*), clay ware, plastics, cast iron, asbestos cement or concrete. Joints may be *spigot and socket*, made tight with mortar pushed hard in against a gasket of old untwisted rope or hemp, or a rubber O-ring joint, etc. In any case the spigot faces uphill, to make the jointing easier.

drain rods Rods made of cane or tightly-coiled steel springs, with threaded brass end fittings which screw together and can be pushed to and fro in a drain to remove a stoppage (*rodding*). *See* inspection chamber.

drain tile American term for *field drains*.

drain well An *absorbing well*.

draughting machine (in USA spelt drafting machine) Equipment clamped on the edge of a *drawing board*, that replaces the older tee-square and set-square. It is lighter and quicker to use but much more expensive. The earliest type may have been the brass parallel ruler with its heavy cylindrical rollers, but the modern ones are much more sophisticated, with straight edges graduated in mm, built-in protractor, etc.

draughtsman [d.o.] One who prepares *drawings* for use on a building site or elsewhere.

draught tube A *draft tube*.

drawbar [mech.] The steel bar by which a locomotive pulls its train, or by which a wagon receives its pull. It passes through the wagon from end to end, transmitting the pull through each wagon to the one behind it.

drawbar pull [rly] *See* tractive force.

drawbridge [stru.] A *movable bridge* with a horizontal hinge and heavy counter-weight at one bank that enables the other end to be raised. Many types exist.

draw cut [min.] *See* bottom cut.

draw-door weir A *weir* with gates which can be raised vertically.

drawdown Lowering of a water level. *See* sudden drawdown.

draw-file [mech.] To grasp a file with both hands and push it across a surface with its length at right angles to the direction of movement. This produces a smoother surface than the usual method of filing, but removes less metal.

drawgear [min.] Chains, shackles, etc., used in hoisting and haulage.

drawing (1) [d.o.] The work of a *draughtsman*, putting on to paper pictorial working instructions, perspective views, etc.

(2) [stru.] A dimensioned and usually true-to-scale elevation, plan, or section, sometimes showing *details* to be constructed by a builder. Drawings which are not to be worked to are generally called sketches.

(3) *See* cold drawing.

drawing board A flat softwood sheet made of several boards fixed edge to edge, measuring about 5 cm more each way than a standard size of *drawing paper*. A common size used by engineering drawing offices is for A1 paper, 594×814 mm, making a board of about 650×920 mm. Modern boards are usually surfaced with plastics sheet 1 mm or so thick that is better to write on than wood, being smoother and less easily deformed. Most drawing boards are fixed to a stand which adds to their cost but makes them much easier to use. Some means of drawing accurate parallel lines is always provided for engineering drawings. The most primitive device is the *tee-square*, which is appropriate for small boards and until about 1950 was the only equipment available. *Parallel motion equipment* is used in many offices. It is easier to use, perhaps more accurate than a tee-square, and very much less expensive than a *draughting machine*.

drawing paper The paper and film, or textile, used for making drawings in drawing offices is of many sorts but is either translucent, and used for making negatives, or is opaque, and not usable for this purpose. Most papers or films can be drawn on and written on with pen or pencil. Paper is commercially described generally by its weight in grams per sq. metre, the best quality usually being the heaviest. For comparison, very good notepaper weighs about 85 g/m², solicitor's notepaper about 100 g/m². The three main types of material are: (*a*) Translucent tracing paper (weighing from 63 to 112 g/m²). The negative formed by drawing on the translucent material is put into a dyeline process from which *contact prints* are produced. This gives a white background that enables the print to be further worked on. More durable but more expensive materials for the same purpose are acetate film or other plastics. Linen has been used for many years. Acetate film is made in thicknesses from 0·075 mm to 0·18 mm. (*b*) *Detail paper*, sometimes called layout paper, can be used for tracing or for drawing preliminary sketches that take little time and not much erasing. It is a lightweight paper, of 45 to 50 g/m². (*c*) Cartridge paper is an opaque, white, very strong paper suitable for making drawings or maps that need much work and erasing. It therefore is very heavy and may weigh from 120 to 200 g/m². When prints are needed from a drawing that has been made on cartridge, a sheet of tracing paper or film is laid all over it and the entire drawing is traced through, usually by hand, though tracings can be made by machines that produce 'true-to-scale' negatives. The standard-sized 'A' sheets listed below are designed to help in the filing of drawings, so that the drawings can be laid flat in the drawer without difficulty. The A sizes listed below are internationally standardized. Their sides are in the ratio of √2. Photographic enlargement and reduction are simplified because of this ratio and so are folding and insertion into envelopes. The same ratio, √2, is used between each size and the next in the series. Larger sizes exist, thus 2A is twice A0, but A0, the basic size, covers an area of 1 m².

SIZES OF A-SHEETS

Millimetres

A0	841 × 1189
A1	594 × 841
A2	420 × 594
A3	297 × 420
A4	210 × 297
A5	148 × 210
A6	105 × 148
A7	74 × 105

dredge [min.] or **dredger** A vessel fitted with *bucket ladder*, *grab*, *or suction dredging* machinery for underwater excavation or for mining alluvial deposits, generally of tin, the noble metals, or gems. Most harbour dredges are sea-going vessels, but mining dredges are more like rafts and may pass their whole life in one small muddy pond. The mining dredge moves the soil from one side of the pond to the other through its concentrating machinery and thus the pond and the dredge move together, often many miles in the course of years. When the deposit is worked out, the dredge is dismantled and moved by road or rail to another small muddy pond. *See also* **stationary dredger, hydraulic dredger, mechanical dredger.**

dredging Excavation, below water level, with a *dredge*.

dredging well The opening in a dredger through which the ladder or suction cutter passes to the bottom of the water.

drift (1) [hyd.] The speed of movement of a body of water.

(2) [air sur.] The angle between the fore-and-aft line of an aircraft and its actual course. The difference between these two lines is caused by the wind.

(3) [mech.] or **drift bolt** A tapered steel bar driven into rivet holes before riveting, to bring them into line, or

used for expanding the end of copper tube before joining. *See* steel erector's tools (*illus.*).

(4) An entry into a mine from the surface, usually dipping at about 1 in 5, enabling men to walk in or out, usually provided with a conveyor to bring out minerals, often also with rail track. It is safer and more flexible, though five times as long (at 1 in 5) as a vertical shaft.

(5) Superficial, geologically recent, loose deposits of gravel, boulder clay, sand, etc., which are often present in river valleys (Thames gravel). They are not shown on *solid* geological maps.

drift barrier [hyd.] An open structure built across a stream to catch driftwood by wire ropes or chains, from which wood can be burnt at low water. *See* debris dam.

drift bolt *See* drift (3).

drift test [mech.] A test of metal plates or tubes in which a *drift* (3) tapered at 1 in 10 is forced into a hole in the plate until it cracks or until a certain specified increase in diameter is obtained.

drill carriage or **jumbo** A movable stage which carries fixed to it several rock drills and is used in tunnelling. It travels on rails or caterpillar tracks.

drill extractor [min.] A *fishing tool* for pulling a drill out of a borehole.

drill feed [mech.] (1) The mechanism for pushing a drilling tool into a hole.

(2) The speed at which a drilling tool is pushed into a hole, and therefore the speed at which it drills rock.

drilling fluid [min.] or **drilling mud** or **mud flush** The mud which is pumped into the drill pipe in *rotary drilling* and rises up outside the pipe, filling the hole, ensuring that gas or oil does not escape and plastering the walls at the same time. It was developed together with rotary drilling about 1890, but can also be used, though with less refinement, in cable drilling. Mud flush was designed to reduce the disastrous *blow outs* of the early holes. Thanks to mud flush, blow outs are now rare. A typical water mud contains *bentonite* to make it *thixotropic*, barytes to increase its density, and water. Specific gravities may be as high as 2·1 but are generally below 1·7. Oil-based muds are used where the water in the mud might penetrate and damage the oil pool. Salt-saturated muds are used for drilling through the Texan salt domes to prevent the mud dissolving the salt and causing the hole to deviate. An ideal mud is thixotropic but not very viscous, unaffected by high temperature (which at 5,000 m depth may rise to 160°C), and has good wall-building (plastering) properties to prevent loss of mud from the hole. *See* drill rods, heaving shale, oil-well cement, turbodrill.

drilling mud *Drilling fluid.*

drill rods [min.] In *rotary drilling*, the hollow rods which form a continuous string in the hole, carry the cutting bit screwed on to the bottom end, and act as pipe for the *drilling fluid* to be injected on to the fresh rock under the bit.

drill steel [min.] In *rock drilling*, the round or hexagonal steel bar (not less than 18 mm across the flats) which enters the hole in the rock. It has a drill bit forged or screwed on to its end. *See* detachable bit.

drive (1) [mech.] The means by which mechanical power is transmitted to an implement or piece of mechanical plant such as a conveyor, rock crusher, vibrator, etc.

(2) In USA a *dedicated street* or road, but in Britain an access to a private house.

drive pipe [s.m.] A pipe driven into the ground, often for *soil investigation* purposes, within which it may sometimes be possible to obtain an *undisturbed sample* of the soil at the bottom of the hole. In sands or gravels it may be quickly sunk by *wash boring*. Like *casing*, it is often re-usable.

driven cast-in-place pile A reinforced-concrete *pile* cast in a hole formed in the ground by driving a steel casing. The casing is then filled with concrete tamped with the *drop hammer*. The casing is usually withdrawn as soon as the concrete is placed. This pile has the advantage in sandy soil that the ground is consolidated during driving but the corresponding disadvantage (particularly in clay) that the ground is disturbed more than with the *bored pile*. *See* **Franki pile, sand piles.**

driven pile A *pile* of steel, wood or reinforced concrete which is forced into the ground by blows from a *pile hammer*. *Compare* **bored/jacked pile, jetting.**

driveway American term for a private access, that is a British *drive*.

driving *See* **pile hammer.**

driving band or **pile hoop** or **pile ring** A steel band fitted round the head of a timber pile to prevent *brooming*.

driving cap or **driving helmet** A steel cap placed over the head of a steel pile to reduce the damage during driving. *See* **pile helmet.**

drop (1) [hyd.] A steep part of a channel or pipe.
(2) The part of a reinforced-concrete *mushroom slab* which is immediately round the column head and is deeper than the rest of the slab.

drop-bottom bucket or **bottom-opening skip** A container for placing concrete.

drop hammer or **beetle head, monkey, ram,** or **tup** A metal block which is raised by a hoist and allowed to drop freely on to a *pile head* to drive it into the ground. For steel or timber piles a drop hammer should, for easy driving, either equal the weight of the pile or be rather lighter. For concrete piles a drop hammer may weigh up to three-quarters the weight of the pile, if the *dolly* effectively protects them, and should weigh at least one third of the weight of the pile and dolly. The weights of steam hammers should be roughly the same

as corresponding drop hammers. *See* **pile hammer.**

drop on A portable rail crossing which can be laid on top of two parallel tracks which are set at a distance apart equal to the gauge of the track. By this means the inner two rails can be used as a track and wagons can be transferred from one track to the other.

drop penetration test [s.m.] A *dynamic penetration test*.

drop shaft or **cylinder caisson** or **open caisson** A method of shaft sinking (or excavating bridge piers, etc.) in soft waterlogged ground, consisting of building up at ground level, on a *cutting curb*, a massive concrete, brick, or iron ring (the drop shaft or caisson) which can serve as or contain the permanent shaft lining. Soil is removed by *grab* within the drop shaft, which gradually sinks under its own weight without dewatering.

drowned weir, submerged weir [hyd.] A weir whose *tailwater* level is above the weir crest. Modern *measuring weirs* can be used for measuring in this condition, which is desirable in several ways. It lowers the cost of the structure and reduces the obstacle that can prevent fish moving upstream.

drum [mech.] A large cylinder (or part cone) on to which steel rope is wound, used for hoists and haulages in mines and elsewhere.

drum curb [min.] A *cutting curb*.

drum gate [hyd.] A spillway gate shaped like a sector of a circle. It is opened or closed by admitting or releasing water through appropriate valves.

drum screen [sewage] A screen shaped like a cylinder or cut-off cone, turning on its centre line.

dry-bulb thermometer An ordinary thermometer. It indicates the dry bulb temperature. *Compare* the **hygrometer.**

dry density [s.m.] The weight of dry material in unit volume of a soil sample after drying at 105°C. *See* **compaction** *and below.*

dry-density/moisture-content relationship [s.m.] The relationship between *dry* *density* and *moisture content* of a soil for a given amount of *compaction*. The relationship is usually drawn on a graph from which the *optimum moisture content* can be deduced.

dry dock or **graving dock** A *dock* into which a ship floats. The dock gates are closed behind it, the water is pumped out, and the ship rests on the *docking blocks* ready for its hull to be repaired or cleaned. *See* **flotation structure.**

dry galvanizing [mech.] A *galvanizing* process in which the steel is first fluxed in hot ammonium chloride solution and then dried in hot air before passing through the bath of molten zinc. *See* **wet galvanizing.**

drying shrinkage *See* **shrinkage.**

dry joint [stru.] A plane of contact between two structures or parts of a structure, to allow relative movement caused by shrinkage, expansion, or settlement. There is no connection between the adjacent parts which may, in fact, be separated by *building paper* (*B*). *See* **expansion joint.**

dry pack Concrete or mortar which is just damp (described as earth-dry), used as filling to join up two load-bearing members by ramming it in with a hammer and cold chisel or piece of wood. It is used between the head of a *cast-in-situ* pile and the building above it which it *underpins*. It is also used for joining precast members in *prestressed* structures. Dry pack gives much less shrinkage than fluid *grout* and can be loaded immediately.

dry weather flow, dwf The rate of flow in a sewer in prolonged dry weather. According to BSCP 2005:1968 'Sewerage', it includes *infiltration*, but apart from infiltration the dwf should equal the water consumption of the population of the area drained. Foul sewers should be designed to carry all quantities between one third and four times the dwf, occasionally six times the dwf but not more than this in a truly *separate system*. A partially separate sewer may have to carry fifty times its dwf after a rainstorm.

dry well (1) An American term for *soakaway* (in Scotland a rummel).

(2) That part of a pump house which contains the machinery, as opposed to the *wet well* or sump which contains water.

Duchemin's formula [stru.] A formula for the *wind pressure* (N) normal to a roof sloping at θ degrees to the horizontal when the wind pressure P on a vertical surface is known.

$$N = \frac{P \times 2 \sin \theta}{1 + \sin^2 \theta}.$$

duct A protective tube or a brick or concrete trench or corridor along which pipes or cables pass through the ground. *See also* **cable duct** *and* (*B*).

duct bank A group of *ducts* together.

ductile [mech.] That which can be drawn into wire. Many metals are ductile, the commonest being mild steel, wrought iron, copper, lead, light alloys.

ductility [mech.] The ability of a metal to undergo cold *plastic deformation* without breaking, particularly by pulling in *cold drawing*.

Ductube An inflated tube used for forming *cable ducts* in concrete. It is tied to the reinforcement, left until the concrete is a few hours old, then deflated and withdrawn.

Duff Abrams' law *See* **Abrams' law.**

dumb barge or **dumb dredger** A barge or *dredger* that has to be towed.

dummy joint or **crack inducer** A *contraction joint* in a concrete road slab, consisting of a groove formed either through the top half of the slab with a fibrous *joint filler* or through the bottom half with a piece of wood. The plane of weakness thus formed ensures that the break is vertical and does relatively little damage.

dumper or **dump truck** A rubber-tyred vehicle ordinarily with two large wheels in front and two small ones behind, having a hopper of up to 250 tons capacity in front. The hopper dumps forwards and the driver sits behind. This arrangement makes the dumper a very useful vehicle for excavation, particularly as it can travel over rough ground. Dumpers may not travel on public roads when the driver's view is obscured by material piled up in front of him. The 250-ton machine has a 3,000 hp electrical generator that supplies the separate motors on each of the six driving wheels. Only two wheels are not driven. Most large dumpers have similar electrical drives for each driven wheel. Many smaller modern dumpers have turntable skips that enable them to dump either side as well as forwards; some are also self-loading. The rate of discharge can now also be slow or fast, at will.

dumpling In a large excavation such as a railway cutting or dry dock, a dumpling is a mass of ground with excavation on two or more sides, left untouched until the end of the dig. It is used as an abutment for timbering the sides of the dig and this saves the expense of long, heavy timbers.

dump test [mech.] or **upending test** A test for the detection of surface defects which shows the suitability of billets, bars, and so on for hot or cold forging. A bar 2 diameters long is shortened by cold-squeezing to 1 diameter and should then show no cracks.

dumpy level [sur.] A simple levelling instrument in which the telescope with its *level tube* is attached rigidly to the vertical spindle.

dune [hyd.] A sandhill formed by wind (or in water by current), usually with a long straight crest, often with *ripples* on its surface. Underwater dunes are much smaller than wind-formed desert dunes that can be 100 m high. *See* antidune.

duplex engine [mech.] A steam-driven pump or compressor engine arranged with two steam pistons each of which drives one pump (or air) piston on the same piston rod. The machinery is simple as there is no rotating motion. *See* free-piston compressor.

duplex-headed nail *See* double-headed nail.

duplex track [rly] A track built on a quay side to carry heavy crane loads. Two *flat-bottom rails* are laid in contact with each other at the flanges. The crane wheels are also double, with the flanges placed centrally and in contact. Each wheel can thus travel on its own rail and the wheel flanges pass down the gap in the middle.

duralumin [stru.] Common *light alloys* of aluminium with about 4% copper and small amounts of magnesium, silicon, and manganese. The 0·1% *proof stress* is about 230 MN/m² and the corresponding working stress in tension is 108 MN/m² compared with 140 for steel. The *modulus of elasticity* is low, 70 GN/m², about one-third that of steel, but the specific gravity is 2·8 instead of 7·8 for steel. These alloys, apart from their high cost, are attractive to the structural designer and they resist corrosion generally better than steel.

duration curve [hyd.] or **rating curve** A curve which shows the amount of flow through a river for power generation. It gives for a certain period, the abscissa, the percentage of the time that the flow equalled or exceeded the ordinate. The area under the curve represents the total quantity (the *run-off*) which flowed down the river in the period under consideration. The Q 95 flow is a low rating, the flow which occurred for 95% of the time. The Q 60 or median flow is the middle rating. The average rating is the arithmetic mean flow.

dusting Said of a concrete floor whose surface is disintegrating and producing dust. It is often caused by lack of *curing* or by excessive water in the mix which may be caused by a dirty sand.

dustpan dredger A *draghead dredger*.

Dutch deep sounding [s.m.] *See* **cone penetration test**.

Dutch mattress [hyd.] A *mattress* of timber and *reed* for protecting a river or sea bed from *scour*.

dyeline [d.o.] A *contact print* which shows

brown-to-black lines on a white-to-pink background. These prints can be made on opaque paper or cloth, or tracing paper or tracing cloth. They are generally not so easy to read as a *blueprint* when printed from faint pencil negatives, but the white ground has made them more popular, since notes and corrections can be written on them.

dyke or **dike** (1) [min.] A tabular-shaped *igneous intrusion*.

(2) [hyd.] A mound of earth along a river bank and at some distance from the river to retain floodwater; but *see* **polder**.

(3) A large ditch.

dynamic consolidation or **ground bashing** [s.m.] The use of the weight-dropping method of *sand piles*, extended all over an area of ground to strengthen it, especially to consolidate *fill*. A safe bearing pressure of 0·16 N/mm² is reached without difficulty but the method cannot be used close to pipes, cables or drains, nor within 20 m of a building, because of the damage that could be caused. The whole area is covered twice with a 10-ton tamper of 4 m² at two weeks' interval. Total settlement of the surface is 50 to 60 cm.

dynamic loading [stru.] Loads which include *impact*.

dynamic penetration test [s.m.] or **drop penetration test** Tests such as the *Raymond standard test* as opposed to *static penetration tests*.

dynamic pile formulae Formulae in which the safe load on a *pile* is calculated from the energy of the hammer-blow and the penetration of the pile for each blow. *See* **Hiley's formula**.

dynamic similarity [hyd.] A principle of *model analysis*, which states that if a model of a hydraulic structure operates at a speed corresponding truly with the full-size project then the resistances R and the densities d, lengths l and velocities v are in the following relationship:

$$\frac{R_1}{R_2} = \frac{d_1 \times l_1{}^2 \times v_1{}^2}{d_2 \times l_2{}^2 \times v_2{}^2}$$

Dynamic similarity implies that the forces in model and prototype are in proportion with the scale of the model. *See* **dimensional analysis**.

dynamic strength [stru.] Resistance to suddenly applied loads.

dynamite [min.] Old term for any *high explosive* consisting of *diatomite* (*B*), as an absorbent containing *nitroglycerin*.

E

E [stru.] The *modulus of elasticity* of a material, the value which tells what is its *stiffness*.

earth auger [s.m.] *See* auger.

earth borer A *truck-mounted drilling rig*.

earthen dam A *dam* built of earth, sand, gravel, or rock (*rock-fill dam*), having a core of clay, concrete, or other impervious material or an impervious skin on the water face, made of concrete, steel plate, etc. Where the soil available is sand or silt and there is a considerable amount of water, a *hydraulic fill dam* is usually economical. If hydraulic fill is not feasible the earth is usually transported and tipped by heavy rubber-tyred vehicles which help to compact the dam by travelling over those parts which need *compaction*. Special *rollers* which weigh up to 200 tons (with water ballast) may also be used for compaction. Earth is a suitable material for a dam whose foundation is likely to move. *See* pore-water pressure.

earth flow *See* flow slide, detritus slide.

earth-leakage protection [elec.] *Protective equipment* which operates as soon as enough power leaks through the *earthing lead* (*B*), to start the protective relays. A very small leakage is enough to operate the relay and break the circuit. Since a fraction of a second is needed to break the circuit, the man on the machine may get an *electric shock* but it is unlikely to be dangerous since it cannot last for long.

earth-moving plant or **muck-shifting plant** Machinery such as *bowl scrapers*, *dozers*, *dumpers*, *excavators*, *graders*, *loading shovels*.

earth pressure [s.m.] Earth pressure is a push from retained earth that varies between two extremes, the minimum, or *active earth pressure*, which is the force from earth tending to overturn a *free retaining wall*, and the maximum,

that is the *passive earth pressure*, which is the resistance of an earth surface to deformation by outside forces. The word '*pressure*' in this sense is not correct, since it is used to mean 'force', but it is used.

earth pressure at rest [s.m.] The thrust from earth on to a *fixed retaining wall*. It is intermediate between the *active* and the *passive earth pressures*.

earthquake Sinking of part of the earth's surface along a fault plane, that is a crack in the earth's crust. Buildings designed to stand up in an earthquake are usually nowadays calculated according to *lateral-force design*. Earthquake intensities are recorded on *seismographs*. *See* Rossi-Forel.

earthwork (1) Any digging or artificial raising of the ground.
(2) The volume of dig or banks which is paid for.

easement curve or **easement** A *transition curve*.

easers [min.] British term for *relief holes*.

easting [sur.] An eastward *departure* from the north–south axis of a survey. A westing is a negative easting.

ebb channel [hyd.] A channel in an estuary made by the river at low water, distinguished by its S-shape in a long estuary. Sand bars have a seaward direction in an ebb channel. *Compare* flood channel.

eccentric [d.o.] Away from the centre, whether purposely or not.

eccentricity [stru.] The distance between the point of application of a direct load to a column or tie and the *centroid* of the member. It is sometimes called the *arm*.

eccentric load [stru.] A load on a column applied at a point away from the column centre and therefore putting a *bending moment* on the column equal in amount to the load multiplied by the *arm*.

echo sounder [sur.] An instrument used by ships and in harbour surveys for determining the depth of water. It measures the time taken for a sound to be echoed back from the sea bed. It is much quicker than *sounding* with a lead and line.

economic ratio [stru.] A design of a reinforced-concrete beam is said to have the economic ratio of steel if the concrete and steel are both stressed to the maximum. Such a design is generally not the cheapest. If cheapness is the aim, the steel should be fully stressed, the concrete should usually be understressed.

economizer [mech.] In any but the smallest boiler plant, a bank of tubes through which the boiler *feedwater* passes. It is placed across the path of the flue gases as they leave the boiler and enter the chimney. By warming the feedwater it saves considerable fuel.

eddy flow [hyd.] *Turbulent flow.*

eddy loss [hyd.] The energy lost by eddies as opposed to that lost by friction. Both are converted into heat.

Eddy's theorem [stru.] In an arch the bending moment at any point is equal to the product of the horizontal thrust and the vertical distance between the arch centre line and the *line of thrust.*

edge preparation [mech.] In the *welding* of steel, grinding and similar preparation of edges is a large part of the expense, some of which may be avoided by deep-penetration welding.

EDM [sur.] *Electronic distance measurement.*

effective area of an orifice [hyd.] The actual area of an orifice multiplied by its *coefficient of discharge.*

effective depth [stru.] In the design of reinforced-concrete beams and slabs, the depth from the outer face of the compression flange of the concrete to the centre line of the stretched steel. The *cover* plus half the bar diameter plus the effective depth are together equal to the overall depth.

effective height of a column [stru.] In the calculation of *slenderness ratio*, a value varying from $0.70 \times$ the actual column length for a column fully restrained in position and direction at both ends, to $2 \times$ the actual column length for a column fully restrained at one end and free at the other end.

effective intergranular pressure [s.m.] *Effective pressure.*

effective length of a strut [stru.] See **effective height of a column.**

effective pressure [s.m.] or **intergranular pressure** or **effective stress** The pressure in a soil between the points of contact of the soil grains. In a soil system in equilibrium it is equal to the *total pressure* minus the *neutral pressure* of the water in the pore space. It increases during the *consolidation* of the soil to a maximum at complete consolidation. In conditions of *hydrostatic excess pressure* the effective pressure is equal to the total pressure minus (neutral pressure plus hydrostatic excess pressure).

effective size [s.m.] Hazen's definition of an effective size of a soil is the following, used in *Hazen's law*. It is the grain size which is larger than 10% by weight of the soil particles, as seen on the *grading curve* of the soil, and is described for short as the D_{10} size. *See also* **coefficient of uniformity, graded filter.**

effective span [stru.] The distance between the centres of the supports of a beam. This length, which is larger than the *clear span*, is used in calculating the *bending moment* of a beam.

effective stress [s.m.] *Effective pressure.*

effective thickness of a wall [stru.] In the calculation of *slenderness ratio* (a) for plain brick or masonry walls it is the actual thickness; (b) for *cavity walls* it is two-thirds of the thickness of the two leaves added together.

efficiency [mech.] or **mechanical efficiency** A very widely misused term which means the work output of a *machine* as a percentage of its theoretically perfect performance. For an engine or motor it is the power output divided by the power input (energy input per unit of time). Efficiency is always less than 100%. *See* **mechanical advantage.**

effluent Liquid or gas that flows away. So far as sewage is concerned, it is some 99.9% water, but a desirable standard of purity was set by the *Royal Commission.*

effluent stream [hyd.] A stream that receives *groundwater*, unlike an *influent stream.*

egg-shaped sewer A sewer shaped like an egg with its small end down, a shape chosen for its satisfactory flow whether empty or full.

ejector (1) [sewage] A pump for raising sewage by injecting compressed air into a pipe containing the sewage, on the principle of the *air-lift pump.*

(2) *See* **hydraulic ejector.**

elastic [stru.] A material is said to be elastic if it expands or contracts by foreseeable amounts when it is pulled or pushed by known forces, and regains its shape when these forces are released. *See* **Hooke's law, modulus of elasticity, resilience.**

elastic constants [stru.] The *modulus of elasticity*, the *shear modulus*, and the bulk modulus (the change in stress per unit change in volume). A fourth constant, *Poisson's ratio*, is sometimes included.

elastic curve [stru.] or **deflection curve** The curve showing the deflected shape of the neutral surface of a bent beam, an essential part of the theory of bending. Its shape was first appreciated by Jakob Bernoulli in 1694 and later by Euler as a circle of radius equal to $\dfrac{EI}{M}$.

elastic design [stru.] The design of a structure to *working stresses* which are about half to two-thirds of the elastic limit. This was the usual method of design, but for redundant frames it is being replaced now by *limit design.*

elastic limit [stru.] The stress beyond which further load causes *permanent set.* In most materials the elastic limit is also the *limit of proportionality.*

elastic moduli [stru.] The *elastic constants.*

elastic rail spike [rly] A rail fastening.

elastic strain [stru.] A *strain* (or deformation per unit of length) produced by a force acting on a body, which disappears when the force is removed. *See* **Hooke's law.**

elbow A sharp corner in a pipe, roadway, etc. *See also* (*B*).

electrical-resistance strain gauge [stru.] A flat coil of fine wire (0·025 mm dia.) wound round an insulating plate between two sheets of insulating paper, of total size about 1×2 cm. The gauge is glued to the surface of metal or cast into concrete and the ends of the wire connected to a sensitive electrical-resistance measuring instrument. As the length of the part increases so also does the resistance increase. An advantage of these gauges is that they can be oriented in any direction to indicate the *strain* in that direction.

electric-arc welding [mech.] *See* **arc welding.**

electric drills Drills driven by an electric motor having a rotating bit and no percussive action are used for drilling coal, wood, and steel, and have also drilled rock. Percussive, rotary-percussive and hydraulic electric drills are well established. *See* **rotary drilling.**

electric eye *See* **photo-electric cell.**

electric motor A *machine* which is forced to rotate by electric power brought usually by a cable. Electric motors, first used about 1890, are the most compact source of power available and are now used for almost every conceivable purpose in industry and construction. *See* **hydraulic power.**

electric shock Injury due to contact with high-voltage electricity. The loss of consciousness which often follows severe shock may prevent the shocked person from disengaging himself. The power should be cut off or short-circuited, whichever is the quicker, the victim removed from the electrical conductors, and artificial respiration applied. If the power supply cannot be interrupted quickly the victim should be dragged away from the contact by his trouser leg or other loose garment so that the rescuer is not shocked also.

electric traction [rly] Haulage of vehicles by electric motor. The motor may be supplied with electric power from trolley wires, storage battery, or diesel-driven generator on the vehicle.

electric welding [mech.] This includes *arc* or *resistance welding* and many *automatic welding* methods.

electro-chemical hardening or **stabilization of soil** [s.m.] Certain clays, especially those that contain monovalent cations (potassium, sodium, lithium), can be strengthened by passing a direct current through them with an anode consisting of a polyvalent metal such as iron, aluminium or calcium. Dissolved additives at the anode may also help the base exchange reaction in the clay; calcium chloride is a common additive. The polyvalent cations form clays that adsorb water less easily.

electrode [elec.] Generally a conductor leading electric current into an electrolytic cell, furnace, or welding implement. In welding, the meaning is specialized as follows: (*a*) in *metal-arc welding* the *filler rod*, bare or *covered*; (*b*) in *carbon-arc welding*, a carbon rod; (*c*) in *atomic-hydrogen welding*, a tungsten rod; (*d*) in *resistance welding*, a bar, wheel, or clamp which presses together the metal parts to be welded.

electro-dialysis, ED A *de-salination* method used in Japan, which cannot reduce the salt content of water below about 500 parts per million without exorbitantly increasing the power consumption. Careful pre-filtration is needed, and bacteria are not removed.

electrogas or **EG welding** A fully *automatic* variation of *MIG welding* that includes some features of *electroslag* welding, with retaining shoes (dams)

that hold the molten weld metal in for vertical position welding. It is normally shielded with carbon dioxide or argon mixed with the CO_2.

electrolysis [elec.] The conduction of electric current through *electrolytes*. Direct current causes metal or hydrogen to be liberated at the *cathode* and acid radicals or oxygen at the *anode*.

electrolyte [elec.] A liquid which conducts electricity, or a salt which makes water highly conductive when dissolved in it. Most soluble salts, acids, or alkalis and many fused salts are electrolytes. *See* **aluminium**.

electrolytic copper, lead, or **zinc** [min.] Copper, lead, or zinc obtained by electrolytic refining, 99·9% pure.

electrolytic corrosion [mech.] *Corrosion*.

electromagnet [elec.] A soft iron bar with thick copper wire wound round it, through which a heavy magnetizing (direct) current passes. An electromagnet is often used for separating tramp iron from ore or coal before it is crushed. *See* **lifting magnet, solenoid**.

electromagnetic length measurement [sur.] *Electronic distance measurement*.

electronic distance measurement or **EDM** or **electromagnetic** or **electro-optical** or **geodetic distance** or **length measurement** or **metering** [sur.] The more than 50 types of these expensive instruments available in 1978 included the *Distomat* made by Wild, the *Geodimeter* made by Aga of Stockholm, the *Mekometer* made by Kern, the *Tellurometer* made by Tellurometer Ltd, also the Zeiss and the Electrotape. An accuracy of 1 part per 100000 is regularly attainable and often more. Three general types exist, according to the length they are designed to measure: up to 100 km; up to 25 km; and less than 1 km. Apart from their high speed of measurement (some ten lengths a day can be measured by an experienced team of only three people) these instruments have revolutionized large-scale surveying because they have enabled the hilltops and mountain tops that were always best for angle measurement to become also the best for length measurements. Formerly, for length measurements, hilly ground had to be avoided because length measurement over it was so awkward and liable to be inaccurate. The first instruments became available about 1957. The principle is, like radar, to use electronic circuitry to measure the transit time of light or radio waves passing between a master and a remote instrument. The remote instrument nowadays is replaced by a simple reflector and a surveyor does not have to be stationed there as a rule. All types have two-way speech by radio. The only long distances that must be taped in the whole of a long *trilateration* are two, one before and one after, so as to check the electronic measurements. Originally intended only for distances above 150 m, these instruments can now be used even for those lengths that can be measured by pocket tape. *Three-tripod traversing* with a theodolite-mounted EDM instrument is particularly fast. Development of these instruments is rapid and competition between makers is strong. A survey that would have taken 15 days by theodolite traverse took 5 days in 1973 by EDM and would probably have taken 2·5 days in 1979. Most of the new EDM instruments used by civil engineers are operated by infra-red light or laser and many of them can function centred over a theodolite telescope. They usually include a microprocessor to do most of the laborious surveying calculations.

electro-optical length measurement [sur.] *Electronic distance measurement*.

electro-osmosis [s.m.] A *groundwater lowering* process, used in silts to speed up natural drainage and to produce a flow of water away from an excavation. (When a direct current is passed through wet soil, water flows to the cathode.) Small quantities of water are pumped away at the cathodes which are about 10 m apart, with anodes intermediately. The process is expensive but greatly increases the strength of silts owing to the change in direction of *capillary* forces in them and is useful since other pumping methods cannot be applied to silts. The cost in electrical energy varies from $\frac{1}{2}$ to 10 kw hours per cu. m of silt excavated. The field of use at present is in those silts which are too fine for the vacuum method of *groundwater lowering*. Voltages of 40 to 180 v direct current have been used, with currents from 15 to 25 amp per well (BSCP 2004). The principle has also been used (*a*) to reduce the voids in concrete and thus increase its strength, somewhat similarly to the *vacuum concrete* process, and (*b*) to dry out walls which have a defective *damp course* (*B*). *See* osmosis, thermo-osmosis.

electroplating [elec.] The deposition of a thin film of one metal on another by *electrolysis*, for instance in electro-tinning or electro-galvanizing. The noble metals, nickel, chromium, copper, cadmium, and others, are also put on by electrolysis.

electroslag welding An *automatic welding* method suitable for welding steel plates usually from 20 to 460 mm thick, with high rates of metal deposition and few weld defects, provided that welding is not interrupted. Once the first arc has been struck and the slag has formed, the process ceases to be *arc welding* but the voltage drop through the slag is similar to what occurs with an arc.

elephant's trunk A *hydraulic ejector*.

elevated railway [rly] A rail track carried on a bridge supported above road level by columns passing through the road.

elevating grader A *grader* equipped with a disc or plough collector and a belt elevator at right angles to its direction of travel. It digs earth or loose materials and discharges it to a height. It is very suitable for excavating road or railway cuttings or wide trenches. Outputs of as much as 300 cu. m per hour have been obtained with these machines in USA, but they have had little success in the wet climate of Britain, where soils are probably too sticky. *See* **multi-bucket excavator.**

elevation (1) [d.o.] A view of (a part of) a machine or a structure drawn without perspective as if projected on to a vertical plane. *See* **sectional elevation.**

(2) [sur.] The altitude of a point, its height above the sea.

elevation head [hyd.] or **position head** or **potential energy** The product of the density of a fluid and its height above a point is its elevation head above that point. It is usually measured in metres (for water) without mention of density.

elevator [min.] A contractor's or mining *conveyor* which raises material up a steep slope usually at about 60°, the material being contained in a series of buckets. It is usually no longer than 15 m and can move from 5 to 120 tons of material per hour.

elevator dredger [hyd.] A *bucket-ladder dredger*.

ellipse of stress [stru.] An ellipse which, drawn proportional to the *principal stresses* in a plane at a point, shows the resultant stress at any angle through the point in magnitude and direction. *See* **Mohr's circle of stress.**

elliptical trammel [d.o.] A *trammel*.

elongation (1) [stru.] *Elastic* or plastic extension of a structural member, particularly the plastic elongation of a piece under tensile test. For mild steel the elongation is often 20% of the *gauge length*. *See* **contraction in area.**

(2) [sur.] The extreme eastern or western position of a star, sometimes observed (in *circumpolars*) for determining the true meridian.

elutriation [s.m.] Size classification of airborne or liquid-borne particles by their settlement speeds. *See* **elutriator, Stokes's law.**

elutriator [s.m.] A *classifier* which works on the principle that large grains sink faster through a fluid than small grains of the same material. Industrial elutriators for mineral washing or classi-

fication usually work by a continuous upward current. Laboratory elutriation is often done by allowing the material to settle in a tall beaker and decanting according to a standard method or measuring the density with a hydrometer. Used in *mechanical analysis* of soils. *See* **Stokes's law, vel.**

embankment or **bank** A ridge of earth or rock thrown up to carry a road, railway, canal, etc., or to contain water (*levée*).

embankment wall A *retaining wall* at the foot of a bank to prevent it from sliding.

emery [min.] A mixture of *corundum* and magnetite or hematite used as an abrasive on emery paper, emery cloth, or emery wheels.

empirical formula A formula based on one or many series of observations but with no theoretical backing.

emulsifier A chemical agent added to a mixture of two or more fluids to help form an *emulsion*.

emulsion A relatively stable suspension of one or more liquids minutely dispersed through another liquid in which it (or they) are not soluble, for example milk, which is a *dispersion* of fat in water. *See* **breakdown,** *also* (*B*).

emulsion injection A process of *artificial cementing* in which a *bituminous emulsion* is injected into soils which have a particle size equal to that of coarse sand (2 to 0·6 mm).

encastré [stru.] or **encastered** Said of a beam which is built in at the ends, that is *end-fixed*.

encroachment [hyd.] or **intrusion** Seawater that travels inland into a freshwater *aquifer* and spoils it. Excessive pumping has caused encroachment in California and other dry areas bordering the sea, and even in wet countries like England.

end-bearing pile or **point-bearing pile** A *bearing pile* which carries its full load down to hard ground at its point. In fact, nearly all end-bearing piles are thought now to be partly supported by friction. *Compare* **friction pile.**

end block [stru.] The concrete at the end of a *tendon*, containing the *anchorage* and reinforced to resist bursting.

end contraction [hyd.] Contraction of the water area flowing over a *measuring weir*. *See* **contracted weir, effective area of an orifice.**

end-fixed [stru.] Said of the end of a beam which is so held that it can develop a *fixing moment*. The term is also applied to columns in the calculation of their *effective height*. An end-fixed column is effectively shorter than a *pinned* column.

end span [stru.] A *span* which is a *continuous beam* or slab only at its interior support and is for this reason often shorter or more heavily reinforced than the *interior spans*. *See* **exterior panel.**

end thrust [mech.] A push from the end of a member, in particular the thrust of a *centrifugal pump* towards the suction end, which must be resisted by a special bearing called a thrust bearing.

endurance limit [mech.] In *fatigue testing*, the maximum stress for any material below which fractures do not occur, however many reversals of stress take place. For steels the endurance limit can be determined at 6 to 10 million cycles of stress. It is roughly three-quarters of the *yield point* in *mild steel*.

energy [mech.] A capacity for doing *work*, usually expressed in work units (Newton-metres or kilogram-metres), sometimes in heat units (kilojoules or calories). Energy may be inherent in the speed of a body (*kinetic energy*) or in its position relative to another body (*potential energy*). *See* **Bernoulli's theorem.**

engine [mech.] A *machine* driven by electrical, hydraulic, compressed-air, steam, internal-combustion, animal, or other power to do *work* such as traction, hoisting, pumping, sawing, ventilation.

engineer One who contrives, designs or constructs electrical or mechanical plant, public works or mining work, or a *tradesman* (*B*), such as a *mechanic* or a fitter and in USA also the driver of any engine. *See* **civil engineer, heating and ventilation** (*B*), **mechanical** (*B*), **structural engineer.**

engineering geology Geology applied to civil engineering. Closely concerned with such matters as the foundations of dams, their stability, *permeability*, etc., it includes *hydrology, soil mechanics, rock mechanics, geomorphology, geophysics*, mineralogy, petrology and related subjects.

Engineering News formula A *dynamic pile formula* developed by Wellington in 1888. The *Hiley formula* is now generally preferred.

engineer's level [sur.] A telescope with a level tube attached. It is often a *dumpy level*.

Engineers Registration Board *See* **technician engineer.**

engineer's transit [sur.] or **surveyor's transit** American description of a *theodolite* having a vertical graduated arc and a telescope bubble, as opposed to a plain *transit* which measures only horizontal angles, since it has no telescope bubble nor vertical circle.

enlarged-base pile A *bored pile* base can be enlarged by hammering a plug of concrete at the bottom of the hole or by *under-reaming* the base.

enrockment *Rip-rap*.

entrance head [hyd.] The head required to cause flow into a conduit or other structure; it includes both *entrance loss* and *velocity head* (ASCE MEP 11).

entrance lock [hyd.] A *lock* which provides access to a *dock* in which the water is at a different level from the water outside.

entrance loss [hyd.] The head lost in eddies and friction at the inlet to a conduit.

environmental engineering A term that has two senses in USA: (1) sewage treatment, sewer networks, and prevention of pollution by gases, dust or noise or other 'insult to the environment'; (2) all the engineering work concerned with central heating and air conditioning – the improvement of the enclosed environment. In Britain in 1979 it had begun to have the sense of (1) only.

Ephemeris [sur.] *See* **American Ephemeris and Nautical Almanac.**

epoxide, epoxy, ethoxylene resin A synthetic, usually two-part material that can set and harden under water or be used for bonding *roof bolts* or for repairing concrete in heavily trafficked areas, etc. One disadvantage is that its fire resistance is low.

equal angle An *angle section* with legs of equal length. *Compare* **unequal angle.**

equal-falling particles [s.m.] Particles of equal *terminal velocity*. They may be found in the *underflow* of a *classifier*.

equalization of boundaries [sur.] A method of calculating areas which have irregular boundaries. The irregular lines are replaced by straight lines which cut off on the one side an amount equal to what they put on on the other side. The area can then be calculated by adding the areas of the triangles so formed. *See* **give-and-take lines.**

equalizing bed A bed of ballast or concrete on which pipes are laid in the bottom of a trench.

equilibrium [stru.] The state of a body which does not move. A body is in stable equilibrium when any slight movement increases its potential energy so that when released it tends to fall back to its original position. A body in unstable equilibrium, when moved slightly, tends to move farther away from its original position.

equilibrium moisture content [s.m.] The moisture content of a soil in a given environment, at which no *moisture movement* occurs. *See also* (*B*).

equilibrium of floating bodies [hyd.] *See* **principle of Archimedes.**

equipotential lines [s.m.] Contours of equal water pressure in the soil mass round a water-retaining structure such as an earth dam or river bank. They can be determined by building a scale model of the bank with the water levels to scale. The soil mass is connected to glass *stand pipes* which show, by the water level in them, the pressure at the points to which they lead. From these elevations the equipotential lines can be plotted. *See* **flow lines, flow net.**

erecting shop A large open workshop or yard where steel frames are joined up after *fabrication* to make sure that they fit, before being sent in separate pieces to the site.

erosion *Scour*.

erratic [stat.] Said of values which seem to vary excessively from the *average*.

error [sur.] A difference from an *average* value. *See* **closing/compensating/gross/probable/systematic error,** *and* **Gaussian curve.**

escape [hyd.] A wasteway for discharging the entire flow of a stream (ASCE MEP 11).

Escherichia coli or **E. coli** or **colon bacillus,** formerly **Bacillus coli,** or **Bacterium coli** A bacterium of exclusively faecal origin, it forms 90% of the coliform bacteria in the human intestine. Its presence is a sign of faecal pollution and its absence is sometimes taken to indicate the absence of bacteriological pollution in water.

estimating draughtsman [d.o.] An experienced draughtsman with or without diplomas who estimates quantities and the costs of work from drawings made by himself or others.

ethane [min.] C_2H_6, a gas found in *natural gas* from oilwells, normally absent from coal mines.

Euler crippling stress [stru.] The *crippling load* (*P*) of a strut divided by its cross-sectional area (*A*). It is calculated from the formula

$$\frac{P}{A} = \pi^2 E \frac{k^2}{l^2}$$

where *E* is the *modulus of elasticity*
k is the *radius of gyration*
l is the *effective length* of the *strut*.
See **slenderness ratio.**

evaporation pan [hyd.] A container, often about 1·3 m dia. and 25 cm deep, from which the loss of water by evaporation can be determined by measuring its depth at various times. Pans serve mainly to determine evaporation losses from lakes or reservoirs. Reservoir losses are less than pan losses so that the evaporation from the pan should be multiplied by 0·7 or 0·75 to determine the reservoir loss. Pans may be sunk in the earth, be 30 cm above it or they may float in the reservoir or lake.

evapo-transpiration [hyd.] Combined loss of water from soils by evaporation and plant transpiration (ASCE MEP 11).

excavating cableway A *cableway* fitted with a clamshell or *orange peel* bucket for digging.

excavation Digging, breaking and removing soil or rock.

excavator or **navvy** A power-driven digging machine, usually mounted on crawler tracks. The *backacter*, *dragline*, *face shovel*, *grab*, and *skimmer* are fittings which can be attached to give a different function to the jib of the usual excavator. It can also be used as a crane. Other excavators are the *dredge*, *elevating grader*, *loading shovel*, *rotary excavator*, *trencher*.

exciter (1) Lime, alkali, sulphates, etc., which, added to a crushed blast-furnace slag, cause it to set when mixed with water. *Portland cement* acts as an exciter in the *Trief process*.

(2) [elec.] A direct current generator which energizes the field magnets of an alternator or similar electric machine.

exfiltration The opposite of *infiltration*. Leakage outwards. *See* sewage.

expanded clay *See* lightweight aggregate *and* (B).

expanded metal Steel or other metal mesh formed by slotting a metal sheet and widening the slots to a diamond shape. It is used for *metal lathing* (B), as a base for plaster and for concrete reinforcement.

expanding cement A hydraulic cement made from cement clinker, gypsum, and blast-furnace slag, developed by Professor Lossier in France. It expands during its setting and first hardening, unlike *Portland cements* which shrink. Expanding cement may eventually result in the making of concretes reinforced with *mild steel* which prestress themselves by their expansion after casting. In 1963 a cement made by a Californian cement-maker was used expansively for building an experimental length of self-prestressing highway in USA. This cement was unlike Lossier's, so far as is known, and the road was prestressed with long steel-wire strand.

expansion bend A loop in a pipe which enables the expansion or contraction due to temperature change to be taken up without danger to the pipe. *See* expansion joint.

expansion bolt An *anchor bolt* into masonry consisting of a split malleable-iron cone inserted thin end first into a drilled or *cored* hole. A bolt between the split halves projects outside the hole. When the head of the bolt is turned, a nut between the halves of the cone is drawn out and tightens the sides of the cone against the walls of the hole. Other expansion bolts work by a *toggle* mechanism or other means. *See* Rawlbolt.

expansion joint (1) In concrete work, a gap in the steel and the concrete to accommodate, at different times, both expansion and contraction. Confusion can arise because of this. A *contraction joint* provides mainly for shrinkage. Both are *movement joints*.

(2) An *expansion bend* or similar device.

expansion rollers Rollers provided at one support of a bridge or truss to allow for thermal movement. The other end is usually fixed.

expansive soils [stru.] *See* swelling soils.

expansive use of steam [mech.] or **expansive working** The expanding of steam in the cylinder or cylinders so that the highest practicable amount of energy is extracted from it. This is usual for stationary steam or compressed-air engines, but to ensure proper expansion engines must be kept in good order.

expending beach A beach designed to use up the energy of the waves. *See* **tetrapod.**

exploder *See* **blasting machine.**

exploration *See* **site exploration.**

explosive compaction [s.m.] *Deep blasting.*

explosives [min.] Materials which are used for demolition or for *breaking ground* by *blasting*. *See* **detonator, dynamite, gelatine explosives, high explosive.**

exterior panel A panel of a slab of which at least one edge has a discontinuous support. Sometimes called an *end span*.

external vibrator A vibrator for concrete placing, fixed to the *formwork*, as opposed to an *internal vibrator*. This method of vibration has the dis-advantage that the shuttering must be unusually strong and it is therefore little used.

extrapolate [d.o.] To continue a curve beyond those points for which data have been obtained for it. Hence to make inferences which are little more than guesses.

extruded sections The commonest *light alloy* structural sections, formed by *extrusion*.

extrusion [mech.] Forming rods, tubes, or *sections* of intricate shape by pushing hot or cold metal or plastics through a *die* shaped to the required section. The *lead sheaths* of electric cables as well as structural sections of *light alloy* or plastics are made in this way. *Compare* **cold drawing,** *see* **ductility, wirecut brick** (*B*).

eye bolt [mech.] A *bolt* with a steel loop forged at one end instead of a head, and a thread formed at the other end. It is screwed into and used for lifting heavy plant.

F

fabric *See* wire-mesh reinforcement.

fabrication [mech.] Preparing the steel members of a building framework or part in the workshop by such operations as shearing, drilling, plate bending or straightening, sawing, flame cutting, planing of castings, squaring the ends of stanchions with ending machines, *notching*, grinding, *automatic welding*, *forging*, etc.

Fabridam A dam made of plastic sheet, which can be inflated with water or air and can thus rise to 6 or 10 m. It is anchored to the river bed, and in torrential rivers has the great advantage that it is completely collapsible and has very little flow-resistance when deflated. *See* **Dracone**.

face left [sur.] The position of a theodolite when its vertical circle is to the left of the telescope, seen from the eyepiece. *See* **face right**.

face piece A *face waling*.

face right [sur.] The position of a theodolite when the vertical circle is to the right of the telescope when viewed from the eyepiece. *See* **change face**, **face left**.

face shovel or **crowd shovel** or **forward shovel** An attachment fitted to an *excavator* by which it digs away from itself into a bank (the face) with a toothed bucket fixed to a rigid arm. It is a most useful digging tool, with a more powerful digging action (since it is more stable) than the other attachments.

face waling or **face piece** A *waling* across the end of a trench. It is held by the ends of the main walings and supports the end of the trench together with the end strut.

facing A protective covering to sea walls, dykes, or cuttings, or a decorative wall surface of brick or stone. *See* also (*B*).

facing points [rly] *See* **points**.

facing wall A concrete, precast, or *in situ* lining used instead of timber sheeting against the earth face of an excavation. It is held by the main timbering (which is later removed) and used as a base for asphalt tanking against which the main retaining wall is eventually built. Timber sheeting cannot be used because it would not be a good base for asphalt and would rot.

factor of safety [stru.] The *stress* at which failure is expected, divided by the design stress (maximum permissible stress). *See* **load factor**.

faggot A *fascine*.

faggoting [hyd.] or **kidding** *Revetment* of river banks with *bat faggots* in submerged places where grass cannot be planted. Faggots, particularly thorn faggots, have the advantage that they collect *silt*.

failure A condition at which a structure reaches a *limit state*. It may be due to leakage, deflection, cracking, etc., but it usually does not involve rupture (fracture) because most structures are considered to be unsafe, therefore unusable, before they collapse.

fairlead (1) A metal fixture to a quay, deck (or ship) which serves to guide the ropes which help ships to berth without damage.

(2) A swivel pulley on the drag rope of a dragline. This pulley is held on the cab.

fall (1) The *gradient* of rivers, roads, or railways, described as a fall of so many m per km or as a percentage.

(2) or **fall rope** The free hoisting rope used with *lifting tackle*.

fall block In *lifting tackle*, a pulley *block* which rises and falls with the load. The load hangs from a hook or eye under the fall block.

falling apron A *revetment* consisting of a *mattress* which is launched by the *scour* beneath it.

falling velocity, fall velocity [hyd.] *See* **Stokes's law.**

fall rope *See* **fall** (2).

false leaders A steel mast set on the ground, held upright by guy ropes and used for guiding a pile during driving and for holding the weight of a *pile hammer* over it. *Compare* **hanging leaders, leaders.**

falsework Support for concrete *formwork* or for an arch during construction.

fan [mech.] A ventilator for delivering large volumes of air at a low pressure. For a colliery main fan, the pressure difference is usually a suction of about 20 cm of *water gauge.*

farm duty [hyd.] The quantity of water delivered to a farm for irrigation (USA). *See* **net duty.**

fascine A brushwood bundle 2·7 to 5·2 m long, firmly tied into a cylindrical shape of about 0·7 m girth. It is used as a protective facing to sea walls or river banks or to float a road over waterlogged soil. Fascines are cut from willow from an osier bed 4 years old, from pollard willow 2 years old, from hazel or sweet chestnut 13 years old, or from ash or birch 6 years old. *See* **faggoting, mattress.**

fatigue [mech.] The lowering of the breaking load of a member by repeated reversals of *stress* so that the member fails at a much lower stress than it can withstand under *static loading*. *See* **corrosion fatigue, endurance limit.**

fatigue test [mech.] The testing of metal testpieces under repeated reversals or fluctuations of stress to determine the *endurance limit*. *See* **stress-number curve.**

feather *See* **plug and feathers,** *also* (*B*).

feed (1) [mech.] The rate of advance of a cutting tool, drill bit, drilling rod, etc.

(2) [mech.] The water supply which has to be pumped into a boiler at the boiler pressure by the *feedpump.*

feeder (1) [elec.] A cable of high current *carrying capacity* (*B*), which connects power stations to substations.

(2) [mech.] A device for delivering coal, ore, or other loose material at a controllable rate.

(3) [hyd.] A channel which supplies a reservoir or canal with water.

feedpump [mech.] The pump which provides a steam boiler with *feedwater.*

feedwater [mech.] Water which in the best practice is *de-mineralized*, heated nearly to boiler temperature, and de-aerated before being pumped into a steam *boiler* by the *feedpump.*

Fellenius's circular-arc method [s.m.] *See* **rotational slide.**

fence [mech.] A guard round machinery to protect people from being drawn into it.

fender A rope mat or ball, an old rubber tyre, etc., which protects a vessel from impact with a pier (and the pier from the vessel).

fender pile An upright, generally free-standing, wooden pile driven into the ground just clear of a berth. It absorbs some of the impact of vessels and thus protects the berth.

fender post or **guard post** A *bollard.*

ferro-concrete An obsolescent term for reinforced concrete.

ferro-prussiate paper [d.o.] Paper treated to make *blueprints*. It is almost obsolete and is superseded by *dyeline* prints.

fetch The free distance which the wind can travel to any point in raising waves, that is the distance from the nearest coast in the direction of the wind. *See* **Stevenson's formula.**

fibre-reinforced concrete or **glassfibre-reinforced concrete (GRC)** or **cement** or **gypsum (GRG)** Such materials have fairly satisfactorily performed as fence posts, when tested by the *Building Research Establishment*. The wall thickness was 12 mm, the bore 10 cm and length 1 m, using randomly oriented glassfibre, 4·5% by weight of the dry cement. The glass has to be alkali resistant, e.g. Cem-FIL. 'Purlin-tiles' also have been made, replacing several tiles, spanning some 2 m and eliminating the need for tiling battens. The fire resistance of the concrete is not good and the units are costly, but that of glassfibre-reinforced gypsum is excellent and it has been tried as the basis for a one-hour fire-resistant door. Steel, carbon and polypropylene fibres have also been tried by the BRE. The Crédit Lyonnais in Queen Victoria Street, London, officially unveiled in December 1978, was perhaps the world's first wholly GRC-clad building, with more than 3,000 GRC units facing the walls of its ground floor and five upper storeys. Leaning outwards at 5° from the vertical, the units drain to a setback at each floor from which dirty water goes to the drainage system and does not flow down the façade.

fibre rope, cordage *Manmade fibre* ropes, less liable to rot, are gradually superseding the old vegetable fibres, some of which are hempen. Cordage is described by its circumference, unlike steel ropes, which are described by their greatest diameter. *See* BS 3724.

Fidler's gear Lifting tackle for laying large blocks at any angle, in *blockwork* below water level.

fiducial line or **fiducial point** [sur.] A reference line or point.

field book [sur.] A surveyor's book recording his field measurements.

field drain or **agricultural** or **land drain** Unsocketed, earthenware, porous concrete, perforated plastics or *pitch fibre pipes* (*B*), about 8 cm bore, laid end to end unjointed so as to drain the ground. The trench is usually backfilled with coarse sand or gravel rather than clay next the drain so as to prevent blockage. *See* **Trammel drain**.

field moisture equivalent [s.m.] The minimum *moisture content* at which a water drop placed on the smoothed surface of a soil will not be absorbed immediately by the soil but spreads over the surface, giving it a shiny look.

field tile American term for *field drain*.

files [mech.] Hand tools more used for cutting metal than wood. They may be of several cross-sections, flat,

round, half-round, square, and triangular (also called three square). *See* cut (4).

fill *Earthwork* in *embankment* or *back filling* (*B*).

filled bitumen *Bitumen* containing *filler*.

filler Fine mineral powder added to road tars and bitumens to make them stiffer. *See also* (*B*).

filler concrete slab A *filler-joist floor*.

filler-joist floor or **filler concrete slab** A floor consisting of 152×89 mm or smaller *rolled steel joists* (filler joists) spaced at intervals of 0·45 to 0·75 m. The intervals may be filled with plain or reinforced concrete or *hollow tile* covered with a concrete topping. This type of floor is common in power stations or other buildings with frequent holes through the floor, particularly when the holes are at positions unknown while the floor is being designed. Generally the filler joists are carried on larger steel beams. *See* **jack arch.**

filler rod [mech.] A rod, often an *electrode*, which provides filler metal to make a *weld*.

fillet weld [mech.] A weld of roughly triangular cross-section between two pieces at right angles.

filling Material used for raising the ground to a higher level. *See also* (*B*).

filter (1) [hyd.] An arrangement for straining harmful matter, including bacteria, from water to make it drinkable or usable for other purposes. *See* **filtration.**

(2) [s.m.] *See* **graded filter.**

filter bed [sewage] A *trickling filter*.

filter blocks Hollow vitrified clay blocks which may be salt glazed and are designed to carry a *trickling filter* (USA).

filter material (1) [s.m.] Granular material which has been so *graded* as to strain solids out of water passing through it.

(2) [sewage] or **filter medium** The strong metallurgical coke, clinker, plastics or broken stone in a *trickling filter*.

filter medium *Filter material*.

filter well [s.m.] A bored well of about 30 cm dia., used as an alternative to *wellpoints*, in which each borehole has its own pump installed at the top. It is more expensive and slower to install, but there is less disturbance to the ground than with wellpoints because there are fewer, though more efficient, wells. The suction lift of each pump is also appreciably better. If the pumps are submersible they can be installed at the foot of each well, and there is then no limit to their depth.

filtrate Liquid (usually water) that has passed through a filter.

filtration An essential part of *water treatment*, the use of a strainer to separate many of the fine solids from water. They are too fine to be removed by sedimentation. Some of the strainers used are: *sand filters*, multi-media filters (like sand filters but with anthracite on the top, sand in the middle and garnet or other dense mineral below), *micro-strainers* and a wide variety of others, even *ultra-filtration*.

final grade American expression for *formation level*.

final setting time The time, determined by the standardized test of BS 1881, during which a fresh paste of cement and water stiffens by a certain amount.

fine-adjustment screw [sur.] A *tangent screw*.

fine aggregate (1) Sand or grit for concrete which passes a sieve of mesh 5 mm square.

(2) Sand or grit for bituminous roadmaking which passes a 3 mm square mesh.

fine cold asphalt A *wearing course* of bitumen and fine aggregate which is spread and compacted while cold or warm.

fine-wire drag, fine-wire sweep [sur.] In *hydrographic surveying*, to ensure there are no upstanding reefs or wrecks on the bed of a waterway, two boats about 100 m apart have to sweep the bed before or after it has been sounded for depth. A light wire, the drag, is held between them, scraping the bed, and wound from a friction-braked drum at one end. When the rope pulls out, the horizontal and vertical angles from the boats along the wire are noted. The obstruction is thus located and, later, mapped.

fineness modulus A number which indicates the fineness of a sand, pigment, cement, etc. It is calculated by determining the percentage residues on each of a series of standard sieves from 37·5 mm opening downwards, each opening being half the preceding one. The percentages are then summed and divided by 100, the quotient being the fineness modulus. The series is as follows: 37·5 mm; 19 mm; 9·5 mm; 4·75 mm; 2·36 mm; 1·18 mm; 0·6 mm; 0·3 mm; 0·15 mm. The test sieves are of perforated plate down to 1·18 mm; below that size they are of woven wire mesh. The largest BS test sieve is 125 mm (previous sizes were in inches). The *grading curve* is often used in Britain and USA instead of the fineness modulus, and for fine powders like cement or fly-ash, the *specific surface* is another common description.

fines [s.m.] The smaller particles in a *mechanical analysis*.

Fink truss or **Belgian/French truss** [stru.] A common, steel roof truss suitable for spans up to 15 m.

fire setting [min.] A method of *breaking ground* practised in ancient Egypt and medieval Europe up to the time of gunpowder. A hot fire is lit next to the rock. As soon as the rock is judged to be hot enough, it is rapidly cooled by pouring water over it. *See* jet drilling.

fire-tube boiler [mech.] A steam boiler in which the smoke passes through tubes surrounded by water, for example locomotive boilers, or the Lancashire, the Cornish, or other relatively small boilers. *See* water-tube boiler.

fire welding *Forge welding*.

firing [mech.] The charging of fuel into a furnace generally of a steam boiler.

firm clay or **firm silt** [s.m.] A *clay* (or

silt) which can be dug with a spade and moulded by firmly squeezing in the hand.

first moment [stru.] *See* **static moment.**

first order [sur.] or **primary triangulation** or **trilateration** A *triangulation* or *trilateration* with sides 20 to 60 km or more in length. *See* **second order.**

fished joint A joint made with *fishplates.*

fishing (1) Bolting up *fishplates* to rails or other members.

(2) [min.] In oilwell or exploratory drilling, letting down recovery tools (fishing tools) into the hole to extract broken tackle.

fishing tools [min.] Tools for cutting off rope or recovering or drilling round or into or through a tool lost in a borehole.

fish ladder or **fish pass** or **fishway** A channel along which fish can travel up or down past a weir or dam.

fishplate The end of a rail is joined to the next *rail* in the track by a pair of specially shaped steel plates called fishplates, one each side, which are bolted through the rails. Fishplates of a simpler, rectangular shape are used for joining a stanchion extension to the stanchion below. For joining timbers, they may be called *splice* plates, splice pieces, cover straps, or flitch plates, and may be of steel or wood.

fish screen [hyd.] A barrier to prevent fish entering a channel.

fishtail bit [min.] A bit used in the oilwell *rotary drill* for drilling through soft ground.

fishtail bolt An *anchor bolt* with its tail split and cast into concrete or masonry.

fishway A *fish ladder.*

fissured clay [s.m.] A *clay* which like the London clay has a network of joints that open up in dry weather. *See* intact/stiff-fissured clay.

fitchering [min.] American description of the jamming of drill steels in a hole.

fitted bolt *See* **turned bolt.**

fitter [mech.] A *skilled man* who can assemble engines in an engineering shop. *See* **black gang.**

fitting [mech.] Skilled work in an engineering shop which involves assembly by a fitter.

fit-up A description of *formwork* which is framed so as to be struck without destroying it. It is therefore suitable for repeated erection.

fix [air sur.] A determination of an aircraft's position when taking photographs of the ground; a form of *ground control.*

fixed beam [stru.] A beam with a *fixed end.*

fixed end [stru.] A fixing to an end of a beam or column which can develop without movement, as much *bending moment* as the *moment of resistance* of the beam or column. *See* fixing moment, *and compare* hinge.

fixed-end moment *See* fixing moment.

fixed retaining walls [stru.] Basement and similar walls which are rigidly supported at top and bottom are subjected to a pressure much higher than that due to *active earth pressure* on *free retaining walls.* The coefficient for the equivalent fluid pressure of sands increases to about 0·5 at 2 m depth instead of the 0·27 value usual for free retaining walls holding up sand. In clayey materials the pressure is higher if the clay can get wet and swell.

fixing moment [stru.] or **fixed-end moment** The *bending moment* at the support of a beam required to fix it in such a way that it cannot rotate, so that it has a *fixed end.*

fixity *See* **continuity.**

flagstone *See* **paving flag.**

flame cutting Cutting steel, iron, or other metal up to 1 m thick with an oxyhydrogen, oxy-coal gas, or oxy-acetylene flame. Less accurate but quicker work can be done with explosive.

flange (1) [mech.] A disc forged or screwed on to the end of a pipe to bolt it to the next pipe or cast on to engine parts which need to be bolted down. *See* **blank flange.**

(2) The wide strips (*compression* or *tension flange*) of a *rolled-steel joist* or girder. *See* **chord.**

(3) [rly] The projecting rim of a railway wheel which holds it on to the rail.

(4) [rly] The flat part of a flanged rail which rests on the sleepers.

flanks The outer quarters of a carriageway, also called shoulders or haunches.

flap trap [sewage] An *antiflood* valve. *See* **flap valve**.

flap valve [mech.] A *check valve* with a hinged disc which opens when the flow is normal and is closed by gravity or by the flow when the flow tends to go backwards.

flared column head A circular column which widens to a cone shape just below the floor slab. It is sometimes used in *mushroom construction*.

flashboard A *stop log*.

flash-butt welding A method of forge-welding butt joints in rails, used by British Rail for joining the rails in *continuously welded track*. A massive machine has to be used, which is rigid enough to hold the 18 m long rails accurately in line with each other. The two rail ends are first butted together and a heavy current passed through the joint of about 10 amp/mm², heating it to red heat. The ends are then separated, and an arc is struck between them, melting the ends. The rails are then forced together to form the weld, the impurities being forced out of the weld as a 'flash' which can be ground off smooth to make a good running surface.

flash set Unusual and inconveniently rapid setting of cement in concrete or elsewhere.

flash welding [mech.] *Resistance flash welding*.

flat [mech.] A thin rectangular iron or steel bar.

flat-bottomed rail [rly] A rail resembling a T upside down, with a thickened foot to the ⊥, on which the wheels travel. This type is universally used on the continent of Europe and is now standard in Britain, having virtually displaced the *bullhead rail*. *See* **rail fastenings**.

flat jack A nearly flat, hollow, steel cushion made of two discs in contact, welded round the edge. It can be inflated by injecting oil or cement grout under a pressure which can be maintained, increased, or reduced as required. Flat jacks were used at *Plougastel* by Freyssinet and are still used particularly at the abutments and crowns of arches to relieve the formwork of load at the moment of striking the *formwork*, or in *prestressing*.

flat slab (1) A reinforced-concrete slab which spans in two directions. Its length is generally less than twice its width, and should preferably be equal to it.

(2) A *mushroom slab*.

flat-slab deck dam [hyd.] or **flat-slab buttress dam** A reinforced-concrete slab with a flat upstream face sloping at about 45°, carried on parallel buttresses. It resembles the *multiple-arch dam* except that its wetted surface is flat.

flattened strand rope [min.] Steel-wire circular ropes built up from strands laid *Lang's lay* round a hemp core. Each strand is made of wires laid round an oval or triangular soft-iron core wire which gives the strands their flattened outer surface. This shape increases the amount of wearing surface and probably, therefore, lengthens the life of the rope.

flexible membrane [s.m.] Sheet, usually of synthetic rubber, that can be laid over the ground under a reservoir or tank or swimming pool to reduce leakages. It is usually less than 1 mm thick and protected against punctures by synthetic foam or felt below and may be protected above by other means. Sometimes the membrane is pervious to hold back silt but not water, when used on a beach, and then it may be of woven polystyrene. Other types of membrane are used for *curing* or waterproofing concrete – bitumen emulsions, rubber emulsions, *epoxy* resins, etc. They can be applied to the outside of concrete retaining walls to waterproof them.

flexible pavement Road or airstrip construction with a waterproof wearing surface of bituminous material which is assumed to have no tensile strength. The load is transferred to the foundation soil by the *base course*, designed from experience of the *California bearing ratio* method. Flexible pavements are considerably cheaper than rigid (concrete) pavements. An innovation was the prestressed-concrete pavement at Orly, France, which is flexible, designed by Freyssinet. *See* pavement.

flexible pipe Pipes made of *pitch fibre* (*B*), unplasticized PVC or steel or ductile iron, suitable for use in ground that may settle with mining or other subsidence. The joints may be rigid or flexible, as with *rigid pipe*.

flexible wall A reinforced-concrete wall in which the stem is designed as a cantilever or as a beam or both. It requires much less concrete than a *gravity retaining wall* but it can be damaged by wave impact.

flexural rigidity [stru.] The *second moment of area* of a beam multiplied by its *modulus of elasticity*, often called its E I value.

flexure [stru.] American word meaning bending.

flints Nodules of silica found in beds in the chalk, believed to have come from the fossil skeletons of sponges.

float (1) [hyd.] A small floating object whose direction and speed of travel are taken to measure the speed of the water which carries it. *See* rod/subsurface float, travelling screen.

(2) [mech.] A body floating in a water tank, which opens a valve in it when the water level falls. *See* float switch.

(3) A tool like a plasterer's *float* (*B*) for spreading mortar or hot asphalt over a road.

float-cut file [mech.] A single-cut file. *See* cut (4).

floater American term for the plasterer's *float* (*B*).

floating boom A boom that may be used for holding back an oil slick if a *Dracone* is used. Another type, used for warning yachtsmen or swimmers of a nearby weir, consists of expanded polystyrene cylinders, 450 mm dia. and 2·4 m long, with a 25 mm dia. plastic tube through a hole along their centre lines; the cylinders are threaded together with a wire rope through the pipe. The foam cylinders resemble the foam blocks used as *void formers*.

floating breakwater Several types of raft exist that can be used as cheap floating breakwaters, that are easily towed away, though they must be anchored. One type proposed originally in 1967 by Harris and Sutherland, consulting engineers, was an assembly of prestressed-concrete beams made light enough to float by their cores of expanded polystyrene *void formers*. The first model was 48 m long and 10 m wide. *See above*.

floating crane [hyd.] A crane carried on a large barge called a pontoon. It forms part of the equipment of any big port, and large ones can lift 200 tons each.

floating dock or **floating dry dock** A steel floating structure with sides. It can be floated or sunk at will. When a vessel at sea needs underwater repairs, the floating dock partly sinks itself beneath the vessel, then makes itself buoyant again by pumping out its water ballast and raises the vessel out of the water with it. The vessel can then be repaired in the dry. *See* dock.

floating foundation A *buoyant foundation*.

floating harbour [hyd.] A *breakwater* of *pontoons* connected end to end.

floating pipeline [hyd.] A pipeline carried on pontoons used for removing the material dredged by a *suction dredger* which pumps fluid sand or silt into the pipeline. The dredged material is deposited on land so as to raise its level, to make a *hydraulic-fill dam*, etc. Pipelines 3 km long have been successfully used like this. *See* **artificial islands.**

float switch [elec.] A pump-house switch for starting or stopping the pump motor when the water level rises or falls. It is operated by a *float*. It is also used for automatically opening or closing spillway gates and is thus a *ball cock* (*B*) on a large scale.

floc A woolly-looking accumulation of solids in a liquid. It settles with difficulty and is the opposite of granular solids like sand, all of which settle easily and are therefore easily removed from water in treatment processes.

flocculation Sticking together of fine solids in water, resulting in *flocs*, sometimes wrongly thought to be the same as *coagulation*. It can be promoted by gentle stirring called mechanical flocculation, or by adding chemical flocculants such as polyelectrolytes, but ordinarily flocculation is a physical process, coagulation a chemical one. Flocs are destroyed by rough stirring.

flood channel [hyd.] The channel in an estuary formed by the flood tide. It is generally wide at the seaward end, narrowing to a point at the upstream end, where there is a *bar*. Generally in a narrow estuary the flood channels branch upstream off the meandering *ebb channel* so that it looks like a poplar tree when mapped.

flood routing [hyd.] Reduction of a flood or its peak by arranging for dams or overflow channels, storage basins and channel widening or deepening.

floor arch Term used in America for a *jack arch*.

floor slab A reinforced-concrete floor, particularly the thin part between reinforced-concrete (or steel) beams.

flotation [stru.] The floating of a structure is a condition that has to be checked by calculation whenever a deep basement is built below water level. After the basement walls and floor have been built and before the building load is put on to them, lifting of the structure by the water pressure under it must be prevented by one of two means; either the water level outside the walls must be kept down by pumping, or the structure may have to be loaded with additional weight. In a *buoyant foundation*, if there is an emergency the extra weight may have to be water.

flotation structure A steel raft built of tubes that can be of 9 m dia. used for transporting an oilwell production *jacket* from the dry dock where it is built to the sea site where it will be used. It must be built before the jacket because the jacket is built on it in the dry dock and slipped off it at the sea site, after which the flotation structure is towed back to the dry dock and the dry dock is pumped out to enable another jacket to be built. The flotation structure may contain 10,000 tons of steel and its tubes are divided by steel bulkheads. The sections of tube so separated from each other can be emptied or flooded at will, enabling the raft to be sunk or floated as required, or rotated under complete control (up-ended) through 90°. The jacket is allowed to slide under control on to its site on the sea bed by up-ending.

floury soil [s.m.] A fine-grained soil which looks like *clay* when wet but is seen to be a powder when dry. It is therefore a *silt* or rock flour, not a clay.

flow curve [s.m.] A graph of the points obtained in the *liquid limit* test showing number of blows on the horizontal, log scale and water contents on the vertical, arithmetic scale. The point where the curve intersects the 25-blows vertical line is the *liquid limit*. The flow curve is a straight line.

flow index [s.m.] The slope of the *flow curve*. Since the abscissae are plotted logarithmically it is equal to the difference between the water content at 10 blows and 1 blow or at 100 and 10 blows.

flow lines (1) [s.m.] Lines in a *flow net* which show the direction of flow of

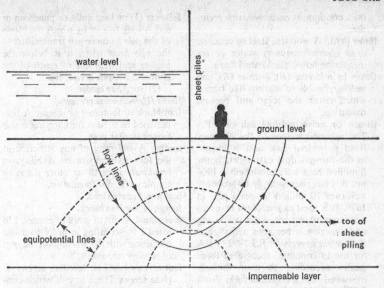

water level

sheet piles

ground level

flow lines

equipotential lines

toe of sheet piling

impermeable layer

Flow net at sheet-pile cofferdam

water through a soil mass near a dam or cofferdam. They intersect the *equipotential lines* at right angles.

(2) [hyd.] The paths traced by particles in flowing water.

flow meter An instrument for measuring the quantity of fluid such as water, air, or gas which flows in a unit of time, for example a *Venturi meter*. The amount of fluid paid for is also measured by a meter (water, gas, or air meter) sometimes called an integrating flow meter. A *current meter* is a flow meter which has not been calibrated to read amounts of fluid or flow, but reads distances.

flow net [hyd., s.m.] A two-dimensional picture of *groundwater* flow, consisting of *equipotential lines* intersecting *flow lines* at right angles in *isotropic* soil. If the soil is not isotropic the lines will not be perpendicular; the flow lines are then likely to follow soil laminations. The flow net shows (*a*) the *neutral pressure* at any point, from which the *uplift* under a dam can be calculated; (*b*) the *effective pressure*, for calculating dam stability; (*c*) the ordinary *seepage* flow; (*d*) the increased pressure due to seepage after rain.

flow slide [s.m.] or **earth flow** or **mud flow** A slide of a liquefied mass of loose sand or silt which spreads out to a very flat slope after the slide. Those slides which have been examined by the methods of *soil mechanics* have had densities below the critical, that is their void ratios were above the *critical voids ratio*. See **landslip, liquefaction.**

flow-table test A standard test for assessing the stiffness of fresh concrete by measuring its spread. See **V.-B. consistometer** and BS 1881.

flue gas [mech.] The smoke from a boiler fire, mainly CO_2, CO, N_2, O_2, and water vapour. Its composition, particularly the CO_2 content, gives a very good idea of the furnace efficiency, and this can be permanently recorded on a continuous *carbon-dioxide recorder*.

flume [hyd.] A wooden, steel or concrete *open channel* to carry water or for measuring flows. *See* **Venturi flume**.

fluxes In *soldering* (*B*), *brazing* (*B*), and *welding*, fusible substances like borax, which cover the joint and prevent oxidation.

fly-ash or **pulverized-fuel ash** or **PFA** The ash which goes to the chimney from *pulverized coal* and is caught in the flue-gas dust extractors. Some 6 million tons were produced in 1964 but this has risen sharply to probably well over 10 million tonnes a year in 1979. It is used as *pozzolana* or as an *admixture* to cement. After pelletizing and sintering it becomes a first-class *lightweight aggregate*. BS 3892 'PFA for use in concrete' recognizes three grades according to their fineness measured by *specific surface*, from 2,750 to 5,750 cm²/gram. Used with a harsh, irregular gravel it can save some 24 % of the cement by its plasticizing action, and it also reduces the heat given out during hardening.

flying buttress A *buttress* which provides support, including lateral thrust, at a high level, usually to a roof. It is not in contact with walls at a lower level, and may pass over them, hence the name.

fly-off or **interception** The catching of rain by plants, followed by evaporation – the opposite of *runoff*.

foamed concrete *Aerated concrete*.

folded-plate or **polygonal shell roof** [stru.] A roof, built of reinforced concrete slabs at an angle to each other (*see illustration*). Such roofs can cover long spans. Other shapes exist.

follower (1) or **long dolly** or **puncheon** or **sett** A long timber by which the blows of the *pile hammer* are transmitted to the *pile head* when it is below the *leaders* and thus out of reach of the hammer. *See* **pile driver**, etc.

(2) [sur.] *See* **leader**.

fondu *High-alumina cement*.

foot block or **footpiece** or **sleeper** A timber used as a base for carrying a *side tree* or similar post.

footing A widening of any structure at the foot to improve its stability, in *breakwaters*, earth or other dams or simple walls. *See* **foundation**.

foot iron *See* **step iron**.

footpiece *See* **foot block**.

foot-pound A unit of work or energy, 1 lb lifted 1 ft, so called in order to avoid confusion with the *pound-foot*, the unit of *bending moment*.

foot screws [sur.] or **levelling screws** or **plate screws** Three screws which connect the *tribrach* of the *theodolite* (and some levels) to the plate which is screwed on to the tripod head. They are used for levelling the instrument at each *set-up*.

foot-ton A unit of *work* or *energy*, 1 ton lifted 1 foot. *See* **foot-pound**.

foot valve [mech.] A *check valve* at the foot of a length of pipe, generally above a pump suction.

footway (sidewalk in USA) That part of the road reserved for pedestrians. *See* **carriageway**.

force [stru.] That which tends to accelerate a body or to change its movement; for example, the weight of a body is a force which tends to move it downwards. *Compare* pressure.

forced drop shaft A method developed

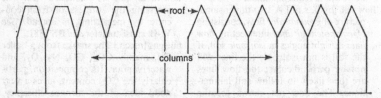

Folded-plate or polygonal shell roof in cross-section

in Germany, by which cylindrical shafts can be sunk in waterlogged ground below the limits of *open* or *pneumatic caissons*. A series of telescopic cast-iron drums is jacked down by hydraulic jacks inside a cylindrical reinforced-concrete curb. Excavation is by dredging followed by a massive rotary boring machine of the diameter of the shaft, called a *trepan*. The broken soil is removed by an *air-lift pump* in the hollow driveshaft of the trepan. The limiting depth is the lowest depth to which the iron lining can be forced. A 6 m dia. drum has been forced to 75 or 100 m before sticking. This method is not generally used now, *cementation* or *freezing* or the *Honigmann method* being preferred.

forced vibration [stru.] Vibration of a structure, due generally to engines or machines, occasionally wind. *See* **damping, free vibration, resonance.**

force pump [mech.] A pump which delivers liquid to a level appreciably higher than the cylinder, as opposed to a *spout-delivery pump*.

forebay (1) [hyd.] A reservoir at the end of a pipeline, particularly above a hydroelectric power station.

(2) The area over which water is taken into the ground, eventually to flow or be pumped from a well. In an *artesian well*, the forebay is higher than the outflow.

fore observation [sur.] or **fore sight** Any observation made by a surveying instrument towards the next station in the direction of progress of a survey. *See* **back observation.**

forepole [min.] or **forepoling board** or **spile** A 5 cm thick board with a sharp edge, driven ahead of an excavation in *forepoling*.

forepoling [min.] or **spiling** In tunnel timbering, driving *forepoles* ahead over the caps of the last *four-piece set* erected, to give temporary protection over miners who are putting up the next permanent timber set or are digging. Forepoling is used in tunnelling or mining loose ground in any

state between hard, unsafe rock to nearly fluid mud.

fore sight [sur.] A *fore observation*, particularly one made during levelling. The ASCE prefers, for levelling, the term minus sight. *See* **back sight.**

forge [mech.] (1) To shape hot metal (wrought iron or steel generally) by pressing or hammering like a blacksmith. *See* **forging.**

(2) The fire where the metal to be forged is heated. *See* **forge welding.**

forge welding [mech.] or **fire/plastic/ smith welding** Joining pieces of steel by hammering like a blacksmith, a form of *pressure welding*. This is the oldest method of joining metal and its origin is unknown. *See* **welding.**

forging [mech.] or **smithing** An ancient craft which originally consisted of the shaping of red-hot wrought iron with a hammer on the anvil, but is now extended to mean work with power hammers, drop stamps, or hydraulic forging machines on steel, light alloys, brasses, bronzes. Web stiffeners may be *joggled* and picks and the bits of drill steels sharpened by forging.

fork-lift truck A power-driven truck with a steel fork projecting forwards which can lift, travel with, and stack heavy packages at a height. The packages are often lifted on a *pallet*.

form A piece of *formwork*.

formation (1) or **grade** in USA The surface of the ground in its final shape after completion of *earthwork*, but before concreting.

(2) Any recognizable sediment in geology. It is the smallest unit in the *stratigraphical* succession.

formation level or **final grade** or **grade level** in USA. The surface level (or elevation) of the ground surface after all digging and filling but before concreting.

form lining Materials such as hardboard or plywood which are placed next the concrete in *formwork* to give it a smooth or textured surface. Being easily bent, they are particularly useful for curved surfaces.

form stop A *stunt end*.

formwork or **casing** or **shuttering** Temporary boarding or sheeting erected to contain concrete during placing and the first few days of hardening. The face texture of the formwork and its stiffness can greatly improve the look of the finished concrete wall or floor. Formwork may be of steel, wood boards, hardboard, plywood, and so on. *See* **form lining, mould, permanent shuttering, shuttering, sliding forms.**

Forth Bridge A *cantilever bridge* over the Firth of Forth near Edinburgh, built in 1890 of plates riveted into shapes like boiler shells. It has two central spans of 520 m clear, slightly less than the *Quebec bridge*. Its overall length is 1,630 m.

Forth Road Bridge A motorway *suspension bridge* completed in 1964 and close to the *Forth Bridge*, which is a railway bridge. The main span is 1,006 m and the overall gap 1,660 m. The towers are 156 m high.

forward shovel A *face shovel*.

foul sewer (in USA **sanitary sewer**) A *sewer* that carries *sewage*, whether in a *separate* or *combined system*.

found (1) To make a *foundation*.

(2) [mech.] To make a metal casting.

foundation (1) The soil or rock upon which a building or other structure rests.

(2) The structure of brick, stone, concrete, steel, wood, or iron which transfers the building load to the ground, sometimes called, together with the rest of the building below ground, the substructure. In a *suspension bridge* contract, the substructure section often includes the towers that may be 150 m high. *See* **buoyant/grillage/pad/piled/raft foundation, caisson, permafrost, pretesting, strip footing** *also* BSCP 2004, 'Foundations'.

foundation bolts *Anchor bolts*.

foundation cylinder *See* **cylinder**.

foundation failure [stru.] Foundations of buildings can fail in one of several ways, first by *differential settlement*, secondly by shear failure of the soil. *See* **circular arc method.**

foundation pier A foundation pier for a bridge is a solid concrete block several metres wide and usually at least the width of the bridge in length.

foundry A works with a cupola for melting pig iron (or other metal) and making metal castings.

four-leg sling [mech.] A *chain sling* or rope *sling* with four hooks hung by chains or ropes from one link or *thimble*.

four-piece set [min.] A frame of squared timbers used when *forepoling* in bad ground with a weak floor. It consists of a cap carried on two posts resting on the sill.

four-stage compression [mech.] Air compression in four stages with *intercoolers* between stages, an *aftercooler*, and sometimes also an antecooler. Three- or four-stage compression is necessary for reaching the pressures required for compressed-air locomotives, about 70 to 80 bars.

fraction [s.m.] Soils which have been subjected to a *mechanical analysis* are described in terms of their weight percentages of each component, the sand fraction, silt fraction, and clay fraction. *See* **classification of soils.**

fractional-horsepower motor [elec.] An electric motor with a rating less than 1 hp. It may be a *universal motor*.

fractional sampling [min.] Mechanical sampling by equipment which divides or decimates a sample without segregation and with less time and labour than coning and quartering.

frame (1) Two or more structural members joined together so as to be stable. A *plane frame* is two-dimensional and only stable in its own plane. A *space frame* is three-dimensional and stable in all directions. Frames may be *redundant* or *perfect*. The typical frame is the portal which is redundant. *See* **bent, steel frame.**

(2) In a timbered trench excavation, the *struts* which separate the boards on the opposite sides of the trench,

together with the *walings* which they hold. Thus in a shaft, all the walings or struts at one level. A frame may include *poling boards* (*see* **setting**). A ground or top frame is a frame of walings or struts set about 0·5 m below ground as a guide for the first setting of *runners*. A guide frame is built above ground to guide the runners and as a stage for the men who drive them.

frame weir [hyd.] or **framed dam** A weir built of timber and steel or cast iron of which some types are propped up by struts against the bed of the river in low water and lowered to the bed or hung above the water when it is in flood. *See* **needle/rolling-up curtain/sliding-panel/suspended-frame weir**.

framework [stru.] The load-carrying frame of a structure, generally of reinforced concrete, steel, timber, or occasionally *light alloy*.

Francis turbine [hyd.] A low-head to medium-head *water turbine* used on many large hydroelectric schemes. The water enters it radially inwards and leaves it, passing downwards. The turbine shaft is usually vertical. *See* **draft tube**.

Franki pile Trade name for a *driven cast-in-place pile* which has, like others, the advantage of a bulbous toe (clubfoot). Its main disadvantage is the large amount of space needed for the pile frame which cannot be accommodated on small city sites. *Bored piles* on the other hand can be driven with a 4 m high three-legged derrick made of steel pipe, which can be carried by two men.

frazil ice [hyd.] or **slush ice** Granular or spiky ice formed in rapids or other agitated water during long cold spells (USA).

freeboard [hyd.] The height between normal water level and the crest of a dam or the top of a *flume*, a height which allows for small waves to splash without overflow.

free end [stru.] A *hinge* of a beam.

free face [min.] In rock blasting, an exposed surface. Generally each *round*

has one free face. Holes with more than one free face need very much less explosive. *See* **burden, line of least resistance**.

free-falling velocity *See* **terminal velocity**.

free flow [hyd.] Flow over a weir or dam which is so high as not to be affected by the *tailwater* level.

free haul The maximum distance which excavated material is transported without extra charge (BS 892). This distance is generally fixed by the item in the *bill of quantities* (*B*), under which the particular excavation is paid for. *See* **overhaul**.

free-piston compressor [mech.] A modern compressor which differs from centrifugal and *reciprocating* compressors in having no important rotating parts. The force of explosion in a Diesel cylinder drives the piston out to compress the air in an air cylinder at the other end of the piston rod. *See* **duplex engine**.

free retaining wall [s.m.] A *retaining wall* which tilts slightly about its base or slides slightly, so that the movement of the top is in the neighbourhood of $\frac{1}{2}\%$ of the wall height. By this means the earth force in granular material is reduced to the fully *active earth pressure*. This value is one half to one third of the *earth pressure at rest* which occurs at a sub-basement or other fixed retaining wall. *See* **creep**.

free vibration [stru.] The vibration which occurs at the *natural frequency* of a structure when it has been displaced, released, and allowed to vibrate freely. In structures this can occur under wind load but is relatively unimportant. *Forced vibration*, however, must sometimes be considered.

free water [s.m.] or **gravity water** American terms for *held water*.

freeway In USA a road for fast through traffic to which abutting owners have no automatic right of access. *See* **parkway**.

freezing For shaft sinking in fine-grained, waterlogged soil, where ordinary excavation and the *grouting method of*

119

shaft sinking are found impracticable, freezing is one way of making strong dry walls within which the ground can safely be excavated in the dry. A ring of cased holes is sunk to the foot of the waterlogged soil, a second tube inserted in each hole, and cold brine circulated at a temperature of about −18°C until the permanent shaft lining is built. This method has been used for shaft sinking in European collieries since the first shaft was sunk by freezing in South Wales in 1862. It was also used for sinking escalator shafts to the Moscow Metro. From 10 to 24 months are needed for drilling and forming the ice wall round the shaft, and the lowest temperature achievable by these methods is −35°C. *Liquid nitrogen* boils at −196°C but is more expensive since it does not re-circulate. *See* **Dehottay process.**

French chalk [d.o.] Finely ground talc.

French drain *Field drains* with the pipe surrounded by filter material like gravel, preferably by a *graded filter*.

French truss A *Fink truss.*

frequency [stat.] The number of observations having a value between two specified limits.

frequency curve [stat.] or **distribution curve** A curve representing ideally the form to which the frequency distribution tends as more and more observations are obtained. *See* **Gaussian curve.**

frequency diagram [stat.] or **histogram** A diagram which shows a *frequency distribution* and is so drawn that the areas under the curve correspond to the frequency.

frequency distribution [stat.] The relation which exists between the magnitude of an observed variable characteristic and the frequency of its occurrence. This can be expressed in tabular form by grouping the observed data according to the magnitude of the variable characteristic and it can be represented either graphically as a *frequency diagram* or *frequency curve* or mathematically as an equation.

fretting or **ravelling** The breaking away of aggregate from a road surface. *See* **scabbing.**

friction [mech.] A force which always opposes motion. *See* **angle of internal friction, coefficient of friction, rolling resistance.**

frictional soil [s.m.] A clean silt or sand or gravel, that is a soil whose shearing strength is mainly decided by the friction between particles. In *Coulomb's equation* its shear strength is given by the statement $S = P \tan \Phi$, since it has no *cohesion. See* **classification of soils.**

friction head [hyd.] The energy lost by friction in a pipe, sometimes considered to include eddy losses at bends and elsewhere.

friction pile [stru.] A *bearing pile* supported wholly by friction with the earth surrounding it. It carries no load at its point, unlike an *end-bearing pile.*

fringe water [s.m.] American term for *held water* just above the water table, which may or may not be permanently held.

frog [rly] or **crossings** or **cross frogs** A piece of rail at intersections, containing V-shaped grooves for the wheel flanges. It is made of a single casting, often of *manganese steel* to reduce wear.

frog rammer or **trench compactor** A man-handled compacting tool, weighing about 500 kg, which lifts itself by the internal combustion of a Diesel or petrol engine. *See* **power rammer.**

front-end equipment [mech.] All attachments to a crane to make of it an *excavator* or *crane*, including the jib and its fittings.

frost Weather during which dew is deposited as ice. The danger to construction caused by frost is that water expands by about 9% of its volume when it freezes. Therefore concrete or mortar which have not set and contain free water are disintegrated by it. Some wet bricks will chip and lose their arrises in hard frost. If a concrete or mortar has begun to set it will generally continue to set without freezing, because of the heat generated by the action of setting. New concrete or brickwork should be covered by at least a tarpaulin in frosty weather.

frost boil The softness of a soil which has thawed after *frost heave*.

frost heave [s.m.] Swelling of soil due to the expansion of water in *frost*, usually upwards. The ice in freezing expands, forces the soil particles apart, increases the void space, and draws more water up from below if the capillary spaces are small enough and the water near enough. In this way layers of ice parallel to the ground surface can be formed in some silts, never in clean, coarse sands, not in clays nor gravels. Soils with less than 1% of grains smaller than 0·02 mm never form cumulative ice layers in this way. For this reason silts are the soils most likely to suffer from frost heave or *frost boil*.

Froude number [hyd.] In an *open channel*, a ratio which should be the same for the *model analysis* as in the full-size project. It is the velocity squared divided by depth times the acceleration of gravity. *See* **Reynolds number**.

frozen ground [min.] *See* **freezing, frost, permafrost**.

fullering [mech.] *Caulking* riveted joints such as boiler plates to make them steam-tight.

fuller's earth [s.m.] A clay composed, like *bentonite*, of montmorillonite, originally used for fulling, that is

absorbing the fats from wool. It is used in paints as an extender, for its *thixotropy*.

full-tide cofferdam or **whole-tide cofferdam** A cofferdam, usually in an estuary, built high enough to keep out the water at all tides. *See* **half-tide cofferdam**.

fully-divided scale [d.o.] A *scale* in which the main divisions are fully subdivided for its full length. *Compare* **open-divided scale**.

fully-fixed [stru.] A description of an end of a member in a structural frame which is a *fixed end*. *Compare* **partially fixed**.

funicular railway An *aerial ropeway* for carrying passengers.

fuse [min.] *See* **detonating fuse, safety fuse**.

fusible plug [mech.] A plug of low-melting-point metal screwed into the part of a boiler just above the furnace, under the water. If the water level drops below the fusible plug, this will melt, steam will blow down into the fire and put the fire out. A similar plug is used in *sprinklers* (*B*).

fusion welding [mech.] The *welding* of metals or plastics by any method which involves melting of the edges of the parts to be joined without pressure. Usually a *filler rod* provides the weld metal. *Thermit, arc, resistance* and *gas welding* are the main fusion welding methods, but *pressure* and *forge welding* are forms of *plastic welding*. *Braze welding* is also excluded.

G

gabion Originally a cylindrical bottom-less wicker basket about 0·6 m dia. placed on the edge of a trench to protect soldiers from rifle fire. It stood, with others, in a row and was filled with earth dug from the trench. It now means a small *cellular coffer-dam* or wire basket to hold soil or rocks. *See* **continuous gabion.**

gad or moil A short pointed steel bar or wedge for wedging out coal in mining or breaking ore in sampling or stone along a line in *broaching*. The Ameri-can bull point is generally longer, about 0·3 to 0·45 m in all.

gage [mech.] The normal American spelling of *gauge*.

gale [stru.] A wind of 75 kph (at 9 m above ground). Blowing steadily on a vertical face, a gale exerts a pressure of about 0·4 kN/m².

gallery [min.] A mine roadway or a tunnel for collecting water in rock or in a concrete dam.

gallium aluminium arsenide [sur.] A substance that forms the essence of the solid-state laser diode. It can produce very short powerful pulses of infra-red (invisible) light and is used in most modern commercial *ED Ms*.

gallon The British Imperial gallon con-tains 4·55 litres of water; one American gallon contains 3·79 litres of water, *but see* p. 9 (conversion factors).

galvanize To dip into molten zinc (hot-dip galvanizing) or to coat with zinc electrolytically. Not all zinc coatings are galvanized (*see* (*B*) *sherardizing* or *metal coating*). *See* **dry galvanizing, sacrificial protection, wet galvanizing.**

galvanized iron [mech.] Not usually iron but steel or steel sheet coated with zinc.

gamma radiography A *non-destructive* method of concrete testing.

ganat, ghanat *See* khanat.

gang (1) A group of workmen, particu-larly of labourers or skilled labourers like *navvies* or concretors.

(2) [mech.] A prefix which indicates that several similar machines operate simultaneously and automatically. A *gang-saw* (*B*) has several saws, a gang-drill several drills, a gang-mortise several mortising machines. *See* **gang mould.**

ganger The man in charge of a group of concretors, *navvies*, or other labourers or skilled labourers (not tradesmen). He may be a working ganger who stays and works with one gang, or a travelling or *walking ganger* who supervises several gangs.

gang mould A mould for casting simul-taneously several similar concrete units. *See* **gang.**

gantry (1) A temporary staging for carry-ing heavy loads such as earth or stones, usually built of square timbers or steel joists.

(2) Permanent gantries also exist and are usually called crane gantries, since they carry the rails for an *over-head travelling crane*.

gantry crane [mech.] A *portal crane*.

gap-graded aggregate *Aggregate* with which an attempt has been made to form a dense concrete by adding a proportion of sand or grit or stone rather than by continuous grading, which implies materials of all sizes in roughly uniform proportions. Excel-lent dense concrete can be made by both methods, but gap grading is usually easier in practice, since two sizes of aggregate are more easily found than a large number. *See* **grad-ing** (3).

garland drain or water ring A gutter cut into the side of a mine shaft, often of cast iron, to catch the shaft water and lead it away to a sump for pumping. In civil engineering excavations gar-lands have been installed on the face of a cut to prevent water reaching the *formation* and softening it.

gas carburizing [mech.] *Carburizing* steel by heating it in a current of gas containing carbon, for instance carbon monoxide, or hydrocarbon gases.

gas concrete *Aerated concrete*.

gas engine [mech.] An internal-combustion engine which uses as fuel a gas such as *blast-furnace/natural gas* or town gas.

gasket [mech.] (1) A sheet of asbestos, often lined with copper sheet on each face, for making gas-tight joints between the cylinder head of an engine and the cylinder block.

(2) Jointing material for pumps, used in the same way as (1) above. It usually consists of sheet rubber.

(3) Material, such as cotton rope soaked in graphite grease, for packing the *stuffing boxes* of pumps.

(4) *See* **drain pipes**.

gas metal-arc or **GMA** or **gas-shielded metal-arc welding** *MIG welding*.

gas tungsten arc or **GTA welding** US terms for *TIG welding*.

gas welding [mech.] Welding of metals (or plastics) by the oxy-hydrogen, oxy-coal gas, or oxy-acetylene flame, generally the last. *See* **autogenous welding, bronze welding**.

gate [hyd.] A barrier across a water-channel which can be removed so as to regulate the flow of water. *See* **crest gate**.

gate chamber [hyd.] or **camber** A recess in a lock wall to take a *ship caisson* or other lock gate when the lock is open.

gate valve [hyd.] A *stop valve* which closes the flow in a pipe by a plate at right angles to the flow. The plate slides in its own plane and beds on a seating round the bore of the pipe when it is closed. When open it offers less resistance to the flow of fluid than any other valve type, since the full bore of the pipe is available for flow.

gauge (USA gage) (1) [mech.] *See* **Standard Wire Gauge** (*B*).

(2) [rly] The distance, normally

1·435 m (standard gauge), between the inner faces of the rails of railway track.

(3) [hyd.] A water-level measuring device which may be an elaborate recording instrument or merely a stick with metres of depth painted on it.

(4) [mech.] An instrument which indicates fluid pressures by a needle moving over a graduated face. *See* **Bourdon pressure gauge**.

(5) [mech.] A *dial gauge*.

gauge length [mech.] The length under test in metal test pieces, on which the percentage *elongation* is calculated. It is frequently 200 mm, and must be marked off before testing.

gauging station [hyd.] A point in a stream channel fitted with a *gauge* and means of measuring the flow, from which continuous records of discharge may be kept.

Gaussian curve [stat.] or **normal curve** A particular type of *frequency curve* with a known equation. It fits a large number of those *frequency distributions* which most often occur.

gelatine explosives [min.] Explosives which have a jelly-like texture but contain no gelatine. All contain *nitroglycerin*, some contain ammonium nitrate. They can be used in wet boreholes but must be treated with great care when they are frozen as they are then liable to detonate if dropped or broken.

general contractor *See* **main contractor** (*B*).

generator [elec.] A machine turned by a *prime mover* such as a steam turbine, steam engine, or Diesel engine. It generates electric power either as alternating current (an alternator) or as direct current (a dynamo).

geodesy *Geodetic surveying*.

geodetic construction [stru.] *Stressed-skin construction*.

geodetic surveying [sur.] or **geodesy** Surveying areas of the earth which are so large that their curvature must be allowed for in calculations. This is specialized work which rarely concerns civil engineers. *Compare* **plane surveying.**

Geodimeter [sur.] An *electronic length-measuring instrument* that uses visible light for measuring the distance between two survey stations. The accuracy is high, about ± 6 mm ± 1 part per million.

geological map A map showing either the *outcrops* of all *formations* or igneous rocks, or only the outcrops of the *solid* with the overlying *drift* removed. Maps of Britain exist on the scale of 1 in. to 1 mile (1:63 360), many have been published, and all can be inspected at the Institute of Geological Sciences, London.

geometric similarity A *dimensional analysis*, if it shows that corresponding dimensions in model and prototype are to the same scale, indicates their geometrical similarity.

geomorphology The study of the surface of the earth and its relation to the geology of the soils and rocks beneath. Geomorphology explains, among other things, how rockfalls, landslips, flow slides, etc., occur or can be forecast, or whether a river is likely to flood and change its course. It is of great interest to the builder of a road, railway, pipeline, dam or canal, who must make sure that his digging will not make the ground unstable.

geophone or **seismometer** A *geophysical* listening instrument planted in the ground or in water to detect the arrival times of sound waves (shocks) in *seismic* surveys. These instruments were used in Japan from A.D. 136 onwards to detect earthquake shocks.

geophysical prospecting, geophysical exploration, geophysical surveying, applied geophysics Searching usually for mineral deposits by making geophysical surveys, i.e. mapping variations in the earth's elastic properties (*seismic* surveys) or gravitational field or magnetic fields. Temperature surveys reveal salt domes that might contain oil. The *resistivity* method has been used in civil engineering to locate bedrock, the thickness of gravel overlying the London clay, the position of old mine workings, etc. *Well logging* makes use of many geophysical methods, but many other methods do not use boreholes at all, e.g. *seismic prospecting*, apart from a small shot hole.

geophysics The study of the earth. It uses information from geodesy, meteorology, oceanography, geography, electromagnetism, the tides, and so on. *See* **geophysical prospecting.**

geotechnical processes [s.m.] *Ground engineering*.

giant [min.] or **monitor** A nozzle for projecting water at (and thus breaking up and washing downhill) sand or gravel. Supply pipe diameters vary from 18 to 45 cm, heads from 30 to 120 m, nozzle diameters from 5 to 25 cm, discharges from 0·04 to 2 cumecs. For all but the very smallest giants, a mechanism called a deflector is needed for turning the jet.

gin pole *See* **derrick** (1).

girder [stru.] A large beam, originally of wood or iron, now usually of steel or concrete, though *light alloys* have occasionally been used. Its *chords* are parallel or nearly so, unlike a *truss*. *See* **bowstring / box / compound / plate / stiffening / Warren girder.**

girder bridge (sometimes called **beam bridge**) A bridge carried by girders or large beams.

give-and-take lines [sur.] In the calculation of land areas, the straight lines used for the *equalization of boundaries*.

gland [mech.] A sleeve or washer which compresses the packing in the *stuffing box* of a pump.

gland bolt [mech.] One of two or more bolts used for tightening or slackening an unthreaded gland.

glassfibre reinforced concrete (GRC) *See* **fibre-reinforced concrete.**

global safety factor [stru.] The combined factor of safety resulting from all the partial safety factors.

goaf, gob, (in Scotland) **cundy,** (in USA) **self-fill** [r.m.] In mining, a void from which mineral has been removed, usually with *caved* roof.

go-devil A ball of sacking, paper, or other available material which is put into the pump end of the pipeline of a *concrete pump* to clean it at the end of the day's concreting. The go-devil is driven through the pipeline by compressed air. It is best to warn the men at the other end before the go-devil comes out, since otherwise they may be spattered with concrete blown out with the air.

Golden Gate Bridge Formerly the largest *suspension bridge*, built in 1937, of main span 1280 m and side spans each 343 m. During an 80 kph gale which lasted for 4 hours this bridge caused some anxiety by vibrating with a double *amplitude* of 3·4 m, 8 times per min. *See* **Tacoma Narrows Bridge, Verrazano Narrows Bridge.**

Goliath crane A heavy *portal* frame, usually of about 50 tons capacity, with a crane *crab* which travels along the beam at the top of the portal. The frame of the portal usually has 4 legs and at least 8 wheels running on 2, 4, or more rails. It is used for shop erection of heavy steel and for other heavy lifting jobs such as harbour or nuclear-power-station construction. *See* **Titan crane.**

goniometer [sur.] An angle measurer, e.g. *compass*, *sextant* or *theodolite*.

go-out [hyd.] A sluice in a tidal embankment which impounds tidal water. The water can pass out through the sluice at low tide.

Gow caisson or **Boston caisson** or **caisson pile** A device for sinking small shafts through soft clay or silt to prevent excessive loss of ground. A short cylinder of steel plate is driven into the clay which is then excavated within it until the clay in the bottom begins to *heave*. Another short cylinder of slightly smaller diameter is then driven inside the first, and so on until the shaft reaches firm ground. The shaft is then filled with concrete and the steel tubes are withdrawn as the concrete rises to their level. *See* **Chicago caisson, loss of ground, underreaming.**

grab or **grab bucket** An excavating attachment hung from a crane or *excavator*. It is a split and hinged bucket fitted with curved jaws or teeth (tines) which dig while the bucket is being dropped and move together to pick up while it is being raised. Grabs are classified according to the shape of the bucket as a mud grab, clamshell grab, dumping grab (for rehandling aggregates), whole-tine grab (for heavy digging in hard clay, dense gravel, or earth), *orange-peel grab*, and heavy-weight grab (for ore, difficult dredging, or general dredging). It is the oldest type of excavator and is superseded in most uses by the dragline, but is still used for specialized work. *See* **excavating cableway.**

grab dredger Two main types of *dredger* (*a*) the dipper dredger, which is a mere *face shovel* mounted on a barge and consequently has very limited depth of excavation, and (*b*) the grab proper, hung on ropes or chains, which therefore has unlimited depth of excavation. Grab dredgers have small output compared with *suction* or *bucket-ladder dredgers* but they can lift solids or pieces of wreckage and can work close to ships or to a dock wall and in a heavy swell of 2·5 m.

grab sampling [min.] *Random sampling* to obtain a general idea of the characteristics of a deposit or shipment when there is not enough time, labour or space to make a representative sample. The sampler takes care with each sample to have the representative proportions of coarse and fine material.

grade Term used in USA for (1) *gradient*, (2) *formation*, (3) ground level.

graded aggregate Aggregate containing selected proportions of different particle sizes, usually chosen to form a concrete or soil of maximum density, but *see* **graded sand.**

graded filter [s.m.] Layers of coarse gravel, fine gravel, coarse sand, and fine sand arranged over each other so that water flowing through one material does not carry it into the next to clog it. Graded filters are placed at the downstream toe of an earth dam to weight it, adding stability while allowing drainage, or at the bottom of an excavation which is *boiling*, or round French drains. In every case the finer material is placed on the side which the water reaches first. To ensure that one layer of the filter will not clog the next, Terzaghi devised the following rule: the grading curve of each layer must be plotted. The grain sizes corresponding to 15% of the total of each layer, their D_{15} sizes (*see* **effective size**) are read off. If the D_{85} size of the finer soil is larger than a quarter or at least one fifth of the D_{15} size of the next coarser soil, there is no fear of the fine material clogging the coarser.

graded sand [s.m.] A sand which contains some coarse, fine and medium sizes, and is thus useful for concreting. It may be well or badly graded but is not a *uniform sand*. Geologists consider a graded sand to be quite different, one of uniform particle size. They think of the grading or classifying action of the river in separating the sand from the gravel or silt and describe single-sized layers as 'well graded' or 'well sorted'. *See* **classification of soils**.

grade level American term for *formation level*.

grader or **blade grader** A road-making implement from 30 to 70 hp usually self-propelled. It is provided with a blade which can be adjusted at any angle to cut or spread the soil. Sometimes the wheels also can be skewed (leaning wheel grader) to help the cut. It cannot usually cut more than 0·5 m depth at a time. It is used for levelling soil, cutting slopes of banks and ditches, and making *windrows*. *See* **autopatrol, elevating grader**.

grade separation Different levels for a road and a railway crossing each other or, on a hillside, of the two directions of a road. An underpass or an overpass are examples.

gradient (In USA **grade**) The fall or rise per unit horizontal (or slope) length of a pipe, road, railway, *flume*, etc. The slope can also be expressed as the number of degrees from the horizontal or as a percentage (USA). Some typical gradients are: locomotive haulage about $\frac{1}{2}$% in favour of the load and against the empties, belt conveyors preferably not more than 30%, never more than 45%, gold sluicing 4 to 8%. *See* **limiting gradient**, and for drainage, **self-cleansing gradient**.

gradienter [sur.] A *micrometer* fitted to the vertical circle of a theodolite or level, which allows the telescope to be moved through a known small angle. In this way the telescope can be used as a *tacheometer* without stadia hairs. It may also enable the telescope to be used as a *grading instrument*.

gradient post [rly] A short post set beside a railway at each change of gradient. It has an arm at each side on which is painted the length of track for one unit rise or fall, or some other simple indication of gradient.

gradient speed The wind speed at 600 m height above ground. It can be calculated by meteorologists from isobars. On land it has only one third of this value because of the friction from obstructions and at sea about two-thirds of it.

grading (1) Shaping the ground surface, usually by *earth-moving* plant such as *graders*.

(2) The percentage by weight of different grain sizes in a sample of soil or aggregate, expressed on a *grading curve*.

(3) The purposeful modification of the proportions of the different grain sizes in an aggregate for concrete or in a soil for an earth dam or other structure, so as to produce the densest or most stable material. *See* **gap-graded aggregate**.

grading curve [s.m.] A curve on which the grain size of a sample is plotted on a horizontal, logarithmic scale, and percentages are plotted on a vertical, arithmetic scale. Any point in the curve shows what percentage by weight of particles in the sample is smaller in size than the given point. It is therefore often called a grain-size accumulation curve. *See* **classification of soils, coefficient of uniformity, effective size, graded filter, mechanical analysis, fineness modulus.**

grading instrument [sur.] or **gradiometer** A surveying level with a telescope which can be raised or lowered to set out precisely a required gradient. *Compare* **gradienter.**

gradiometer *See* **grading instrument.**

graduation of tapes [sur.] Most accurate tapes or steel bands of 100 ft or more were graduated only at every foot. To obtain the precise length it was therefore necessary to apply a *reglette* to the foot mark nearest to the point whose distance was required. The other end of the band was set at a precise foot or read similarly with another scale.

grafting tool or **clay spade** or **graft** A narrow stiff spade for digging hard clay, often used on the London blue clay. It may be driven in by the foot or by compressed air. In the latter case it may also be called a clay digger or spader and weighs about 10 kg. *See* **rock drill** (*illus.*).

Graham's law of diffusion [min.] The rates of diffusion of different gases at the same temperature and pressure are inversely proportional to the square roots of their densities (molecular weights). *See* **diffusion.**

grain *See* **rift.**

grain-size classification [s.m.] Any *classification of soils* based on grain size. *See* **grading curve.**

granite A rock formed of relatively large, interlocking crystals (indicating that the fluid rock cooled and crystallized slowly) of *quartz*, felspars, and mica. The crystals are often half an inch in size or larger. Its *crushing strength* can reach 140 N/mm^2 (Aberdeen), which is stronger than blue bricks. Since it is not easy to achieve this strength with concretes it is conceivable that *pre-stressed* structures of the future may use granite. The relative density is from 2·4 to 2·8. It is a typical *igneous intrusion*. Its fire resistance is low.

granolithic or **grano** A *screed* of cement, sand, and granite chippings floated over concrete floors to give a smooth, hard-wearing surface about 38 mm thick. Emery or Carborundum may be incorporated in the surface to make it non-slipping. *See* **jointless flooring** (*B*).

granular stabilization [s.m.] *Soil stabilization.*

granulator A *breaker* for making small aggregate from large stone.

graph [d.o.] A line drawn, usually on squared paper, to show the variation of one quantity with another; for instance the increase of concrete strength with age or the temperature increase of the rock in a tunnel as the depth of the tunnel increases. A vertical measurement to a graph from the *origin* is an ordinate, a horizontal one an abscissa. Both are *coordinates*.

grass A *revetment* for river banks, obtainable by turfing or sowing grass seed. *See* **maritime plants.**

graticule (1) [sur.] The *reticule* of a surveying telescope.

(2) [d.o.] A squared grid.

grating A wooden *grillage* foundation. Wooden foundations must be well below the permanent water level to prevent them rotting.

gravel (1) Untreated or only slightly washed, rounded, natural building aggregate, larger than 5 mm (for concrete 10 mm).

(2) [s.m.] Granular material, smaller than 60 mm, which remains on a 2 mm square mesh.

gravel pump A *centrifugal pump* with renewable shoes on the impellers and a renewable lining, used for raising gravel loosened hydraulically. Sometimes the linings to pump and pipes are of rubber, which lasts longer than steel or iron. *See* **rubber-lined pipe.**

graving dock A *dry dock*, originally a dock where ships' bottoms were scraped and smeared with graves (the dregs of tallow).

gravitational water (1) [s.m.] Groundwater moving downwards in the unsaturated ground above the water table.

(2) *Irrigation* water that is not pumped.

gravity The force which attracts matter towards the centre of the earth and gives it its weight. The acceleration due to gravity is 9·81 m per sec. each second at sea level, but decreases slightly as the distance from the centre of the earth increases.

gravity-arch dam A dam which obtains its resistance to the thrust of water both from arch action and from its own weight. *See* **arch dam.**

gravity correction [sur.] A *tape correction* to a band standardized at one place and used at another place of different *gravity*. This correction is only made for the most exact work in which the tension to the tape is applied by weights on a cord running over a pulley.

gravity current *See* **density current.**

gravity dam A *dam* which is prevented from overturning by its weight alone. If it is high it is very heavy and expensive, therefore other types are preferred where possible. *See* **arch/gravity-arch dam, gravity retaining wall.**

gravity main The pipeline in which water flows downhill from an *impounding reservoir* to a *waterworks*. Its diameter is fixed by the designer, who calculates the friction loss of the maximum flow through it. This friction loss in metres must not exceed the difference in level between the bottom water level of the impounding reservoir and the top water level at the waterworks. *See* **break-pressure tank.**

gravity retaining wall A *retaining wall* which, like a gravity dam, is prevented from overturning by its own weight alone, not by the weight of any soil it carries. It must therefore be designed to take no tension, that is the *line of thrust* must pass through the middle third of the wall. The design is usually massive and, for deep walls, extravagant compared with reinforced-concrete walls. Gravity walls are of masonry, brick, mass concrete, or they may be *crib dams*. *See* **flexible wall·**

gravity scheme [hyd.] A water-supply scheme in which all flow (or most of it) into or out of the *impounding reservoir* is by gravity and no pumping is therefore needed.

gravity water (1) [s.m.] A term used in USA for *gravitational water*.

(2) [hyd.] A water supply from a *gravity scheme*.

GRC, GRG *See* **fibre-reinforced concrete.**

grease trap A large household *gulley* for kitchen waste fitted with a metal tray in the bottom, fixed to a handle reaching above water level. The grease carried into the gulley by the sink waste congeals and floats to the surface of the water in the trap. The rest of the waste water flows out at a low level. If the tray is pulled out and emptied daily, the drains are kept free of grease and stoppages of drains are unlikely.

Greathead shield A protection to workmen tunnelling in soft ground, first used successfully in London by Greathead in 1879, and later for driving the circular London *tube railway* tunnels. *See* **shield.**

green pellets *See* **briquette.**

gribble A crustacean *marine borer*.

grid (1) An open frame of wooden beams resting on the foreshore where a vessel can float in, moor, and be repaired lying on the grid when the tide is low.

(2) [d.o.] Any rectangular layout of straight lines, generally used in locat-

ing points on a plan. *See* **grid plan** (*B*).

(3) [stru.] In plane frames the members are simple and repetitive, therefore cheap. These properties have been copied in the space frames known as space grids or space decks, but the spans are so large that the structures are extremely expensive. Many types of grid are used as space frames. A two-way grid has two sets of trusses of the same depth throughout, intersecting each other at right angles. A three-way grid has three sets intersecting each other at 120°, forming a triangular mesh. Hexagonal meshes have also been built. *See* **double-layer grid.**

grid bearing [sur.] The angle between a line in a *grid*, generally a north–south line, and a required direction.

grillage foundation or **grillage** A *foundation* for concentrated loads such as columns, consisting usually of two layers of rolled steel joists (occasionally timbers, *see* **grating**) on top of, and at right angles to each other. The lowest layer is placed on the concrete foundation, the next laid across it. Steel joists are invariably covered with concrete as a protection from rust. By this means an intense column load can be spread over an area large enough to carry it.

grinding (1) [min.] The final size reduction of ore from about 18 mm down to about 0·06 mm (slime) depending on the size of the mineral particles to be extracted from the ore. *See* **ball mill, breaker.**

(2) [mech.] The removal of metal by a *grinder* (*B*).

grip (1) or **catch drain** or **intercepting channel** or **drain** A small channel cut into the ground on the uphill side of an excavation to lead rainwater clear of it. *See* **catchwater.**

(2) A shallow channel dug into the *verge* of a road to lead rainwater from the road to the ditch or drain.

(3) *See* **bond** *and below.*

grip length [stru.] or **bond length** The length of straight reinforcing bar, ex-

pressed in bar diameters, required to anchor the bar in concrete. For round bars it is taken in Britain as equal to the stress in the bar divided by four times the permissible *bond stress. See* **transmission length.**

grit blasting [mech.] *Sand blasting* with grit.

grit chamber [sewage] A *detritus tank*.

gritter (1) A towed or self-propelled implement which spreads chippings over the surface of a road in *surface dressing*.

(2) or **winter gritter** A similar machine for spreading chippings, grit, or salt over a frosty road.

gritting *Blinding* on a road surface.

gritting material Small chips for *surface dressing* or for making a temporary non-skid layer on a road.

groin American spelling of *groyne. See also* (*B*).

grommet or **grummet** (1) A circular washer made of hemp and red lead, inserted on to a fixing bolt on the flange of cast iron *tubbing* or tunnel lining to make it watertight. Grommets are also used for making a watertight packing between steel pipes in holes bored in rock (for cementation) and the rock itself.

(2) A coil of rope placed on top of a *dolly*.

gross duty of water [hyd.] or **diversion requirement** The irrigation water diverted to the intake of a canal system, usually expressed in depth on the irrigable area under the system (ASCE, MEP 11).

gross error [sur.] or **mistake** An error which is easily detected because it is large, in proportion to the value being measured. This error would be detected by making three measurements. Two of the measurements would show that one measurement was incorrect and could be rejected. The value used would then be the average of the two more accurate measurements.

gross loading intensity [stru.] The total load per unit area at the base of a foundation. In order to calculate the likely *settlement* of a structure the *net loading intensity* has to be calculated. This is the gross loading intensity less the pressure of the earth that has been removed from the dig. It is possible for the net loading intensity to be less than the gross, in which case there will be no settlement. The earth removed is then heavier than the structure put in its place. *See* BSCP 2004.

gross ton *See* **long ton.**

ground anchor A *roof bolt* or *tension pile* used as an *anchorage* to support a *sheet-pile wall*, *diaphragm wall* or merely the vertical face of an excavation.

ground bashing [s.m.] *Dynamic consolidation.*

ground beam [stru.] A reinforced-concrete beam at or near ground level which acts as a foundation for the walls or floors of the superstructure. It may span between foundation piers or piles or be itself a *strip foundation*.

ground control [sur.] In *photogrammetry*, the marking of points on the ground so that they can be recognized in the photograph. In addition some surveying work must be done to verify or measure the positions and altitudes of these points. *Radar* can now *fix* the aircraft position at the instant at which each photograph is taken, and this is another very important sort of ground control. *See* **stereoscopic pair.**

ground engineering or **geotechnical processes** [s.m.] Improvement of the ground from the viewpoint of the structural engineer. With *site exploration* it includes all the processes of *ground improvement*.

ground frame *See* **top frame.**

ground improvement [s.m.] *Compaction, deep blasting, dynamic consolidation, electro-osmosis, freezing, groundwater lowering, injection, sand piles, vibro-flotation*, etc.

ground prop A *puncheon* between the lowest *frame* and a foot block on the formation level of a timbered excavation. It carries the weight of the timbering.

groundwater [s.m.] Water contained in the soil or rocks below the *water table*; if this is lowered too much, the ground may settle disastrously. Venice has suffered *subsidence* at about 5 mm a year because of excessive withdrawal of sweet water from wells and fountains. To prevent subsidence and in the hope of raising the city by 30 to 50 mm yearly, ICOS proposed in 1973 to sink a *diaphragm wall* 120 m deep and 60 cm wide in the lagoon around it, inside which the water level could be raised by pumping fresh water into recharging shafts within the watertight ring. All the diaphragm wall work would be done from barges in the lagoon. Such a deep diaphragm wall has never been attempted, the previous maximum depth being about 30 m.

groundwater lowering [s.m.] Lowering the level of *groundwater* to ensure a dry excavation in sand or gravel or to enable the sides of the excavation to stand up. Groundwater lowering in this sense is always carried out from outside the excavation either by *wellpoints*, or from *filter wells*. Filter wells have the advantage for deep lowering that the pump can be submerged in the bottom of the well. There is therefore no limit to their depth. The limit to the depth of a wellpoint is about 4·5 m; for greater depths than this, two or more series of wellpoints must be installed in succession. Filter wells and wellpoints must be provided with a *graded filter* surrounding the pump suction to ensure that fine material is not removed from the ground with the water. Water cannot be lowered in soils of an *effective size* below 0·05 mm although wellpoints may still be used in such soil in the so-called vacuum method. In this method although the water level is lowered not at all or very little, the strength of the silt is greatly increased; the increase

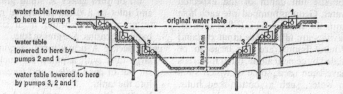

Groundwater lowering by wellpoints in series for a deep excavation

in strength is proportional to the vacuum and may be about 50 kN/m². All groundwater lowering installations, except those in the purest coarse gravel, tend to remove fine material from the ground with the water they pump out. The water should therefore, before discharge from the site, be led to a tank where any soil pumped out can be seen. If soil is pumped out the ground will settle, and damage may be caused to buried cables or pipelines or drains or other structures. Such *loss of ground* can be prevented by installing properly *graded filters* at the *wellpoints* or *filter wells. See* **electro-osmosis.**

grout [s.m.] (1) To fill with grout. *See* **artificial cementing.**

(2) Fluid or semi-fluid cement *slurry* or a slurry made with other materials for pouring into the joints of brickwork or masonry or for injection into the ground or prestressing ducts. Grouting of ducts improves the bond and may reduce corrosion of the tendons but it prevents their inspection and re-tensioning or renewal and so is opposed by BS 4975:1973. Grouts injected for *ground improvement* can include slurries of cement alone or with sand or *fly-ash* or clay or alum, or bentonite alone or with silicate; the *Joosten process* and other two-shot processes are effective and include epoxy resin or polyester resin injections, acrylamides, chrome lignin (calcium lignosulphonate with sodium dichromate), urea formaldehyde, resorcinol formaldehyde, etc. *Ordinary Portland* cement particles are often as large as 100 microns, limiting its use to grouts for coarse sands and fine gravels. *High-early-strength* cements have particles up to about 20 microns so can be used for grouting finer soils. *Bentonites* are also fine, usually smaller than 10 microns. The main division of grouts is into two types: (*a*) particulates, of cement, fly-ash, bentonite, etc., ordinarily injected first to close the coarse gaps; (*b*) chemical grouts, very much finer, injected last, to close the finest gaps.

grout box A conical *expanded-metal* box, cast into concrete, with an anchor plate at the foot (the narrow end of the cone) through which an *anchor bolt* passes.

grout curtain A row of holes drilled downwards under the *cut-off wall* beneath a dam. The holes are drilled vertically down, also upstream and downstream, and are filled with grout at one pressure. They are then drilled out and filled at a higher pressure and so on until the engineer is satisfied that the fissures in the rocks are all filled or that the rock can take no higher pressure without danger of breaking up.

grouted concrete [stru.] *See* **Colcrete.**

grouted macadam A road built with coarse aggregate in which the voids are filled by pouring in bituminous grout or cement grout. *See* **Colcrete.**

grouting machine, grout pan A *boojee pump.*

grouting method of shaft sinking [min.] or **cementation** In fissured water-bearing rock a ring of holes is drilled parallel to the shaft and just outside it for the full depth of the expected water. Grout is pumped into each hole until the engineer is satisfied that the cavities are filled. (*See* grout curtain.) Where fissures are too large to be sealed by cement alone, other materials have been used, some of which swell in water, such as cotton-seed hulls, chopped straw, *bentonite* clay, sawdust, or *bituminous emulsion*.

groutnick *See* joggle.

groyne (or jetty or groin in USA) A wall built out from a river bank or seashore to check or increase scour as appropriate. It may be built of piling, fascines, stone, etc. *See* spur.

grub axe A tool with an adze-like blade for pulling up roots and an axe blade at the other end of the head.

grubbing *See* clearing.

grummet *A grommet.*

guard lock [hyd.] A lock which separates a *dock* from tidal water.

guard post A *bollard*.

guard rail A *check rail* or a handrail.

guide frame *See* frame.

guide pile In an excavation supported by sheet piles, a heavy vertical square timber which is driven close to them and carries the horizontal members (walings) which first guide, and later support the sheet piles. It is strutted to a similar timber on the far side of the dig or to a *dumpling* or to a raking shore. It carries the full *earth pressure* from the walings.

guide rail [rly] A *check rail*.

guide runner A *runner* driven ahead of others to guide them.

gullet A narrow trench dug to formation level in an earth or rock cutting, wide enough to take a track for the wagons which remove the soil. The trench is widened as convenient to the full width.

gulley or gully (1) A pit in the gutter by the side of a road. It is covered with a grating and water drains away from it through a trap, but silt can collect in the pit. The silt is periodically removed by a *gulley sucker*.

(2) or yard gulley A small grating and inlet to a drain to receive rainwater and waste water from sinks, baths, or basins. *See* grease trap.

gulley sucker A heavy lorry carrying a large tank with a pump for sucking silt out of road *gulleys* and forcing it into the tank.

gulley trap [sewage] or yard trap A water seal provided in all gulleys to keep foul gases in the drains. It may get unsealed in very hot weather if the water evaporates. The remedy is to pour water into it.

gully *See* gulley.

guncotton *Nitrocellulose.*

gunite (Shotcrete in USA) or sprayed concrete A cement-sand mortar, thrown on to formwork or walls or rock by a compressed-air ejector, which forms a very dense, high-strength concrete. It is used for repairing reinforced concrete, for making the circular walls of *preload* tanks, the wearing surfaces of coal bunkers, for covering the walls of mine airways or water tunnels and so on. An interesting development since the late 1950s, mainly in Austrian hydroelectric tunnels, has been the application of accelerated mixes in thicknesses of several centimetres at one pass, containing gravel up to 30 mm max. size. This technique enables a thick lining to be placed quickly, giving immediate support to the rock (sometimes setting in as little as 15 minutes) and enabling men to work safely in very large openings with no props to obstruct mechanical plant. It has on occasion eliminated the need for *pilot tunnels*, e.g. the tunnels in the Italian motorway from Milan to Rome about 24 m diameter were driven in this way in about 1960. *See* pneumatic mortar.

gunmetal [mech.] An alloy of copper, tin, lead, and zinc.

Gunter's chain [sur.] A surveyor's 66-ft chain for land measurement in Britain. One chain is one tenth of a furlong and 10 sq. chains (4840 sq. yd) are one acre.

gusset [stru.] or gusset plate A piece of steel plate, usually roughly rectangular or triangular, which connects the members of a *truss*.

gusset plate See gusset.

GUTS [stru.] Guaranteed Ultimate Tensile Strength of a tendon, the strength of the weakest tendon, therefore a value below which none of the tensile tests fall.

gutter [hyd.] (1) A paved channel beside a street, to lead rainwater away.

(2) A trench beside a canal, lined with *clay puddle*.

guy or guy rope A rope which stays a mast, *shear legs*, *derrick*, or other temporary structure.

guy derrick or guyed derrick See derrick (3).

guyed-mast See derrick (1).

gyratory breaker [min.] or gyratory crusher A fixed, crushing surface of the shape of a hollow erect cone, within which a solid erect cone gyrates on an eccentric bearing. This is a very widely used machine, for the first breaking of mineral or stone (*primary breaking*). It has a reduction ratio of about 6 and breaks down to a size of about 50 mm like the *jaw breaker*.

H

half-hour rating [elec.] *See* **rating**.

half-joist [stru.] A joist cut in two along the web, to form a T-section often used in welded steelwork. *See also* **castellated beam**.

half-lattice girder [stru.] A *Warren girder*.

half-silvered mirror [sur.] A mirror of which half the area is silvered, the other half clear. It can bring a mirror image into line with a direct image so is very conveniently used in many instruments, modern or ancient, including the *optical square*, *sextant*, *prismatic coincidence bubble*, etc.

half-sized aggregate *See* **single-sized aggregate**.

half-socket pipe A *subsoil drain* socketed in the lower half only. If of concrete, the upper half of the barrel may be made porous and the lower half impervious.

half-tide cofferdam A cofferdam in the sea or an estuary which is not built high enough to exclude the water at high tide and therefore needs dewatering after every full tide. *See* **full-tide cofferdam**.

half-track tractor A *tractor* with wheels in front and *crawler tracks* in the rear.

Hallinger shield A Hungarian *shield*, successfully used in tunnelling under the Danube, also at Dortmund, Germany, in very soft ground. It is provided with a mechanical excavator and no timbering is therefore needed to protect the miners. *See* **rotary excavator**.

hammer *See* **pile hammer, water hammer,** *also* (*B*).

hammer drill [min.] The usual compressed-air-operated rock drill which has superseded the piston drill.

hand boring [s.m.] Holes can be drilled in earth by *shell and auger* from 4 to 60 cm dia., single handed or by as many as three men with a derrick.

hand distributor A *hand sprayer*.

hand finisher A tool such as a *screed* rail for forming a surface of compacted concrete to the right level and shape. It may carry a *vibrator*.

hand lead [sur.] or **sounding lead** A lead weight for attaching to a *lead line* of 100 fathoms or less in *hydrography*.

hand level [sur.] A hand-held instrument such as the *Abney level* having a spirit level which provides a level line of sight. Contours can be made with these instruments at distances of up to 120 m from a point of known level.

handling plant [mech.] *See* **materials handling**.

hand rammer *See* **punner**.

hand sprayer or **hand distributor** A hand-directed spray for spreading road binder, in which the pressure is developed by hand pump or power-operated pump. *See* **spray lance**.

hanging leaders A steel frame hung from a pivot at the top of a crane or excavator jib. It is used to guide a *driven pile* on its downward path. Unlike *false leaders* the steam hammer or *drop hammer* is carried by the crane rope. Hanging leaders do not rest on the ground but are anchored back to the crane by a strut at the foot of the jib. *See* **leaders**.

harbour An area of sheltered water where ships can lie and, in some harbours, load or unload. It may be natural or artificially sheltered (by breakwaters). *See* **harbour of refuge**.

harbour models [hyd.] Before building a harbour a scale model of the harbour is built, to such a scale that waves of measurable height can be generated. Harbour models are built to horizontal scales from 1 in 50 to 1 in 180, with a vertical scale that may be 5 times as large, resulting in waves outside, of about 18 mm height. The height of the waves in the model generally gives to scale an accurate measure of those at the harbour. Models are also used for solving problems of silting and scour. Harbour designs are frequently modified by the information given in the *model analysis*. Their main drawback is the difficulty in obtaining any true information about *silting* or *scour*. The particle size of the *silt* in the harbour cannot be reduced to scale in the model or it would become a different material (*clay*) with different settling properties and might not settle at all.

harbour of refuge A *harbour* without loading facilities, provided at an inhospitable coastline merely to allow shipping to shelter during storms. Every harbour must serve as a harbour of refuge, so the term is applied only to those that serve no other purpose.

hardcore Hard lumps of stone, brick, furnace slag, old concrete, etc., suitable for filling soft ground in a foundation or under a road, etc.

hardenability [mech.] In *welding*, a loss of ductility between weld and parent metal, a defect which causes cracking and may bring about failure of a weld. It usually increases with the carbon content of the steel. It is the opposite of *weldability*.

hardening (1) [mech.] Steel with more than about 0·5% carbon can be hardened by rapid cooling (quenching) from about 800°C, often in water but also in oil or air. This is usually followed by *tempering*.

(2) [stru.] The expression is also used for less precisely controlled changes such as the increase in strength of an aluminium alloy or a concrete with age, or the brittleness and tensile strength acquired by steel in *cold drawing* or of copper during *cold working*.

hard facing [mech.] Welding on to steel or other metal a hard surface of *Stellite* or *tungsten carbide* to form an abrasion-resistant cutting edge to an oil-well drilling tool, excavator bucket, etc.

hardness [mech.] (1) The hardness of metals is measured by elaborate methods since hardness is related to the *tensile strength* of a metal. Metal hardness is measured by tests such as the *Brinell*, *diamond-pyramid*, or *scleroscope* hardness tests, which have been standardized to give hardness scales of several hundred numbers.

(2) The surface hardness of compacted concrete is related to the strength of the material near the surface and is measured by the *rebound hammer* or by indentation testing. The method cannot be used for concrete that is honeycombed whether unintentionally or purposely as in concrete blocks or no-fines concrete. Wet surfaces are at least 20% weaker than dry ones. Hardness testing is, however, a good measure of the uniformity of concrete pieces cast in similar conditions. *See* **non-destructive testing**.

hardpan [s.m.] (1) The lower part of the topsoil which has been cemented by iron or calcium salts leached from the upper part. *See* **B-horizon**.

(2) In USA a glacial drift cemented by the weathering of overlying rocks. It may or may not contain boulders, sand, or clay.

hard standing Any hard surface suitable for parking vehicles.

Hardy Cross method [stru.] This usually refers to the method of *moment distribution* in continuous beams described by Professor Hardy Cross in 1936. Another valuable short cut due to him is the *column analogy*. His method of successive approximations can be used also for calculating the flows in pipe networks.

hatching [d.o.] Drawing parallel lines in sections of buildings or machines to distinguish between different materials. New brickwork is usually shown in Britain by pairs of lines at 45° to the horizontal drawn across the sectioned walls.

haulage rope A *traction rope* in an *aerial ropeway* or *cableway*, etc.

hauling plant For short hauls of about 30 m or less, *dozers*, *draglines*, or similar excavators are used; for big hauls, *wheeled tractors* drawing *bowl scrapers*; for intermediate hauls, bowl scrapers pulled by *crawler tractors*. *Slackline cableways* and *hydraulicking* are used each for their special conditions. Tipping lorries are used for road transport and large towed dump wagons or smaller self-propelled *dumpers* are used for transport over the rough ground of a building site.

haunch (1) The part of an arch near the springing, roughly one quarter of the span.

(2) In USA the haunch may mean a complete half-arch from springing to crown.

(3) or **flank** The outermost strip of a road.

Hazen's law [s.m.] Since the *permeabilities* of soils vary from 10^{-7} cm/sec. for clays to 1 mm/sec. for coarse sand, it is helpful to have an approximation to the permeability based on the particle size. Hazen's law, based on the *effective size* (mm), does this. It states that the permeability is approximately equal to the D_{10} size squared in cm/sec.

head [hyd.] The potential energy per unit weight of fluid above a certain point, that is the height, usually in metres, of the free-water level above this point. Theoretically the velocity head and pressure head should also be included, but in water problems these are often small by comparison.

head bay [hyd.] The part of a canal lock upstream of the lock gates.

head board A horizontal board in the roof of a heading which touches the earth above and is carried by *head trees* at each side. *See also* (*B*).

header [mech.] Generally any conduit or pipe which distributes fluid to or extracts fluid from other conduits or pipes, for example a pipe through which a pump draws water from *well-points*, or the part of a boiler to which the boiler tubes are connected.

head gate [hyd.] The upstream gate of a lock or a conduit. *See* **tail gate**.

heading (1) Any small tunnel in construction work.

(2) In making a large tunnel a *pilot tunnel* (or heading) is sometimes first driven. Headings may be as small as 1.8×1.2 m in UK but Iranian *khanats* are only 1 m high, 0.8 m wide.

head race [hyd.] The channel bringing water to a turbine or water wheel from the *forebay*.

head tree or **side tree** A horizontal timber at each side of a rectangular heading, supporting *head boards*. The word may also mean a *head board*.

head wall A retaining wall at the end of a culvert or drain.

headwater [hyd.] The water upstream, or the source of a stream.

headway The amount of time that elapses between vehicles in the same lane on a road.

headworks [hyd.] (**intake heading** in USA) In irrigation, the structure at the head of a channel for diverting water into it.

heating value *See* **calorific value.**

heat treatment [mech.] Of steel, any heating (including controlled cooling) to change its properties. *Quenching*, blank carburizing, *tempering*, and *normalizing* are examples, some of which are also applied to metals other than steel.

heave (1) [s.m.] Rising of the floor of a deep excavation in soft silt or clay.

(2) *See below and* **frost heave.**

heaving shale [min.] When a shale at depth (and therefore dry) is penetrated by a tunnel or by an oilwell, the moisture in the air or in the mud of the *drilling fluid* enters the shale and may cause it to expand and lumps to break off. In tunnelling this is troublesome but not disastrous before the tunnel is lined. If it occurs after the lining is built much costly lining may be destroyed. One solution is to seal the shale with *gunite* as soon as it is exposed. In oilwell drilling, shales can be prevented from heaving by using special *drilling fluids* containing no water (oil-based muds) or water-based muds containing dissolved sodium silicate. Before these techniques were learnt many costly miles of well had to be abandoned.

heavy soil [s.m.] A soil which is largely clay (therefore damper than a sand and for this reason heavier).

hecto- A prefix denoting one hundred times.

heel (1) The part of the base of a dam or *retaining wall* which is on the water side of a dam or on the earth side of a retaining wall. *See* **toe**.

(2) [rly] The hinge of *points*.

heel post [hyd.] or **quoin post** The corner post of a lock gate, carried on the *hollow quoin*.

height of instrument method [sur.] The *collimation method*.

held water [s.m.] or **capillary water** (in USA **free water** or **vadose water**) Water held in the soil by surface tension above the *standing-water level* against the action of gravity. The term is sometimes, in Britain, reserved for adsorbed water which can be driven off only by baking for 24 hours at 105°C. *See* **fringe water, hygroscopic moisture, specific retention.**

helical conveyor [mech.] or **screw/worm conveyor** A conveyor for small coal, grain, and similar material which consists mainly of a horizontal shaft with helical paddles or ribbons, rotating on its centre line within a stationary tube filled with the material. It is compact and cheap but has a low capacity and a power consumption about 20 times that of a belt conveyor. It is therefore only suitable for small outputs or for condensing and expelling air from very fine material, like cement, before delivering it to a belt conveyor. In the screw-tube conveyor the helical ribbon is fixed to the tube, which itself rotates, and there is no central shaft.

helical reinforcement Steel rod reinforcement bent into a spiral curve, some-

times used as a *binder* in columns.

heliograph [sur.] An instrument for reflecting the sunlight in flashes so as to make a distant surveying station visible.

helium [min.] A gas found in some uranium minerals and used in USA for lighter-than-air craft. The richest wells are reserved for the US government. Helium is also used as a breathing atmosphere mixed with oxygen in deep diving suits or *caissons*, since it is less soluble in the blood than nitrogen, and diffuses out of the blood more quickly, being less dense. *See* **caisson disease.**

helium diving bell A *diving bell* in which the men breathe a *helium*-oxygen mixture instead of the nitrogen-oxygen mixture which is ordinary air.

helmet *See* **pile helmet.**

hemp Vegetable fibres used for making *fibre rope* or the absorbent oil-filled cores of steel ropes. Rope fibres are usually named after their place of origin. Manila is the strongest, but like sisal and cotton, is not a hemp.

herringbone drain A *chevron drain*.

high-alumina cement or **aluminous cement** or **Ciment Fondu** or **fondu** A *refractory* cement with more alumina than *Portland*. It hardens enough for normal loads in 24 hours but heats up during hardening, so it can be cast only in thin layers. Because of failures of precast concrete roof beams made with this cement, such critical uses are no longer common, but it resists acids and sulphates well and can sometimes be used below ground, particularly for temporary work. *See* **calcium aluminate.**

high-angle eyepiece [sur.] The eyepiece of a *prismatic telescope*.

high-carbon steel [mech.] *Carbon steel* containing over 0·5% of carbon and up to 1·5% C, such as spring steels which are stronger and more easily tempered but less ductile than *mild steels*. Low-carbon steel has 0·04% to 0·25% C and medium-carbon steel has 0·25% to 0·5% C. *See* **high-tensile steel.**

high-early-strength cement *Rapid-hardening cement.*

high explosive [min.] An explosive which contains at least one chemical compound which, when fired, decomposes at high speed, a process called *detonation.* Most explosives are now of this type and are thus the opposite of low explosives like black powder or liquid oxygen explosives in which at least two materials combine with a rending or heaving slow explosion, very different from the shattering detonation of high explosives.

high-pressure steam-curing *See* **autoclaving.**

high-strength friction-grip bolts Fixings for steelwork, which originated in Britain in the 1930s and were developed in N. America and reintroduced into Britain about 1950 by British manufacturers. They have superseded *turned bolts* and *rivets* for site work, though *black bolts*, which are cheaper, are also used. Friction-grip bolts are much more convenient than rivets, since one man alone can place a bolt; three are needed for riveting, and it is noisier and less reliable. These bolts fit into a clearance hole and are supplied with hard steel washers at the head and nut which also is of high-strength steel. The nut is screwed tight by one of several methods; *impact spanners* are often used, and in the *Torshear bolt* (1960) the end shears off to indicate that the right stress has been reached. Friction-grip bolts are tightened to such a shank tension that they hold the steel members purely by friction, and not in shear or bearing, since the bolt does not fill the hole. (They are not allowed to be driven.) BS 3139:1959 gives the dimensions of the bolts (from 13 to 38 mm) with their nuts and washers. BS 3294:1960 describes their use. Friction-grip bolts are made of high-tensile steel of ultimate strength above 770 N/mm^2 and 0·1% *proof stress* about 540 N/mm^2. *See* **interference-body bolt, load-indicating bolt.**

high-tensile steel Steel for bridges, buildings, and similar purposes is made in Britain with a yield point up to 350 N/mm^2 as compared with *mild* steel 230 N/mm^2. It may contain up to 0·3% C, up to 0·5% copper, and up to 1·5% manganese. *See* **high-carbon steel,** *and above.*

highway A road where traffic has the right to pass and to which owners of abutting property have access. *Compare* **freeway.**

Hiley's formula A *dynamic pile formula* for the resistance of a pile to driving. It states

$$\text{Ultimate driving resistance in tons} = \frac{Whn}{s + \dfrac{c}{2}}$$

in which W = weight of *drop hammer* in tons
h = height of free drop in centimetres
n = efficiency of the blow
s = penetration of pile per blow of hammer, cm
c = temporary elastic compression in centimetres of the soil, pile, packing, and *dolly.*

The safe load on the pile is taken as half the ultimate driving resistance. The formula is fairly reliable in sand but is not recommended for clays. Dynamic pile formulae are not recommended where avoidable. They provide information too late, while the pile is going in, not beforehand at the design stage and they are unreliable, though still occasionally used. *See* **ultimate bearing capacity of a pile.**

hindered settling [s.m.] The condition in which closely packed particles sink in a liquid. They settle more slowly than when one particle sinks freely alone and the latter is the case to which *Stokes's law* truly applies.

hinge [stru.] A point in a structure at which a member can rotate slightly, sufficiently to eliminate all bending moment in the members at the joint. *Compare* **fixed end**. *See also* (*B*).

histogram [stat.] A *frequency diagram*.

hoe scraper [min.] A bucket for a *scraper loader*, shaped like a hoe with two sides to contain the ore.

hog [stru.] or **camber** Upward bending, that is a shape which is concave below, the opposite of sag. A beam may be built with hog to counteract its sag, like all prestressed-concrete beams.

hoggin [s.m.] A well-graded gravel containing enough clay binder to be used in its natural form for making roads or paths.

hogging moment [stru.] or **negative moment** or **support moment** A *bending moment* which tends to cause *hog* such as occurs at the supports of a beam. *See* **sagging moment**.

hoist (1) [mech.] A drum driven by a prime mover or electric motor. The drum winds or unwinds a steel rope which passes over a hoisting sheave and raises or lowers the load. *See* **platform hoist**.

(2) A set of *lifting tackle*.

hoist controller [elec.] Plant which controls the speed of an electric motor for a hoist or winding engine.

holdfast A temporary anchorage for guy ropes, consisting of masonry or logs with a weight of earth or other material over it. *See* **dead man**.

holding-down bolt An *anchor bolt*.

hollow-block floor *See* **hollow-tile floor**.

hollow clay tile *See* (*B*) and **hollow-tile floor**.

hollow dam A reinforced-concrete, plain-concrete, or masonry dam in which the thrust of the water is taken on a sloping slab or vault carried by a row of regularly spaced buttresses. *See* **multiple-arch dam**.

hollow quoin [hyd.] Recessed masonry carrying the *heel post* of a lock gate in a hole drilled in its upper surface.

hollow sections [stru.] *See* **tubular sections**.

hollow tile or **pot** Concrete or burnt-clay hollow blocks. Flooring blocks in UK measure 0.3×0.3 m and are from 7·5

to 30 cm deep. Similar blocks are used for building outside walls (rendered outside, plastered inside).

hollow-tile floor or **hollow-block floor** or **pot floor** or **ribbed floor** A reinforced-concrete floor in which the load-bearing part consists of *tee-beams* reinforced with steel bars in the bottom of the span, usually bent up over the support. Between each pair of ribs with this reinforcement, a row of burnt-clay *hollow tiles* is placed, generally 0·3 m wide. These are laid on the shuttering and are later plastered. They reduce the dead load of the concrete by an amount which varies between 100 and 250 kg per sq. m according to the thickness of the pot. These floors are therefore very suitable for spans of 6 m or more, but not if many holes are to be cut through them in positions which are unknown at the design stage. *See* **plate floor**.

hollow-web girder [stru.] A *box girder*.

honeycombing Local roughness of the face of a concrete wall caused by the concrete having *segregated* so badly that there is very little sand to fill the gaps between the stones at this point. Such concrete is weak and should be cut out and rebuilt if the wall is heavily loaded.

Honigmann method of shaft sinking [min.] A method of sinking shafts in soft waterlogged ground with a *trepan* as in the *forced drop shaft* method. It differs from this method in that the full depth of the shaft is excavated before any lining is lowered. Furthermore the water level in the shaft is kept above that in the ground and liquid clay is added to it to plaster the walls and strengthen them. The earth excavated by the trepan is removed by an air-lift pump in its central shaft.

Hooghly bridge, Calcutta [stru.] *See* **cable-stayed bridge**.

Hooke's law [mech.] The deformation in an *elastic* material is proportional to the load on it. Expressed in modern terms, stress is proportional to strain, which is one basic principle of present-day engineering design. *See* **modulus of elasticity.**

hook gauge [hyd.] A pointed hook fixed to a vernier moving along a vertical graduated staff. The hook is lowered into the water and raised until the surface is just pierced. It is an accurate laboratory instrument for measuring water level, and a skilled observer can measure a change in level of one tenth of a millimetre. *See* **point gauge.**

hooping Curved reinforcement such as the steel in a circular concrete tank which resists *ring tension.*

hoop stress [stru.] or **hoop tension.** *See* **ring tension.**

hopper dredger [hyd.] A dredger which can act as its own hopper and can thus transport the mud which it picks up to dump it at the desired place.

hoppit [min.] A *kibble.*

horizon [sur.] At any point, a plane at right angles to a plumb line. *See* **artificial horizon, sensible horizon.**

horizon glass [sur.] Part of the *sextant,* a glass which is half silvered and half clear.

horizontal circle of a theodolite or transit [sur.] The circular, graduated *plate* under a *theodolite* telescope, by which horizontal angles can be accurately measured.

horizontal control [sur.] Connecting a survey with *triangulation* or *trilateration* points that are well within the accuracy needed.

horizontal curve A *curve* in plan.

horsepower [mech.] In Britain and USA originally 550 ft-lb/sec. and on the European continent 75 kg-m/sec. Since 550 ft-lb = 76 kg-m, not 75, the hp is now avoided by British engineers and for precision they prefer the kilowatt. 1 UK hp = 746 watts.

horsepower-hour [mech.] The work done when one horsepower is spent for one hour. In precise statements, kilowatt-hours are now preferred in the UK so as to avoid the confusion that is possible between continental and UK hp.

hose coupling [mech.] A joint from hose to metal pipe or to another hose.

hot-dip coating [mech.] Dipping metal parts in molten tin or zinc to give them a protective coating. *See* **galvanize.**

hot miller [mech.] A compressed-air tool with cutting wheels which mill the hot cutting edges of rock drill bits.

hot rolling [mech.] The method by which *rolled-steel sections* are made in a rolling mill, by passing hot steel bars through pairs of massive steel rolls. *See* **hot working.**

hot shortness [mech.] or **red shortness** Brittleness when working hot metal, caused in steel by a low manganese and a high sulphur content.

hot working [mech.] The shaping of metal parts by *extrusion,* smith *forging, hot rolling,* and so on at temperatures (for steel around red heat) high enough to prevent the *hardening* and brittleness which may be caused by *cold working.*

house drain A drain which takes all waste or sewage from a house, in USA also called a collection line. In Britain it extends from the house to the *water authority's* sewer.

Howe truss [stru.] A roof truss used in spans up to 24 m. As used in USA it has steel verticals and timber (or timber and steel) horizontal members and sloping members, but it may also be entirely of steel.

Hoyer method of prestressing *See* **pretensioning.**

Humber Bridge [stru.] The longest UK *suspension bridge,* due for completion in 1980, resembling the *Severn Bridge* in design, but of 1410 m span. This span would make it the world's longest except for the *Akashi-Kaikyo Bridge,* though the *Verrazano Narrows Bridge* with 12 lanes of traffic on two decks would probably be the heaviest.

humidity of air or **absolute humidity** The weight of moisture present in unit volume of air, to be contrasted with *relative humidity* which is a percentage or ratio.

humus (1) [s.m.] Dark-brown fertile material in topsoil, largely rotting vegetation, a useless foundation material.

(2) The solids that flow out in the *effluent* from *trickling filters*.

humus tank [sewage] A sedimentation tank in which the so-called *humus* from *trickling filters* settles out. Humus sludge may be de-watered and disposed of either directly or together with other sludges.

hundredweight A British unit of weight, 112 lb, 20 of which make 1 *long ton*, 2240 lb.

hurdle work or **wattle work** Osiers (*laths*) interlaced with vertical sticks to make a low fence on a river bank which encourages silting or discourages scour.

hurricane A wind of 120 kph. (*Beaufort's* number 12.)

hydration The combination of water with any substance such as lime or minerals, responsible for the alteration of minerals in weathering, the formation of *hydrated lime* (*B*), the setting of cement and so on.

hydraulic Relating to the flow of fluids, particularly water. *See* **hydraulics** *and* (*B*).

hydraulic dredger A *suction* or *suction-cutter* or *draghead dredger*.

hydraulic ejector or **elephant's trunk** or **silt ejector** A pipe for removing sand, mud, or small gravel from the *working chamber* of a *pneumatic caisson*. At the bottom end of the pipe, in the sump of the working chamber, water is injected into the pipe from a pump at the surface. This jet sucks up mud through a suction branch into the pipe. The device can pump stiff silt which will not flow through a pump. Fifteen tons of silt per hour have been removed with 8 tons of jetting water at 45 m head.

hydraulic elements [hyd.] The depth, cross-sectional area, *wetted perimeter*, velocity, and so on, of water flowing in a channel.

hydraulic elevator A *hydraulic ejector*.

hydraulic engineering [mech.] The design and manufacture of pumping plant,

reservoir valves, penstocks, pipelines, and so on.

hydraulic excavation Excavation by *giants* delivering a jet of water at high velocity against an earth or gravel bank and breaking it up. The flowing water carrying the mud and soil is led to *flumes* and from there to the embankment or treatment plant as required. The gradient for carrying fine material in a flume must be at least 2% and for coarse material 6 to 8%. *See* **hydraulic fill dam**.

hydraulic fill Embankment material carried by water in flumes or pipelines. *See* **hydraulic excavation**.

hydraulic fill dam An embankment or *dam* built up from water-borne clay, sand, and gravel carried through a pipeline or flume. The discharges from the pipe are arranged at both edges of the dam flowing inwards towards the centre. By this means the heaviest material settles near the edges and the finest, most impervious material settles at the centre, forming what amounts to a clay *cut-off wall*. The water is removed at the centre over the clay core, sometimes by a *floating pipeline*. Hydraulic fill is in suitable conditions the cheapest method of transporting fill and building dams.

hydraulic friction [hyd.] or **loss of head** The resistance to flow caused by roughness or obstructions in a pipe or channel. *See* **lost head**.

hydraulic gradient (1) [hyd.] (or **hydraulic grade line** in USA) An imaginary curve along a flowing pipeline which shows the levels to which the water could rise in open pipes leading up from it. It can be expressed as a ratio, the slope of the curve, or as a fractional drop in m per km. It is also the slope of the surface of water flowing uniformly in an open conduit.

(2) [s.m.] The difference in the water level between two points, divided by the length of the shortest soil path between them. *See* **Darcy's law**.

hydraulic jack [mech.] A ram which works

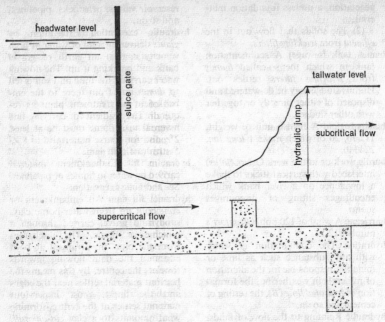

headwater level

sluice gate

tailwater level

hydraulic jump

subcritical flow

supercritical flow

Sluice gate, with supercritical and subcritical flow, and hydraulic jump

on the principle of the hydrostatic press, used in civil engineering for loading up and testing driven or bored piles or other structures or for *prestressing* concrete beams and slabs. It is generally oil-filled and loaded up by a hand pump.

hydraulic jump [hyd.] In an *open channel* of uniform slope the flow is in equilibrium at a single depth (the normal depth) at which the gravitational pull just balances the friction of the bed and walls. When, because of obstacles, a fast flow meets a slower flow downstream, there is a sudden change of depth called the hydraulic jump as the stream gradually recovers the 'normal depth'. The jump can be artificially induced in a measuring flume, or at an outlet from a sluice gate, and involves violent eddying, turbulence and loss of energy.

hydraulicking [min.] Earth-moving by

flowing water, *hydraulic excavation*.

hydraulic lift or **electro-hydraulic lift** [mech.] A lift operated by hydraulic ram. The hydraulic pressure for it is obtained from an electrically-driven pump nearby. Compared with rope-hoisted lifts, hydraulic lifts have many advantages; they need no overhead hoist and the siting of the pump and control room is not critical. They are smooth and accurate in operation, need little maintenance (no adjustment of the rope) and have no counterweights so they need a smaller lift shaft. They can be installed in an existing building without strengthening it because all the load can be carried on the ram and this takes it down to the ground through a borehole in the cellar. *See* BS 2655.

hydraulic main A pipeline which supplies water under a pressure of tens or hundreds of newtons per sq. mm to subscribers who use it for driving hydraulic cranes, lifts, presses, etc. *See* **hydraulic power.**

hydraulic mean depth [hyd.] or **hydraulic radius** The cross-section of the water flowing through a channel divided by the *wetted perimeter* of the channel. The greatest hydraulic radius gives the largest flow for a given channel and slope.

hydraulic pile driving A method of driving *sheet piles* silently by hydraulic force. A driving head is clamped on to a group of about seven piles; while the jack forces each pile down it reacts against the other six.

hydraulic power Hydraulic power has many advantages for the driving of machines but is not often nowadays taken from a *hydraulic main*. Anywhere in an industrialized country it can be generated by a simple electric motor driving a hydraulic pump. This combination is made use of for electro-*hydraulic lifts*, for driving rock drills that are appreciably quieter than those driven by compressed air, and for other purposes.

hydraulic press [mech.] *See* **hydrostatic press.**

hydraulic radius *Hydraulic mean depth.*

hydraulic ram [mech.] (1) The *ram* or plunger in a *hydraulic press*.

(2) An automatic pump, usually placed beside a stream. It uses the energy of the stream to pump some of the water to a considerable height. The stream is diverted into a pipe, its flow is checked at intervals by a valve and the resulting increased pressure in the pipe drives the water to the required level up a branch-pipe. *See* **water hammer.**

hydraulics The study of the flow of fluids. In civil engineering this concerns mainly the flow of water, that is rivers, water supply, dam building, irrigation, and drainage; and in mining the flow of viscous *drilling fluids*, ore pulps, and *hydraulic filling*. *Compare* **hydrostatics.**

hydraulic tensor [rly] A *tensor.*

hydraulic test (1) [mech.] A test for pipes, boilers, pressure vessels, etc., which are filled with water to the design pressure or slightly above it.

(2) or **water test** A test for new *drains*. They are stopped at the lower end and filled with water for an hour to a maximum head of 2 m. If no fall of level occurs during the hour the drain is accepted. The test is a severe one. *Compare* **rocket tester** (*B*).

Hydrodist [sur.] A land-based *EDM* instrument that works with a ship at sea, made by Tellurometer Ltd from 1959 onwards. It helped the location of the boreholes in the Channel tunnel survey in the early 1960s but has been superseded.

hydrodynamics The branch of *hydraulics* which deals with flow over weirs, through openings and pipes and channels.

hydroelectric power station A power station at which electricity is generated by the energy of falling water, causing turbines to turn and drive generators. If a hydroelectric power station with its associated dams and canals may be considered to be one structure, the biggest excavations in existence are Kuibyshev power station (USSR) which required 165 million cu. m and Stalingrad power station, 90 million cu. m. *See* **hydraulic fill dam.**

hydroelectric scheme A project or completed structure for generating water power, including the building of a dam, the diversion tunnels or channels, spillways, power station, intake structures, penstocks, and any roads, bridges, houses, irrigation works, villages, and cement works which may be required.

hydrofracture [s.m.] Breakage or disturbance of ground, near an injection point, by a grouting pressure that exceeds the *overburden pressure* and consequently can lift individual rock masses. It may sometimes purposely be used to increase the permeability of the ground. *See* **artificial cementing.**

hydrogeology *Hydrology*, but with emphasis on geology, chemistry and water exploration.

hydrograph [hyd.] A graph showing, against time as abscissa, the level or flow rate or velocity of water in a channel, indispensable for the planning of a water supply or hydroelectric or drainage scheme. *See* **unit hydrograph.**

hydrographer [hyd.] A person who records measurements of water level, flow, rainfall, run-off, and so on.

hydrography [sur.] or **hydrographic surveying** The surveying and mapping of waterways.

hydrological cycle, water cycle The circulation of water from hills and streams down to lakes or seas, through evaporation up into clouds, then as rain or snow on to the hills again and back to the streams. Some of the rain enters the earth as *infiltration* to recharge the groundwater that flows out elsewhere as springs, often in a stream or lake bed, or the sea.

hydrology The study of water; for civil engineers, mainly what lies on or under the earth's surface, including water discovery, storage and flow.

hydrometer An instrument which when floated in water or any fluid gives a measurement of the specific gravity of the fluid by the level on the stem to which it is submerged. It is used in the *wet analysis* of soils.

hydrometry (1) The use of *hydrometers*.
(2) The measurement and analysis of the flow of water (ASCE MEP 11).

hydrophobic cement *Water repellent cement.*

hydrostatic catenary [stru.] The curve taken by an inextensible cord which is pulled by a load proportional to the distance of the cord below its supports. It is the shape taken by a *flume* which bridges a gap.

hydrostatic excess pressure [s.m.] The pressure per unit area of soil which exists in the pore water at any time in excess of the hydrostatic pressure, due to applied loads. The hydrostatic excess pressure is equal to the *total*

pressure minus (*effective pressure* plus the *neutral pressure*). *See* **pore-water pressure.**

hydrostatic joint A spigot-and-socket joint in a large water main formed by forcing lead into the socket with a hydraulic ram.

hydrostatic press or **hydraulic press** [hyd.] A large ram whose surface is acted on by a fluid in contact with a small ram. The small ram is moved to and fro to increase the liquid pressure thus producing a large force on the large ram. The original example of this was Bramah's press (1796); modern industrial examples of it are used for many purposes, including clamping plywood during gluing.

hydrostatic pressure The pressure at any point in a liquid at rest is the hydrostatic pressure. This is equal to the depth of the liquid multiplied by its density.

hydrostatic pressure ratio In calculations of *active earth pressure*, the ratio between the pressure on a vertical plane due to the soil and that which would exist at the same point in a liquid of the same density as the soil. It is Rankine's coefficient of *active earth pressure*.

hydrostatics [hyd.] That part of *hydraulics* which concerns the pressures in fluids at rest.

hydrostatic test A *hydraulic test.*

hydro-stressor [rly] A *tensor.*

hydroxylated polymers or **polyhydroxylated po'ymers** *Admixtures* to concrete that were developed in the 1970s and are claimed to improve workability, surface finish, homogeneity, cohesion, pumpability and durability in the concrete.

hygrometer A device for estimating the *relative humidity* of the air. The commonest hygrometer is called the wet-and-dry bulb thermometer. It consists of two thermometers, the wet-bulb thermometer whose bulb is covered with a wet muslin bag dipping in water, and an identical dry-bulb thermometer beside it with no muslin bag. The temperature of the wet bulb is usually lower than the dry bulb because it is cooled by the evaporation of the water. At 100% relative humidity no evaporation is possible and this is the only occasion when the wet- and dry-bulb temperatures are the same. The humidity of the air can be determined by noting the wet- and dry-bulb temperatures and reading from a table or graph the relative or absolute humidity for any given dry-bulb temperature with the observed wet-bulb depression.

hygrometry The measurement of the *humidity* of the air.

hygroscopic coefficient [s.m.] The moisture, in percentage of its dry weight, that a dry soil will absorb in saturated air at a given temperature (ASCE MEP 11).

hygroscopic moisture [s.m.] Moisture which is contained in an air-dried soil but evaporates if the soil is dried at 105°C.

hypar or **hyperbolic paraboloid roof** A roof of unusual shape often used in recent years for building thin shells in concrete or timber. Although the surface is doubly curved, every point on it is at an intersection of two straight lines on the surface. Therefore the shuttering for it (or the timber roof itself) can be conveniently built from straight strips of wood.

hyperbaric chamber A device in which, like a *diving bell*, men can breathe under water. It was used for repairing underwater pipelines by welding, when *wet welding* was only beginning to be practicable.

hyperstatic frame *See* **redundant frame, statically-indeterminate frame.**

hypsometer [sur.] An instrument in which water is boiled and the boiling temperature is measured, either for determining the air pressure as a measure of altitude or for *calibrating* the thermometer.

hysteresis The loop formed in the stress-strain curve when a specimen is strained beyond the elastic limit in alternating cycles of tension and compression.

145

I

I [stru.] *See* **moment of inertia.**

I-beam [stru.] A rolled steel joist, generally implying one which is tall and narrow.

ice apron or **ice breaker** A ramp on the upstream side of a bridge pier which slopes up from well below water level. Ice carried down by the stream is lifted and harmlessly broken by this simple device.

idler [mech.] (1) A wheel interposed between two others in a gear train. It does not alter the relative speeds of the wheels but enables them to turn in the same direction instead of turning in opposite directions which they would do if they meshed together.

(2) A broad pulley carrying the weight of a *belt conveyor* and its load. Idler pulleys are symmetrically placed about the belt centre line in sets of three, sometimes five, at an angle to each other so as to bend the belt into a trough shape and form a troughed belt conveyor.

igneous intrusion [min.] Rock forced out molten from the centre of the earth to form thick masses or thin flat deposits (sills) covered by other rocks. They cool and crystallize relatively slowly and therefore have crystals large enough to be seen by the naked eye, unlike volcanic (extruded) rocks which have very few visible crystals. Many valuable ores are found near igneous intrusions such as *granite*.

ignition powder [mech.] A mixture usually of powdered aluminium and oxidizing material, which starts the reaction in *thermit* welding.

Imhoff tank [sewage] A deep two-storeyed tank in which sewage ferments to form *methane* and the sludge settles to be drawn off.

immersed tube or **submerged tunnel** Road tunnels under relatively narrow waterways can now be built by dredging a trench across the waterway and laying precast tunnel units in it. Concrete tunnel units weighing thousands of tons are cast in a nearby dock and made watertight by a temporary bulkhead built across each end. The dock is then flooded and the units are floated to their final destination, sunk and joined to their neighbours.

immersion vibrator *See* **internal vibrator.**

impact [stru.] The collision of bodies. From the viewpoint of the structural engineer, even the small weight of a person walking gently over a floor produces an impact effect on it which must be allowed for by adding something to the weight of the person to calculate his full effect on the floor. *See below.*

impact factor [stru.] A factor between 1 and 2 by which the weight of a moving load is multiplied to give its full effect on a bridge or floor. For a long span the factor for the same load is smaller than for a short span. The greatest impact factor for a short single-line road bridge is 1·6. For a bridge with more than one traffic line the biggest factor is 1·5. *See* **Pencoyd formula.**

impact spanner or **impact wrench** or **power wrench** A compressed-air-operated spanner which tightens *high-strength friction-grip bolts* until it reaches the correct *torque* for the nut being tightened. These impact spanners must be re-calibrated every shift and for every change of bolt diameter. A torque spanner is a hand-operated spanner for doing the same work, but for reasons of labour cost it should only be used for tightening a small number of bolts where no air supply is available. The *Torshear bolt* is tightened by a specialized impact spanner.

impact test [mech.] A test on a notched bar which is broken by a pendulum or other striker while the energy absorbed by the broken specimen is recorded. It is a measure of the brittleness of the material, in particular, its sensitivity to the *notch effect*. Common tests are the *Izod* and the *Charpy* tests.

impact wrench *See* **impact spanner.**

impeller [mech.] The rotating curved blades of a centrifugal (or rotary) pump or blower or compressor or fan.

imperfect frame [stru.] A frame which has fewer members than are needed to make it stable. Some writers also consider that a *redundant frame* is imperfect.

impermeability factor [hyd.] or **run-off coefficient,** in USA **coefficient of imperviousness** The ratio of the amount of rain which runs off a surface to that which falls on it. It is therefore a factor from which the *run-off* can be calculated. It is as follows:

watertight roof surfaces	0·70 to 0·95
cobblestones	0·40 to 0·50
macadam road	0·25 to 0·60
gravel road	0·15 to 0·30
parks	0·05 to 0·30
woodland	0·01 to 0·20

See **Lloyd Davies formula.**

impervious [s.m.] A description of relatively waterproof soils such as clays through which water percolates at about one millionth of the speed with which it passes through gravel.

imposed load [stru.] Live load.

impounding or **storage reservoir** A large reservoir in which water is stored from the wet to the dry season, as opposed to the smaller *service reservoir*.

impregnation The soaking of wood with creosote, zinc chloride, mercuric chloride, or other *preservatives*.

improved Venturi flume [hyd.] The *Parshall measuring flume*.

impulse turbine [mech.] A steam or water turbine (such as a Pelton wheel) in which the driving energy is provided by the speed of the fluid rather than by its change in pressure. *Compare* **reaction turbine.**

incinerator A furnace where rubbish is burnt.

incise To put regularly spaced shallow wounds into a log so that it can absorb preservative such as creosote. *See also* (B).

incline [rly] A length of track laid at a uniform slope.

inclined cableway A monocable *cableway* in which the track cable has a slope along its full length (about 1 in 4) steep enough to allow the carrier to run down under its own weight.

inclined gauge [hyd.] A sloping staff graduated to read vertical heights (or depths) above a certain datum.

inclinometer [sur.] A *clinometer* or *dip needle*.

indented bars Steel reinforcement for concrete, which has indentations. These indentations increase the *mechanical bond* between the steel and the concrete.

indented bolt An *anchor bolt* which consists of a plain bar with indentations forged on it to increase its grip in concrete or grout.

indenting roller or **branding iron** or **crimper** A roller with a pattern cast on its surface which it impresses into hot asphalt when pushed over it, making a non-slip texture.

index [sur.] A *plane table* alidade.

index glass [sur.] The movable reflecting glass of a *sextant*.

index of liquidity [s.m.] or **liquidity index** It is equal to the

$$\frac{\text{(water content of sample) minus}}{\text{(water content at plastic limit)}}$$
$$\text{index of plasticity.}$$

This figure is the reverse of the *consistency index* and gives a value of 100% for a clay at the *liquid limit* and 0 for a clay at the *plastic limit*.

index of plasticity [s.m.] or **plasticity index** The difference between the water contents of a clay at the *liquid* and at the *plastic limits*. It shows the range of water contents for which the clay is plastic. A clay with a high plasticity

index is said to be very plastic. *See*
toughness index.

index properties [s.m.] Those properties
which distinguish one soil from another. They are of two types, the soil
grain properties (size, shape, and
chemical constitution) and secondly
the soil aggregate properties, *dry density*, *moisture content*, and *consistency
limits*. The former refer mainly to
sands, the latter mainly to clays and
silts. *See* **classification of soils.**

industrial diamond [min.] *Black diamond*
or *bort*.

inertia (1) [stru.] The resistance to bending of a beam section, dependent on its
shape and size. *See* **moment of inertia.**

(2) [mech.] The resistance of a mass
to rotation, equal to its mass times
the distance from its centre of rotation
squared.

infiltration (1) Entry of rainwater into
the soil, as opposed to *runoff*.

(2) The entry of groundwater into
an old *sewer*, laid below the water
table, through cracks in the pipe and
loose joints, common in a wet climate.
In dry countries, sewers leak outwards
– exfiltration.

infiltration capacity [hyd.] The maximum
rate at which a soil can absorb rainfall
in a given condition. It decreases as
the rainfall continues, enabling the
clay particles to swell and block the
soil pores.

inflexion [stru.] or **inflection** *Contraflexure.*

influence line [stru.] A graph used for
examining the effects of different
loads on beams. The curve extends
the full span (or half span) of the
beam. Its ordinates show, for any
point of particular interest on the
beam, such as the support, or midspan,
either the *shears* or the *bending
moments* caused by unit load at any
position.

influent stream [hyd.] A stream that loses
water to the ground, thus recharging
the *groundwater*, unlike an *effluent
stream*.

infra-red distancer [sur.] An instrument

for *electronic distance measurement*,
built by Wild.

infra-red photography [air sur.] Photography on special film which is more
sensitive to heat radiation (infra-red
rays) than to light. It can therefore be
effectively used in misty weather
(though not in dense fog) for *photogrammetry*.

ingot [mech.] A metal bar which, if of
steel, may be up to 50 cm square in
cross-section and about 2 m long,
cast into this shape for *hot working*,
usually *cogging*. Modern steel makers
are now using continuous-casting
machines in which ingots of any
length can be cast at a speed of 300 m
per hr (for a 5×5 cm ingot, 7 tons).
Non-ferrous metals are cast into ingots
which are generally smaller. *Compare*
pig.

inherent settlement [stru.] The sinking of
a foundation due only to the loads
which it puts on the soil below it and
not to the loads on any nearby
foundations. In city sites where the
foundations are on clay, as in London,
all foundations suffer both inherent
and *interference settlement*.

initial setting time The time required
before a concrete mix can carry a
small load without sinking like a mud.
This is after about one hour in warm
weather with wet concrete. However,
with ordinary *vibrated concrete* or
vacuum concrete, no impression with
the full weight of the foot can be
made immediately after vibration or
vacuum treatment. Nevertheless such
concretes do have an initial set which
increases their strength in the same
way as that of wet concretes. They
have initially a much higher strength
due to their lower water content.

initial surface absorption test A test of
water absorption by a concrete surface, aimed at proving the quality of
concrete roofing tiles (BS 1881).

injection [min.] *See* **grout, grouting
method of shaft sinking.**

injection well [hyd.] A *disposal well* or
one for *artificial recharge*.

inlet or **street inlet** US term for a *gulley*.

innings Land regained from the sea or from a marsh.

insert A metal or precast concrete piece left in concrete after casting and used for any purpose such as carrying load or joining one part to another.

in situ *See* **cast-in-situ,** *and below.*

in-situ concrete piles Concrete *bored piles* poured in place in holes bored or driven in the ground, as opposed to precast piles which are always fixed in the ground by driving or jacking or *jetting*.

in-situ soil tests [s.m.] Tests made on soil in a borehole, tunnel, or trial pit. For example static or *dynamic penetration tests, vane tests*, field *permeability* tests made by pumping from boreholes, measurement of soil density in place, and vertical or lateral loading tests.

inspection chamber or **manhole** A shaft down to a sewer or duct arranged so that a man can enter it from the surface. In sewers less than 0·9 m dia. a manhole should be provided at every change of direction or at every 75 to 90 m on straight lengths, since this is the greatest length which can be *rodded*. For a sewer larger than 0·9 m dia., manholes may be unnecessary on long straight lengths if a man can walk through them. *Deep manholes* can be built very conveniently and quickly of precast concrete pipe (0·9 in dia.) with step irons cast in.

inspector or **inspector of works** An experienced *tradesman* (*B*), ganger, or foreman, employed under the supervision of a clerk of works or a resident engineer to report on progress and to control a contractor on a section of civil engineering work. *Compare* **building inspector** (*B*).

instrument [sur.] A measuring appliance which requires more than ordinary skill or care or instruction to be used effectively, for example a *theodolite, dumpy level, sextant*, or *planimeter*.

instrumental shaft plumbing [min.] Looking down a shaft with a *theodolite* to obtain the bearing of a point at the foot of a shaft from a *set-up* at the top of the shaft. (The set-up may be at the bottom and the point at the top.) *See* **optical plummet, shaft plumbing.**

intact clay [s.m.] A *clay* with no visible fissures. *Compare* **fissured clay.**

intake heading American term for *headworks.*

integrally-stiffened plating [stru.] Extruded aluminium sheet shaped like an L upside down (⌐) and used for decking.

integrating meter A *meter* which records the total of fluid or electricity which has passed it. It is usually simply called a meter. *See also* **flow meter.**

intensity of rainfall The rainfall in mm per unit of time.

intensity of stress [mech.] An American term for *stress*.

intercept [sur.] The length of a staff which is seen between the two *stadia hairs* of a telescope in *stadia work*.

intercepting channel or **intercepting drain** A *grip*.

intercepting drain *See* **intercepting channel.**

interception [hyd.] US term for *fly-off*.

intercooler [mech.] A device for cooling air or gas between one stage of compression and the next in a blower or compressor. Its function is similar to that of the *aftercooler*.

interface strength *See* **bond.**

interference-body bolt Bolts made by the Bethlehem Steel Co. in USA and first publicized by them in 1963, which were in their way as revolutionary as *high-strength friction-grip bolts*. Like these, they are used in a clearance hole, but unlike them they are driven in and they completely fill the hole. They thus have high bearing strength and shear strength, which are claimed to be better than those of rivets. They carry V-shaped corrugations on the unthreaded part of the shank, and these are deformed during driving.

The head is cup-shaped and cannot be turned, but this is unimportant since the shank is fully gripped by the slightly crushed corrugations pressing against the walls of the hole.

interference settlement [stru.] The sinking of a foundation due to loads on foundations near it and the natural extension of their *settlement craters* beyond their own boundaries. *Compare* **inherent settlement.**

interflow [hyd.] Flow of groundwater from one *aquifer* often at a *perched water table* to another at a lower level.

intergranular pressure [s.m.] *Effective pressure.*

interheater [mech.] A *reheater.*

interior span [stru.] A *continuous beam* or slab of which both supports are continuous with neighbouring spans. *Compare* **end span.**

interlock A *clutch* in steel-sheet piling.

interlocking piles *Steel sheet piling.* Occasionally concrete or timber piles are made with a projecting tongue, but this *clutch* is much less likely to be waterproof than with steel sheet piling.

intermediate sight [s.m.] In levelling, a staff reading which is neither a *back sight* nor a *fore sight.*

intermittent filtration [sewage] or **land treatment** The spreading of sewage effluent over land and the removal of the water by field drains. *Compare* **broad irrigation.**

internal-combustion engine [mech] An engine such as a petrol, gas, or *Diesel engine* in which the burning of a gas or vapour provides the energy which turns the wheels round. Generally the burning takes place in a cylinder in which a piston is driven down by the increased gas pressure formed by burning, but jet engines and turbo-jets have neither piston nor cylinder.

internal flow [hyd.] *See* **density current.**

internal friction [s.m.] *See* **angle of internal friction.**

internally-focusing telescope [sur.] *See* **anallatic telescope.**

internal vibrator or **immersion vibrator** or **poker vibrator** A cylinder of 3 to 8 cm dia. containing a vibrating mechanism. It is inserted into wet concrete so as to compact it. *See* **vibrator.**

interpolation Inferring the position of a point between two known points on a graph by assuming that the variation between them is smooth. Usually the assumption is that the variation is linear, a straight-line variation. *See* **extrapolate.**

intersection [sur.] A method of using the *plane table* at each end of a measured base line alternately. The points to be mapped are sighted at each *set-up* and located on the plan by the intersection of corresponding pairs of sight lines.

intersection angle [sur.] A *deflection* angle.

intersection point [sur.] The point at which two straights or tangents to a road or railway curve meet when produced. *See* **tangent distance.**

interstitial water *Groundwater.*

intrusion [hyd.] *See* **encroachment.**

intrusive rock [min.] *See* **igneous intrusion.**

invar [sur.] An alloy of one third nickel, two-thirds iron and other elements, used for making measuring *tapes* because of its very low *coefficient of expansion* which varies with different tapes and is even occasionally negative but is usually less than 0·0000014 per degree C. Invar tapes vary in length with time and therefore need fairly frequent *standardization.*

invert The lowest visible surface, the floor, of a *culvert*, *drain*, *sewer*, channel, or tunnel. *Compare* **crown.**

inverted siphon [hyd.] *See* **sag pipe.**

inverting eyepiece *See* **astronomical eyepiece.**

invert level The level of the lowest part of the invert; the level by which the elevation and slope of a drain, sewer, or channel is defined, since however much the diameter changes, the invert is usually kept smooth.

ion [elec.] That part of an electrolyte which moves to one or other *electrode* in *electrolysis*. Cations move to the cathode, anions move to the anode.

ion exchange [hyd.] Chemical exchange of a dissolved substance, usually harmful to water, for another that is less harmful. Thus the zeolites used in *base exchange* water softening take in calcium and magnesium in exchange for the sodium they give out. The sodium salts thus introduced to the water do not form curds with soap, but soften the water. Artificial resins used in ion exchange in power stations reduce the solids content of water below one part per million in *demineralized water*.

Irish bridge A paved ford, a watersplash.

iron (1) [mech.] *Pig* iron or *cast iron*.

(2) [mech.] *Wrought iron*, the purest form of iron, much purer than cast iron or steel and with none of the brittleness of cast iron. It is unfortunate that these two very different materials should be similarly named.

(3) A smoothing iron for sealing and smoothing an *asphalt* surface.

iron fighter Either a *bar bender* or a *steel erector*.

iron pan [s.m.] *Hardpan*, sometimes impervious, cemented by iron oxides.

iron paving A non-skid surface of studded cast-iron blocks.

irrigable area The amount of arable land which is low enough to be irrigated. The area includes houses, roads, and other areas never irrigated.

irrigating head (1) The flow used for irrigation of a particular tract of land.

(2) The flow of water distributed at a single irrigation or that in a single farm lateral.

(3) The flow rotated among a group of irrigators (ASCE MEP 11).

irrigation (1) [hyd.] Distribution of water to land for farming. It usually involves digging canals and building civil engineering structures such as dams or aqueducts.

(2) [sewage] The disposal of sewage by spreading it over land.

irrigation requirement [hyd.] The quantity of water, including wastes but excluding rain, that is needed to grow a crop.

isochromatic lines [stru.] In *photo-elastic* stress analysis, coloured streaks which are lines of equal difference of principal stress.

isoclinic lines [stru.] In *photo-elasticity* or other studies of stress concentration, dark lines which join all points at which the principal stresses are parallel to the planes of polarization.

isohyet [hyd.] A line joining points of equal rainfall.

isolator [elec.] or **link** A part of a circuit which can be removed from it so as to break the circuit when no current is flowing. It is usually a copper bar bolted in position.

isometric projection [d.o.] In mechanical drawing a (seemingly) perspective view of an object in which, for a cube as an example, the nearest three edges would be drawn at 120° to each other with the vertical edges vertical. All three edges would be seen, as they would not in the usual mechanical plan or elevation, which shows only two edges. The perspective is not true but the measurements along the edges are true to scale. *See* **projection.**

isostatic frame *See* **statically-determinate frame.**

isotherm A line joining places at the same temperature.

isothermal compression [mech.] Compression of air at constant temperature, a condition which is approached by using *intercoolers* between stages.

isotropic [stru.] Having the same physical properties in all directions. Metals are practically isotropic. Wood is not, being very much stronger along the grain than in either of the two directions across the grain. Some *aquifers* are isotropic. *See* **orthotropic.**

Izod test [mech.] An *impact test* in which

151

a notched bar is broken by a blow from a pendulum. The height to which the pendulum rises is recorded after the test piece is broken. From this height, and the height from which the pendulum was released, the energy absorbed in breaking the specimen can be deduced.

J

jack [mech.] A piece of equipment for raising heavy loads from below. The smallest jacks are operated by screw and called screw jacks; larger jacks work by a hydraulic ram. They are used in civil engineering for tensioning *prestressing* wires. *See* **kentledge.**

jack arch (1) (or **floor arch** in USA) A brick or concrete arch of about 1 m span springing from the bottom flange of a rolled-steel joist or rail. Jack arches were much used before reinforced concrete was developed and are still used to a limited extent in short-span bridge decks or heavy floors, but they have generally been replaced by the *filler-joist floor* in which the soffit is flat.

(2) American term for a *Welsh arch* (*B*) or *flat arch* (*B*).

jackblock method Building a multi-storey block by an idea developed from *lift-slab construction.* The first building of this type was a 17-storey block of flats for old people at Barras Heath, Coventry, completed in 1963. One real advantage of the method was that its completion was not delayed by the extremely hard frosts from January to March 1963. As in lift-slab, the floors are cast at ground level, and as soon as each floor has been cast, matured, and stressed up by its pre-stressing cables (with rapid-hardening cement, after about 4 days), it is jacked up one storey. The ground-floor slab is an exception to this rule, because it is cast first, remains in position throughout its life, and acts as casting bed for the other floors and roof. The roof slab is cast next. As soon as the roof slab has been raised one storey, the top floor is cast, its walls are built, and with the roof it is jacked up one storey. The main difference from lift-slab is that the supporting walls are built at the same time as the floors and are jacked up with them. With lift-slab, only the floors are lifted; the columns are already in place to their full height. The finishing trades work at about two storeys above ground, the wet trades at one storey below this, and the basic concreting is at ground level. The contractor claims that this converts the building site into a factory which is relatively easy to keep warm and well-organized; the work flows efficiently because the building moves upwards, like a conveyor, and completion is fast and efficient. The name originates from the precision-made precast concrete blocks, equal in height to one stroke of the jacking rams (about 20 cm) which are laid dry for the full height of the building. With their enclosing vertical strips of high-alumina cement concrete, the jackblocks form the supporting walls.

jacked pile A *pile* forced into the ground by jacking against the building above it in underpinning, usually installed in short lengths. *See* **pretesting.**

jacket A usually tubular steel structure standing on the sea bed, often with eight or four legs and containing many thousands of tons of steel, sometimes 150 m high, used for producing oil or gas from a well under the sea, and originally built in a dock on a *flotation structure*. The term was originally used in the Gulf of Mexico because each leg contained a driven pile forced into the sea bed, so that each leg was a jacket for its pile. The nodes on jackets can be very large and difficult to weld, involving junctions between 6·5 cm thick walls of tubes of 4·25 m dia.

jack roll A windlass used for hand-hoisting from pits. A bucket is hung from each end of the rope so that an empty bucket goes down as every full one comes up.

jaw breaker [min.] or **Blake breaker** or **jaw crusher** A machine for breaking ore or rock. The jaw opening in different machines varies from the laboratory size, 18×25 cm, to the mammoth size 2×3 m. Jaw breakers have roughly the same duty as *gyratory crushers*.

jet drilling [min.] An American method of rock drilling by fire (1946). Fuel is injected through a water-cooled pipe with oxygen and burnt within the hole. Drilling speeds are usually 5 m per hour but may reach 11 m. About 65 cu. m of oxygen are burnt per m of hole, the usual dia. being 18 cm. It is very suitable for quarrying. Holes can be *chambered* without explosives. *See* **fire setting, thermic boring.**

jetting A method of sinking piles (or *wellpoints*) into sands, used when a *pile hammer* is impracticable because it might damage the piles or neighbouring buildings. A concrete pile can be cast with jetting holes in it. Timber piles are driven with jetting pipes fixed to opposite sides of the piles. Considerable quantities of water with or without compressed air must be used, but the method is often effective after piles have been driven to refusal. Air alone has been used. The water jet may break up the ground so it must be used with caution (apart from the dangers of flooding). It is ineffective in clay soils.

jetty [hyd.] (1) A deck carried usually on piles at the water's edge and used as a landing stage. *See* **open jetty** (*illustration*).

(2) A *groyne* to check scour or encourage silting.

jetty cylinder *See* **screw pile.**

jib [mech.] (1) or **boom** The lifting arm of a *crane* or *derrick*. At the outer end is a pulley over which the hoisting rope passes.

(2) The arm carrying the cutting chain of a coalcutter, power-operated *chain saw*, etc.

jib crane [mech.] A crane with a jib, as opposed to *overhead travelling cranes*,

transporter cranes, etc., which usually have none.

jig [mech.] A template shaped to guide a cutting tool, such as a drill, quickly and accurately to the right places. *See* **manipulator.**

jig back [min.] (or **reversible tramway USA**) or **to-and-fro aerial ropeway** An *aerial ropeway* with one or two track cables and only one carrier on each track cable. A single traction rope is connected to both carriers which travel in opposite directions on the two track cables, reversing at the end of each run. The intermittent action limits the capacity to about 25 trips per hour or 100 tons maximum.

jiggle bars A *rumble strip*.

jim crow [rly] A hand-operated rail bender with a heavy *buttress screw thread*. *See* **railway tools** (*illustration*).

joggle (1) or **groutnick** In block work or masonry walls, a recess on one block which fits a projection on another block, or which forms, with a similar recess on the other block, a cavity into which mortar is poured, making a *cement joggle.*

(2) [mech.] The slight sharp bending of a steel angle needed to make it fit as a web *stiffener* over the angles at the top and bottom of a built-up girder and to fit tightly on to the web plate. This bend is usually made cold in a joggling press but for a heavy bar may need to be done by *forging.*

joint (1) A discontinuity in rock, where it breaks easily. *See* **rift.**

(2) In steel sheet piling, a *clutch.*

joint box [elec.] A cast-iron box which is built up around a joint formed between the end of one cable and the beginning of the next. The wire armouring or lead sheath is gripped by bolted glands outside the box. The box is often filled with insulating compound after the joint is made.

joint filler Compressible strip material used as a spacer between precast or in-situ concrete units, permitting them to expand without developing serious compressive stress in the concrete (after BS 892). Bitumen, bituminized felt, granulated cork or loose cork are used, some of them with a **sealant**.

joint-sealing material *See* **sealing compound** (*B*), **sealer** (*B*), *and above, also* **sealant**.

joist In Britain, a wood or steel or precast concrete beam directly supporting a floor, usually a wooden joist. Steel joists are usually distinguished by calling them RSJs or *rolled-steel joists*.

Joosten process [s.m.] Injection of two separate solutions through pipes driven or *jetted* into the soil. The solutions injected are calcium chloride after sodium silicate. The two solutions meet in the ground and react to form a gel which strengthens the soil and makes it watertight. The method is suitable only for sands and gravels, but in them it forms a solid cylinder of about 0·6 m dia. round each injection tube. (First used about 1920.) *See* **artificial cementing**.

joule The SI unit of work, energy, or heat. It is therefore the ideal unit for expressing the *mechanical equivalent of heat*. One joule = 1 newton-metre and 1 MJ = 1 MN-m. 1 watt-second = 1 joule and 1 MW-second = 1 megajoule.

jubilee wagon A *tipping wagon*.

jumbo [min.] A *drill carriage*.

jumper A heavy steel bar with a chisel point used for boring holes in rock or soft ground by raising it, twisting it, and dropping it repeatedly on the same point. For making horizontal holes it is usually struck with a hammer, with two men working together.

jumping up [mech.] *Upsetting*.

jump join [mech.] A forge weld made by *upsetting* the ends of two bars before welding them.

junction point [sur.] A point on a curve where the circular part joins a non-circular part, either a straight or a transition curve.

jute fibre The fibres of plants grown in India and America used for making *fibre rope*, hessian canvas, reinforcement for plaster, and so on.

K

kanat [hyd.] A *khanat*.

Kaplan turbine [hyd.] A *water turbine* of the propeller type, having blades of a pitch which can be automatically varied with the load to increase the efficiency.

kathode *See* **cathode**.

keel blocks *Docking blocks*.

kelly [min.] The topmost drilling pipe of a *rotary drilling* rig, carrying the water swivel.

kelly bar In certain piling rigs, a massive bar that guides the pile hammer.

Kennedy's critical velocity *See* **critical velocity**.

kentledge or **cantledge** Loading to give weight and thus stability to a crane, to provide a reaction over a *jack*, to push down a plate in the *plate bearing test*, or to test a caisson or a bearing pile. It may be scrap metal, large stones, tanks filled with water, or any other convenient material.

kerb (In USA **curb**) A hard stone like granite or good-quality precast concrete used for bordering a road and limiting the footway. Usually it raises the footway above the road level by about 15 cm.

kerf Any saw-cut.

kern [stru.] The *core* of a section.

key (1) *Mechanical bond* or that type of it achieved by an irregular or serrated surface in any construction joint. *See also* (*B*).

(2) [rly] A steel spring or a hardwood wedge driven between a *chair* and the rail to hold the rail firmly.

khanat [hyd.] or **kanat, ganat, ghanat, infiltration gallery**, or in Mexico, **galeria** A long, ancient tunnel or network of tunnels dug to collect groundwater, usually from alluvial deposits, certainly used 2,500 years ago in Persia, possibly 1,000 years earlier in Armenia. They are also in use in Afghanistan, Egypt, Mexico and Chile. About 25,000 are said to be in use in Iran. A khanat is an *adit* or several adits branching off each other, dug by sinking shafts from vertically above them, at a spacing of around 100 m to enable the rock to be removed from the tunnel and to provide ventilation for the tunnellers. The adits are about 1 m high and 0·8 m wide and slope at 0·5 m to 5 m per km. The shafts may serve as wells when the khanat is completed. If there is enough water it is distributed, when the adit reaches the surface, through irrigation canals to the farmers nearby.

kibble [min.] or **bowk** or **hoppit** or **sinking bucket** or **skip** A large bucket used in shaft sinking for hoisting rock, water, men, and tools. It may be from 60 to 600 litres capacity.

kicker or **starter stub** A concrete plinth at least 7 cm high above the concrete floor, forming the start of a concrete wall or column. It is accurately set and sometimes cast with the floor slab. It thus forms a strong and very convenient way of clamping the feet of the wall shutters.

kicking piece A short timber spiked to a waling to take the thrust from a raking strut.

kid [hyd.] or **faggot** A bundle of brushwood used as a *fascine*.

kidding *Faggoting*.

Kill Van Kull Bridge A steel, two-hinged trussed-arch bridge of 510 m clear span built in 1931, the longest of its type in the world. Unlike *Sydney Harbour Bridge* it was built with the help of intermediate supports.

kilo- A prefix meaning 1000 times, thus a kilogram is 1000 grams.

kilowatt hour [elec.] or **Board of Trade unit** or **kilowatt unit** or **kWh** The commercial unit of electrical energy, the unit of payment. It is equivalent

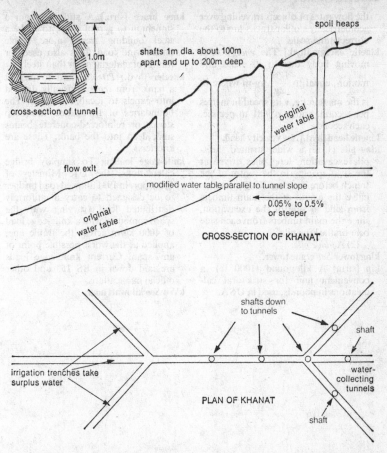

cross-section of tunnel

1.0m

shafts 1m dia. about 100m apart and up to 200m deep

spoil heaps

original water table

flow exit

modified water table parallel to tunnel slope

0.05% to 0.5% or steeper

original water table

CROSS-SECTION OF KHANAT

shafts down to tunnels

shaft

irrigation trenches take surplus water

water-collecting tunnels

PLAN OF KHANAT

shaft

The khanat is one of the most useful and ancient of man's creations. It cannot be called a structure because it is entirely dug and not built. In Iran they reach to 70 km in length

to 1·34 UK horsepower-hours.

Kind-Chaudron method of shaft sinking [min.] A method of sinking circular shafts in heavily water-bearing rock beneath an impervious stratum. It is suitable where there is too much water for pumping to be practicable. Boring is done by a massive rotary tool, the *trepan* of diameter equal to the shaft diameter. The water stands at its normal level in the shaft until sinking is completed. The shaft is then lined with cast-iron tubbing which is entirely assembled at the shaft mouth and then gradually lowered to the bottom. The shaft is not dewatered until the lining is completed.

kinematic similarity *A dimensional analysis* of a *harbour model* and prototype indicates kinematic similarity if the flow rates of objects travelling over geometrically similar tracks are to the correct time scale.

kinetic energy [hyd.] The *energy* of a moving body due to its mass and motion, equal to $\dfrac{Wv^2}{2g}$ kg-m where W is the mass in kg, v its speed in metres per second, and g is 9·81 m per sec. each second.

kinetic head [hyd.] *See* **velocity head.**

king pile (1) In a wide, strutted sheet-pile excavation, long piles driven at the strut spacing in the centre of the trench before it is dug. King piles thus halve the length of the main timbers from side to side of the excavation, since the main timbers from each side bear on the king piles.

(2) A *guide pile*.

king tower *See* **crane tower.**

kip [stru.] A kilopound (1000 lb): a convenient unit for structural calculations in pounds, used in USA.

knee brace [stru.] A stiffener from a stanchion to a roof truss, to make a steel building frame more stable under wind load. It is also used for frames of material other than steel.

kneeler [hyd.] *Pitching* laid to protect a bank from *scour* is usually divided into panels to localize damage. The boundaries of the panels are deep stones or reinforced-concrete beams sunk deep into the bank. These are kneelers.

knife-edge loading To simplify bridge calculations, the UK Ministry of Transport in 1931 allowed road bridges to be designed to carry a uniformly distributed load (varying with the span) combined with a knife-edge load of 4000 kg/m across the traffic line, applied at the worst possible point of any span. Current knife-edge loads are laid down in BS 153 and other official publications.

kWh *See* **kilowatt hour.**

L

laced column [stru.] A column built up with *lacing* from several members.

lacing (1) [stru.] Light metal members fixed diagonally to two channels or four angle sections to form a composite strut or beam (laced or lattice strut or girder). *Compare* **batten plate**.

(2) [stru.] Light wooden bars fixed diagonally to the square wooden posts at each corner of a laced timber column to make of them a single strut.

(3) [stru.] The *distribution steel* of a reinforced-concrete slab.

(4) In the timbering of excavations, a light timber spiked to pairs of walings or struts to tie them together and ensure that one cannot move relatively to the other.

ladder The mud buckets of a *bucket-ladder dredger*.

lagging [min.] Scrap wood, wire mesh, corrugated steel sheet, etc., laid over the main supports in a tunnel to prevent stones or soil falling.

laitance A scum on cement concrete or over-trowelled mortar. It is weaker than the rest of the concrete and should be cut away and covered with a pure cement wash before laying more concrete on it.

Lake Washington Bridge *See* **pontoon bridge**.

Lally column [stru.] Trade name for a hollow, *cold-rolled* steel column, sometimes filled with concrete (USA).

lamella roof [stru.] A large-span vault or dome built of concrete, wooden, or metal members joined by bolts or other means, connected in a diamond pattern. Since trusses are not used, the space below can be well lit by roof lights and has a feeling of volume. The system was patented by a German engineer in 1925. Steel lamellas can span 425 m.

laminar flow [hyd.] *Streamline flow*.

laminar velocity [hyd.] That speed in a particular channel for a certain liquid, below which *streamline flow* always occurs and above which the flow may be streamline or turbulent.

laminate *See* (*B*).

lamphole A small, vertical shaft centred over a *sewer* so that a lamp can be lowered into it on a string. If a man at a manhole then looks along the sewer towards the lamp he can see whether there is any obstruction in the flow, or damage to the sewer.

land accretion or **land reclamation** Gaining land from the sea or from a marsh. The cheapest method is by planting reeds or other *maritime plants* to encourage the deposition of silt, a method used in Holland many centuries ago. Other methods are the dumping of dredged mud or other material on the enclosure and pumping out.

land drain A *field drain*.

land drainage *See* **water authority**.

land reclamation *See* **land accretion**.

landslip or **landslide** A sliding down of the soil on a slope because of an increase of load (due to rain, new building, etc.), or a removal of support at the foot due to cutting a railway or road or canal. Clays are particularly liable to slips. *See also* **detritus slide, flow slide, rotational slide, shear slide.**

land surveyor [sur.] or **topographical surveyor** A person who measures land and buildings for mapping. His professional qualification may be membership of the Royal Institution of Chartered Surveyors and possibly also a university degree. Most engineers (structural, civil, mechanical) can act as surveyors since *setting out* requires a knowledge of surveying. *See* **cartographer**.

land tie A tie-rod holding a *sheet-pile* or other retaining wall to a buried *dead* *man* or *stay pile*. *See* **barge bed** (*illustration*).

land treatment [sewage] *Intermittent filtration.*

Lang lay [mech.] or **Lang's lay** A wire-rope construction in which the strands are twisted in the same direction as the wires in them. This sort of rope can only be used for hoisting a guided load because it spins dangerously and loses its twist when hoisting a free bucket, but it wears less than a rope of *ordinary lay*

lap The length by which one reinforcing bar must overlap another bar which takes its place. It is equal to the *grip length.*

lap joint A simple joint between steel plates, of which the end of one overlaps the end of the other. The two plates may be welded or bolted or riveted together. *See also* (*B*).

large calorie A kilogram *calorie* (*B*); 1 kg cal = 3·97 Btu = 4·19 kilojoules.

laser [sur.] Lasers were first generated around 1960 and at that time consisted of infra-red (invisible) light only. They were subsequently made usable by surveyors and visible. The beam is intense, more sharply defined than is possible with ordinary light, and can be maintained over distances above 1 km, so it has been used for aligning tunnels during driving and for plumbing tall buildings during construction. Nearly all makers of modern *E D Ms* now use infra-red laser beams because of their small divergence. *See also* **gallium aluminium arsenide.**

lateral [hyd.] A small *irrigation* channel, also a branch sewer.

lateral canal [hyd.] A canal dug parallel to a river which flows too fast to be easily navigable, such as the Canal Latéral du Rhône. *See* **lateral.**

lateral-force design [stru.] A method of designing a building in an earthquake region, so that it shall carry safely a horizontal force (lateral force) in any direction equal to a proportion of its deadweight (plus some live load). *See*

reinforced grouted brick masonry.

lateral support [stru.] Horizontal propping to a column or wall or pier across its least dimension. A wall or column supported at close intervals in this way to prevent it buckling is a *short column* and thus carries much higher loads than a *long column.*

lath [hyd.] The lengthwise, horizontal osiers of *hurdle work.*

latitude [sur.] The distance in metres north or south of a reference line which runs east and west. *Compare* **departure.**

lattice Description of an open girder, beam, column, etc., built up from members joined by intersecting diagonal bars of wood, steel, or light alloy. *See* **lacing, space lattice.**

launching of a bridge [stru.] Bridge spans that can be part-built on the bank can usually be launched, i.e. pushed slowly over the gap until they rest on the next pier or meet and are joined to their other half. This is generally both safer and cheaper than building the span over the gap on *falsework*. A launching beam sometimes must be built to help in this work. Usually only beam type bridges are launched, not *suspension bridges*, nor *arches*, nor *movable bridges.*

lay [mech.] (1) The lay of a wire rope is its method of twist which may be either *Lang lay* or *ordinary lay*, further classified as right-hand or left-hand. Right-hand lay is the standard lay, in which the *strands* (not the wires) bend round to the right, that is clockwise looking along the rope.

(2) Numerically the lay is that number of helix diameters in which a strand makes one complete turn of 360° in its helix. A lay of twenty means that each strand turns round the rope in twenty rope diameters.

lay barge A barge for laying pipes on the sea bed, or in any other watercourse. It carries pipes, cranes and welding plant for joining lengths of pipe together on the barge, and is followed by a *stinger.*

lay-by A part of a road or railway out of the traffic lanes, where vehicles may wait.

layered flow [hyd.] *See* **density current.**

layered map [sur.] A *contour* map in which the areas enclosed by the different contours are given different colours.

laying-and-finishing machine A self-propelled machine which receives road material, spreads it, and compacts it into a finished road surfacing which may be rolled later. *See* **Barber Greene tamping levelling finisher.**

layout [d.o.] A drawing showing the general arrangement of plant or of proposed construction.

leach [s.m.] To remove salts or other substances from anything by passing water through it. *See* **leachate.**

leachate Water that has dissolved salts from materials it has passed through. The word is often applied to water that has flowed from refuse tips, which is usually more polluting than sewage. Six cavities in rock salt are being made by the leaching out of the salt with seawater pumped down to them 1650 m below ground. These cavities near Humberside, UK, will be 150 m high, each providing 230,000 m³ of storage for North Sea gas. The cavities are being made in pairs and each pair is expected to take two years to make.

lead [rly] A *turnout*.

leader [sur.] The man holding the leading end of a chain or tape, who is aligned by the follower.

leaders or **leads** The guides in a *pile frame* for the drop hammer of a pile driver. *See* **false/hanging leaders.**

leading draughtsman *See* **section leader.**

lead line [sur.] or **sounding line** A strong cord marked at metre intervals for taking soundings in *hydrography*. It is weighted with a lump of lead.

lead sheath [elec.] A lead tube covering a power cable or cable for electrical communication. *See* **extrusion,** *also* (*B*).

least count [sur.] The smallest direct measurement made with a vernier.

leat [min.] A channel dug along a contour to carry a stream of water (generally a mill stream) for power purposes.

Leca Light Expanded Clay Aggregate, a *lightweight aggregate.*

ledge rock or **ledge** American terms for *bedrock.*

leech A *limpet.*

Leipzig market halls [stru.] Circular buildings of 75 m span which are remarkable for their concrete dome roofs, the first large *shells* built according to the *membrane theory*. Like all such shells they are remarkably light, having a weight per sq. m of floor area about one tenth that of St Peter's, Rome, which has a span of 40 m.

letting down [mech.] Reducing the hardness and brittleness of a quenched steel by *tempering* it.

levée [hyd.] An embankment built to prevent flooding of low-lying land. It may or may not have an impervious core.

level (1) [sur.] A *dumpy level*, or similar instrument with a telescope and bubble tube which enable the surveyor to take level sights over considerable distances, shots of 30 m being normal practice. It is used with a *levelling staff*. *See* **tilting, automatic level.**

(2) [sur.] To use a level of any sort for measuring differences in altitude.

(3) [sur.] The elevation of a point, corresponding in Britain to *grade* in USA.

(4) To form a horizontal earth surface.

(5) [hyd.] A drainage canal in the English fen country.

level book [sur.] A field book with special vertical rulings for recording the staff readings taken with a *dumpy level.*

levelling rod *See* **levelling staff.**

levelling screw [sur.] A *foot screw.*

levelling staff [sur.] or **levelling rod** A staff from 2 to 5 m long carried by a staff man in *level* or *stadia work*. For

161

most work it is graduated in metres and centimetres and can easily be read to 5 mm. A staff is either *self-reading* or a *target rod* and is almost always telescopic so as to be carried easily.

level-luffing crane [mech.] A *crane* in which, during any alteration of radius (luffing or *derricking*), an automatic device causes the load to move horizontally. The crane therefore operates more quickly and with a smaller power output than simpler cranes.

level of control [stat.] A measure of the producer's mastery over his production processes. In concrete it is often measured by the cube strength and its *standard deviation. See* **statistical uniformity.**

level recorder [hyd.] A pressure-operated or float-operated instrument which records continuously the level of the water in a channel.

level trier [sur.] or **bubble trier** An instrument which measures the slope corresponding to a noted number of graduations through which the bubble has moved.

level tube [sur.] or **bubble** or **bubble tube** or **vial** A glass (or other transparent) tube filled with liquid. The upper surface, which is graduated, is barrel-shaped and the bubble therefore tends to remain near the summit at all times. It is an indispensable part of all *levels*, dumpy or spirit, and of the *theodolite.*

lever [mech.] A rigid rod which rotates about a fixed point called the fulcrum. A force applied at the distant end is multiplied at the near end in proportion to the ratio of the distances of the ends from the fulcrum.

lever arm [stru.] The arm of a *bending moment*, that is the bending moment divided by the force producing the moment.

Levy facing [hyd.] A watertight facing to the water face of a French dam. The facing is built on to a row of small arches in a horizontal plane which form vertical openings the full

height of the dam. The arches are drained at the foot. Any leakages which occur through the facing can thus not produce dangerous hydro-static pressures within the masonry of the dam, since the water within the Levy facing can never be at a pressure higher than atmospheric.

Lewis bolt or **rag bolt** A steel *anchor bolt* with an enlarged indented conical base for anchoring it into the concrete. It is fixed by casting it into the concrete or by leaving a hole and grouting it in later with cement mortar or other *grout.*

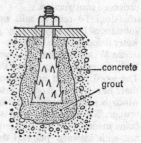

Lewis bolt

life linesman A diver's helper, who stays at the diver's lifeline as long as the diver is under water. He lowers the diver into the water and pulls him up as signalled by the diver on his lifeline (a stout cord). He often also works the air-pump controlling the diver's air supply.

lift (1) When pouring a concrete column or wall, the height shuttered at one time (not necessarily all poured together) is one lift. Generally in buildings it is one storey height.

(2) [hyd.] The distance through which a vessel rises or falls in passing through a lock.

(3) [hyd.] A power-operated hoist for raising or lowering vessels from one reach to the next without using a lock.

lifter *See* **devil** (2).

lifter hole [min.] A shot hole in tunnelling drilled near the floor and fired after the *cut holes* and *relief holes*.

lift gate [hyd.] A lock gate which opens by rising vertically.

lifting block [mech.] An arrangement of pulleys to enable heavy weights to be lifted, such as a *differential pulley block*.

lifting magnet An *electromagnet* which hangs from a crane hook and is used for lifting iron or steel. It has the further advantage that it lifts only magnetic material and thus separates it from non-magnetic material (non-ferrous metal).

lifting tackle [mech.] Lifting blocks, hooks, ropes, chains, slings, eye-bolts, bulldog grips, *Bordeaux connections*, and hand-operated pulleys or hoists for raising or lowering heavy weights. Power-operated lifting tackle is usually a *crane* or a *derrick*.

lift pump [mech.] A suction pump. *See* suction head.

lift-slab construction Pouring reinforced-concrete floor slabs and roof slab on the ground floor, one on top of the other, separated by sheets of building paper. Before the slabs are poured, the columns which will eventually carry them are erected to their full height. After hardening, the roof slab is raised into position by lifting jacks. The lower slabs are then jacked into position after the roof. One method of fixing slabs to steel columns has been the welding of the columns to metal lugs cast into the slab. The method was first used in USA in 1948 but was proposed by Lafaille in 1947 for flats at Saint-Ouen near Paris. *See* jackblock method.

light alloys *Alloys* of aluminium, which have been used in building for about 30 years, and alloys of magnesium, which have only recently been developed but are even lighter. Their specific gravities are: aluminium alloys 2·7, magnesium alloys 1·8, compared to steel 7·8. *See* duralumin.

lighthouse A structure having a recognizable flashing light which guides ships or warns them of danger. The famous beacon or lighthouse 134 m high on the island of Pharos near Alexandria was built about 285 B.C.

light railway [rly] A railway with light traffic; because of this it is subject to less strenuous regulations than most railways. It may be a narrow-gauge railway.

lightweight aggregate *Foamed slag* (*B*), *clinker* (*B*), *vermiculite* (*B*) and *perlite* (*B*) have been used in lightweight unreinforced concrete and in insulating screeds for many years, and this is likely to continue, except that the supply of clinker in Britain is dropping by about a million tons a year and the same tonnage of *fly-ash* is taking its place. Fly-ash itself can be used as a lightweight aggregate, though it has the disadvantage of being about as fine as cement. To the structural engineer the most interesting lightweight aggregates are *expanded clay* (*B*) (also called sintered or bloated clay), sintered fly-ash, and foamed slag, because these can be used for making reinforced or prestressed concrete structures of low weight and high insulation. Three synthetic lightweight aggregates, Aglite, Lytag and Leca, are available in the UK.

lightweight concretes *No-fines concretes* (*B*), *aerated concretes*, and concretes made of *lightweight aggregate*. Sometimes two of these types are combined. For example a no-fines concrete made of coarse foamed slag or clinker or other lightweight aggregate is not only more insulating and lighter in weight than a no-fines wall of dense stone and the same thickness, but it is nailable, which is very convenient. Generally speaking, aerated concretes are the most highly insulating and the lightest in weight, having a conductivity (k-value) of about 0·1 watt/ metre degree C at 500 kg/m^3, and loadbearing roof slabs are made at this density with a wet *crushing strength* of 1·9 N/mm^2 and a modulus of elasticity of 1380 N/mm^2. Concretes

163

made of lightweight aggregates can reach cube strengths as high as dense concretes, but their insulation value is much better and they are usually at least 25% lighter. A typical k-value for lightweight aggregate concretes would be 0·3 watt/metre degree C at 1440 kg/m³, with a 28-day cube strength of 20 N/mm².

limb [sur.] or **lower plate** That part of a *theodolite* which pivots on the *tribrach*, and is graduated from 0° to 360°. Both the upper *plate* and the lower plate may be called limbs, but at present 'limb' usually means lower plate.

limiting gradient, ruling gradient [rly] The maximum gradient on a route. This gradient dictates the size of the trains that can use the route, unless a second locomotive is used, which is unusual.

limiting span *See* **long span.**

limit of liquidity, of plasticity [s.m.] *See* **liquid limit, plastic limit.**

limit of proportionality [mech.] The point on a *stress-strain curve* at which the strain ceases to be proportional to the stress and begins to increase more rapidly than before. For mild steel this point is very near the *yield point* and the *elastic limit*, and commercially all three are generally taken to be the same.

limit state [stru.] The condition, under BSCP 110:1972, at which a structure begins to become unfit for use. A structure can have several possible limit states, e.g. when water leaks in or out or when it begins to overturn or when the steel is stressed to its yield point or corrosion eats it away. One serviceability limit results when the downward deflection reaches one 250th of the span or when cracks in reinforced concrete reach 0·3 mm thick. In prestressed concrete often no cracking at all is allowed. Another limit state results from vibration, because of the sensitiveness of humans to it. *Plastic design* is *limit state design* in steel.

limit state design [stru.] BSCP 110:1972, the 'Structural Use of Concrete', also called the unified code, introduced several new ideas that clarify the procedure of structural design. Based in part on the *characteristic strength* of the material, partial safety factors were introduced for each *limit state*.

limit switch [elec.] A control and safety device for an electrically-driven lift or winding engine or hoist. Limit switches come into operation at the end of the journey, and prevent the cage overwinding or underwinding.

limpet [hyd.] or **leech** or **limpet dam** A small '*open caisson*' shaped to fit a dock wall. It is lowered by crane into the water, placed in contact with the section of wall to be repaired, and pumped out. The water pressure forces it into close contact with the wall at the edges and holds it in place. Access is through the open top. Most large harbours possess a limpet, since it is very much more convenient, easier, and quicker to work in a limpet which is open to the air than in a diving suit or a *diving bell*.

line drilling [min.] *Broaching*.

line drop [elec.] The loss in electrical pressure (voltage) due to the resistance of the conductors (the line) between the power station and the consumer.

line of least resistance [min.] In blasting, the shortest distance between the centre of the explosive charge and the nearest *free face*. It is usually slightly shorter than the *burden*.

line of thrust [stru.] The locus of the points through which the resultant force in an arch or retaining wall passes. In an unreinforced arch or wall, it should be within the *middle third* throughout. *See* **gravity retaining wall, Eddy's theorem.**

liner or **stretcher** In timbering, a board cut to the length available between opposite members of a frame and spiked between them to lock them in place. *See* **sill,** *also* **pipe liners.**

lining (1) [hyd.] A layer of clay, concrete, brick, stone, or wood on the bed of a canal to reduce scour, friction, and leakage.

(2) [min.] A concreted or *gunited* or bricked surface to a tunnel or shaft.

link (1) [sur.] One hundredth of an *engineer's chain*, in which one link is 1 ft, or of a *Gunter's chain*, in which one link is 7·92 in. *See* tally.

(2) [elec.] An *isolator*.

Linville truss *See* Pratt truss.

lip block or lip piece or lipping A piece of wood spiked over a strut in trench timbering. It overhangs the waling which the strut supports, so that if the sides of the trench fall away the strut will not drop on the men below.

liquefaction [s.m.] A saturated sand which has a *voids ratio* higher than the *critical voids ratio*, that is a loose sand, is liable to liquefaction when it is shocked by earth tremors or by more water flowing into it or by sudden loading. The sand becomes temporarily quick and a *flow slide* is caused.

liquidity index [s.m.] *See* index of liquidity.

liquid limit [s.m.] The *moisture content* at the point between the liquid and the plastic states of a clay. A mixture of soil and water is placed in a standard cup and divided by a standard grooving-tool along a diameter of the cup. A curve is plotted of moisture content against the number of blows on the cup which make the two divided parts rejoin for 12 mm at the bottom of the cup. The curve should be smooth (normally a straight line) from 10 blows to 50 blows, and the water content at 25 blows is the liquid limit. *See* consistency limits, flow curve.

liquid-membrane curing compound A *sealant* (3).

liquid nitrogen method of freezing ground [s.m.] Liquid nitrogen, a by-product of the manufacture of oxygen, boils at −196°C and can be applied to tubes for *freezing* ground through 5 cm pipes at about 1 atmosphere pressure; but it is expensive since normally it is not re-circulated. The discharge point,

where the used nitrogen is released, must be well ventilated, since being devoid of oxygen it could suffocate people.

littoral drift The moving of beach material along a coast line by the sea. The waves are one cause since they move and break heavy stones, but transport of fine material over large distances is by marine currents which hold sand in suspension.

live load [stru.] or superload A *load* which may be removed or replaced on a structure, not necessarily a dynamic load and including neither *wind force* nor *earthquake* loads. *See* moving load.

Liverpool datum [sur.] A levelling datum used in England, based on a fortnight's observations of the mean sea level at Liverpool in 1844. This datum is still shown on old maps but has been replaced on newer maps by *Newlyn* (Cornwall) datum.

Lloyd-Davies formula or rational method for the design of sewers An old way of estimating *runoff* by the simple formula:

$$Q = 0.167 \, ARC$$

in which Q is the rate of runoff in cu. m per minute, A is the catchment area in hectares, R is the rainfall in mm per hour and C is the *impermeability coefficient*.

load (1) [stru.] The weight carried by a structure, its *dead load* and *live load*.

(2) [mech.] The work being done by an engine or motor.

loadbearing wall [stru.] A wall which carries any load in addition to its own weight and the *wind force* on it. Partitions and panel walls are generally not loadbearing.

loaded filter [s.m.] or reversed filter or weighted filter A *graded filter* at the foot of an earth dam or elsewhere, which stabilizes the toe of the dam by its weight and permeability, since no water can exist in it under pressure.

load-extension curve [mech.] A curve showing the results of a *tensile test* on a metal test piece, and relating the load to the elongation of the piece throughout the test. For mild steel it generally shows the *yield point*. The curve is very like the *stress-strain curve*.

load factor (1) [stru.] The ratio of the load, which causes *failure* of a structure or member, to the design load. It varies from 1¼ upwards according to the working conditions of the structure. Although load factor occasionally means the same as *factor of safety* there is now a tendency to use the term to refer to *limit state design* exclusively.

(2) [elec.] The ratio of the average to the maximum electrical load over a certain period for a certain consumer or power station.

load-indicating bolt A development in 1963 of the *high-strength friction-grip bolt*, which gives a reliable easily-inspected direct indication that the specified minimum tension has been achieved. The head of the bolt carries small projections on its underside, which compress as the bolt is tightened. The gap thus indicates the amount of the bolt tension, and this can be measured quite simply by feeler gauges pushed under the bolt head. A more recent innovation is the load-indicating washer, which carries corresponding projections, enabling an ordinary bolt to be used, but it requires also that a second, hard steel washer be inserted next to it.

loading boom Any overhanging structure from which material is loaded into wagons or lorries.

loading gauge [rly] The limiting dimensions of height and width of rolling stock and their loads to ensure that they clear tunnels and bridges.

loading shovel or **tractor shovel** or **wheel loader** A mechanical shovel on four pneumatic-tyred road wheels, originally designed for lifting and loading rubbish, sand, coal, coke, and so on. It can also be used for digging or calfdozing and even as a crane. When calfdozing, the *mouldboard* is

bolted on ahead of the loading scoop, which does not have to be removed. For digging, a digging bucket replaces the light sheet-metal loading scoop. It can also be used as a *fork-lift truck* for stacking bricks or raising them up to scaffolding. It is therefore a very light and fast-moving *excavator* unsuitable for travelling on bad ground because of its rubber tyres. It moves at 30 kph without difficulty. *See* **tractor shovel**.

loam [s.m.] A roughly equal mixture of sand, clay, and *humus*.

local attraction [sur.] Deviation of the magnetic needle from the magnetic north at any point. It may be due to iron or steel in the ground or a penknife in the surveyor's pocket.

lock [hyd.] A *chamber* separated from the two reaches of a canal or river each side of it by gates through which barges or ships can pass up- or downstream, usually for a small payment. *See* **slack-water navigation**.

lockage [hyd.] The water lost from the upper to the lower reach of a canal by passing a vessel through a lock.

lock bay [hyd.] A lock *chamber*.

lock cut *See* **cut**.

Locke level [sur.] A *hand level*.

locked-coil rope [mech.] A steel-wire rope which is not stranded but built of concentric rings of specially-shaped, closely-packed wires in opposite *lays*. The outer ring is of S-shaped wires locked together so that if one breaks it cannot work loose. The surface of the new rope is very smooth but the ropes are stiff; they are therefore well suited for use as shaft guide ropes or as ropeway or *cableway* tracks.

lock gate [hyd.] A gate which separates the water in an upper or lower *reach* from that in the lock chamber. Sometimes a third lock gate divides the chamber into two compartments.

lock nut [mech.] A second nut screwed on to a bolt after the nut which carries the load, to prevent it from unscrewing. Measured along the bolt length, it is usually half the depth of an ordinary nut. A castle nut is a particular type of lock nut with notches cut in its outer face through which a split pin can enter a hole in the bolt. The nut in this case is doubly secured.

lock paddle [hyd.] A *sluice* for filling or for emptying a lock chamber.

lock sill [hyd.] or **clap sill** or **mitre sill** That part of the floor of a lock chamber against which the gates bear when shut.

locomotive [rly] A railway engine which draws trains by its own steam engine, diesel engine, electric motor, or gas turbine.

locomotive crane A diesel-powered crane which travels on *standard-gauge* track. It is commonly used for its simplicity and robustness, but its lifting range is limited. It weighs about five times the maximum load which it can lift. *See* **mobile crane.**

locomotive haulage [rly] Haulage by loco is feasible and economical where tracks are strong, straight, and flat, preferably under 3% gradient, always less than 6%, above which a rope or *rack railway* or rubber-tyred haulage must be used.

loess [s.m.] Wind-borne *silt*, found in Europe, USA, and Asia. When dry it can stand vertically in cuts, having some cohesion. Its grain size is between 0·02 and 0·006 mm. *See* **classification of soils.**

log chute [hyd.] or **logway** A way through or beside a dam, for logs and driftwood.

logway A *log chute.*

London clay [s.m.] *See* **stiff-fissured clay.**

long column [stru.] or **strut** A column which fails when overloaded, by buckling rather than by crushing. In reinforced-concrete work this is assumed to happen with columns which are longer than fifteen times their least dimension, but with *lightweight aggregate* concrete the ratio is 10. The permitted stress on a column is reduced as its length increases. *See* **reduction factor, short column, slenderness ratio.**

long dolly A *follower.*

longitudinal bead test [mech.] or **slow bend test** A test for *weldability.* A steel plate on which a welding bead is deposited is bent double. If the plate or weld metal is not weldable it will crack.

longitudinal profile or **longitudinal section** or **vertical alignment** A section vertically through the centre line of a road, railway, pipeline, etc., to show the original and final ground levels.

long-line method of prestressing *See* **pretensioning.**

long span [stru.] or **limiting span** A span is long for a particular slab, beam, girder, or *bridge* type if it is near the greatest economical length for that type. Some long spans are: solid concrete slab 10 m; hollow-tile concrete slab 11 m; arches 300 m; *cantilever bridges* 600 m; *suspension bridges,* the *Golden Gate bridge* (1937) 1280 m between centres of support. *See* **Parramatta Bridge.**

long ton or **gross ton** The ton of 2240 lb equivalent to 1·016 metric tons (tonnes). *Compare* **short ton,** *see* **hundredweight.**

loose-boundary hydraulics [hyd.] The study of the flow of a fluid along uncertain boundaries involving air-borne or water-borne transport of sand. In a stream with banks and bed of loose sand, with rising water level the sand is picked up, while with falling water level sand is dropped, so that the stream boundaries change with the water level. It includes the study of *antidunes, dunes, bed load, hydraulics, layered flow, saltation* and *turbulent flow.*

loose core Large aggregate which has become segregated from the concrete by mishandling between mixing and placing.

loose ground Granular soil with a relative compaction below 90%, which can be dug with a shovel. Unlike *compact material,* a pick is not needed to break it up.

Lossier's cement *See* **expanding cement.**

loss of ground In excavating soft ground the volume of silt, clay, or sand dug out is greater than the volume of the excavation because material flows into it even when no *boil* occurs. This ground is lost from outside the excavation and may cause settlement of neighbouring buildings. To avoid this, excavation must be done in sheet-piled *cofferdams*, *Gow caissons*, etc. *See* **groundwater lowering**.

loss of head *Hydraulic friction*.

loss of prestress [stru.] Losses of pre-stressing force after *transfer* arise mainly through elastic shortening, *shrinkage* and *creep* of the concrete and creep of the steel. The use of high-quality concrete can reduce these losses considerably. Correspondingly, if lightweight aggregate is used, the losses can be expected to be 50% more.

lost head [hyd.] *Hydraulic friction* in a pipe or channel expressed as a loss in potential energy (metres head).

low-carbon steel [mech.] Steel with 0·04 to 0·25% C, generally called *dead mild* or *mild steel* according to its carbon content.

lower plate The *limb* of a *theodolite*.

low-heat Portland cement A cement that is made with different chemical composition from *ordinary Portland cement* so as to liberate less heat in dams or other massive concrete blocks. These may take many months or years to cool to the ambient temperature, and therefore could crack badly if built with other cements. Even though it is more finely ground, it is not so strong as ordinary Portland cement. It is only made to special order in the UK, but *sulphate-resisting cement* is sometimes a good substitute. *See* BS 1370.

low-water valve [mech.] A valve which operates on the same principle as the *fusible plug*.

luffing *Derricking*.

luffing cableway mast A *cableway* tower hinged at the foot and held up by guys which can be adjusted to allow some lateral movement either way at the head so as to move the *track cable*.

luffing jib crane or **derricking jib crane** A crane like most civil engineering cranes with a jib hinged at the foot to allow the hoisting rope to work at different radii. *Compare* **level-luffing crane**.

lumping [rly] A method of renewing rail track in which a crane pulls out a complete pair of rails with its sleepers and inserts a new pair built up in the railway workshops with its sleepers.

lurching allowance [rly] An allowance for extra load on the outer girders and stringers of a railway bridge caused by the swaying of the loco and train. The greatest allowance for lurching is in Britain one eighth of the total *live load*, that is an increase of one quarter of the live load on one rail. *See also* **impact, nosing**.

Lytag A *lightweight aggregate* made by sintering *fly-ash*.

M

macadam Uniformly sized stones rolled to form a road. The road may be *waterbound*, cement bound, or coated with tar or bitumen and may be laid by hand or machine. Coated macadam is the commonest road construction in Britain. *See* **tarmacadam, single-sized**.

macadam spreader A machine like the *Barber Greene* machine.

machine [mech.] A tool or device for overcoming force by applying another, usually smaller, force elsewhere. The lever, the screw, screwdriver, wheel, lifting tackle, jack, are all machines. *See* **mechanical advantage**.

machine tools [mech.] Metal-cutting machines such as boring machines, drills, grinders, planers, key seaters, hobbing machines, tapping machines, shapers and slotters, lathes, etc.; in general, those machines which make other machines.

Magic Mole A Russian compressed-air driven soil-drilling tool that can make holes of 14 to 25 mm dia., suitable for installation of pipe or cable under a road. It is useful where the expense of *pipe-pushing* would not be justified. In 1973 a Magic Mole cost about £700, but it should not be confused with a Mole tunnelling machine, of a diameter about 200 times larger.

magnesite [min.] $MgCO_3$, magnesium carbonate. When heated it is used for making a basic *refractory* lining to steel furnaces which can be used at temperatures up to 1800°C. As with lime the heating drives off CO_2 so that magnesite refractory is really magnesia (MgO).

magnetic bearing [sur.] The horizontal angle measured from magnetic north to a survey line. *See* **bearing**.

magnetic compass [sur.] *See* **compass**.

magnetic declination [sur.] *See* **declination** (2).

magnetic north or **south pole** [sur.] Centres of magnetic attraction in the north of Canada and in Antarctica. They are continually moving and these movements account for the continual alteration of *declination* throughout the world.

magnetic variation [sur.] (1) *Declination* (2).

(2) Small daily variations in the declination which nowhere exceed 1°. Slight annual variations also exist and the dip also varies regularly.

magneto [elec.] or **magneto generator** A small electric generator which carries its magnetic field in a permanent magnet.

magnetometer [sur.] An instrument for measuring the intensity of a magnetic field. It is particularly useful in *geophysical prospecting* in conjunction with an air survey of the ground. An aeroplane carrying a recording magnetometer flies low over the ground and its indications are later plotted as contours of magnetic force over the *mosaic*, showing in a striking way where magnetic rocks are most likely to be found.

MAG welding or **metallic active-gas welding** *MIG welding* in which carbon dioxide or oxygen either alone or mixed with argon are used to shield the weld. It is so called because oxygen is never inert and carbon dioxide is rarely so.

Maihak strain gauge An *acoustic strain gauge* from Germany.

main A large supply pipe for water, gas, etc. For water it may be a *gravity main*. The word is also used to describe the 'service main' bringing the gas or water service into each house.

main beam [stru.] A beam which bears directly on to a column or wall, not on to another beam.

main canal [hyd.] An irrigation conduit taking water from the supply. It delivers water to the *laterals*.

main contractor or **general contractor** *See* (*B*).

main drain or **main sewer** A sewer which leads direct to an *outfall*.

main holes [min.] *Relief holes*.

main sewer *See* **main drain**.

maintenance period *See* (*B*).

main tie [stru.] The tension members joining the feet of a roof *truss*, generally at wall-plate level.

malleability [mech.] That property of a metal which enables it to be hammered or bent without breaking.

malleable cast iron [mech.] Iron castings which have been heat treated by packing in an oxidizing agent and then holding at 800°C for about four days. Surface oxidation and change of internal chemical structure are both believed to cause the improvement in toughness and strength. The average tensile strength is more than double that of ordinary *cast iron*. It is not really malleable but has noticeable ductility in the tensile test.

mammoth pump [min.] The *air-lift pump* within the hollow boring rods of a *trepan*.

mandrel or **mandril** [mech.] An accurately turned rod which fits into a bored hole to be enlarged on the lathe. The American term is arbor. *See* **pile core**.

manganese [min.] Chemical symbol Mn. A metal which is added in the proportion of at least 0·8% to nearly all steels.

manganese steel [mech.] Steels containing more than 1% of Mn, which are appreciably tougher than ordinary steels with only about 0·8%. Colliery *drawgear* made of 1·5% manganese steel has the advantage that it does not need annealing every six months like *wrought iron*. Steels with about 10% Mn are used for dredger buckets and similar hard use.

manhole (1) [mech.] An access hole to a tank or boiler drum, just large enough for a man to enter. It is normally covered with a cast-iron or steel plate called the manhole cover.

(2) An *inspection chamber*.

manhole cover A cast-iron plate fitting into a cast-iron frame bedded in the concrete slab over an *inspection chamber*. Manhole covers over foul drains are sealed by a tongue projecting down from the cover all the way round its edge into a grease-filled groove corresponding with it on the frame. *See* **double-seal manhole cover**.

manifold [mech.] A thick pipe, generally curved, into which or from which several smaller pipes lead. *See* **header**.

Manila rope The best vegetable *fibre rope*.

manipulator [mech.] A jig to which work is clamped during *welding*. The work can thus be rotated or raised into convenient positions.

man-lock An *air lock* through which men, not materials, pass. It is an access to a tunnel, shaft, or *caisson*, driven in *compressed air*. A separate man-lock is needed because men may spend more than 60 min. decompressing from high pressures. *See* **decanting, working chamber**.

manmade fibre rope Synthetic fibre ropes are usually formed from one of three materials: polyamide (nylon), polyester or polypropylene. They are stronger than, and for many purposes preferable to, the vegetable *fibre ropes* of conventional cordage. Many BS describe twisted, plaited or hawser types.

manometer [hyd.] A gauge for measuring pressure differences in a water pipe. It usually consists of a U-tube containing a liquid such as kerosene or mercury which does not mix with water. The two ends of the U-tube are joined to the two points in the pipe between which the pressure difference is required.

manual metal-arc welding (in USA **shielded metal-arc, SMA** or **stick welding**) A common but highly skilled welding method using consumable electrodes, usually coated with material that shields the arc and excludes the atmosphere with its harmful oxygen and water. No hoses or gas cylinder are needed, consequently welds can be made even on remote parts of a building site. The equipment is relatively cheap and portable. All steels except high-alloy steels can be welded, also cast iron, aluminium, copper and their alloys. With heavy coatings the electrode is positive because this is the hotter electrode. Medium-coated or bare electrodes are connected to the negative so that they do not melt too fast. The best welding voltages are between 20 and 45 volts DC and welding currents can vary from 20 to 600 amp.

map [sur.] A drawing of part of the earth's surface. Countries are usually mapped by Government organizations such as the Ordnance Survey of Great Britain or the French General Staff. However, private bodies such as mining or air survey companies also make their own maps, usually on a larger scale than those provided by the Government. Maps of the whole of Britain are obtainable at the scale of 6 in. per mile (1:10 560) and all except mountains can be obtained at 25 in. per mile (1:2534). Air photo *mosaics* of many built-up areas exist at 51 in. per mile (1:1242).

margin *See* **verge.**

marigraph [sur.] A gauge at a tidal observation station which records the levels of the tides.

marine borers Molluscs and crustaceans which live usually in warm water and destroy wood by eating it. The gribble (Limnoria lignorum) and shipworm (Teredo navalis) are the best known, since they can penetrate any wood in favourable water. The best antidote usually is full-cell treatment with creosote, but concrete or Monel metal encasement have sometimes been found necessary. Light explosive charges set off in the water will kill the borers but will not ensure that they do not return.

marine surveying [sur.] or **marine hydro-**

graphic surveying The mapping of the sea bed and the estimation of the currents, *scour*, and *silting* near the coast.

maritime plants [hyd.] Plants which grow on foreshores in salty conditions may prevent or reduce *scour*. Rice grass (cord grass or Spartina townsendii) grows best in foreshore muds 0·6 to 1·2 m below high water. Marram grass (Psamma arenaria) flourishes in the arid conditions of the sand dunes which it helps to stabilize. Shrubby seablite (sea gorse or Suaeda frutosa) will grow in shingle beaches. These plants may be a very cheap *revetment*.

marl [s.m.] Now any soil or rock containing a vague quantity of lime. The term originally meant any soil or rock suitable for liming (marling) arable land.

marram grass *See* **maritime plants.**

masonry cement A cement, usually a *Portland*, that hardens slowly and holds water well, sometimes containing a plasticizer and other additives. BS 5224:1976 describes one with a Portland base.

mass centre *Centre of gravity.*

mass concrete Concrete without reinforcement. *See* **plain concrete.**

mass curve [hyd.] or **mass diagram** A graph of accumulated monthly inflow volumes plotted as ordinates against the time in years or months of the period likely to be critical for a *reservoir*. The mass curve provides a first approximation to the size of reservoir that will be needed.

mass-haul curve A curve which shows the amount of excavation in a cutting, which is available for fill. The abscissa shows the distance from the centre line, the ordinate shows the amount of fill available, that is the amount of excavation up to that point. *See* **balance point.**

mast [stru.] (1) A slender tower held upright by guy ropes, for instance in a *cableway.*

(2) The upright member in a *derrick* from which the *jib* is supported.

masthead gear Any gear carried on a mast or jib; this has come to mean two drums carried on a crane jib to control two subsidiary ropes over pulleys near the head of the jib. These two ropes can exactly orient a chisel grab digging a trench for a *diaphragm wall* and can thus control the direction of the wall. Any diaphragm wall during excavation is liable to be overloaded by the crane standing near its edge. This device enables the crane to stand well away from the wall, so that it does not *surcharge* the edge of the trench.

mastic *See* **sealant** *and* (*B*).

mastic asphalt A wearing course to a road or a waterproofing to a roof, consisting of liquid *asphalt* spread hot by hand floats. Some clean sand or chips may be mixed with it. It is laid in two or three coats, the latter being 18 mm thick in all.

mat (1) American term for a *raft*, or a footing of steel or concrete under a post. A *blinding*.

(2) A heavy mesh of reinforcement in a concrete slab.

match lines [air sur.] The lines along which mosaics are cut so as to hide the joints between them. Edges of fields or roads or railways or streams are best.

materials handling [mech.] or **mechanical handling** Machinery for handling stone, coal, and other granular material, including *conveyors* of every sort, cranes, *transporter cranes*, grabs, elevators, railways, *cableways*, and ropeways. It merges into *earth moving*.

materials lock An *air lock* through which rubbish is sent out and building materials sent into a pneumatic caisson or shaft being driven in compressed air. *See* **working chamber**.

matrix The material of a solid, in which the larger grains are embedded. Cement or lime is the matrix of mortar; tar or bitumen is the matrix of a tarred road surface; mortar is the matrix of concrete. Quartz is the matrix of a *quartzite*, often also of a granite.

mattress (1) A concrete slab at ground level used as a base for a transformer or for other plant.

(2) A layer of *blinding* concrete.

(3) [hyd.] A flexible layer of brushwood *fascines* often over 50 m long, weighted with stones or concrete blocks, towed into position and sunk on to a river or sea bed to prevent *scour*. It may also be made of precast concrete pieces strung on to steel wire ropes, woven polypropylene sheet, *continuous gabions*, *wiepen*, *reed*, *Dutch mattress*, etc.

maturing *See* **curing**.

maximum cement content [stru.] The maximum cement content in concrete under BSCP 110:1972 is 550 kg/m^3, to prevent overheating in thick sections and cracking in thin sections.

maximum dry density [s.m.] The dry density obtained by a stated amount of compaction of a soil at the *optimum moisture content*.

mean [stat.] An arithmetic mean is an *average* in which all signs are taken as positive. In an algebraic mean the signs of the quantities are considered and the mean may be either positive or negative.

mean depth [hyd.] The cross-sectional area of a stream divided by its width of free surface.

mean velocity [hyd.] *See* **current metre**.

measuring chain [sur.] *See* **chain, Gunter's chain**.

measuring weir [hyd.] A *weir* built to measure the flow of the stream. Since the weir crest is horizontal, the water depth over it is more easily measured than from the rough, stony or muddy bed. It may extend across part of the width of the stream, in which case it has *end* (or side) *contractions*. If it covers the full width of the stream, the contractions are suppressed and it becomes a *suppressed weir*. Near a weir, the water level drops fairly steeply. The *head* at a weir must therefore be measured upstream of this part. This is best done by a *float* gauge that continuously records the depth of water. *See* **Venturi flume.**

mechanic (1) [mech.] A *fitter*, a man skilled in mechanical engineering.

(2) A *tradesman* (*B*).

mechanical advantage [mech.] The ratio of the load raised by a *machine* such as *lifting tackle* to the applied force. The mechanical advantage divided by the *velocity ratio* is the *efficiency* of the machine.

mechanical analysis [s.m.] The determination of the proportions of the different particle sizes in a given soil sample to help in *classification* of the soil. Grains larger than 0·06 mm can be sieved. Smaller particles cannot be measured by sieving; their effective diameters are estimated from their settling velocities in water by *wet analysis. See* **consistency limits, fineness modulus, grading, mesh.**

mechanical bond or **key** Adhesion obtained by indentations in reinforcing bars or similar serrated shapes which enable concrete or mortar to grip *Lewis bolts*, bricks, and so on. *Compare* **specific adhesion.**

mechanical dredger A *bucket-ladder dredger* or a *grab dredger*.

mechanical efficiency [mech.] *See* **efficiency.**

mechanical equivalent of heat, Joule's equivalent The amount of mechanical energy which can be transformed into one heat unit. In imperial units it is 778 ft-lb per British thermal unit. In metric units, one kilowatt-hour is one kilowatt for 3600 seconds, so 1 kWh = 3·6 MJ. *See also* **joule.**

mechanical handling *Materials handling*.

mechanical key *See* **mechanical bond.**

mechanical loading *See* **excavator.**

mechanical rammer A machine carrying a weight which it lifts and allows to drop on the soil. *See* **frog rammer, power rammer.**

mechanical sampler *See* **sampler.**

mechanical shovel or **power shovel** An *excavator*.

median strip or **median** or **central reservation** or **central reserve** A strip of land between the two carriageways of a

motorway, sometimes with shrubs growing or a crash barrier along its centre line.

medical lock or **medical air lock** or **compression** or **decompression chamber** An air chamber consisting of a steel cylinder 2 m dia. and about 5·5 m long, closed at one end, with air-tight doors (or one door) at the other end. It is connected to a compressed-air supply and fitted with a bed, telephone, pressure gauge, and clock. *See* **caisson disease.**

medium-carbon steel [mech.] *See* **high-carbon steel.**

meeting post [hyd.] or **mitre post** Vertical timbers at the outer end of each of a pair of lock gates. They are chamfered so that they fit each other to close the gate.

mega- A prefix meaning one million times.

mekometer [sur.] An *EDM* instrument, developed at the UK National Physical Laboratory, capable of measuring lengths up to 500 m with an accuracy of the order of 1 in 1 million or better.

member [stru.] A structural member is a wall, *column, beam*, or *tie*, or a combination of these. A building or building frame consists of a number of members fixed together.

membrane [stru.] A thin film or skin, such as the skin of a soap bubble or a waterproof skin. *See* **sealant** (3).

membrane analogy [stru.] In the determination of the stress in a twisted bar, lines of equal shear stress are well represented by the contour lines of a soap bubble (membrane) of the same shape. There is therefore an *analogy* between these contour lines and the stress lines. This enables the lines of stress to be more easily understood than would otherwise be possible.

membrane processes This usually means the de-salination processes that use a filtering skin (membrane), including *electro-dialysis, reverse osmosis*, and *ultra-filtration*. They are usually best for brackish waters with not more than about 1500 parts per million of dissolved salts.

membrane theory [stru.] A theory of design of thin *shells* which is based on the assumption that the shell cannot resist bending because it deflects like a balloon or bubble. Only shear stresses and direct tension or compression therefore can exist in any section. The conditions necessary for a membrane state of stress are uniform loading and edge support and uniform or smoothly varying thickness and curvature.

meniscus *See* **surface tension.**

meridian [sur.] or **meridian of longitude** or **meridian plane** or **true meridian** A plane passing through the earth's axis of rotation and the point under consideration. It coincides with the true north–south line through the point.

meridian passage [sur.] The *culmination* of a star.

Merrison committee *See* **box girder.**

mesh (1) A woven wire cloth used for screening sand or gravel or for the laboratory *mechanical analysis* of soils. *See* **fineness modulus.**

(2) Light woven or welded steel *reinforcement.*

metal Broken stone for making roads.

metal-arc welding Electric-*arc welding,* often with a consumable metal electrode, generally using low-voltage DC. *See* **manual metal-arc, automatic welding.**

metallic-electrode inert-gas welding. *See* **MIG welding.**

metalling A road surface.

metallurgical cement *Supersulphated cement.*

meter (1) An instrument which measures the flow or quantity of a fluid. *See* **current meter, flow meter, integrating meter.**

(2) American spelling of *metre.*

methane CH_4, known as **marsh gas** in marshes or **firedamp** in coal mines. Firedamp is released from coal seams and the rocks around them into the mine air. It occurs also in the natural gas from oil formations, and has been

ignited during tunnelling under the Thames, in the Orange-Fish *tunnel* and for the north anchorage (in dolerite) of the *Forth Road Bridge.*

method of slices [s.m.] A method of calculating the stability of an earth slope. The wedge of soil is divided into vertical slices of uniform width. The equilibrium of the whole wedge is calculated by summing the effects on all the slices. *Compare* **circular-arc method.**

metre (or **meter** in USA) The length unit that is now coming to be used throughout the world. It is equal to 39·37 in. or to 1000 millimetres or to 100 centimetres. 1000 metres are equal to 1 kilometre. *See also* **meter.**

metric system The weights and measures system based on the metre and its decimal divisions. A cubic centimetre (1 cc) of water weighs 1 gram. A litre of water (1000 cc) weighs 1 kilogram. A pressure of 1 kilogram per sq. cm is thus equivalent to a column of 10 metres of water or 1 atmosphere of pressure. A cubic metre of water weighs 1 tonne. The millilitre (ml) has superseded the cubic centimetre (cm^3 or cc) but for engineering purposes there is no difference between them. The litre is one decimetre^3.

micro- A prefix meaning one millionth.

micrometer (1) A measuring device which works on the principle of the *micrometer gauge.*

(2) [sur.] A fitting on the eyepiece of a good-quality *dumpy level,* which enables the levelling staff to be read to high precision.

micrometer gauge [mech.] or **micrometer** A length-measuring instrument which measures to one thousandth of an inch or less. It consists of a G-shaped steel frame, one leg of which is a round bar accurately threaded with 100 divisions per inch. A nut running on it is marked outside with lines which represent 0·001 in. Precise micrometers are obtainable with metric graduation.

micron (1) One thousandth of a millimeter, 0·001 mm, now written one μm.

(2) A pressure equivalent to 0·001 mm of mercury, written μmHg.

microptic theodolite [sur.] An extremely compact, lightweight *theodolite*, weighing only 4 kg, with an 11·5 cm long telescope. Both the horizontal and the vertical circles are of glass, and have *optical reading* to 20 seconds of arc.

microscope or **optical microscope** An instrument which gives a magnification of several hundred times and is indispensable to the mineralogist. *See* **petrographic microscope.**

micro-strainer or **micro-screen** [sewage] A device, also sometimes used in *raw water* treatment, that uses very fine stainless steel wire mesh to strain out solids from water or sewage *effluent*.

middle third [stru.] That part of the thickness of a wall or arch which is one third of the total thickness and is central in it. If all the forces, including the wall weight, combine to form a resultant which is everywhere within the middle third there can be no tensile stress in the wall. This is aimed at in the design of walls without reinforcement, whether brick, masonry, or concrete. *See* **core, gravity dam.**

middling frame *See* **tucking frame.**

mid-ordinate [d.o.] An ordinate which occurs half-way between the extremes.

midpoint [stat.] or **midrange** The value which is the average of the two extreme observations.

midspan [stru.] A point half-way between the supports of a beam.

MIG welding or **metallic-electrode inert-gas welding** or **gas-shielded metal-arc welding** Welding of light alloys, mild and carbon steels, stainless and heat-resisting steels and non-ferrous metals with a consumable filler wire (electrode) of metal that is chosen to suit the metal being welded. The arc is shielded by various possible gases, including argon, carbon dioxide (CO_2) or mixtures of argon with oxygen or CO_2 or both together. The gas also is varied to suit the metal in question. The welding torch is air-cooled for currents up to about 400 amp; but it must be water-cooled for higher currents up to about 600 amp. Manual or *automatic welding* are possible. It is fast, but unsuitable for sheet thinner than 1 mm. *See* **MAG welding.**

mil (1) One thousandth of an inch, a unit used in measuring the thickness of *metal coating* (B). *See* **circular mil.**

(2) [air sur.] 0·001 radian.

mild steel [mech.] Steel containing from 0·15 to 0·25% C, which because of its low carbon content cannot be hardened by quenching but is much more ductile than *high-carbon steel*. Steel made to BS 4360, 'Weldable structural steels', has a yield point of 230 N/mm^2, but higher yield points are obtainable and the standard also states the chemical analyses of the steels concerned. Mild steel is used for making pipes, joists, etc. *See* **dead-mild/high-tensile steel.**

mill (1) [mech.] A machine for grinding or crushing, such as a ball mill, hammer mill, or pug mill.

(2) A building containing (particularly woodworking) machinery.

millimetre Abbreviation mm. One thousandth of a metre. 25·4 mm = 1 in.

millimicron One millionth of a millimetre, formerly written mμ or $\mu\mu$. *See* **micron.**

milling [mech.] Removing metal shavings from a surface by pushing it on a moving table past a rotating toothed cutter.

milling machine [mech.] A *machine tool* for *milling* invented by E. Whitney in 1818. It can be an extremely complicated machine used for making drills and gears as well as for cutting channels and making plane surfaces.

mill scale Black iron oxide formed on steel sections during *hot rolling*. Because of this scale, bars which come untreated from the rolling mill are called *black* bars.

mill tail [hyd.] A *tail race*.

miner's dip needle A *dip needle* which shows the presence of magnetic material in the ground.

minimum cement content [stru.] For 'designed mixes' (designed by the contractor so as to achieve the cube strength demanded) the engineer specifies a minimum cement content under BSCP 110. This is considered to ensure resistance of the concrete to corrosion, especially by concretes in the ground. Contractors tend to dispute the need for a minimum cement content. A *maximum cement content* also exists.

Ministry of Transport loading This loading for bridge calculations has been superseded by BS 153.

minus sight [sur.] This term is recommended by the ASCE instead of the term *fore sight* in levelling.

miser [s.m.] A large hand *auger* for exploring loose soils.

mistake [sur.] *See* gross error.

mitre post *See* meeting post.

mitre sill [hyd.] A *lock sill*.

mix The proportions of a batch of concrete (or mortar or plaster), usually varying for concrete between 200 and 400 kg of cement per cu. m of concrete, with a stated water/cement ratio.

mix design [stru.] The choice and proportioning of the cement, sand, coarse aggregate and water in a concrete mix, usually the responsibility of a specialist civil engineer. He may design for low heat evolution or for low cracking, not necessarily for strength, but he usually does aim at a minimum *cube strength*, and may specify a *minimum cement content*.

mixed-flow turbine [hyd.] An inward-flow reaction *water turbine* in which the water acts on the runners both radially and axially. Various types exist.

mixer *See* concrete/soil mixer, pug mill (*B*).

mix-in-place [s.m.] *Soil stabilization* in which the soil is mixed by a *travel mixer* without being removed from the site. *Compare* plant mix.

MMA welding *Manual metal-arc welding*.

mnemonic [d.o.] A device to aid the memory. Mnemonics are often used in engineering formulae; the symbols being chosen so that they are easily remembered. One engineering mnemonic is the *bending formula*:

$$\frac{M}{I} = \frac{f}{y} = \frac{E}{R} \text{ remembered as Mifyer.}$$

Others are:

Thirty days hath September,
April, June, and November;
All the rest have thirty-one
Excepting February alone.

Sir Humphry Davy
Abominated gravy.
He lived in the odium
Of having discovered sodium.

The *compressive strength* of a concrete is roughly related to its *water/cement ratio* and *aggregate/cement ratio* by mnemonics.

mobile crane, truck-mounted crane A crane which is driven by petrol or diesel engine and travels either on *crawler tracks* or rubber tyres. When lifting at one point they are usually stabilized by *outriggers*, often with jacks to lift them off their tyres. One large British mobile crane is powered by two Diesel engines providing electric power to the separate electric motors of each motion. Its biggest lifting capacity is 200 tons at 4 m radius. Not all mobile cranes can slew through 360°. *Loading shovels* although fully mobile are not called mobile cranes nor are *locomotive cranes*. Mobile cranes generally weigh only about twice the maximum load which they can lift.

mobile hoist A *platform hoist* carried on a pair of rubber-tyred road wheels on which it can be towed. It can lift 500 kg to a height which varies with the hoist from 6 to 24 m. Mobile hoists were developed in 1945 for house-building in Britain.

model analysis [stru.] The building of models to scale, their subsequent testing by loading them up to design loads and measuring their deflections, or, for hydraulic models, measuring the heads and flows of water and finally the interpretation of the results in terms of the proposed structure. *See* **deformeter, dimensional analysis, harbour models, photo-elasticity.**

modular ratio [stru.] (abbreviation m) In any composite construction such as reinforced concrete or reinforced brickwork, the ratio of the *modulus of elasticity* of the reinforcement to the modulus of elasticity of the masonry. In Britain for reinforced concrete loaded over a long period it is usually taken as 15 and, for lightweight concrete, 30. Loaded over a short period, strong concrete has m about 6. For reinforced brickwork with weak bricks (10 to 15 meganewton/m² crushing strength) m is 33. For strong bricks (more than 55 MN/m²) 12 is the accepted value of modular ratio.

modulus of elasticity [stru.] or **stiffness** or **Young's modulus (E)** For any material the ratio of the stress (force per unit area) to the strain (deformation per unit length). It is expressed in units of stress, and is usually constant up to the *yield point*. (*See* **Hooke's law.**) The values for some common materials in GN/m² are about as follows: steel 200, *light alloys* of aluminium 69, of magnesium 45, concrete loaded over long periods 14, over short periods 30 (increasing with the strength of the concrete), greenheart 23, Douglas fir 11, English oak 10, most softwoods about 10, English ash and beech 13, resin-bonded chipboard, or *lightweight concretes* (of density around 960 kg/m³) about 3. *See* **elastic constants.**

modulus of incompressibility [s.m.] The ratio of the pressure in a soil mass to the volume change caused by the pressure.

modulus of resilience [mech.] *See* **resilience.**

modulus of rigidity [stru.] or **shear modulus** The ratio of the *shear stress* to the *shear strain* in a material. *See* **Poisson's ratio.**

modulus of rupture [stru.] The breaking stress of a cast-iron or wooden or mass concrete rectangular beam, calculated on the assumptions that the tensile strains in the beam are equal to the compressive strains at equal distances from the *neutral axis*. The strain at any point is also, as in the usual theory of bending, assumed to be proportional to the distance of the point from the neutral axis. The beam formula discussed under *modulus of section* is applied to calculate the assumed breaking stress. Breaking stress $f = \dfrac{M}{Z}$. *See* **beam test.**

modulus of section or **Z** [stru.] The second moment of area of a beam section (also called its *I* or *moment of inertia*) divided by the distance *y* from the extreme fibre to the neutral axis, used in the formula $f = \dfrac{M}{Z}$.

For a symmetrical beam there is one section modulus:
$$Z = \frac{I}{y = \text{half beam depth}}$$
but for an unsymmetrical beam there are two, one corresponding to each distance from the neutral axis. ($M = $ bending moment, $f = $ stress.) *See* **mnemonic, modulus of rupture, plastic modulus.**

modulus of subgrade reaction [s.m.] The value K in the empirical equation: Soil pressure $= K \times$ settlement. This equation is not always reliable but may be a useful working assumption up to a limiting pressure.

modulus of volume change [s.m.] or **co-efficient of volume decrease** The *coefficient of compressibility* divided by $(1 + \text{initial } voids ratio)$.

Mohr's circle of stress [stru.] A graphical construction which enables the stresses in a cross-section oriented at any direction to be easily determined if the *principal stresses* are known. It is commonly used for determining stresses in two directions but also, with slight further complication, can be used for determining three-dimensional stresses. *See* **ellipse.**

moil *See* gad.

moisture content [s.m.] The weight of water in a soil mass divided by the weight of the solids and multiplied by 100. *See* **optimum moisture content.** *See also* (*B*).

moisture index [s.m.] *See* **index of liquidity.**

moisture meters Electrical meters exist for determining the moisture content of concrete, timber, plaster, etc., but they generally measure only the moisture of the surface material.

moisture movement A property which causes a material to increase in length when its *moisture content* increases. Most of these materials also shrink when their moisture content falls (all soils, cement products, timbers, wood products, bricks). The reversible moisture movement of concrete or concrete bricks varies from 0·01 to 0·055%, the first and non-reversible drying *shrinkage* being from 0·02 to 0·08%. The moisture movement of clay building bricks is usually below 0·01% and that of sand-lime bricks may vary from 0·001 to 0·05%. Clinker concrete may have up to 0·2% and for this reason clinker blocks must be kept dry before they are built in, otherwise severe cracking of the plaster over the blocks must be expected when the blocks dry out as the house is warmed by its occupants. Redwood along the grain has 0·17% but across the grain the much larger value of 0·7%. This is the expansion which causes panelled softwood doors to be too tight in winter if they fit the frame well in summer. Soils, particularly clays, expand with increasing moisture content. *Clays* shrink with decreasing moisture content until the *shrinkage limit* is reached. *See* **bulking.**

mole (1) A *breakwater*.

(2) A large tunnel excavator, used in soft rock in USA. *Compare* **Magic Mole.**

mole drain A drainage slot cut in a stiff clay by drawing a *mole plough* through it. This method is cheaper and quicker than laying *field drains* and lasts for many years.

mole plough A vertical knife blade with a horizontal bullet shape at its lower end about 8 cm dia., pulled through the soil to form a *mole drain*. A caterpillar tractor making an 8 cm dia. mole drain at 0·6 m depth uphill (and this is the correct direction) needs to be of at least 50 hp. Mole ploughs have also been used for laying copper or polythene water-pipe by towing it on a rope behind the mole plough. The pipe is uncoiled from a drum set up at the exit from the drain to the ditch. Speed of laying can reach 36 m/min. and diameters up to 35 cm can be laid to a depth of 2 m.

moling Making drains or laying pipe with a *mole plough*.

moment distribution [stru.] A method of solving the *bending moments* in continuous beams and redundant frames by successive approximations. Every span is first assumed *end fixed* at each support. Each end fixing is then relaxed in turn and the released support moments are distributed to the different supports in proportion to the *stiffnesses* of the spans, the stiffness being

the $\dfrac{I}{L}$ (inertia ÷ length). *See* **Hardy Cross.**

moment of a force [stru.] The turning effect of a force about a given point. It is equal to the force multiplied by the shortest distance between the force and the point. *See* **bending moment.**

moment of inertia [stru.] or *I* or **second moment of area** About a line in the plane of a section, it is equal to the sum of the products of all the elementary areas times their distances squared from the line. When no line is specified, the least moment of inertia is usually intended, that is, the I about an axis through the centroid. This is the I of the *bending formula*. Its unit is length to the 4th power. *See* **polar moment of inertia, static moment.**

moment of resistance [stru.] or **resistance moment** The couple produced by the internal forces in a bent beam when it is bent to the highest allowable stress. It is the highest bending moment which the beam can carry without allowable stresses being exceeded.

momentum [mech.] The product of the mass of a body and its velocity.

monitor [min.] A *giant*.

monkey (1) A *drop hammer*.
(2) Scots term for the trip gear which detaches the drop hammer from the rope which raises it.

monocable An *aerial ropeway* with one rope which fulfils the double function of haulage and track rope. A large monocable installed in 1930 from Tilmanstone colliery to Dover harbour delivered 120 tons of coal per hour to dockside bunkers. This unusually long monocable passed through a tunnel, and was laid out in two sections of 6·5 and 5·2 km.

monolith A large hollow rectangular, concrete, stone, or brick foundation sunk as an *open caisson* and excavated by grabbing crane. It has several compartments or wells of which the bottoms are sealed to the foundation when this is reached. The wells are often also filled with concrete. A monolith may also be sunk as a *box caisson*, or be built from the foundation within a cofferdam or pneumatic caisson. A *cylinder* is a circular monolith.

monolithic Forming a single block without joints, a description often applied to the whole of a reinforced-concrete structure between successive *movement joints*.

monorail (1) A *telpher*.
(2) A rail track laid over a building site for placing concrete. The track

consists of one deep rail laid on sleepers on the ground.

monotower crane A *tower crane*.

monument [sur.] or **beacon** A stone set by a surveyor to mark a corner or line of a site boundary, etc.

mooring forces *See* **berthing impact.**

mortar A paste of cement, sand and water laid between bricks, blocks or stones, and usually now made with *masonry cement*, formerly with cement and lime putty. The matrix of a concrete also is a mortar.

mosaic [air sur.] A map made by fitting together a large number of *vertical photographs* which have been enlarged to the same scale. It is not called a map because its inaccuracy though slight may be more than that of a map of the same scale, or at least of a different sort. A mosaic is much more quickly made than a map to the same scale.

motion study The study of the movements of workers with the intention of reducing their labour and increasing their output by laying out their work carefully or providing them with work-saving tools.

motor grader An *auto-patrol*.

motor starter [elec.] *See* **starter.**

motorway A fast road, like a *freeway*, for some motor vehicles only.

mould A temporary, usually wooden structure built to hold concrete or plaster while it is setting. The use of this word is usually restricted to factory work. For site concrete the words *formwork* or shuttering are more usual.

mouldboard In a farmer's plough, the steel blade which turns over the slice of earth. Hence the flat blade of a *dozer* which pushes the earth in front of it.

mould oil Oil, soft soap, worthless paint or similar liquids which are not absorbed by *formwork*, laid over it to prevent it sticking to concrete. *See* **release agent.**

mound breakwater A *rubble-mound breakwater.*

mountain railway [rly] A railway so steep that trains are pulled by ropes or a rack locomotive. *See* **locomotive haulage, rack railway.**

movable bridge [stru.] Many types of *drawbridge, swing bridge, traversing bridge* and others that can be moved to allow vessels to pass. They often have a deck built of orthotropic steel plate, i.e. steel plate, stiffened by joists welded under it, that is extremely light in weight. Occasionally they have been built of *light alloy*.

movable dam [hyd.] A dam of which part or all may be removed during floods to increase the flow past it. *See* **stop log.**

movement joints in concrete Movement joints, according to BSCP 110:1972, may be of five types, though it is possible for one to combine the properties of one or more others. They reduce or prevent cracking or buckling caused by temperature changes, *shrinkage, creep, subsidence* and so on. Their location is important. Where possible they should be placed at points where cracking (or buckling) might start. The five types are: *contraction, expansion, hinge* or hinged joint, *settlement* and *sliding joints.*

moving forms A term which has been used in three different senses, *climbing forms, travelling forms,* and *sliding forms.*

moving load [stru.] A *live load* which is moving, for example, pedestrians, wheeled traffic, and so on.

muck Waste rock, or rubbish, or excavated earth.

mucking, mucking out [min.] Removal of *waste* rock in tunnelling.

muck-shifting plant *See* **earth-moving plant.**

mud flow *See* **flow slide.**

mud flush [min.] *Drilling fluid.*

mud jacking Boring a hole through a concrete road slab which has sunk and connecting it to a mud jack by flexible pipe. The mud jack is a lorry on which is a mixer for water–soil–cement slurry and a pump which forces the mix under the slab and raises it (USA).

Mulberry harbour A harbour made on the north-west coast of France in June 1944 by the invading Allies, who towed precast concrete quays from England and sank them in position offshore.

multi-bucket excavator or **scraper excavator** A machine like a *bucket-ladder dredger* designed for digging sand or ballast in long cuttings for road, railway, or canal excavation. One large machine digs 80 cu. m per hour on a slope 8 m high. The bucket chain is sloped at the angle of repose or slightly flatter. The driving engine is at the upper end, which is the delivery end of the bucket ladder, and is carried on a truck moving on rails along the top of the excavation. *Compare* **rotary excavator** (2).

multi-media filter *See* **filtration.**

multi-phase flow [hyd.] Underground this refers to the movement of oil, gas and water, sometimes also to fresh water, brackish water and salt water.

multiple-arch dam [hyd.] A *dam* built of repeating arches whose axes slope at about 45° to the horizontal. The arches are carried on parallel buttress walls. This is a lightweight dam suitable for a weak foundation, as for example the dam of La Girotte at 1750 m altitude in the French Alps. *See* **flat-slab deck dam, round-headed buttress dam.**

multiple-dome dam [hyd.] A development of the *multiple-arch dam.*

multiple-expansion engine [mech.] An engine driven by steam or compressed air which expands in two or more stages. A *compound engine* has 2, a triple-expansion engine 3, a quadruple-expansion engine 4 stages. *See* **compounding.**

multiple wedge [min.] The *plug and feathers.*

multiplying constant [sur.] In *stadia work,* a constant by which the staff *intercept* is multiplied to give the distance between the staff and the *tacheometer*. It is usually 100.

multi-wheel roller A *pneumatic-tyred roller*.

municipal engineering The design and maintenance of roads, streets, sewers, water supply, public transport, lighting, airfields, and other public services for a town, with concern for the environment.

mushroom construction [stru.] or **mush-room slab, flat slab** Reinforced-concrete solid slabs carried by columns which may be *flared* at the top but are not joined by beams. The slabs may be thickened round the columns with *drops*. The *plate floor* and other floors with a flat soffit are generally preferred, both by architects and by contractors.

mushroom slab *See* **mushroom construction.**

N

nappe [hyd.] A sheet of water which flows over a crest of a weir or dam.

narrow gauge [rly] A railway gauge narrower than 1·435 m, the *standard gauge*.

natural asphalt *Asphalt* as it is excavated. *See* natural rock asphalt.

natural frequency of a foundation The frequency of *free vibration* of a foundation-soil system. It is important that this frequency should be appreciably different from that of any machines which the foundation carries, to avoid *resonance*.

natural gas [min.] Gas which flows from the ground and can be used as a fuel. It is mainly methane, with other paraffins and olefins.

natural harbour [hyd.] A harbour made by the shape of the coastline. *Compare* artificial harbour.

natural rock asphalt Rock such as sandstone or limestone containing *asphalt* or bitumen in its voids.

natural scale [d.o.] A drawing made to equal vertical and horizontal scales is said to be to natural scale.

Nautical Almanac [sur.] An astronomical calendar published annually several years in advance by the Astronomer Royal, for astronomers, surveyors, and navigators, like the *American Ephemeris*.

Navier's hypothesis An assumption made use of by engineers in the design of beams. The stress (or strain) at any point due to bending is assumed to be proportional to its distance from the *neutral axis*. This hypothesis is nearly true and together with Bernoulli's assumption and Hooke's law it greatly simplifies beam calculations. Galileo made the first recorded attempt at formulating this idea early in the 17th century.

navigation [hyd.] A river canalized for shipping. *See* slack-water navigation.

navvy (1) A labourer who specializes in digging foundations, trenches, sewers, drains, railways, and roads with pick, shovel, and *graft*. He may also be able to do concreting and timbering and tunnelling. The word is believed to be derived from the *navigation* labourers who dug the English canals in the 19th century.

(2) Any crawler-mounted crane with *excavator* attachments.

NDT *Non-destructive testing.*

neat lines or net lines The lines defining the sides of an excavation to be paid for in tunnelling. Any material removed beyond the neat line is *overbreak*.

necking [mech.] The *contraction in area* and *elongation* which occur when a *ductile* metal fails in tension. It is seen in broken tensile test-pieces of ductile mild steel and is an example of *plastic deformation*.

needle instrument [sur.] A surveying instrument which includes a *compass* needle.

needle traverse [sur.] A *compass traverse*.

needle valve [hyd.] A cone-shaped valve which ends in a point, used for regulating the flow to large turbines.

needle weir [hyd.] A fixed *frame weir* which carries heavy vertical timbers (needles) in contact. The timbers can be withdrawn as required to lower the water level.

needling To insert a *needle* (B) into a wall.

negative moment [stru.] *Hogging moment.*

negative skin friction [s.m.] *Fill*, unless well compacted, tends to settle. Therefore a pile or caisson driven through recent fill may be pulled further down by the settling material. This negative friction is added to the other vertical loads in the design of a deep foundation under fill.

net duty [hyd.] or farm duty The water supplied to a farm expressed as the depth of water over the irrigated area.

net lines *See* **neat lines.**

net loading intensity [stru.] At the base of a foundation, the additional pressure caused by the weight of a structure, including backfill. Usually it is the difference between the load in kg/m² before digging starts (vertical earth load only) and the load per m² after the structure is complete and fully loaded (*gross loading intensity*).

net ton The US short ton of 2000 lb.

neutral axis [stru.] or **neutral plane** or **neutral surface** In a beam bent downwards, the line or surface of zero stress, below which all fibres are stressed in tension and above which they are compressed. The neutral axis passes through the centre of area of the section (*centroid*), if it is of homogeneous material.

neutral pressure [s.m.] or **neutral stress** The *hydrostatic pressure* in the pore water of the soil. *See* **effective pressure, hydrostatic excess pressure.**

Newlyn datum [sur.] The levelling datum now used by the *Ordnance Survey* of Great Britain, determined by several years of observation of mean sea level at Newlyn, Cornwall. It differs by more than 0·3 m from levels at different points (for example in London) based on *Liverpool datum*.

Nicol prism [min.] A crystal of Iceland spar which has been cut and cemented with Canada balsam so as to exclude the ordinary ray of light and to allow only the extraordinary, plane-polarized ray to pass through it. It is also called a polarizer or an analyser from its function in the microscopic analysis of rock sections. *See* **petrographic microscope, polariscope.**

nip A wound caused to a diver by a fold of the diving suit at considerable depth crushing his skin. Nips are prevented by wearing several layers of very thick underclothing.

nitriding [mech.] or **nitrarding** or **nitrogen hardening** *Case-hardening* of alloy steels containing aluminium by holding at about 500°C for 2½ days in ammonia gas to introduce nitrogen into the surface of the metal. No subsequent heat treatment is needed. It distorts the steel less than *carburizing* or *cyanide hardening*.

nitrocellulose [min.] or **cellulose nitrate** or **guncotton** A solid *high explosive* used with nitroglycerin in gelatine explosives.

nitrogen hardening *See* **nitriding.**

nitrogen method of freezing ground [s.m.] *See* **liquid nitrogen.**

nitroglycerin [min.] A liquid *high explosive* which evolves carbon dioxide, nitrogen, water, and oxygen when detonated. It is the main part of *dynamite*.

nitrous fumes [min.] Reddish fumes of NO_2 and N_2O_3 which are produced when *nitroglycerin* explosives burn instead of detonating. They are poisonous and may be fatal to breathe.

node [stru.] A *panel point* in a framed structure, particularly a truss, where two or more members meet.

nomogram [d.o.] or **alignment chart** A diagram used like a graph for eliminating or shortening calculations. In its simplest form it consists of three straight lines each graduated for one of the variables in a relationship. By joining any two of them with a straight edge the third can be read off. One line showing the velocity of flow in a water pipe can be related to a second showing the internal diameter and to a third showing either the quantity flowing or the friction loss, or both (one value each side of the line). Nomograms are very much simpler to read than graphs showing the same amount of information, because they have no confusing background of squared lines. However, they give no picture of variation, as a curve gives it, and this is a disadvantage.

non-cohesive soil [s.m.] A *frictional soil* (sand, gravel, etc.).

non-destructive testing, NDT A branch of physics that includes any way of checking the quality of materials that does not damage them, e.g. the weighing of coins in a bank, the tapping of railway wheels to see if they 'ring', the filling of a length of drain with water to find leaks, etc. There are at least seven main groups of methods: electrical (conductivity, eddy current, electro-chemical, dielectric); magnetic; penetrant dye; *radiography* and *radiometry*; thermal; ultrasonic and sonic; and visual testing. Many British standards cover this fast-growing subject, including BS 3683, a glossary, and BS 4408, 'NDT methods for concrete', which describes electromagnetic *cover meters*, gamma radiography, surface *hardness*, *rebound hammers*, *strain gauges* and the measurement of the speed of *ultrasonic pulses*.

non-metallic minerals [min.] Abrasives, asbestos, asphalt, building stone, clay, lime, coals and carbon minerals, petroleum, gems, fossil gums, natural gas, pigments.

non-return valve [mech.] A *check valve*.

non-slip floor or **non-skid floor** A concrete floor surface treated with iron filings or carborundum powder or indented while it is wet to roughen it.

non-tilting mixer A drum-shaped *concrete mixer* with two openings which rotates about a horizontal axis. The mixed concrete is extracted from it by inserting a chute which catches the concrete as it drops from the side baffles. There are several standard sizes in Britain, up to about 4 cu. m.

normal curve *See* **Gaussian curve**.

normalizing [mech.] Heating of steel to above the range of *critical points* followed by cooling in air. It softens the steel and makes it less brittle. Other metals also are normalized. *Compare* **stress relieving**. *See* **heat treatment**.

normal law of error [stat.] The equation of the *Gaussian* error curve.

normal stress [stru.] *Direct stress*.

nosing A lateral load from the wheels of a locomotive in either direction, usually taken in bridge design as 10 tons at rail level, perpendicularly to the track. *See* **lurching allowance**.

notch [hyd.] or **notch plate** A small *measuring weir* with its upper edge above water level.

notched bar test [mech.] An *impact test*.

notched weir [hyd.] A *measuring weir*.

notch effect [stru.] The locally increased stress at a point in a member which changes in section at a sharp angle. Close to a right angle notch the stress can be three times as high as the average across the reduced section. Notches are therefore avoided in highly stressed members. *See* **impact test, stress concentration**.

notcher [mech.] A machine in a steel *fabrication* shop, which strips the flanges from the ends of rolled joists.

notching (1) Excavating a cutting in a series of horizontal steps advancing in sequence.

(2) [mech.] Cutting a steel joist in *fabrication* with a *notcher*.

N-truss [stru.] A *Pratt truss*.

O

oblique photograph [air sur.] or oblique aerial photograph An air photograph taken with the camera axis inclined away from the vertical. A high oblique is one which shows the horizon, a low oblique does not include the horizon. *Compare* vertical photograph.

oblique offset [sur.] A distance from a survey line measured at an angle to it which is not a right angle.

oblique projection [d.o.] A pictorial view of an object showing its elevation, plan, or section to scale with parallel lines projected from the corners (at 45° or any other angle) to indicate the other sides. *See* projection.

OBM *Ordnance Bench Mark.*

OD *Ordnance Datum.*

oedometer [s.m.] A *consolidation press.*

offset [sur.] A horizontal distance measured at right angles to a survey line to locate a point off the line.

offset scale [d.o.] A short scale used for plotting details on a map, which have been fixed by measured *offsets* in the field.

Ohio cofferdam A *double-wall cofferdam* built of two lines of vertical timbers, held by tie-rods across the gap, anchored to horizontal *walings* along the outside of each wall. It is built on land or near the shore, floated into the river and fixed by filling it with material dropped in by crane or pumped in by a suction dredger.

oil-well cement A *hydraulic cement* (*B*) which sets much more slowly than *ordinary Portland cement* at the high temperatures in oil-wells. The process of fixing *casing* into an oil-well (usually called cementing) consists of lowering the casing to the full depth, then pumping the calculated volume of cement slurry followed by drilling fluid in through the drilling rods and up outside the casing until all the *drilling fluid* outside the casing is displaced by cement slurry. This is not before the cement slurry begins to appear at the surface. Half an hour's pumping may well be needed before the slurry can be allowed to set, therefore a slow initial set at high temperature is essential. *See* slug.

oil-well derrick *See* derrick (5).

on center [d.o.] An American term for *centres.*

open caisson A *caisson* which may be a *cylinder*, *monolith*, or *drop shaft* and is open both at top and bottom. *Compare* pneumatic caisson.

open channel [hyd.] A conduit in which the upper surface of the water is not in contact with the crown of the channel but with the air. It may be covered over but is the contrary of a pressure pipe.

open cut Excavation in the open, not in tunnel. *See* cut and cover.

open-divided scale [d.o.] A *scale* divided in such a way that only the main divisions at each end are fully subdivided into the smallest units. For instance a 12 in. long scale of 1 in. to 1 ft would have 10 marked but undivided inches in the middle and 1 in. at each end subdivided into twelfths, or other fractions, corresponding to inches on the drawing. An open-divided scale is preferred by most draughtsmen as it is clearer to read and cheaper than a *fully-divided scale.* The *Armstrong scale* is a scale of this type.

open-frame girder [stru.] A *Vierendeel girder.*

open jetty *See* jetty, *also illustration on p.* 186.

open sheeting (1) Vertical poling boards not touching each other, held up by walings and struts.

(2) Horizontal sheeting at open spacing held by *soldiers* and struts. Both types of timbering can be used

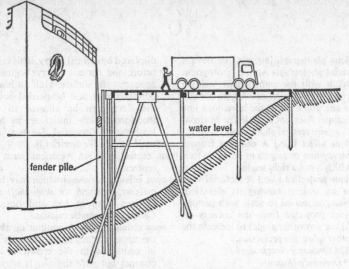

Open jetty, built on driven piles

only in ground which neither flows nor crumbles.

open-tank treatment Immersion of timber in warm zinc chloride solution, a method of preserving timbers which requires only small capital outlay. *Pressure-tank* treatment with zinc chloride solution is quicker and often more effective than the open-tank treatment but requires twice the capital. *See* **preservatives.**

open traverse [sur.] A *traverse* in which the last line is not joined to the starting point of the traverse. It therefore cannot be checked.

open-web girder [stru.] A *lattice* girder.

operation waste [hyd.] Water lost from an irrigation system through spillways or otherwise, after being diverted into it.

optical coincidence bubble [sur.] A *prismatic coincidence bubble.*

optical compensation [sur.] *Autocollimation* of a level.

optical distance measurement [sur.] *Stadia work,* distance measurement with a *subtense bar* suitable for detail map-

ping. Electro-optical distance measurement, on the other hand, is a type of *electronic length measurement.*

optical microscope *See* **microscope.**

optical plummet [sur.] or **autoplumb (1)** An auxiliary telescope, of small magnification, now provided on most *optical-reading theodolites,* which has a line of sight, via prisms, through the centre of the hollow vertical axis of the theodolite. A centring device, giving some 25 mm of movement, enables the instrument, previously levelled, to be centred while the point on the ground (or in the roof) is being sighted through the small telescope. No string or plumb bob is needed. For underground work a refinement, invented by the surveyors of Warsop Main Colliery of the National Coal Board, projects an image of the telescope cross-hairs on to the roof, enabling the instrument to be even more easily centred. A miner's lamp shines through the telescope to provide the necessary light.

(2) Other means of optical plumbing

include the fitting of a pentagonal prism to the object end of the telescope, turning the horizontal line of sight through 90°, thus eliminating the auxiliary telescope.

optical-reading theodolite [sur.] Modern theodolites that have largely superseded vernier or micrometer theodolites since they are smaller, lighter, more accurate, quicker and more convenient to read. Also, being totally enclosed, they need less maintenance than older instruments. The horizontal and vertical circles are of glass, which is more precisely graduated than the earlier circles of metal, and the physical centre of a glass circle is also more easily found. An optical image of the glass circle is transmitted through prisms into an eyepiece next to the main telescope eyepiece. The surveyor thus does not need to move from one side of the instrument to the other when he reads the circles. *See* **microptic theodolite.**

optical square [sur.] A compact, hand-held instrument, more accurate than the *cross staff* but less so than the *theodolite* or the *sextant*, which enables the observer by mirrors or prisms to view a point straight ahead as well as one perpendicular to it, and thus to set out a right angle on the ground. It usually measures no more than 7·6 cm dia. and 2 cm thick.

optical wedge [sur.] A prism placed in front of the object glass of a theodolite telescope in *optical distance measurement*. It deviates the line of sight of the theodolite by an amount that can be read on a horizontal measuring staff.

optimum moisture content [s.m.] That moisture content of a soil at which a precise amount of *compaction* produces the highest *dry density*. It is particularly important to achieve this in *soil stabilization* before the road is completed. *See* **dry-density/moisture-content relationship, Proctor compaction test.**

orange-peel bucket A *grab* shaped like a

half orange cut into segments, used for digging sand, gravel, or clay inside small *cylinders* and elsewhere.

ordinary lay [min.] A description of the *lay* of a steel wire *rope* in which each strand twists in the opposite direction from the wires of which it is made. It is therefore much less likely to untwist than a *Lang lay rope* and can be used to hoist a bucket without guides.

ordinary Portland cement A *cement* made by heating to clinker in a kiln a slurry of clay and crushed limestone, the most generally available and the cheapest *Portland cement* used in building. It is governed by BS 12 which also specifies *rapid-hardening cement.*

ordinates *See* **graph.**

Ordnance Bench Mark [sur.] A levelling *bench mark* in Britain established by the *Ordnance Survey* at a level shown on their maps.

Ordnance Datum [sur.] The levelling datum for the Government agency responsible for mapping in Britain (*Ordnance Survey*). *See* **Newlyn datum, Liverpool datum.**

Ordnance Survey [sur.] The Government agency responsible for mapping in Britain. It belongs to and is organized by a branch of the army, the Royal Engineers.

organic silt or **clay** [s.m.] A silt or clay containing plant remains, occasionally animal remains. It is recognizable by its stink when disturbed and its dark colour. It has very low bearing capacity, being highly compressible.

oriented-core barrel [min.] A *borehole surveying* instrument which takes and marks a core to show its orientation, and at the same time records the bearing and slope of the hole.

orifice meter [mech.] A plate with a hole in it, placed across a pipeline of flowing fluid. The pressure difference between the two sides of the plate is measured and indicates the amount of the flow through the pipe. *Compare* **measuring weir.**

origin [d.o.] A point of intersection between two axes of a *graph*, the zero point of a graph where both y (abscissa) and x (ordinate) equal 0. *See* **Cartesian coordinates.**

orthogonal [d.o.] At right angles, a term sometimes used for orthographic.

orthographic projection [d.o.] The usual method of mechanical drawing by making *projections* such as plans, elevations, and sections, on to a horizontal or vertical plane. The projection lines are at right angles to the plane on which the drawing is made. *See* **plan.**

orthophoto [air sur.] An air photo, usually a *vertical photo*, from which height distortion has been removed by *rectification.*

orthophotoscope [air sur.], **orthoscan, orthophotomat, orthoprojector,** etc. Trade names for *plotting instruments* for *rectification.*

orthotropic [stru.] A description of the physical properties of any material which, like wood, has pronounced differences in two or more directions at right angles to each other. Also called orthogonally anisotropic. For wood, the variations are in strength, but any elastic or flow property may well interest an engineer. *Compare* **isotropic.**

orthotropic plate floor or **deck** [stru.] A floor or bridge deck which is markedly stiffer in one direction (the direction of the span) than in the direction perpendicular to the span, e.g. a hollow-tile floor or a steel-plate deck with joists welded under it. The opposite, an isotropic floor, is less common but *plate floors* are an example.

OS *Ordnance Survey.*

osmosis In chemistry, the diffusion of a solvent or of a dilute liquid through a skin (permeable in only one direction) into the more concentrated solution. It is analogous to the movement of water in soil during electro-osmosis. *See below and* **thermo-osmosis.**

osmotic pressure The pressure in *osmosis* exerted by a solvent when its entry

through the skin into the more concentrated solution is prevented.

outburst bank [hyd.] The middle part of the slope of a sea embankment, between the footing and the swash bank.

outcrop [min.] An exposure of a stratum or orebody at the earth's surface. A buried outcrop is one which would be seen if the recent loose deposits over the *bedrock* were removed.

outfall [hyd.] The point at which a sewer or land drainage channel discharges to the sea or to a river. It may be controlled by a gate or flap valve to prevent tidal water backing up.

outrigger [mech.] A steel beam or lattice girder projecting from a *mobile crane* or other crane. It gives stability to the crane by widening its base.

oven-dry soil [s.m.] Soil dried in an oven at 105°C.

overbreak [min.] or **overbreakage** The amount of rock excavated beyond the *neat lines* of a cutting or tunnel. This additional excavation is not paid for and its cost must therefore be included by the contractor in the price he tenders for the rock within the neat lines.

overburden [min.] (In USA **capping**) The worthless rock or soil over the valuable material in an open cut or mine.

overburden pressure The weight per unit horizontal area of the rocks at a certain level. In mines it is often taken as about $2 \cdot 5$ ton/m^2 for each metre depth.

over-consolidated clay [s.m.] A clay that in previous geological times was loaded more heavily than it is now and consequently has a tendency to expand if it has access to water.

overfall [hyd.] (1) The part of a dam or weir over which the water pours.

(2) The overpouring water (ASCE MEP 11). *See* **nappe.**

overflow [s.m.] *See* **classifier.**

overflow stand [hyd.] A stand pipe in which water rises and overflows at the hydraulic grad eline (ASCE MEP 11).

overhaul (1) In excavation, a distance of

haul in excess of the *free haul*, for which, therefore, extra payment must be made.

(2) [mech.] or **overrun** The condition in a haulage engine when the load runs towards the engine faster than the rope and thus slackens and tangles the rope on the drum.

overhead ropeway An *aerial ropeway*.

overhead travelling crane Lifting plant which is usually power-operated at least in its hoisting motion. It is carried on a horizontal girder spanning between rails above window level at each side of a workshop and consists of a hoisting *crab* which can itself travel from end to end of the girder. The whole area of the workshop between the rails can thus be traversed by the crab. *See* **gantry, traveller.**

overload In structures, a weight greater than the structure is designed to carry. In electrical or mechanical engineering a *load* greater than the plant is designed for.

overload trip [elec.] *Protective equipment* on a motor starter or on a circuit breaker, which ensures that the power is cut when the current exceeds a certain value. It is usually operated by a *solenoid*.

overplanted *See* **underplanting.**

overrun [mech.] *See* **overhaul.**

overrun brake [mech.] or **overriding brake** A brake fitted to a towed vehicle such as a rubber-tyred concrete mixer or a trailer. It operates as soon as the towing lorry slows down and the towed vehicle tends to push into it. This relative movement of the towed vehicle towards the towing vehicle applies the overrun brake. High-speed towing is thus safe.

oversize [s.m.] or **underflow** In classifying mineral, aggregate, etc., into two sizes, the larger size; the smaller size is the undersize or overflow. For screened material the terms undersize and oversize only are used. *See* **classifier.**

overturning [stru.] Tipping over. Every structure, in its stability calculations, must be checked that it cannot turn over.

oxy-acetylene flame [mech.] A flame obtained from compressed oxygen and acetylene in separate steel cylinders, used for cutting metals. Oxy-coal gas and oxy-hydrogen flames are also used. These gas flames are used for *brazing* (B) or welding copper, but for structural steel, *arc welding* methods are usual.

ozonizing *Disinfection* of water by injecting it with ozone; often used in France.

pack or **packing** A steel plate inserted between two others to fill a gap and fit them tightly together.

packer [s.m.] An inflatable rubber ring, like a small inner tube, that is fixed on to a perforated grouting tube to go into a borehole, and inflated when the tube has been lowered to its correct level. The inflated packer prevents grout passing beyond it. The *tube à manchette* uses packers.

packing (1) [mech.] Hemp or similar material inserted in the stuffing box of a pump to make it watertight.

(2) A sand cushion between the helmet and the head of a driven *pile*. *See* **pack**.

paddle [hyd.] A wooden panel for closing the water passage in a lock or sluice or culvert.

paddle hole [hyd.] A hole which allows water to pass into or out of a lock.

pad foundation An isolated foundation for a separate column.

page A small wooden wedge used in timbering trenches.

pallet A lifting tray used for stacking material with the *fork-lift truck*.

pan Steel **telescopic centering** (*B*).

panel [stru.] In a *lattice* girder, the amount of the girder enclosed between adjoining vertical members. *See* **panel point**.

panel point [stru.] or **node** A junction on a *truss* chord, particularly one where a vertical meets the chord.

pan head A head shaped like a cut-off cone, to a rivet or screw.

pannier A basket used like a *gabion*.

pantograph (1) [d.o.] Rods connected like a parallelogram, used for copying a drawing to the same or any other scale.

(2) [rly] An expanding, hinged diamond-shaped structure over an electric loco for collecting power from an overhead trolley wire. It is of the same shape as (1).

parabola [d.o.] The shape made by cutting a cone. It is also the curve of the *bending-moment diagram* for a uniformly distributed load on a simply supported beam. For this reason arches are often made parabolic, since they need to be under no tension if they are subjected to uniform loading.

parallel-flanged beam A *universal beam*.

parallel-motion equipment Equipment fitted to a *drawing board*, that is a considerable improvement on the tee-square and less expensive than the *draughting machine*. It consists of a thick, transparent, Perspex straight edge, some 10 cm wide, lying flat on the board and some 15 cm longer than the board. It runs absolutely parallel to itself. This is arranged by two tensioned endless wires fixed to it, one each side, which run over a pulley at the top and the bottom of the board. There are thus four pulleys. The two at the top, which are of precisely the same diameter, are locked to one shaft so that their motion and that of the wires is exactly the same. Tensioning is either by a spring or by a weight on the bottom part of the endless wires.

park-and-ride In *transportation engineering*, a stratagem to encourage private motorists to abandon their cars at car parks in the suburbs close to bus, rail or underground stations from which public transport to the city centre is easy and fast.

parkway In USA a *freeway* which passes through a park and is administered by a local authority, often a park authority. It is not open to commercial traffic. *Compare* **street**.

Parramatta Bridge An elegant arch, and the longest concrete span in the world,

305 m clear span, completed in 1964 over the Parramatta river at Glades-ville, Sydney, New South Wales, a short distance from the *Sydney Harbour Bridge* over the same river. This arch bridge, built of 50-ton precast concrete blocks, is a revival of the ancient technique of the *voussoir arch*, which had been moribund for 50 years. The 6-lane carriageway is 22 m wide and has 1·8 m footways. Maunsell and Partners of London designed it.

Parshall measuring flume [hyd.] The improved *Venturi flume* of the US Department of Agriculture for measuring the flow in *open channels*. It has a contracting length and an expanding length separated by a throat at which there is a sill.

partially fixed [stru.] An end support to a beam or column which cannot develop the full *fixing moment* to the beam or column is called partially fixed.

partially-separate system A drainage system in which the rainwater from house roofs and backyards flows away with the house sewage and the rest of the rainwater flows off in a different *sewer*. *See* **combined/separate system**.

partial prestressing [stru.] Prestressing to a stress level such that under design loads, tensile stresses exist in the pre-compressed tensile zone (A C I).

particle-size analysis [s.m.] or **grading** or **particle-size distribution** The proportions by weight of the different particle sizes in a soil or sand determined by *mechanical analysis* so as to build up a *grading curve*.

parting agent, parting compound A *release agent*.

Pascal's law [hyd.] A law of hydrostatics (1646) which states that in a perfect fluid the pressure exerted on it anywhere is transmitted undiminished in all directions.

passing place (1) A local widening of a narrow road where vehicles can pass each other.

(2) A railway siding.

passive earth pressure [s.m.] or **passive resistance** The resistance of a vertical earth face to deformation by a horizontal force (usually due to *active earth pressure*). The passive earth force in sand is equivalent to that of a fluid weighing three to four times as much as the sand. It is the reciprocal of the coefficient of active earth pressure in *Rankine's theory*, that is $\frac{1+\sin\phi}{1-\sin\phi}$. *See* **earth pressure**.

passive resistance *Passive earth pressure*.

pavement (1) In Britain, the lay term for a *footway*.

(2) The whole construction of a road, the paved part, including *stabilized soil*, in particular the hard road surface whether of asphalt, concrete, wooden or stone blocks, etc. (BS 892). They are either rigid or *flexible pavements*. *See* **paving**.

(3) A hard floor of tiles, bricks, concrete, wood blocks, etc. (mainly USA).

paver *See* **concrete paver, slip-form paver**.

paving A surfacing over the ground of wood blocks or stone setts or bricks or precast slabs, or a layer of concrete, asphalt, or coated macadam.

paving brick A hard brick of *engineering brick* (*B*) quality for paving.

paving flag or **flagstone** A thin flat stone for surfacing a footway. Cast-stone flags are now usually cheaper than natural stone and they are made without reinforcement 50 or 63 mm thick, 0·3 or 0·6 m wide and 0·3 to 1 m long.

peat blasting [s.m.] or **bog blasting** or **swamp shooting** A method of road building over peat deposits. Hard fill is first dumped on the road site over the peat to a height equal to the depth of the peat. Holes are then drilled or jetted (*see* **jetting**) through the fill into the bottom of the peat at the centre and edges of the road. Charges of explosive are fired at the edges, followed one second later by the detonation of the charges at the

191

centre. The peat is displaced outwards and the fill sinks into the space which was occupied by the peat. If exploratory drilling shows that the fill has not settled sufficiently, the process can be repeated until the settlement is complete. This was done in the Middle West of USA in the 1920s and in Germany for the autobahn roads of about 1935 in peat to some 20 m depth.

pedestrian-controlled dumper A small *dumper* of about 250 litres capacity controlled by a man walking beside it. This machine carries a full mixer load of concrete and thus considerably increases the mixer output above what is possible, even with 3 to 6 barrow men, each wheeling a barrow.

peg [sur.] A short pointed wooden rod driven into the ground to mark a line or a level. A nail driven into the top of the peg usually shows the position of the point.

peg-top paving Paving with very small *setts*.

pellicular water or **adhesive water** [hyd.] A film of water over soil particles, so thin that it is under strong forces of molecular adhesion and cannot be removed in a centrifuge even with a power of 70,000 g. It can, however, be removed by evaporation and the 'pellicular zone' is the depth to which evaporation effects penetrate.

Pelton wheel [hyd.] The commonest *impulse turbine*, a wheel carrying buckets at its perimeter which are struck by a fast-flowing water jet. When the wheel is to be stopped the jet must first be deflected away from the wheel and then shut off slowly enough to avoid *water hammer* in the pipeline. The Pelton wheel is used for medium to very high heads, of 250 m to over 1000 m. *See* **water turbine.**

Pencoyd formula for impact [stru.] A formula used in the design of railway bridges which gives the proportion of the live load due to *impact* to be added for a given span. This proportion diminishes as the span increases.

Fractional impact allowance =
$$\frac{300}{3 \cdot 28 \text{ (span in metres)} + 300}$$
A development of the formula used by Indian engineers is
Fractional impact allowance =
$$\frac{65}{3 \cdot 28 \text{ (span in metres)} + 45}$$

penetration (1) Of sheet piling, its *cut-off depth*.

(2) Of a *monolith* or *caisson*, its depth below ground surface.

penetration needle *See* **Proctor plasticity needle.**

penetration tests [s.m.] Tests of the soil in place which give a surer indication of its load-bearing capacity than tests in the *soil mechanics* laboratory. Broadly they can be divided into *static* and *dynamic penetration tests*. Evidence from penetration tests should always be interpreted with the help of information from boreholes.

penetrometer [s.m.] The wash-point penetrometer is a cone-shaped instrument which is *jetted* into the ground to the required level and then forced in at a measured pressure. It is thus a *static penetration test*.

penning *See* **pitching.**

penning gate [hyd.] Specifically UK term for a rectangular sluice gate which opens by lifting upwards. *See* **penstock.**

penstock [hyd.] (1) A pressure pipe which supplies water to a *water turbine*.

(2) A *penning gate*. In USA only the first sense is used, and this first sense is coming to be accepted in Britain but not, unfortunately, to the exclusion of (2).

peptizing agents Materials which can lower the viscosity of a liquid when they are added in small amounts. This may occur chemically by de-polymerization or by reducing *flocculation*.

perched water table [min.] *Groundwater* maintained temporarily or permanently above the *standing-water level* in the ground below it, usually by an impervious stratum between them.

percolating filter [sewage] A *trickling filter*.

percolation [s.m.] The movement of gas or water through the pore spaces of the ground. *See* **Darcy's law.**

percussion drill *See* **cable drill.**

percussion tools Tools which work by striking rapid blows. Most of them are driven by compressed air like the *hammer drill*; but whether they are driven by electricity or compressed air or hydraulically, they drill rock, chip slag or excess metal from a weld, caulk joints between steel plates, close rivets, and *bush-hammer* stone or in other ways tool the surface.

percussive-rotary drilling [min.] *Rotary drilling* (2) combined with a vibratory or percussion motion on the bit; a fast modern method of rock drilling.

percussive welding [mech.] *See* **resistance percussive welding.**

perfect frame [stru.] A *frame* which is stable under loading from any direction and would become unstable if one of its members were removed or if one of its *fixed ends* became hinged. *Compare* **redundant frame.**

permafrost Permanently frozen ground such as is found in Siberia, Alaska, and northern Canada. It amounts to a quarter of the world's land area. *Foundations* must be based below the *active layer* on frozen ground, and should be prevented from thawing with the warmth of the building by good insulation under the ground floor. *See* **frost heave, refrigerator foundations.**

permanent adjustment [sur.] An *adjustment* to a surveying instrument which is made only occasionally and not at each *set-up. Compare* **temporary adjustment.**

permanent set [stru.] Deformation of a structure or test piece which remains indefinitely after all load has been removed from it. It includes *yield* and *creep*, but not *elastic strain*.

permanent shuttering A lining to *form-work* which encases concrete throughout the life of the structure. Woodwool or insulating board have been used as an insulating permanent shuttering.

permanent way [rly] The *rails, sleepers,* and *ballast* laid for a railway. *Compare* **construction way.**

permeability [s.m.] The rate of diffusion of a fluid under pressure through a soil. It is measured in the field by pumping at a constant rate from a borehole until the level of the water in the borehole is constant. The amount of flow related to the slope of the water table provides the data from which the *coefficient of permeability* in *Darcy's law* can be obtained. Several other boreholes must be drilled to determine the level of the water table during pumping. For sands or silts, the permeability generally varies inversely with the *specific surface*, but is always highly variable. *See also* **Hazen's law, permeameter.**

permeameter [s.m.] A laboratory instrument for measuring the coefficient of *permeability* of a soil sample. The constant head permeameter is used for permeable materials like sand or gravel, the falling head permeameter is used for impermeable materials like clay or fine silt.

personal equation [sur.] In accurate instrument work (not only surveying) it is found that each observer tends to measure every value with a consistent difference from the average of all observers. An observer's personal equation states the correction which must be applied to all his readings to bring them up or down to the average. (The average is the surveyor's closest approximation to the truth.)

pervibration A term sometimes used for internal *vibration* of concrete.

PETN [min.] Pentaerythrite tetranitrate, used in *detonating fuse*.

petrographic microscope [min.] A *microscope* used for studying *thin sections* of rocks to determine the minerals they contain and their particle size. It is fitted with two *Nicol prisms* (a polarizer and an analyser) in addition to the apparatus of all microscopes.

PFA or **pulverized fuel ash** *Fly-ash*.

photo-elasticity [stru.] A technique for examining by *model analysis* the distribution of stresses in unusual shapes under load. *Polarized light* is passed through a transparent model which shows *isochromatic* and *isoclinic* lines. This technique gives the directions of the axes of *principal stress* at any point and the magnitude of the difference of principal stresses. As in the *petrographic* microscope a polarizer and an analyser are needed. The method has been used for determining the stresses in models of soil structures, dams, and other exceedingly complicated structures.

photo-electric cell or **electric eye** An electric circuit using the *photo-electric effect*, for opening and closing doors when individuals approach them, for counting the wagons in a train, etc.

photo-electric effect When light falls on certain electrical conductors a current flows in them; similarly when a ray of light ceases to flow the current is interrupted. This interruption of a circuit is used in the *photo-electric cell*.

photogrammetry [air sur.] or **aerial surveying** The making of maps by photographs mainly from the air, now rarely from the ground. Certain points of known level and position on the ground must be known and recognizable on the photographs. With the help of a *plotting instrument* a contoured map can be drawn from the photographs. Photogrammetry from a land camera was first used by Col. Laussedat in 1849 in France for mapping, only 10 years after Daguerre had invented his photographic process. Laussedat also took photos from the air using kites and balloons but abandoned this in favour of ground photos. Aeroplanes were first used for photography about 1913. *See* **fix, ground control, mosaic, oblique/vertical photograph.**

photomicrograph A photograph of an object as seen under, and magnified by, the microscope.

phreatic surface The *water table* (mainly USA).

phreatic water [s.m.] A little-used term for *groundwater*.

phreatic zone or **zone of saturation** The ground below the *water table*. It is saturated with water but a small amount above it, the lower part of the *capillary fringe*, is also saturated.

picket [sur.] A *range pole*.

pickling of metal The dipping of steelwork in hot sulphuric acid, then hot water, then hot phosphoric acid to remove scale as a preparation for painting or galvanizing. The steel is then dried and painted while still warm. *Compare* **phosphating** (*B*).

pier (1) A wide column or short wall of masonry or plain or reinforced concrete for carrying heavy loads, such as a support for a *bridge*.

(2) A *breakwater* used as a quay.

pier cap or **pier template** The top part of a bridge *pier* which distributes uniformly over the pier the concentrated loads from the bridge. Pier caps used to be of large thick stones but generally now they are of reinforced or mass concrete. Granite pier caps are allowed to be loaded at about the same stress in compression as lightly reinforced concrete, at $5N/mm^2$. Other types of rock are allowed much less than this.

piercing *See* probing.

pier template *Pier cap*.

piezometer tube [hyd.] An open-topped tube (*stand pipe*) for measuring moderate pressures. It contains water or kerosene for low, or mercury for higher pressures.

piezometric surface [hyd.] An imaginary surface above or within the ground, at which the water level would settle in a *piezometer tube* whose lower end passes below the *water table*. It indicates the level to which the water from an *artesian well* could rise. It corresponds to the line of the *hydraulic gradient* in a pipe, except that the water in the pipe flows. A piezometric surface is more responsive to pumping than a water table. It can be lowered in a few minutes by pumping 2 km away, though the water table may take months to settle.

pig [mech.] An iron or lead block as cast at the smelting furnace for remelting at the foundry. The word *ingot* is used for other metals.

pile A timber, steel, or reinforced-concrete post usually vertical and less than 60 cm square, *driven*, *jacked*, or *jetted* into or cast into the ground (*bored pile*). Piles carry vertical load on *bearing piles*, or horizontal load from earth or water pressure on *sheet piles*. *See also* **batter/bored/displacement/sand/screw pile**, *and* **cylinder, pile-placing methods, precast concrete, pretesting.**

pile bridge A bridge carried on *piles* or piled *bents*.

pile cap (1) A reinforced-concrete mass cast around the head of a group of piles to ensure that they act together and distribute the load among them from the structure above.

   (2) A steel plate fixed on top of a steel *cylinder* to distribute the load on to the concrete filling within it.

pile core or **mandrel** A withdrawable steel rod or stiff pipe inserted into a hollow steel *cylinder* pile when the pile is sunk by driving rather than by jetting or grabbing. The force of the pile hammer is spent on the pile core which makes contact with the pile shoe. The cylinder is therefore not damaged by driving.

piled foundation A *foundation* carried on *piles* to ground considerably beneath the surface.

pile-drawer A *pile extractor*.

pile-driver or **pile frame** A hoist and movable frame (usually on skids) which can handle the weight of a *pile* and drive it into the ground. *See* **dolly, leaders, pile frame, pile hammer, silent pile-drivers.**

pile extractor or **pile-drawer** Any *pile-driver* which strikes a pile upwards and loosens the grip of the pile on the ground. The actual pull of with-drawal of the pile is done by the crane from which the pile extractor hangs. It is therefore essential to have a crane which is strong enough for the job. If the pile and extractor weigh 3 tons and the total lift of the crane is 4 tons, only 1 ton of upward force will reach the pile. This is the minimum required – more than 1 ton lift should be available.

pile frame A *pile-driver*. It must be appreciably taller than the longest pile to be driven.

pile group Several driven or bored piles placed close together to take a heavier load than a single pile could carry. A pile group whether of steel, concrete, or timber piles is generally capped by a reinforced-concrete *pile cap*.

pile hammer Generally either a *drop hammer* or a *double-acting* hammer. A steam hammer may be fully automatic, or semi-automatic. Semi-automatic hammers are single-acting, have a steam admission controlled by hand line, give about 40 blows per minute and drive timber or concrete piles. They are extravagant with steam but very simple, trouble free, and easy to use. Steam hammers can also work on compressed air. A Diesel hammer is a drop hammer in which the ram is raised by a *Diesel-engine* piston. About 60 blows are delivered per minute. The blow of the drop hammer is slightly cushioned by compression of the combustible charge in the cylinder.

pile head The top of a pile. The heads of precast-concrete piles are protected by *packing* under a *pile helmet* during driving and sometimes also by a timber *dolly*. The heads of wooden piles are encircled by a *driving band*.

pile helmet A cast-steel cap which covers and protects the head of a precast-concrete pile during driving and holds the *packing* in place between it and the pile head. It is recessed on top for a plastics or hardwood *dolly* to cushion the blow from the drop hammer.

pile hoop A *driving band*.

pile-placing methods Driving by *drop*

hammer or stream hammer, *jetting*, jacking (*pretesting*), boring, pulling down, washing out, blowing out, coring, drilling, grabbing out with a grabbing crane, or explosives or vibration. *See* **bored/driven/screw pile, silent pile-drivers.**

pile ring A *driving band*.

pile shoe A high-grade cast-iron point on the foot of a wooden or concrete *driven pile* to help it penetrate the soil. Its sides slope at about 1 horizontal in 6 vertical. For driving through uniform clay, silt or sand, it may be unnecessary.

pillar [min.] A mass of coal or ore which is left in to support the overlying ground. Pillars, except shaft pillars, are little used at great depths because they crush, sometimes dangerously.

pilot circuit [elec.] A control circuit such as that used in *remote control* or for *contractors*. *See* **relay.**

pilot lamp [elec.] A small electric lamp which shows whether the power is turned on to a circuit, often used to indicate the attitude of a *circuit breaker*.

pilot shaft or **pilot tunnel** [min.] A shaft or tunnel driven to a small part of the dimensions of a large shaft or tunnel. The full-sized shaft or tunnel is later excavated from either end as desired, with full information about ground and water, with good ventilation, and the simplest method of removal of rock.

pinchers Two *poling boards* strutted apart on opposite sides of a trench.

pin joint [stru.] A *hinge* in a structure.

pinned [stru.] or **pin jointed** A description of a beam or a column which has a *hinge* at the end.

pipe liners Polythene (polyethylene) pipe liners up to 500 mm dia. have been inserted into old gas mains and sewers, effectively making them tight, prolonging their useful life, and making them smooth inside.

pipe-pushing or **pipe jacking** or **thrust boring** Building underground pipelines by assembly at the foot of an access shaft and pushing them through the ground, instead of assembling them in situ. There are two main ways in which this is done, which depend on two facts: the first is that a 1 m diameter tunnel is about the smallest in which a heading driver can work, and the second is that some pipes can be pushed through the ground without tunnelling for them, the diameter depending on the pushing force available. For 1 m pipes or larger, miners or tunnelling machines excavate the soil, working inside or beyond the end of the pipe. The pipe is pushed by powerful hydraulic rams in the access shaft, reacting against the wall of the shaft. The whole length of pipe is thus pushed at once; at the point where the pushing load becomes excessive for the rams installed, another shaft must be sunk on the pipeline. The method has been used for driving pipes under rivers, main roads, and railway embankments, and is developing rapidly. *See* **vibrating pile-driver, Magic Mole.**

piping [s.m.] or **subsurface erosion** The movement through a dam or cofferdam of a stream of water and sand. Piping is a subsurface *boil*, and may, like boiling, become disastrous. *See* **critical hydraulic gradient, toe filter.**

pit (1) A surface excavation to obtain sand, clay, gravel, etc.; a *borrow pit* or a *trial pit* for exploration of the ground.

(2) A rectangular hole dug for *underpinning* or for building foundations, *retaining walls*, etc.

pit boards *Well curbing*.

pitched work A stone *revetment* for the slopes of a reservoir or river bank, also called *pitching*.

pitcher A granite *sett*.

pitcher paving *Paving* with granite *setts*.

pitching (1) Lifting a *runner* or a *pile* and placing it in position for driving. In a small steel sheet pile *cofferdam*, all the piles are pitched before any are driven, ensuring that they fit.

(2) or **penning** or **soling** Large stones 18 to 45 cm deep placed on edge and

wedged by small stones called spalls (or rolled) to form a road foundation or a *revetment* to protect an earth slope from scour. Road pitching is usually placed directly on the ground. Embankment or river-bank pitching should be placed on about 23 cm of quarry rubble, chips, or pebbles. For heavy waves the stones should be at least 50 cm deep and at least 15 cm square on the face. The principle is that of the *graded filter*. See **beaching**.

pitching ferrules One or two short lengths of galvanized steel pipe cast into a reinforced-concrete pile and used as holes for lifting it. The exact position is calculated so as to give the least possible *bending moment*, since this is the biggest bending stress which occurs in the life of the pile.

Pitot tube [hyd.] A device used in measuring the pressures and the velocities of flowing air and water. Two tubes enter the stream, one orifice facing the current, the other at right angles to it. The latter measures the static pressure, the former the total (velocity+static heads). The difference between the two readings is the velocity head and from it the velocity can be calculated. Because the Pitot tube is so small, it can be used without disturbing the flow in small pipes or air ducts and can therefore be very accurate.

pivot bridge A *swing bridge*.

placing boom A three-axle lorry with a collapsible crane jib up to about 22 m long, that carries the delivery pipe from a *concrete pump*. It enables floor slabs to be concreted several storeys above ground level with no delays for fixing pipework.

placing plant Plant for placing wet concrete in position. This may consist of *cableways*, *concrete pumps*, *conveyors*, *dumpers*, lorries, *pedestrian-controlled dumpers*, *placing booms*, *platform hoists*, *telpher* cranes, *trémies* or merely of one barrow and a road made of scaffold boards.

plain concrete Concrete with no reinforcement to carry weight or bending

forces but with light steel to reduce shrinkage and temperature cracking, generally about 0·6% of the volume of the concrete. Mass concrete has less steel than this, sometimes none.

plan [d.o.] A view from above of an object or an area in *orthographic projection*.

plane frame [stru.] A frame in which the centre lines of all the members are in the same vertical plane. Most building frames are of this type for the reason that calculation and fabrication are simple. Three-dimensional frames (*space frames*) usually cost more in labour of design and construction, though they may also provide a roof over an area which could not be covered in any other way. A single plane frame is not stable against wind but needs support from walls or from bracing to neighbouring frames.

plane of rupture [s.m.] The plane along which retained earth is imagined to fail when a wall is being designed to retain it in the *wedge theory*. The angle of elevation of the plane determines the weight of the earth retained.

plane of saturation [s.m.] The *water table*.

planer A machine fitted with milling cutters for smoothing a road surface which is usually first heated to soften it.

plane surveying [sur.] The measurement of areas on the assumption that the earth is flat and has no curvature. This assumption leads to no noticeable error for small areas. *Compare* **geodetic surveying**.

plane table [sur.] A drawing board set on a tripod for use in the field. The fixing to the tripod includes a swivel head which enables the board to be rotated and oriented as required to the surrounding country. An *alidade* enables the bearings of objects sighted to be ruled in pencil on the drawing board. The positions of the objects along the ruled line can be fixed by taping or by *stadia work* from a tacheometer beside the plane table, or by a second plane table *set-up*. See intersection, progression, radiation, re-section.

plane-tabling [sur.] Mapping with a *plane table* and *alidade*. It is a very quick way of mapping small areas of open country and is one of the earliest methods of surveying, being several hundred years old.

planimeter [d.o.] An *instrument* which measures the area of a plan whose perimeter has been traced out by its moving arm.

planish [mech.] To smooth or polish by light hammering with a smooth hammer.

planning engineer A civil engineering assistant or qualified civil engineer who plans for a contractor his requirements of cranes, mixers, and other plant and materials in a contract.

planometric projection [d.o.] A pictorial view of an object showing it in *plan* with oblique parallel lines from the corners showing the front, side, and thickness. *See* **projection**.

planoscope [sur.] A levelled instrument set up on a tripod and observable from 150 metres distance or so. Thus a bulldozer operator or a foreman digging a trench can tell, without leaving their work, whether enough has been dug. Viewing from the correct height, the observer can immediately see from the appearance of the image on the planoscope, whether the ground level is correct. Control of formation levels and slopes is thus easier than with the *dumpy level* or other instruments that always need an observer at the instrument.

plant Roads, railways, buildings, conveyors, scaffolding, lifting tackle, pipelines, reservoirs, quarries, mines, offices, and any machines needed to work them effectively. Plant generally means working apparatus which is not machinery, but it may include machinery.

plant mix *Soil stabilization* by carrying the soil to a stationary mixer, returning it to the site and re-spreading it. *See* **soil mixer**.

plant-mixed concrete *Ready-mixed concrete*.

plashing Weaving sticks to make *gabions*. The word also means to weave living sticks horizontally in a hedge.

plastic deformation [stru.] or **plastic flow** or **plastic yield** The flow without fracture of a plastic material during loading. Mild steel and other *ductile* metals show plastic yield during tensile testing above the *yield point*. Clays also are plastic. Any metal which yields plastically is usually preferred in structural design to one which breaks suddenly as in *cleavage fracture*. *See* **plastic fracture**.

plastic design [stru.] or **collapse design** The structural design of steel or reinforced-concrete frames on the assumption that *plastic hinges* form at points of maximum bending moment. The intention in design is to obtain as many simultaneous plastic hinges as possible. *See* **elastic design, limit state design, load factor, plastic modulus**.

plastic flow *See* **plastic deformation**.

plastic fracture Breakage of a metal in tension by drawing out (*necking*). The necking produces a work-hardening effect on steel and the eventual failure is more gradual than the abrupt and therefore dangerous cleavage fracture. *See* **cup-and-cone fracture**.

plastic hinge [stru.] A point of maximum bending moment, which is assumed in *plastic design* to be stressed up to the yield point of the steel. If the hinge is in fact stressed to the yield point it does yield slightly and throws some bending moment on to other parts of the structure, forming eventually more plastic hinges. However, the greatest load applied to the structure (design load) is never more than two-thirds of that which causes a plastic hinge and usually considerably less.

plasticity index [s.m.] *See* **index of plasticity**.

plasticizer or **water reducer** An *admixture* in mortar or concrete which can increase the *workability* of a mix so much that the water content can be extremely low and the mortar or concrete strength can thus be increased. However, plasticizers do exist which have the effect of reducing concrete strengths.

plastic limit [s.m.] The water content at the lower limit of the plastic state of a clay. It is the minimum water content at which a soil can be rolled into a thread 3 mm dia. without crumbling. *See* **consistency limits.**

plastic modulus [stru.] A value used in the *plastic design* of steel structures, which is a constant for each particular shape of section and corresponds to the *modulus of section* used in *elastic design.* The plastic modulus of a rectangular beam is 50% larger than its section modulus. For I-section beams the plastic modulus is generally within 1% of 1·15× the modulus of section.

plastics *See* (B).

plastic welding [mech.] Welding with steel or iron in the plastic state, such as *forge welding* and, usually, *pressure welding.*

plastic yield [stru.] The usual term for *plastic deformation.*

plat [sur.] Term used in USA for a plan showing land ownership, boundaries, and subdivisions with their descriptions but nothing else.

plate (1) [mech.] Copper thicker than 10 mm and wider than 0·3 m, or steel thicker than about 3 mm (11 SWG, but see **steel sheet**). *Compare* **sheet** (B).

(2) [sur.] The upper plate of a *theodolite* is the vernier plate carrying the telescope and the vernier within the lower, outer plate, which is graduated from 0 to 360°. The upper plate is often called the plate, the lower plate is the *limb. See also* (B).

plate bearing test [s.m.] An old method of estimating the bearing capacity of a soil by digging a pit down to the proposed foundation level, placing a stiff steel plate about 0·3 m square on the foundation, and loading it until it fails by sinking rapidly. The method has been somewhat discredited since it has

been proved that on compressible soils the results only apply to a depth of about $1\frac{1}{2}$ times the plate width. If the soil below this depth is softer, the building as a whole will probably settle faster than the plate at the same load. However, if the soil is homogeneous to a depth, below the building, equal to twice the building width, or if the underlying soil is harder than that at the plate, the method may be useful. *See* **ultimate bearing pressure, side jacking.**

plated beam *See* **compound girder.**

plate floor [stru.] or **beamless floor** A reinforced-concrete floor with a flat soffit, commonly used in office buildings because it enables the shapes and sizes of rooms to be altered without difficulty. Careful structural design is needed for the hidden beams, as well as large amounts of steel in them, but some contractors find this the cheapest concrete floor to build. There is a saving in shuttering, resulting from the smooth soffit; compared with the *hollow tile floor* there is also a saving from the labour cost of placing the hollow blocks. A weight-saving, equivalent to that given by hollow blocks, can be achieved by using a *lightweight aggregate.*

plate girder [stru.] Formerly a girder with angles riveted to plates, now usually a unit with two flange plates welded to a web plate. *See* **Britannia Bridge.**

platen [mech.] In a compression-testing machine such as those used for concrete cubes, the smooth steel plates which are in contact with the concrete faces during the test. *See also* (B).

plate screws [sur.] *Foot screws.*

plate vibrator [s.m.] A self-propelled mechanical *vibrator* with a flat base, used for compacting fill which is to be built on.

platform gantry A *gantry* built to carry a *portal crane* or for other purposes.

platform hoist A power-driven hoist (with petrol, Diesel, or electric motor) which lifts a platform carrying a load

199

of 100 to 2500 kg up to as much as 60 m height. The platform is so built that a barrow of concrete or bricks can be wheeled on to it at ground or any other level and wheeled off at the floor where it is needed. The hoist engine is usually at the foot of the tower, controlled by a rope leading to the storey from which it is being used. *See* **mobile hoist.**

plot [d.o.] (1) To draw a map of the ground from field notes made by a surveyor.

(2) To draw a *graph*.

(3) An area of land for building, called a 'lot' in USA.

plotting instrument [air sur.] or **plotting machine** or **stereoplotter** A large drawing machine provided with a mechanically-operated plotting arm and pencil as well as a viewing window in which *vertical photographs* or their projections can be viewed *stereoscopically* together with their *ground-control* points. The draughtsman is thus enabled to fit his ground-control points to his photographs at the correct scale and altitude, to draw *contours* and so on. The machine operates the drawing pencil at a distance by a mechanical linkage as he views the photographs in the window.

Plougastel Bridge A bridge first built in 1930 over the Elorn river in northwest France, having three arch spans at 187 m centres. It is of reinforced concrete with a very small amount of reinforcement (less than 0·3% total) and is also known as one of the earliest sites where Freyssinet used *flat jacks*. The *formwork* for one arch was built on the shore and floated out on barges into position under the first arch. When this arch was built, the formwork was lowered and floated away to the next arch. The bridge was breached in 1944 but rebuilt to the original design.

plough An agricultural implement for loosening *topsoil*. *See also* **mole/snow plough.**

plough steel [mech.] A name used for the

steel from which wire is drawn for making steel ropes, or for *prestressed concrete.*

plug and feathers [min.] or **multiple wedge** Feathers are two steel bars which fit together. They are flat on the inner face, curved on the outer face, and inserted into a hole drilled in rock. The plug is a wedge which is inserted between them and driven in. A line of holes is drilled and then wedged simultaneously to split the rock along the line. It is used for cutting out rock in foundations where the rock must not be shattered, like *broaching*, or for cutting dimension stone. The plug can be driven by hand-hammer or with a *rock drill.*

plum or **displacer** A large stone of any shape dropped into a mass concrete structure such as a dam to reduce the volume (and cost) of the concrete.

plumbago Graphite used as a *refractory* for making crucibles.

plumb bob [sur.] or **plummet** A weight hanging on a string called a *plumb line* to show the direction of the vertical.

plumbing [sur.] Transferring a point at one level to a point vertically below or above it, usually with a *plumb bob*, *optical plummet*, etc.

plumb line [sur.] A string on which a weight is hung to stretch it in a vertical direction. The string should be braided like fishing line to avoid spinning of the bob. Wire is used for *shaft plumbing.*

plummet *See* **plumb bob.**

plunger *See* **ram** (3).

plus sight [sur.] In levelling, the term recommended by ASCE for what is called in Britain a *back sight.*

pneumatic Acting by the pressure of air or gas.

pneumatic caisson A *caisson* in which the *working chamber* is kept full of *compressed air* at a pressure nearly equal to the water pressure outside it. Its advantage over the *open caisson* is that men can work in it in the dry and without wearing diving suits, but they are under an air pressure considerably above atmospheric. Its limiting depth is about 35 m of water, 3·5 bars of pressure. Open caissons have been sunk to much greater depths – as much as 80 m below water level. Pneumatic caissons are much more expensive and are used only when circumstances compel it for one or more of the following reasons: (*a*) when the *formation* below water level has to be inspected and other means of de-watering are not possible; (*b*) when the ground contains rock or boulders, making a sheet pile *cofferdam* impracticable; (*c*) when the caisson forms the starting point for a tunnel to be driven under compressed air; (*d*) when the adjoining ground must be properly supported and not allowed to flow in as may happen with grabbing from an open caisson. *See also* **decanting, hydraulic ejector, weighting, sealing pneumatic shafts to rock.**

pneumatic conveyor [mech.] A tube through which powder or granular material is transported by an air blast. It is used for cement, wheat, pulverized coal, etc.

pneumatic drill [mech.] A compressed-air drill, *see* **rock drill.**

pneumatic mortar Mortar thrown on as *gunite*. For *preload tanks*, very strong, thin walls can be made by guniting the mortar on to the shuttering. Cube strengths of 20 N/mm^2 at 7 days and 40 N/mm^2 at 28 days are easily obtainable since the water/cement ratio is low (less than 0·45). The mortar is built up in layers 25 mm thick by successive passes of the cement gun. It cannot be used with heavily reinforced concrete. It is therefore particularly suitable for *prestressed concrete* and is the only method for covering the prestressed wires of pre-load tanks with mortar.

pneumatic pick A light *concrete breaker* (9 to 14 kg).

pneumatic sewer ejector A *displacement pump* for sewage, which works by compressed air.

pneumatic shaft sinking The use of a *pneumatic caisson.*

pneumatic tool [mech.] Any tool worked by compressed air, usually a hand tool.

pneumatic-tyred roller or **multi-wheel roller** A *compaction* unit. It is a towed *roller* carried on two axles, each of which carries several rubber tyres. It can be loaded with water tanks or other ballast and may weigh up to 200 tons. It compacts earth dams and similar fills in 10 to 15 cm thick layers by from 8 to 10 passes of the roller. *See* **wobble-wheel roller.**

podger or **construction spanner** A single-ended, open-jaw spanner with a pointed handle, 25 cm long for 10 mm bolts, up to 1 m long for 35 mm bolts. The pointed end is used for aligning two or more drilled steel plates which are to be bolted, such as fishplates to rails, or stanchions. The point is inserted through the holes and moved about until they are brought into line. It is used for railway work and building steel frames. *See* **steel erector's tools** (*illus.*).

podzol [s.m.] A relatively acid, surface soil from the *A-horizon* of temperate climates, from which much soluble material (iron and aluminium oxides) has been leached into underlying soils. It has more silica than iron and aluminium oxides together, and may have up to seven times as much.

point-bearing pile An *end-bearing pile.*

point gauge [hyd.] A sharp point fixed to an attachment which slides on a graduated rod for measuring the water level. The point is lowered until it barely touches the water surface. *See* **hook gauge.**

point load [stru.] A *concentrated load.*

points [rly] or **switch** Hinged, tapered *rails* which can be arranged to direct a train on to one or another of the tracks at a junction. The hinge is at the heel of the rail, the toe of the movable rail being locked against the *stock rail.* According to the direction of approach of a train, points are called facing or trailing points. If the train first meets the heel they are trailing points, if it first meets the toe they are facing points. *See* **catch points, spring points, turnout.**

Poisson's ratio [stru.] For elastic materials strained by a force in one direction, there will be a corresponding strain in all directions perpendicular to this, equal to p times the strain in the direction of the force. Poisson's ratio, p, for steel and aluminium is 0·30. The relationship between the *modulus of elasticity* E, the *shear modulus* G, and Poisson's ratio is as follows: $E = 2G(1+p)$.

poker vibrator The usual name for an *internal vibrator*.

polariscope The optical apparatus used in the *petrographic microscope* and in the *photo-elastic* analysis of stressed models. The object to be examined under polarized light is placed between two *Nicol prisms*, a polarizer and an analyser.

polarized light Light in which the vibrations are in one plane only is said to be polarized. A *Nicol prism* filters out all light except that vibrating in one plane, and thus conveniently polarizes the light in a *petrographic microscope*.

polarizer One of the *Nicol prisms* used in a *polariscope*.

polar moment of inertia [stru.] The polar moment of inertia of a plane section is its second moment of area about an axis perpendicular to its plane. If the axis passes through the *centroid*, the polar moment is equal to the sum of the other two moments of inertia about axes passing through the centroid and in the plane but perpendicular to each other.

polder Low-lying land reclaimed from the sea by enclosure with *dykes* (Holland), followed by pumping.

pole (1) [elec.] A terminal of an electric supply, an *electrode*.

(2) *See* **derrick.**

poling back Excavating behind timbering which has already been placed.

poling boards (1) [min.] or **forepoling boards** Horizontal boards in the roof which protect miners in running ground. *See* **forepole.**

(2) Vertical boards which support the sides of a trench or pit being sunk in loose ground. They measure about 1·2 m long and 3 to 5 cm thick. *See* **tucking frame.**

poling frame A *tucking frame*.

polysulphide sealant Many firms in USA and Europe make polysulphide *sealants* of high resilience, that will accept movement up to half the thickness of the joint.

pond (1) [hyd.] or **reach** or **pound** The stretch of water between two locks on a canal or a river.

(2) A German unit of force equivalent to one gram, thus one kilopond (kp) is equal to one kilogram force.

pontoon A vessel, generally flat-bottomed, for carrying plant or materials or for carrying a part of a floating bridge (*pontoon bridge*).

pontoon bridge A temporary or permanent bridge which floats on pontoons moored to the river bed. Permanent bridges are built in this way when the foundation material is very poor. In this case the pontoons may be of reinforced concrete (Lake Washington Bridge, near Seattle).

population [stat.] A number of units from one source which have one variable characteristic (at least) which is the subject of *statistical* examination, for example a consignment of bricks or a number of concrete cubes (crushing strengths).

pores [s.m.] Small cavities in soils, particularly granular soils like sand.

pore-water pressure [s.m.] The pressure of water in a saturated soil, sometimes measured by inserting open-topped tubes into the soil, or tubes leading to a *Bourdon pressure gauge*. Pore-water pressure is often measured in earth dams during and after their construction because the amount of the pressure gives an indication of the *consolidation* process. If the pressure is zero it means that consolidation is complete. *See* **hydrostatic excess pressure.**

pore-water-pressure cells [s.m.] Sensitive instruments for measuring pore-water pressures due to load changes such as the rise and fall of the tide.

porosity [s.m.] The ratio of the volume of voids to the total volume of a soil sample. In sands it is from 30 to 50% but in clays may be above 90%. If the *voids ratio* is e, the porosity is

$$\frac{e}{1+e}.$$

portable crane A crane which is not self-propelling but can be moved about on wheels. It has a power-driven hoist and sometimes also power slewing and *derricking*.

portal (1) [stru.] or **portal frame** (*See* **Titan crane**) A *frame* consisting of two uprights rigidly connected at the top by a third member which may be horizontal, sloping, or curved. It is a *redundant* frame.

(2) [min.] The entrance to a tunnel.

portal crane [mech.] or **portal jib crane** or **gantry crane** A *jib crane* carried on a four-legged *portal*. The portal is built to run on rails set parallel to the quayside in the floor of a quay. Wagons and lorries can pass under the portal or the portal can pass over them.

Portland blast-furnace cement A *cement* with at least 35% of *ordinary Portland* and up to 65% of blast-furnace slag crushed with it. This is good for making the concrete in dams, which does not need high early strength. It resists leaching well and has a lower heat of hydration than Portland cement. *See* BS 146, *also* **Trief process**.

Portland cement Many different cements now in use are Portland cements or at least contain some; the varieties include: *ordinary*, *rapid-hardening*, *ultra-high-early-strength*, *Portland blast-furnace*, *sulphate-resisting* and *water-repellent cements*, apart from coloured cements. Portland cement is made by heating to clinker, in a kiln, a slurry of crushed chalk or limestone and clay. The clinker is finely ground and

some gypsum ($CaSO_4$) is added.

Portland-cement concrete The commonest *concrete* in use today.

Portland pozzolana cement A cement made by adding about 20% of finely ground burnt clay or shale to Portland cement so as to combine with its free lime and reduce its liability to *leaching* by aggressive water such as that containing sulphates or to increase its fire resistance. It hardens more slowly than Portland cement but reaches the same final strength. If the percentage by weight of *pozzolana* rises to 40%, it is described as a pozzolanic cement. *See* **fly-ash**.

position head [hyd.] The *elevation head* of a fluid.

post-hole auger [s.m.] A tool rotated by one or two men, by which 15 cm dia. or larger borings can be made down to about 6 m in unsupported holes and deeper in cased holes. *See* **shell-and-auger boring**.

post-stressing *Post-tensioning*.

post-tensioning A method of *prestressing concrete* in which the cables are pulled or the concrete is jacked up after it has been poured. This method is usual for bridges and heavy structures which are poured in place. The losses of prestress are slightly smaller than with pre-tensioning. *See* **anchorage** (2).

pot A *hollow tile*.

potable water Drinking water.

potential energy [mech.] *Energy* due to position such as the *elevation head* of water or the elastic energy of a spring or structure caused by its deformation.

pot floor A *hollow-tile floor*.

pound (abbreviation lb) A unit of weight in some English-speaking countries, equal to 454 grams (0·454 kilogram). 2240 lb are equivalent to 1 long ton. *Also see* **pond**, *and* conversion factors, p. 9.

pound-foot [stru.] A unit of *bending moment*, the effect of 1 lb force at a distance of 1 ft. *Compare* **foot-pound**.

powder spreader A *bulk spreader*.

power [mech.] Mechanical power can be provided by portable *internal-combus-*

Cement type and BS	Setting in relation to ordinary Portland	Minimum strengths, N/mm^2				In relation to ordinary Portland	
		Vibrated cubes		Hand-made cubes		early heat evolution	resistance to sulphate attack
		3-day	7-day	3-day	7-day		
Portland cements							
BS 12 ordinary	2–8 hrs	15	23	8	14	—	—
BS 12 rapid hardening	similar	21	28	12	17	higher	similar
BS 146 blast-furnace	slower	15	23	8	14	lower	better
BS 1370 low-heat	slower	7·5	14	3·5	7	lower	similar
BS 4027 sulphate-resisting	similar	15	23	8	14	lower	better
BS 4246 low-heat blast-furnace	slower	7·5	14	3·5	7	less	better
White or coloured or hydrophobic (water-repellent) (No BS) Generally similar to Portland cement							similar
Ultra-high early strength (No BS)	faster	30	32	16	20	higher	similar
non-Portland cements							
BS 4248 super-sulphated	slower	14	24	7	17	low	better
BS 915 high-alumina	similar	42 (24-hour)	49 (3-day)	—	—	much higher	much better

The table states the average strengths of 3 mortar cubes, crushed at 3 days and 7 days, using 300 kg/m³ of cement, cured in air for 24 hours at 19°C and 90% relative humidity, then stored in water until crushed. The strengths are the minima required by the BS for the cement, though for some there are no BS. 28-days strengths are, very roughly, double 7-day values except for high-alumina cement, which reaches its full strength in 24 hours. All the BS for Portland cements insist that 7-day strengths shall show an increase on the 3-day values. Rapid-hardening and ultra-high early strength cements are 30 to 40% dearer than ordinary; white and coloured cements from 70 to 500% dearer and high-alumina about 100% dearer. (BS CP 110) *tion engines* or by stationary plants such as electric power stations or air compressors with power lines running out from them to small motors. The sources of power are generally only fuel and falling water, though occasionally the sun, winds, and the warmth of rivers are used. In electricity, power is the product of current squared times resistance, I^2R, which is the same as voltage times resistance, EI, and is expressed in watts or *kilowatts*. Mechanical power is expressed in *horsepower* or kilowatts. *See* conversion factors, p. 9.

power barrow A *pedestrian-controlled dumper*.

power earth auger [s.m.] A *truck-mounted drilling rig*.

power rammer A hand-operated compacting machine which weighs about 90 kg and is raised by its own internal-combustion engine. It rams the earth by dropping on it. *See* **frog rammer.**

power shovel A loose term for any *excavator*.

power take-off [mech.] An external splined shaft on a *tractor* used generally while the tractor is stationary for driving plant such as winches, pumps, threshing machines, etc.

power wrench *See* **impact spanner.**

pozzolana, pozzolan Originally a volcanic dust used at Pozzuoli, Italy, as a *hydraulic cement* (*B*) when mixed with lime. It can be made artificially by burning and grinding clay or shale. *Fly-ash* counts as pozzolana in the UK. Pozzolanic implies an ability to combine with lime under water, in the same way as any hydraulic cement. *See* Portland pozzolana cement.

pozzuolana *See* **pozzolana.**

Pratt truss [stru.] or **Linville truss** or **N-truss** or **Whipple-Murphy truss** A bridge- or roof-truss with vertical struts separating the panels. Many variations of the panel shape exist, one extreme being the *queen-post truss* (*B*) with only two verticals.

pre-boring for piles *Spudding* or boring holes for timber piles through ground

which is too hard for them to be *driven* in without damage.

precast concrete Concrete beams, columns, lintels, *piles*, and parts of walls and floors which are cast and partly matured on the site or in a factory before being lifted into their position in a structure. Where many of the same unit are required, precasting may be more economical than casting in place, may give a better surface finish, reduce shrinkage of the concrete on the site, and make stronger concrete. *See* **pre-tensioning.** *Compare* **cast-in-situ.**

precipitation All the water which falls as rain, hail, snow or dew, expressed as daily, monthly, or annual millimetres of rainfall.

precise levelling [sur.] When L is the distance between two points in km, precise levelling can determine the difference in level between the points in two successive determinations which do not differ more than $1 \cdot 2 \sqrt{L}$ mm. In ordinary levelling the allowable difference is about $12 \sqrt{L}$ mm.

precision [sur.] The precision of a measurement is the fineness with which it has been read. For instance a precise tape measurement may be taken to $0 \cdot 001$ m but may nevertheless be grossly inaccurate because of *tape corrections* which have not been allowed for. Precision is therefore different from *accuracy*.

pre-coated chippings or **grit** *Coated chippings* or *grit*.

pre-consolidation load [s.m.] By drawing the curve of compression of a clay which is compressed in the *consolidation press*, an estimate can be made of the highest load to which it has been subjected in the past. This pressure can be translated into a depth of soil and compared with the existing depth of soil. The difference is the erosion caused by glaciation and other processes.

pre-formed rope [min.] A steel-wire rope made of strands which are bent to their *lay* before they are laid together. The rope therefore does not spin or kink.

preliminary treatment [sewage] Removal of gross solids, grit, oil, grease, synthetic wrapping film and other plastics before *primary treatment*. Sometimes the solids are broken up by a *comminutor*, so that they are then not removed until the next stage – primary treatment.

pre-load tank A circular concrete tank prestressed by winding round the walls a single *post-tensioned* high-tensile wire in a continuous spiral. The tension is applied by a machine hung from wheels travelling round the top of the wall, with the wire gradually climbing to the top. The wire is tensioned on this machine by passing (for instance) a 5 mm dia. wire through a *cold drawing* die of 4·8 mm bore during winding. The stress induced is thus about 1 GN/m². For large tanks the preload system can be economical, a 21 m dia. tank for instance can be built to carry 5·8 m depth of liquid with a wall of *pneumatic mortar* which is 15 cm thick for its full height.

prepacked concrete or **grouted aggregate** Colcrete.

preservatives for timber Civil engineering timbers for harbour work or others that do not need much handling are best treated against fungus and termites by *pressure creosoting* (BS 913), but pressure-creosoted timbers are not pleasant to touch. BS 4072 specifies suitable copper-chrome-arsenic mixtures and their application. They are said to be as effective as creosote, not unpleasant to the touch, but being waterborne are not recommended for river or harbour work. *Open-tank treatment* is occasionally used. General guidance is given by BS 1282 and by Building Research Digest 201. Many BS describe the individual preservatives.

press In steel *fabrication*, presses are used for punching holes, notching, shearing, *joggling*, and so on. *See* **hydrostatic press.**

pressure (1) *Force* per unit area. In this sense it is similar to stress but stresses are usually estimated on solids, pressures on fluids. *See* conversion factors, p. 9.

(2) [min.] The air pressure for compressed-air *rock drills* can be from 5 to 7 bars, the most economical pressure being 6·2 to 6·6 bars, since although breakages are high at this pressure, drilling speeds are also high.

(3) [min.] *Drilling fluid* pressures require to be balanced against the gas pressure in an oil-well. Gas pressures vary between 90 and 120 millibars per metre depth.

(4) [s.m.] Ground pressure in shafts may reach, in loose ground above the water table, 5 KN per sq. m of shaft exposed per metre of depth. Below the *water table*, 10 KN per sq. m per metre depth is the usual maximum but this figure rises to 15 in fluid silt or clay. *See* **effective pressure, hydrostatic excess pressure.**

pressure creosoting The most effective way of preserving timber by creosoting, under pressure in tanks. *See* **preservatives for timber.**

pressure gauge [mech.] An instrument for measuring fluid pressure. The *Bourdon pressure gauge* is a simple and popular device, but needs calibrating for precise work. *See* **manometer.**

pressure head [hyd.] The head of water at a certain point in a pipeline due to the pressure in it.

Pressuremeter [s.m.] An *in-situ soil testing* device lowered into an uncased borehole, which expands into the soil, compressing it at pressures that are recorded. This pressure/deformation relationship is used to determine the strength of the soil.

pressure tank (1) A tank in which timber is inserted for impregnating with creosote or zinc chloride or other *preservative*. *Compare* **open-tank treatment.**

(2) A closed tank for heating tar or bitumen and spraying it through jets on to a road. *See* **tank sprayer.**

pressure vessel A vessel to contain fluid under pressure. The commonest types are steel boilers that contain steam, but the safety demands of nuclear power stations have brought in a new type of purely civil engineering pressure vessel, made of prestressed concrete (PCPV) and controlled by BS 4975:1973 'Prestressed Concrete Pressure Vessels for Nuclear Reactors'. In the UK in 1973, four PCPV contained Magnox reactors and ten more contained, or were to contain when built, advanced gas-cooled reactors. Their great safety advantage is that unlike steel vessels they can be made very large, to contain both the reactor and its boilers with all the primary coolant. The operating conditions, of pressurizing and heating, improve the safety of the vessel by reducing the compressive stresses in the concrete formed during tensioning. Internal dia. of a PCPV is above 25 m with wall thickness of over 3 m.

pressure welding [mech.] Welding by pressing the joint parts together while the weld metal is plastic. Many methods of electrical *resistance welding* use pressure. *See* forge welding.

prestressed concrete [stru.] Concrete in which cracking and tensile forces are eliminated or greatly reduced by compressing it by stretched cables within it, or by pressure from *abutments*. The two main methods both use bars or wires in the concrete: *post-tensioning* and *pre-tensioning*. Prestressed concrete is economical for spans which are large or where the beam depth must be reduced to a minimum.

A possible development may be the prestressing of concrete by the use of *expanding cement*, but this is not yet past the experimental stage. The *cold drawn* wires used in prestressing are of carbon steel containing 0·7 to 0·8 % C with a breaking strength of 1540 N/mm² at 7 mm dia. increased by further cold drawing to 2300 N/mm² at 2 mm dia. The 0·2 % *proof stress* is often used to define the strength of the

wires. The working stress allowed is generally 0·65 of the breaking strength or 0·80 of the 0·2 % proof stress, whichever is the lesser. The behaviour of these wires on stressing varies considerably with the period which has elapsed since cold drawing. *See* steam curing, tendon.

prestressed concrete cylinder pipe or **cylinder prestressed concrete pipe** A welded steel pipe at whose ends a steel socket and a spigot are welded. Inside it is lined with spun concrete. Outside it is radially prestressed by high-tensile wires wrapped round it, and protected by cement mortar all round. These pressure pipes are used in pipelines.

prestressing [stru.] Applying forces to a structure to deform it in such a way that it will withstand its working loads more effectively or with less total deflection. When concrete beams are prestressed they deflect upwards slightly by an amount about equal to their total downward deflection under design load. Downward deflection is thus less than half that of a reinforced-concrete beam of the same shape. The struts (or braces in USA) to deep excavations in bad ground are prestressed to prevent settlement of the surface and damage to neighbouring structures. *See* pretesting, *and above*.

pre-tensioning [stru.] or **Hoyer method of prestressing** Concrete members are precast, in a works, with the tensioned wires embedded in them. The wires are anchored either against the moulds or against permanent abutments in the ground. After hardening, the concrete is released from the mould and the wires are cut at the anchorage. This method may give a larger loss of prestress than with post-tensioning but is usually economical for small members and may produce better concrete since it is always factory controlled. In long-line prestressing, used for the precasting of pre-tensioned concrete floor slabs or beams, the casting bed may be as much as 180 m

207

long, enabling units to be cut to any desired length with a *diamond saw*. The width of the units may be 1·2 m, and their thickness 15, 20 or 25 cm. They usually have tubular voids running down the length and occupying about 30% of the cross-section.

pretesting A term used by Lazarus White and Edmund Prentis to describe their patented method of *underpinning* tall buildings in New York. Steel-cylinder piles are sunk by jacking or grabbing (or both) to the rock, which may be 12 m down. The piles are filled with concrete. When the concrete has hardened they are jacked against the structure one at a time and pinned against it while the load is on the jack. In this way the elastic shortening of the pile, which in 12 m is appreciable, has no effect and the building is underpinned to new foundations without movement. Pretesting is the jacking of the piles, so called because it tests them to a load about 50% more than their design load. The word is also used for the prestressing of struts (braces USA) in timbered excavations.

Primacord fuse [min.] American *detonating fuse* with a core of PETN (pentaerythrite tetranitrate).

primary breaker [min.] A breaker such as a *gyratory* or *jaw breaker* which breaks ore down to about 5 cm max.

primary treatment [sewage] Sedimentation – the settling of solids out of *sewage* and their removal in the form of a *sludge* of well over 90% water. Sedimentation removes about half the pollutants from the sewage. Its efficiency is improved by *preliminary treatment*.

prime mover [mech.] An *internal-combustion/steam engine*, *water wheel*, or *steam/water turbine* or windmill which converts fuel or other natural energy into mechanical power.

primer (1) [min.] A cartridge which sets off the other cartridges in a hole. It is one in which a *detonator* is inserted and is usually either the first or the last of the charge.

(2) [s.m.] In *soil stabilization* a bituminous spray with which soil is covered after compaction so as to waterproof it.

priming (1) [mech.] Filling a pump or siphon with water so that it is enabled to flow.

(2) [hyd.] The first filling of a canal or reservoir with water. It may occur annually or only once in the lifetime of a reservoir.

principal point [air sur.] The point on an air photograph where the optical axis of the camera intersects the film.

principal stress [stru.] If a piece is loaded by several forces in different directions, these *stresses* may be resolved into three simple *direct stresses* which are in planes at right angles to each other. Of these three planes, two are called principal planes and the stresses across them (which are greater than that across the third plane) are called principal stresses. *See* **Mohr's circle of stress, photo-elasticity.**

principle of Archimedes [hyd.] When a body is immersed in a fluid it loses weight by an amount equal to the weight of the fluid which it displaces, called its *buoyancy*. This principle applies to floating or submerged bodies as well as to those which neither float nor are submerged. *See* displacement.

principle of superposition [stru.] *See* superposition.

prismatic coincidence bubble or **split bubble** [sur.] A refinement fitted to most modern, precise levelling instruments. An arrangement of prisms enables the surveyor to sight half of each end of the bubble at the same time, with the images of the two halves conveniently alongside each other. Exact levelling is thus made easier.

prismatic compass [sur.] A pocket compass by which bearings as close as 1° of arc can be read by holding the instrument to the eye and looking through the prism at the compass card while sighting the object.

prismatic telescope [sur.] A *theodolite*

telescope with an eyepiece fitted with a prism reflecting at 90°. By this means steep sights can be taken easily.

prismoidal formula A formula for obtaining the volume of earth from the length of the excavation L, the two end areas A_1, A_2 and the area Am at the midpoint.

$$\text{Volume} = \frac{L}{6}(A_1 + A_2 + 4 \times Am).$$

Compare **Simpson's rule.**

prism square [sur.] An *optical square* containing a prism.

probability [stat.] In *statistics* the estimation of the number of chances by which an event may happen, compared with the total number of chances. It is used in engineering for estimating probable strengths from occasional test results, and in *surveying* for estimating *probable error*.

probable error [stat.] A *deviation* equal to 0·6745 times the *standard deviation*. For a *Gaussian* distribution of values, ordinates placed at amounts equal to the probable error each side of the average value include half of the observations. It is therefore the most probable error. The idea is used in *surveying*, in construction, and in sampling.

probing [min.] or **piercing** Pushing or driving a pointed steel rod up to 6 m long into the ground for determining the position of bedrock or hard lumps. In Burma, bamboo rods are used in probing for gem gravels.

processing [s.m.] The various operations of *soil stabilization*, including *pulverizing*, moisture control, addition of *stabilizer*, mixing, rolling, and covering with a *primer*. *See* **plant mix.**

Proctor compaction test [s.m.] A way of compacting soils in the laboratory, standardized to give results which can be compared. By weighing different compacted samples of the same soil the *optimum moisture content* can be determined. The test is used for soils in earth structures such as *earth dams*,

soil-stabilized roads, and so on. *See* **compaction.**

Proctor plasticity needle [s.m.] or **penetration needle** A rough but convenient instrument for measuring the resistance of a soil to penetration at a standard rate of 13 mm per second. Needles of area varying from 645 to 32 sq. mm are used and a spring balance shows the force needed to push the needle in. Granular soil must be screened to remove coarse material which gives erratic results. *Compare* **California bearing ratio.**

profile (1) *See* **longitudinal profile.**

(2) [sur.] Two upright posts driven into the ground, joined by a horizontal board (*sight rail*) nailed to them. With other profiles it shows the amount of earth that must be dug out.

profile paper [d.o.] Squared paper on which profiles of ground levels can be drawn.

progression [sur.] or **traversing** Doing a *traverse* with a *plane table* set up at each station in turn, using the *alidade* to align the backsight and foresight and taping (or determining by *stadia*) the distance between stations. The traverse lines are drawn on the plane table as they are made.

projection [d.o.] Drawing on a plane surface (usually paper or cloth) such objects as machines, buildings, or the earth's surface, which are not plane. To make the drawing practicable it is assumed that parallel lines are projected from each point on the object towards the paper. *See* **axonometric/isometric/oblique/orthographic/planometric projection.**

projection welding [mech.] An electrical *resistance welding* process like *resistance spot welding*, except that projections are formed at the places to be welded before they are put in contact between the *electrodes*.

proof stress [mech.] A means of comparing the strengths of metals which have no definite *yield point*. The 0·2% proof stress, for example, is that stress

209

which causes a *permanent set* of 0·2% in the material; it is often used as a basis for the safe working stresses of light alloys, both in compression and in tension. *See* **high-strength friction-grip bolts, prestressed concrete, secant modulus of elasticity,** *also* BS 4461 *and* BS 4486 on cold worked steels.

propeller fan [min.] or **axial-flow fan** A modern fan evolved from the airscrew. It is easy to reverse and adjust, efficient but noisy. Several airscrews can be placed in series and the power of the fan thus increased without difficulty and at reasonable extra cost.

proportionality [stru.] *See* **limit of proportionality.**

proportioning The measurement by weighing or volume-batching of the constituents of a concrete, mortar, or plaster before they are mixed. *See* **batching plant.**

protective equipment [elec.] Electrical circuits and switches such as relays, *circuit breakers, overload trips, earth-leakage protection,* which protect a machine or its operator from faults or overloads.

proving ring [stru.] A steel ring accurately turned, *heat-treated,* ground, and polished. It is precisely *calibrated* in a testing machine by measuring its diametral deformation for different loads. It is used with a *dial gauge* for measuring a load applied to a structure during testing, as well as for small-scale laboratory work.

pudding stone *See* **conglomerate.**

puddle or **pug** To pack with *clay puddle* and thus to make watertight.

puddle clay or **pug** *Clay puddle.*

pull [min.] The depth of ground which can be shattered at each cut, that is 'pulled' out of the face of a tunnel or shaft during driving. When the *cut* is well designed it is generally not more than 15 cm shorter than the longest hole. With the popular *wedge cut,* pulls of 2 m can be obtained in almost any ground.

pull-lift A chain-operated or rope-operated pulling device, giving a pull of up to 5 tons, and light enough to be carried by one man.

pull-out test A strength test on a concrete structure, preceded by casting a hole in it 32 mm dia. and 76 to 100 mm deep, to contain a bolt with an end clamp, that is pulled hydraulically. If the concrete is strong enough the pulling can be stopped at any stage and no damage is caused. If the concrete is weak and the bolt pulls out, a hole about 100 mm deep and 150 mm dia. has to be patched unless the structure is scrapped.

pulverized coal Finely ground coal of which 99% is smaller than 0·25 mm dia. The ash may go up the chimney as *fly-ash* unless an ash-catching plant is provided and this is the source of fly-ash for civil engineering and building purposes.

pulverizing mixer A soil mixer used in *soil stabilization* for pulverizing the ground over which it passes with its revolving tines, and mixing it with the *stabilizer* spread over the ground. *See* **spotting.**

pump [mech.] A machine used for raising liquids in a pipe. The main types are *air lift, centrifugal/diaphragm/displacement/reciprocating/rotary pump, hydraulic ejector.*

pun To ram wet concrete or earth with a rod or *punner* so as to consolidate it by driving the air out.

punch or **puncheon** A *follower. See also* (B).

puncheon (1) An upright from a waling to the ground in a timbered excavation. (2) A *follower. See also* (B).

punching [mech.] Forming rivet holes in metal with a press. The method is quicker than drilling but weakens the metal round the hole. The strength can be increased to that of a drilled hole if the hole is reamed out after punching, and the weakened metal removed.

punching shear [stru.] When a heavily loaded column punches a hole through a base, the base is said to fail by punching shear. Punching shear is prevented by thickening the base or enlarging the foot of the column so that the shear stress (assumed uniform) round the perimeter of the column does not exceed twice the allowable shear stress in concrete.

punner (1) or **hand rammer** A wood or metal block at the bottom of a handle. It is raised and dropped to compact earth or to bed paving slabs. *See* **rock drill** (*illus.*).

(2) A steel bar plunged up and down in wet concrete to compact it.

pusher tractor A crawler tractor used for pushing, particularly during the filling of a large *bowl scraper* towed by a *wheeled tractor*. Since one bowl scraper does not provide enough work for one pusher tractor, it usually pushes two or more scrapers in turn.

push shovel A *face shovel*.

puzzolane *See* **pozzolana.**

pycnometer [s.m.] An instrument used for determining the density of soils, the simplest type of *relative density* bottle. It may be merely a jam jar. It is weighed three times: empty, then full of soil, then full of soil and water. If the density of the soil particles is known, these three weighings will also enable the moisture content of the soil to be calculated, otherwise a fourth weighing is needed, after drying.

pyramid cut [min.] A method of blasting several rings of holes in tunnelling or shaft sinking. The holes of the central ring (*cut holes*) are shaped like a pyramid, with their toes close together.

pyrometer An electrically-operated instrument for determining temperatures of furnaces, etc. It is usually worked by the radiant heat of the furnace acting on a *thermocouple*.

211

Q

qanat *See* khanat.

quadrant (1) A quarter circle; an arc of 90°.

  (2) A granite sett 46×23 cm shaped like a quadrant.

quadrantal bearing [sur.] or **reduced bearing** A *bearing* less than 90° measured from east, west, north, or south.

quadrilateral [d.o.] A four-sided figure of any shape. Its area is equal to the product of the diagonals times half the sine of the angle between them.

quarry An open pit from which building stone, sand, gravel, mineral, or fill is taken. *See also* (*B*).

quarter The *flank* of a road.

quartering way *See* rift.

quarter peg Pegs placed at the quarter width of a road which, in conjunction with centre pegs, define the road surface.

quartz SiO_2. Crystalline *silica*. The main part of sand, gravel, or sandstone; the transparent part of *granite*; the commonest known mineral and one of the hardest. Silica exists in many crystalline or non-crystalline forms, some of which are gems.

quartzite [min.] A strong *sandstone* cemented by quartz, therefore about 98 % silica.

Quebec Bridge One of the largest *cantilever bridges* in the world, built in 1917. The clear opening of its central span is 549 m, which is larger than that of the *Forth Bridge*, but the Forth Bridge has two main spans and is therefore considerably longer.

quenching [mech.] Cooling steel from above the *critical point* to *harden* it. This is done for most carbon-steel cutting tools such as miners' picks, drill steels, carpenters' chisels, and so on.

quick-levelling head [sur.] A ball-and-socket fitting under a *dumpy level* instead of the three levelling screws.

quicksand [s.m.] A sand through which water moves upwards so fast that the sand is held in suspension by the water. It therefore has no bearing capacity. Quicksands are made stable by reducing the flow of water. Fine sands are more dangerous than coarse sands, and uniform sands are more dangerous than well-graded sands. The worst sands so far investigated have a *coefficient of uniformity* less than 5 and an effective size less than 0·1 mm. *See also* boil, critical hydraulic gradient, uplift, wellpoint.

quickset level [sur.] A level with a *quick-levelling head*.

quick test [s.m.] or **undrained shear test** A *box shear test* or a *triaxial compression test* of a cohesive soil carried out without allowing the sample to drain. *See* consolidated quick test, drained shear test.

quoin post [hyd.] A *heel post*.

R

race (1) [hyd.] A channel to or from a *water wheel* (headrace or tailrace).

(2) [mech.] A groove in which a machine part moves (ball race).

rack (1) [mech.] A toothed bar which in a *rack railway* is engaged by a cog wheel.

(2) [hyd.] A *trash rack*.

racked timbering *Timbering* which is diagonally braced to prevent deformation.

racking [stru.] *See* **wracking forces**.

racking course A layer of graded stone spread over stone *pitching* to fill cavities and form the road shape before surfacing it.

rack railway A mountain railway which can safely be used on gradients from 8 to 15% at which gradient it becomes uneconomical and a rope haulage is preferable. A toothed *rack* bar beside or between the rails provides extra adhesion by connecting with a driving pinion on the locomotive called the climber. *See* **locomotive haulage**.

radar [air sur.] The position and altitude of an aircraft at the moment of exposure of a *vertical photograph* can now be fixed by radar. This has greatly reduced the need for closely spaced *ground-control* points.

radial gate [hyd.] or **segmental sluice gate** or **Tainter gate** A dam gate with a curved water face and a horizontal pivot axis which is usually also the centre of curvature of the water face.

radial-sett paving Paving of small *setts* laid in concentric arcs to form fan shapes.

radiation [sur.] Plotting the surrounding points on a *plane table* set up by radiating lines drawn with the *alidade*, marking off on each line the distance of the point to scale.

radiography *Non-destructive testing* methods involving detection of radiation by photography rather than by instru-

ments (*radiometry*). Gamma rays have been used for detecting variable compaction in concrete up to 60 cm thick, as well as for measuring its density or depth of corrosion or the quality of grouting around prestressing *tendons*.

radiometry *Non-destructive testing* methods involving detection of radiation by instruments such as Geiger counters or scintillation counters, combined with radiation measurement by electronics. Gamma radiation is used for testing concrete because the sources, cobalt 60 or caesium 137, are much more portable than X-ray equipment.

radius [mech.] The horizontal distance from the centre of the crane hook to the centre of the slewing pivot, a distance needed for calculating the allowable load on a crane hook.

radius-and-safe-load indicator [mech.] A pendulum which hangs freely on a crane jib over a board on which are painted the crane radius for any angle and the safe load for this radius.

radius of gyration [stru.] A value used in calculating the *slenderness ratio* of a strut. If A is the cross-sectional area and I the moment of inertia of the strut the radius of gyration equals $\sqrt{\dfrac{I}{A}}$, usually known as k.

raft foundation A continuous slab of concrete, generally reinforced, laid over the ground as a foundation for a structure. It is as large as, or slightly larger than, the area of the building which it carries. A *buoyant raft* is a particular and very expensive raft foundation.

rag bolt A *Lewis bolt*.

rail [rly] One of two parallel steel bars in a railway, laid on *sleepers* to form a track for wagons or trams with flanged wheels. For surface work on passenger track, rails weighing up to 55 kg/m are used in Britain, always *flat-bottomed*, and up to 77 kg/m elsewhere. In mines on steep gradients in USA, wooden rails of 5 by 8 cm section are used, where their high friction is helpful. Also, when a locked wheel does skid, no flat is formed on the wheel. Early railways used wooden rails and, later, cast-iron ones. *See* **continuously welded track**.

rail bender [rly] A tool for bending rails, usually a *jim crow*.

rail chair [rly] *See* **chair, rail fastening**.

rail fastening [rly] For the British *bullhead rail* the cast-iron rail chair with steel or wooden keys to wedge it to the rails was essential. It was held down by spikes or screws through three holes. *Flat-bottomed rails*, now standard in Britain, are fastened down by various proprietary fixings usually with a resilient pad between rail and sleeper, made of rubber sheet. On timber sleepers there is also a metal baseplate, next the wood.

rail gauge [rly] The distance between the inner vertical faces of the track rails of a railway. The usual gauge in Western Europe and USA is 1·435 m but gauges of one metre exist. On sites, gauges vary from 0·3 m up to the standard gauge (1·435 m). *See* **broad/narrow gauge**.

rail key [rly] A wedge which fixes a bullhead rail into a *rail chair*. It may be a steel spring or a hardwood wedge. The key is driven in on the outer side of the rail so as to maintain the correct gauge.

rail test A test for brittleness of rails in which a weight of 1 ton drops from different heights on to a rail on supports 0·9 m apart.

rail tie [rly] American term for a *sleeper*.

railway curves [d.o.] A set of templates for arcs or spirals cut out in wood or celluloid, of different radii, used for drawing to scale the curves of railways.

railway transit [sur.] A *theodolite* with no vertical circle (USA).

rainfall or **intensity of rainfall** The amount of rain as measured in a *rain gauge*, usually expressed as millimetres depth calculated on the area of the funnel.

rain gauge An instrument which collects the rain falling on it and can thus indicate the *rainfall*. It usually consists of a funnel from which the rain drips into a cylinder graduated in millimetres of rain falling on the funnel area.

rainwash [s.m.] The movement of surface soil and rock down a slope with the help of rain.

rake or **batter** An angle of inclination to the vertical.

raking pile or **batter pile** or **raking prop** A *pile* (or prop) which is not vertical.

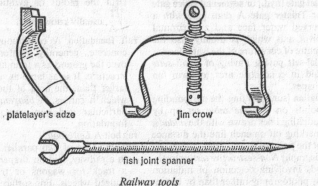

platelayer's adze   Jim crow

fish joint spanner

Railway tools

raking shore *See* (*B*).

ram (1) The cast-iron weight of a *drop hammer*.

(2) To compact loose material with a punner, to tamp.

(3) [hyd.] or **plunger** The moving cylindrical block in the working chamber of a hydraulic press or of a ram pump.

(4) [hyd.] *See* **hydraulic ram.**

rammer (1) A *punner*.

(2) *See* **power rammer.**

ramp (1) A steeply sloping road or floor.

(2) A short length of drain laid much more steeply than the usual gradient.

ram pump [mech.] A *single-acting* reciprocating pump which has no piston but a ram. Unlike pistons the ram is of constant diameter and does not fit closely in the cylinder. The ram passes through *packing* in the end of the cylinder, without a connecting rod. Rams pump by *displacement* only. Pistons pump by end pressure and displacement.

random sample [min.] A *sample* selected without bias so that each part has an equal chance of inclusion. *See* **representative sample.**

range (1) [stat.] The difference between the highest and the lowest value.

(2) [sur.] To align points by eye with *range poles* or with a telescope.

range line [sur.] *See* **township.**

range pole [sur.] or **banderolle** or **range rod** or **ranging rod** A straight staff 2 m long held upright by a surveyor's chainman, or planted in the ground when setting out points in a straight line.

ranging a curve [sur.] *Setting out* a curve for a road, railway, etc.

ranging rod A *range pole*.

Rankine's theory [s.m.] or state of stress theory of granular earth pressures developed by Rankine about 1860. His value for the pressure on a vertical wall retaining earth with a horizontal surface is $\dfrac{1-\sin \phi}{1+\sin \phi} \times$ soil density for

each metre depth of earth retained, where ϕ is the angle of friction of the soil. This value $\dfrac{1-\sin \phi}{1+\sin \phi}$ is called the co-efficient of *active earth pressure*. Compare **passive earth pressure, wedge theory.**

rapid-hardening or high-early-strength cement A *Portland cement* to BS 12 which hardens more quickly than *ordinary Portland cement* and is more costly because it is more finely ground, having a *specific surface* of at least 3250 cm²/g. Vibrated cubes should have a strength at 72 hours of at least 21 N/mm², compared with only 15 N/mm² required for *ordinary Portland cement*.

rapid-transit system US term for (*a*) a suburban railway, (*b*) express trams that travel in special traffic lanes, or (*c*) other fast public transport.

ratchet-and-pawl mechanism [mech.] A cogwheel (ratchet) with which a single tooth (pawl) engages to prevent it turning backwards and allow it to turn forwards. The pawl is held down on to the ratchet by a spring.

rate of spread *See* **spread.**

rating (1) [hyd.] The relationship between the water level and the discharge of a stream or well or *aquifer*, or the work of taking the observations and making the calculations needed to establish this relationship.

(2) [hyd.] The greatest amount of water per unit time that can safely be drawn from a stream, well or aquifer without damage to it. If the water source is overrated the pipeline and pumps will be underworked and consequently will have cost too much.

(3) [elec.] The power output of an electric motor over a certain period as certified by the maker. A continuous rating of so many kilowatts means that the motor is designed to work permanently without overheating at the power stated. A half-hour rating is the possible power output for half an hour only. Since the rating is

based on the rate of heating and cooling of the electrical part, the half-hour rating of a motor is appreciably higher than its continuous rating.

rating curve or **stage-discharge curve** [hyd.] A graph of the water level of a stream against its flow rate. *See also* **duration curve.**

rating flume [hyd.] (1) A *control* flume.

(2) A flume containing still water in which *current meters* or *Pitot tubes* are drawn at known velocity so as to calibrate them.

rat-tail file [mech.] A round *file* tapering to a smaller diameter at the end away from the handle.

ravelling *See* **fretting.** *Compare* **scabbing.**

raw water Water which, after treatment at a *waterworks*, becomes a *water supply*.

Rawlbolt A bolt screwed into a hole in masonry to anchor a machine or building part. The hole is lined with a drilled lead plug which is gripped by the bolt and expanded against the walls of the hole. For heavy loads the lead plug is replaced by an *expansion bolt*. Both these anchors have the advantage over grouted anchors that they can be removed without damaging the building.

Raymond standard test A *dynamic penetration test* used by Terzaghi to compare the bearing capacities of soils. A hole is first bored to the proposed foundation level and a *soil sampler* of 5 cm outside dia. is then lowered into the hole and pressed 15 cm into the soil. Its position is then measured and it is given a number of blows from a 64 kg hammer which drops 76 cm. The number of blows required to drive it 0·3 m into the soil is recorded and gives a measure of the *relative density* of a sand. The sample tube is withdrawn with a 0·3 m long soil specimen inside it.

reach [hyd.] or **pond** One stretch of water between two locks.

reaction [stru.] The upward resistance of a support such as a wall or column against the downward pressure of a

loaded member such as a beam.

reaction turbine [mech.] A steam or *water turbine* in which the jets or nozzles are on the moving wheel, as opposed to an *impulse turbine* which has only fixed jets.

ready-mixed concrete Concrete that is mixed at a distant batching plant and carried to the site in a *truck mixer*. This economical way of buying concrete for small concreting jobs is for some very congested sites the only possible way. Its use is steadily increasing.

realignment An alteration to the line of a road, railway, etc., which may affect only its slope (vertical alignment) but more usually alters its layout in plan (horizontal alignment).

ream [mech.] To enlarge or smooth a *borehole* or a hole in metal with a *reamer*.

reamer (1) [mech.] A hand or machine tool for finishing a drilled hole. It has a cylindrical or conical shaft with cutting flutes or teeth.

(2) or **belling tool** Reamers for *bored piles* are now in use which can enlarge the base of a 1·5 m dia. pile to 5 m dia.

rebound hammer or **Schmidt rebound hammer** A quick testing method that, in conjunction with careful cube or *ultrasonic* pulse velocity testing of the same concrete, enables its strength to be determined within $\pm$ 3 N/mm^2. There may be differences in rebound from faces that are trowelled and those that are cast against formwork. Other differences come from variations of moisture content, curing, concrete composition, surface texture and depth of carbonation from the surface.

recalescent point [mech.] *See* **critical point.**

receiver [min.] An air container interposed near the rock drills in a compressed-air pipeline to store air for the short but frequent periods when the air demand exceeds the supply. It is also convenient to use it as a sump for withdrawing water which

216

has condensed in the pipeline. A drain cock is provided for this purpose.

recharge [hyd.] Refilling of an *aquifer* either by *artificial recharge*, or naturally by rainfall and *infiltration*.

reciprocal levelling [sur.] A method of eliminating instrumental error in levelling between two points by taking levels on them from two set-ups, one near each point. The average of the differences in level is the true difference.

reciprocating [mech.] A description of anything with a to-and-fro motion. *See* **percussion tools, single-acting.**

reciprocating engine [mech.] A *steam engine* or an *internal-combustion engine* with cylinder and piston, not a turbine nor a jet engine.

reciprocating pump or compressor [mech.] A pump or compressor worked by pistons or rams (*see* **ram pump**), but not a centrifugal pump or compressor, nor an *air-lift pump.*

recording gauge [hyd.] or **recorder** A gauge which records automatically the level of the water in a stream or tank, sometimes also the velocity and pressure in a pipe. It often works by a float or by a submerged air tank with a rubber diaphragm which moves inward as the water level rises, causing a pressure increase in the air, which is recorded by the pen. *See* **stilling well.**

recovery peg [sur.] or **reference peg** A peg placed at a known relationship in level, direction, and distance to another peg to enable this one to be re-established, if disturbed.

rectangular coordinates [d.o.] *Cartesian coordinates.*

rectangular hollow sections [stru.] *See* **tubular sections.**

rectangular weir [hyd.] A *measuring weir* with a rectangular notch. Unless a suppressed weir is specified the term may be taken to mean a *contracted weir* (ASCE MEP 11).

rectification [air sur.] or **differential rectification** Elimination of the image displacements in *vertical photos*. They are caused by aircraft *tilt* or hills and valleys. Removal of the image displacements gradually corrects the errors in scale.

red shortness [mech.] *Hot shortness* of steel or other metal.

reduced bearing *See* **quadrantal bearing.**

reduced level [sur.] An elevation calculated from an agreed datum.

reduction [min.] The extraction of a mineral from its ores, derived from the chemical term meaning the removal of oxygen from an oxide to produce a metal or other element.

reduction factor [stru.] A factor by which for a given *slenderness ratio* the permissible stress on a long column is reduced below that allowed on a short column, so as to prevent *buckling*. Building regulations state the reduction factors for any given slenderness ratio in any material, steel, timber, masonry, reinforced concrete.

reduction in area [mech.] The *contraction in area* of a *tensile test* piece.

reduction of levels [sur.] The calculation of the differences in level between various points from the staff readings in a field book.

redundant frame [stru.] or **statically-indeterminate frame** A frame which has more members or more *fixity* than is needed for it to be a *perfect frame*. It is therefore necessary to remove a member or members or some fixity to make it perfect. *See* **superposition.**

reed Phragmites communis, a plant about 2 m long tied into bundles of 76 cm girth for use in the *Dutch mattress. See also (B).*

reeving thimble or **link** [mech.] An end loop to a crane *sling*, through which the remainder of the sling can be passed. It is usually pear-shaped. Round *thimbles* are non-reeving.

reference mark [sur.] or **reference object** A distant point chosen so that the *bearings* to other points can be measured from it at a station.

reference peg [sur.] A *recovery peg.*

reflecting level [sur.] A vertically hanging mirror separated from an unsilvered part by a horizontal line. The position of the eye is adjusted until the image of the pupil is bisected by the cross-line. The staff reading is then noted since the line of sight is horizontal.

reflux valve [hyd.] A *check valve*.

refractories *See* **refractory linings**.

refractory A material from which refractory bricks, and therefore *refractory linings*, are made.

refractory clay A clay used for making a *refractory lining*.

refractory linings or **refractories** Bricks or rocks that are hard to melt and therefore used for lining furnaces. Service temperature limits are controlled more often by the aggregate than by the cement. *High-alumina cement* can withstand 1200°C but concrete made from it with silica gravel and sand should not be used at temperatures above 300°C; limestone 500°C; blast-furnace slag (dense or foamed), brick, or calcined *diatomite* (B) 800°C; some igneous rocks, including basalt, dolerite, pumice, as well as expanded clay aggregate, will resist at least 1000°C; dead-burned magnesite 1400°C; bauxite 1500°C; chromite 1600°C. *See also* **basic refractory, bauxite, calcium aluminate, Carborundum, silica brick, silicon carbide, zirconia.**

refrigerator foundations Since a large refrigerator can, even if fairly well insulated, freeze the ground beneath it and thus cause *frost heave* which may raise the building dangerously, it is advisable to ventilate foundations or otherwise to ensure that they are not frozen. With boiler houses on clay a similar problem occurs due to the shrinkage of the clay by drying out when heated. In this case the building sinks unevenly, more below the boiler than elsewhere. A similar problem occurs with the foundations of every heated building in a *permafrost* region. One way is to have shallow foundations and to ventilate over them, keeping the ground floor of the building above ground. Another,

rather more expensive method, is to carry the building on piles. Both foundations should rest on permanently frozen soil, well below the *active layer*.

refuge An island in the traffic, separated from it by a *kerb*, sited so as to divide the traffic streams and to provide a safe area for pedestrians. *See* **bollard** (2).

refusal A pile which sinks only about 13 mm in five blows is said to be driven to refusal.

regime [hyd.] (also **regimen** in USA) A stream or canal is said to be in regime if its rate of flow is such that it neither picks up material from its bed nor deposits it. This is unusual in the whole length of a stream and only short lengths of it can be expected to be in regime at any one time. However, in the course of the years after construction, canals generally tend towards a regime condition.

reglette [sur.] The short, usually 12-in. scale, divided into hundredths of a foot, formerly used for accurate measurements of length with a steel band graduated in feet only. *See* **graduation of tapes.**

regulating course A layer of stone put over an old road to shape it before it is surfaced.

reheater [mech.] or **interheater** An accessory to steam or compressed-air engines, which greatly reduces their consumption of air or steam. A reheater superheats the steam or reheats the air between expansion stages, increasing its pressure and reducing the likelihood of freezing.

reinforced brickwork Brickwork with expanded metal, steel-wire mesh, hoop iron, or thin rods in the bed joints. Rods also can be arranged to pass vertically through a properly bonded wall at the points where the vertical joints intersect. Reinforced brickwork has been used in India (*Quetta bond* (B)) and in California to ensure against the collapse of walls in earthquakes. Hoop iron has been occasionally used in the bed joints of English brickwork for hundreds of years. Wall ties are not considered to be reinforcement but they do strengthen walls which they tie together. *See* **reinforced grouted-brick masonry.**

reinforced concrete Concrete containing more than 0·6% by volume of reinforcement consisting of steel rods or mesh. The steel takes all the tensile stresses (theoretically) so that the cracks which always occur in reinforced concrete do not appreciably weaken it. In good design the reinforcement is sufficiently distributed so that the cracks are not conspicuous. *See* **bond, creep, plain concrete, prestressed concrete, shrinkage,** *and below.*

reinforced grouted-brick masonry [stru.] In USA brickwork built like the *cavity wall* (*B*) except that the cavity, known as a collar joint, is filled with fluid mortar as the wall rises and reinforced with mesh or rod reinforcement. The bricklayer can work only on one side of the wall at a time, nevertheless this construction is much used in the earthquake region of California. The cross joints have been found to be completely filled by grout. *See* **lateral-force design, reinforced brickwork.**

reinforcement (1) Rods or mesh embedded in concrete or mortar to strengthen it, usually of steel but occasionally of other material like glassfibre or even bamboo in countries where it is plentiful. Reed or hessian have been used in British *fibrous plaster* (*B*). Unlike *tendons*, reinforcement is not designed to stress the concrete. *See* **deformed bars,** *and above.*

(2) In a weld, the amount by which the weld metal projects above the parent metal.

reiteration [sur.] or **repetition** A method of increasing the *precision* of a measurement of an angle with a given instrument by repeatedly measuring it. (The precision is proportional to the square root of the number of readings.) With a *theodolite* the technique is as follows: after the first measurement the lower plate is unclamped (the vernier being kept clamped) and the telescope turned back to the first point. The lower plate is then clamped, the upper plate released, and the angle is measured again. The total angle should now be double the first angle. The procedure is repeated until the desired precision is obtained.

relative compaction [s.m.] The *dry density* of the soil in situ divided by the maximum dry density of the soil as determined by the *Proctor compaction test* or other standard test. It is generally expressed as a percentage. *Compare* **degree of compaction.**

relative density (formerly **specific gravity**) The weight of a substance divided by the weight of the same volume of water at 4°C. It is therefore a number without units – a ratio. To determine the density of a substance its relative density must be multiplied by the density of water – 1 g/cc or 1000 kg/m³ as convenient.

relative density of a sand [s.m.] A measure of the density of a sand which gives a better impression of its *compaction* than the *voids ratio*. The densities of the sand are measured in the laboratory in its loosest possible dry state and in its densest possible state. The relative density of a field sample of the same sand is as follows (d = field density):

$$\frac{d \max (d - d \min)}{d (d \max - d \min)}$$

relative humidity [min.] The ratio of the weight of the water vapour in the air to that in saturated air at the same temperature. This is the same as the corresponding ratio of the vapour pressures.

relative settlement [stru.] *Differential settlement.*

relaxation [stru.] A *loss of prestress* in a tendon, caused by its own *creep* under stress. Since creep is uncertain, manufacturers of tendons may be asked to undertake the expense of making 100-hour constant-strain tests of their tendons. The tendons are held at a constant stretch, equivalent to that which would result from 70% of the characteristic load specified, for example, by BS 4486, 'Cold-worked high-tensile alloy steel tendons'.

relay [elec.] A device which responds to a specific current or power and opens or closes a *pilot circuit*. The pilot circuit operates a second circuit often by a *solenoid* of a *circuit breaker* or *contactor* or by other *protective equipment*.

release agent or **parting agent** or **parting compound** or **bond breaker** A general term that includes any greases, *mould oils*, or *sealants* (2) laid over forms or form linings either to ensure a good finish to the concrete or to improve the durability of the *form* or for both reasons.

relief holes [min.] (or **easers** in Britain) In breaking ground for tunnelling or shaft sinking, American term for the holes which are fired after the *cut holes* and before the *lifter holes* or *rib holes*.

relief well [s.m.] A borehole drilled at the foot of an earth dam or of an excavation to relieve high *pore-water pressures* caused by the weight of the dam. It is not pumped. *See* boil.

relieving platform A deck at the land side of a *retaining wall* such as a sheet-piled jetty to transmit heavy loads (loaded lorries or wagons) vertically down to the wall and to prevent them becoming a *surcharge* on the earth behind the wall. A relieving platform is usually carried partly on the wall and partly on bearing piles or raking piles.

remedial works *Underpinning* and many *ground improvement* processes.

remote control [hyd.] Hydroelectric power stations in the mountains are sometimes operated by radio (*tele-control*), the valves and circuits being opened and closed electrically from the parent station in the valley. No attendants are on duty at the mountain station, which is visited only at weekly or monthly intervals by a maintenance gang for greasing and replacing electrical contact-points.

remoulding [s.m.] The disturbance of the internal structure of a clay or silt. When remoulded a clay loses shearing strength and gains compressibility. For this reason pile-driving is inadvisable in some clays. *See* remoulding index.

remoulding index [s.m.] The ratio of the load per millimetre of compression of undisturbed clay to the load per millimetre of compression of the remoulded clay. *See* sensitivity ratio.

Reno mattress A *continuous gabion*.

repetition [sur.] *Reiteration*.

repose [s.m.] *See* angle of repose.

representative sample [stat.] A *sample* which can be selected only by planned action to ensure that a fair proportion is drawn from the various parts of the whole. The sampling within the parts may be *random*.

resection [sur.] A method of locating a point away from the base line in *plane-tabling* when only one end of the base can be occupied by the plane table. In principle it involves knowing the length of the base line, measuring two angles, deducing the third angle of a triangle and calculating the other two sides. It is therefore not checked within itself and needs checking from nearby set-ups.

reservoir A tank or artificial lake where water is stored. *See* impounding reservoir, service reservoir.

reservoir roofs Reservoirs for drinking water are usually roofed to keep out leaves and other dirt. Lightweight roofs are cheap and quick to build because they need no foundations. A plastics sheet of 1500 gauge black polythene was installed on Horsley reservoir by the Newcastle and Gateshead Water Co. in 1973. The 30×45 m sheet floats on the water. Rainwater on top of it helps to filter out ultraviolet light and so protects the polythene. Another type of lightweight roof, more complicated but with the advantage of allowing access to the water, is the *air house* (*B*) which has often been used over reservoirs in earthquake areas.

resident engineer A civil engineer who watches the interests of the *client* at a site, working under the *consulting engineer*.

residual errors [sur.] Errors which cannot be eliminated from a measurement despite the most careful work.

residual stress [stru.] Stress that remains in a material from its manufacturing process. In steel joists the outer parts of flanges and the centre of a deep thin web cool faster than the junctions between web and flanges. Cold straightening often relieves the stress. Heating in a stress-relieving furnace is usually not practicable so stress-relief is usually achieved by heavy proof loading or by the onset of the first working loads. Welded metal particularly suffers from residual stresses.

resilience [stru.] The *strain energy* stored in an elastic material per unit of volume. The modulus of resilience is the greatest quantity of energy per unit volume which can be stored in a material without *permanent set*. Steel has a modulus of resilience of 0·027 kilogram-metres per cu. cm, rubber about 0·54 kilogram-metres per cu. cm.

resistance (1) [hyd.] or **resistance losses** The resistance of a pipe or channel to flow is usually expressed in metres head of water.

(2) [rly] *See* rolling resistance, tractive resistance.

resistance flash welding [mech.] *Resistance welding* by first striking an arc between the two parts to be welded until the required temperature is reached. The power is then turned off and the parts joined by pressing them together. *Compare* flash-butt welding.

resistance losses [hyd.] *See* resistance.

resistance moment [stru.] *See* moment of resistance.

resistance percussive welding [mech.]

Resistance welding in which the heavy welding current is passed at the same time as a mechanical pressure forces the parts together.

resistance projection welding [mech.] *See* projection welding.

resistance seam welding [mech.] *Resistance welding* in which the welding electrodes consist of two rollers moving along the seam to be welded, that are pressed together at the moment when the welding current passes. It is often *automatic*.

resistance spot welding [mech.] *Resistance welding* by electrodes of small end area which cause fusion where they touch the parts to be welded.

resistance strain gauge [stru.] *See* electrical-resistance strain gauge.

resistance welding [mech.] The *welding* of two parts held tightly in contact by *electrodes* through which a heavy alternating current flows momentarily and causes them to fuse together. *See* stud welding (*B*) *and above*.

resistivity logging, electrical logging A *well logging* method in which electric current is applied to the drilling fluid in an uncased hole in order to determine the resistivity of the rocks penetrated. Wet clays have low resistivity, granites very high, often one million times as large. Other electrical methods include induction logging and the investigation of electric currents that exist naturally in the well.

resoiling or **soiling** Levelling the ground after building or dredging is finished and replacing topsoil so as to make the ground fit for vegetation.

resonance [stru.] When the *vibration* of a machine corresponds closely with the *natural frequency* of its *foundation* it is very likely that the foundation will vibrate excessively. It is therefore important to design foundations so that their natural frequency is different from that of the machines which they carry. *See* soft-suspension theory.

retaining wall A wall built to hold back earth or other solid material (a dam holds back liquid). Important differ-

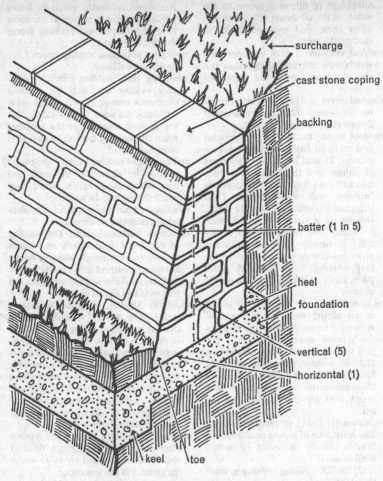

- surcharge
- cast stone coping
- backing
- batter (1 in 5)
- heel
- foundation
- vertical (5)
- horizontal (1)
- keel
- toe

Retaining wall

ences in design exist between free and *fixed retaining walls*. Fixed retaining walls are supported both at top and bottom and they cannot tilt, so that the earth pressure does not fall to the reduced value of the *active earth pressure*. *Free retaining walls*, however, can be *gravity retaining walls*. They need not be designed to bend, but must be able to tilt or slide enough to

bring on the reduced value of the active earth pressure. They may be of *sheet-pile* construction (timber, steel, or reinforced concrete). Bridge abutments are usually free retaining walls except for those which are fixed arches and portal frames. Cantilever walls are free and may be counterforted or buttressed, sometimes with a keel in the base to prevent sliding or a *reliev-*

ing platform at the top to reduce earth pressure due to *surcharge*. *See* **diaphragm wall, flexible wall, Rankine's theory, wedge theory,** *and opposite* for illustration.

retarder (1) or **retarder of set** An *admixture* which slows up the setting rate of concrete. It is sometimes applied to *formwork* so that when the shuttering is stripped the concrete in contact with it can be removed by brushing. A rough texture is thus formed which may be needed for its appearance or as backing for plaster. *See also* (*B*).

(2) [rly] or **wagon retarder** Braking bars parallel with the running rails in a shunting yard. When the signalman wants to slow down the wagons he pulls a lever which causes the braking bars to grip the wheel flanges tightly against the rails.

reticule [sur.] or **graticule** or **reticle** A set of intersecting fine spider webs held by the diaphragm at the optical focus of a telescope. The intersection of the central lines defines the line of sight (collimation line) of the telescope. *See* **graticule, stadia hairs.**

retreading roads A method of repairing roads whose surface is breaking up or which are misshapen. The surface is first scarified 7 cm deep, the road is then shaped with a grader, rolled, and surfaced.

return sheave [min.] A pulley at a distance from a haulage drum. A rope from the drum passes round it (tail rope) and enables the haulage engine to pull away from itself.

reverse curve [sur.] or **reversed curve** A *curve* of S-shape.

reversed filter *See* **loaded filter.**

reverse face [sur.] or **reversing face** *See* **change face.**

reverse osmosis, RO A *de-salination* process, rather expensive, although about 30 plants existed in Japan in 1976. Bacteria are removed.

reverse-rotary drilling *Rotary drilling* in which the direction of flow of the drilling fluid is reversed, in other words

the fluid is pumped down outside the drilling pipe and rises up inside it. Because the area of the pipe bore is smaller than the area outside the pipe, the rising mud has a high velocity and can carry large pieces easily. Consequently the method is suitable for drilling in deposits that break easily into coarse lumps or for drilling in deserts where water is too valuable to be used in mud, and air must be used instead.

reversible tramway *See* **jig back.**

revet To protect a surface with *revetment*.

revetment A protective covering to a soil or rock surface to prevent scour by weather or water. It may be a wall, but differs from the usual wall in that its function is to protect the earth, not to withstand its thrust. Common revetments are asphalt sheets, *beaching*, concrete slabs precast or cast-in-place, faggots, *falling aprons, fascines, grass, mattresses, maritime plants, pitching, rip-rap.*

revolver crane A crane of unusually large lifting capacity. Two at Graythorp on the Tees, near Hartlepool, in use in 1973 for building North Sea oil production jackets, could lift 800 tons at 21 m radius or 112 tons at 61 m radius. They had jibs 73 m long and travelled on concrete tracks 23 m apart. The cranes were erected on steel towers 49 m high above the dock floor, which travelled under load, at 5 m/min. by jacking.

revolving screen [hyd.] A *trash rack* which may be a cylinder or a belt, turned mechanically or by the force of the water passing through it. As the screen appears above the water it is freed of rubbish by a scraper, a water jet, etc.

Reynolds number [hyd.] or **Reynolds criterion** Reynolds established the principle used in hydraulics and aerodynamics that

$$\frac{\text{fluid velocity} \times \text{pipe radius}}{\text{viscosity}}$$

is the same for all fluids at the *critical*

velocity. This number, which differs with the velocity, is the Reynolds number for the given flow condition. It is much used in *model analysis*, since the Reynolds number in model and structure should be the same. *See* **Froude number.**

Reynolds's critical velocity [hyd.] *See* **critical velocity.**

rib (1) or **rib centre** The curved beam which carries the centering of an arch.

(2) A small beam projecting from a reinforced-concrete slab, whether flat or arched. It stiffens the slab.

ribbed slab A *hollow-tile floor*.

rib holes (**trimmers** in Britain) American term for holes in tunnelling or shaft sinking which are drilled at the sides of the tunnel or shaft and therefore are fired last, after the *cut holes*, *relief holes* (and *lifter holes* if any).

rice grass *See* **maritime plants.**

riffle sampler [min.] A *sampler* designed to reduce a batch of ore to half its original size. It consists of a rack of vertical parallel plates a uniform distance apart, each of which diverts the ore falling on to it. Alternate pairs of plates divert the ore to alternate sides. The volume reduction is rapid for dry ores crushed to suitable fineness. To reduce the sample to one quarter or one eighth its original size the sampler can be built of several riffles in series. Riffle sampling is much quicker and less laborious than coning and quartering.

rift or **grain** or **quartering way** Quarrymen's words for the roughly perpendicular joints and cleavage planes in most rocks. Rift is the easiest plane of splitting, grain may be a secondary cleavage at right angles to it. Some writers mention a third plane, head. *See also* **tough way.**

rigger (1) A semi-skilled or skilled man who erects and maintains *lifting tackle*, hand-operated *derricks*, *ropes*, *slings*, *cradles* (*B*), and other scaffolding.

(2) A less widely-skilled man who erects tubular or other metal scaffolding.

rigid arch [stru.] An arch without *hinges*, *fully fixed* throughout.

rigid frame [stru.] A structural frame in which the columns and beams are rigidly connected together without *hinges*.

rigidity [stru.] The resistance of a material to shearing or twisting.

rigid pavement Road or airstrip construction of concrete slabs. *Compare* **flexible pavement.**

rigid pipe Unglazed or glazed pipes made of vitrified clay, concrete, asbestos cement or grey cast iron. Flexible or rigid joints may be used, as with *flexible pipe*.

ring In the lining of tunnels and shafts with cast iron, pressed steel, or precast concrete segments of circles, a complete circle formed by these segments is called a ring. In the London *tube railways* these are 508 mm wide, of cast iron and about 25 mm thick. *See* **steel ring, tubbing.**

ring tension [stru.] or **hoop tension** The tension which occurs in the wall of a circular bunker or tank containing solid or liquid. The force of the material pressing outwards on the walls, at the top of an open tank, is carried wholly by ring tension, at the bottom wholly by tension in the floor, and intermediately in proportion.

riparian [hyd.] Concerning the banks of a stream, lake, or canal. A riparian owner owns at least part of one bank.

ripper (1) A tractor with downward-pointing, massive steel teeth at the rear, which can be forced into the ground hydraulically. Forward motion of the tractor breaks up the ground if it is not too hard. Sometimes the teeth are on a towed frame and forced into the ground by weight alone.

(2) A *concrete breaker*.

ripple [hyd.] A small wave on a water surface or a repetitive wave on a sand bed, with a flat upstream face and steep downstream face, caused by slow flow slightly above the least flow needed to move the sand.

rip-rap [hyd.] Stones for *revetment* from

7 to 70 kg weight. They protect the bed of a river or its banks from *scour*.

rise The vertical distance from the crown of a road to its lowest point.

rise and fall [sur.] A method of reducing staff readings by working out the rise or fall from each point to the one following it. The rises or falls are entered in the level book in special columns parallel to those for the staff readings. *Compare* **collimation method**.

river purification board, RPB Bodies in Scotland that correspond generally to the English and Welsh *water authorities*, with the important difference that RPBs set *effluent* standards and do not, like water authorities, operate *sewage treatment* plants.

rivet [mech.] A round bar of *dead-mild steel* with a cup-shaped or conical or pan-shaped head, driven while red-hot into a hole through two pieces of steel which are to be joined. The head is held in position by a holder-up with a dolly while another man strikes (sets up or *upsets*) the other end, forming a head on it with a hand hammer or pneumatic or hydraulic riveter. Rivets of smaller diameter than 18 mm can be driven cold. Aluminium, copper, and other materials are also used for making rivets. *Light alloy* is riveted with light alloy rivets to avoid corrosion at the rivet hole, but steel rivets can be used with protective painting. The *high-strength friction-grip bolt* is much more convenient and quicker than riveting, which is not now used on sites, at least in Britain.

road (1) A concrete, *stabilized soil*, earth, *hoggin*, tarred or other surface for vehicles or animals to travel on.

(2) [rly] A rail track.

road bed [rly] The *ballast* which carries the *sleepers* and *rails* of a *permanent way*.

road breaker *See* **concrete breaker**.

road forms or **side forms** Wooden or steel planks on edge which form the side of a concrete slab and are set with their upper surfaces at the correct levels for the road so as to guide the men screeding.

road heater A machine which heats a road surface by blowing flame or hot air on to it.

road-making plant Plant which is specialized for making roads and is not used for other construction, for example *concrete paver, gritter, planer, pressure tank, pulverizing mixer, road heater, roller, scarifier, smoothing iron, spreader*, etc.

road panel An area of concrete laid in one operation and bounded by free edges or joints on all sides, some of which may be *dummy joints*.

road roller A power-driven *roller* weighing from ½ to 12 tons. *See* **compaction, roller, tandem**.

road surface Also called the carpet, topping, or *wearing course*.

rock A mass of different grains cemented together by a *matrix*. Sandstone is a rock consisting of quartz grains cemented by an iron oxide (red sandstone) or by calcite (pale sandstones). Quartzite is a sandstone cemented by quartz.

rock anchor, rock bolt *See* **roof bolt**.

rock burst [r.m.] In mines deeper than about 1000 m, in strong rock, an explosion of virgin rock that takes place at the face or away from it. From 50 kg to many tons of rock are crushed in one rock burst. Rock bursts have occasionally occurred in quarries but not in coal mines, except as *sudden outbursts*. Coal mine rocks are too weak to cause rock bursts. Bad rock bursts have occurred in the South African gold mines (up to 3000 m deep) and in the Kolar gold field in India and in mines in Canada, USA and elsewhere. Severe rock bursts were suffered in the driving of the Mont Blanc tunnel between France and Italy, opened in 1965. It is 11·6 km long and is under 2000 m of rock for half its length. The worst rock bursts occurred at the deepest part with 2450 m of the Aiguille du Midi above.

Unfissured rock created the worst bursts, and very few if any occurred in the roof and floor. All were in the sides. Rock that suffers rock bursts is usually as hard as granite. Rock bursts are a special part of *rock mechanics*.

rock drill [min.] Any drill (electric or compressed air) for making holes in rock whether for broaching, blasting, or other purpose. *See* **hammer drill, percussive-rotary drilling.**

rocker bearing A bridge or truss support which is free to rotate but not to move horizontally unless it is also carried on rollers.

rocker shovel [min.] A high speed mechanical shovel used in tunnelling.

rock-fill dam [hyd.] An *earthen dam* built of any available stone or broken rock. If built of random stone it is likely to be faced with a flexible watertight skin of steel plate or timber on the water side. If the watertight skin is brittle, like reinforced concrete, or if the dam has a watertight concrete core wall instead of a watertight skin, the stone must be carefully

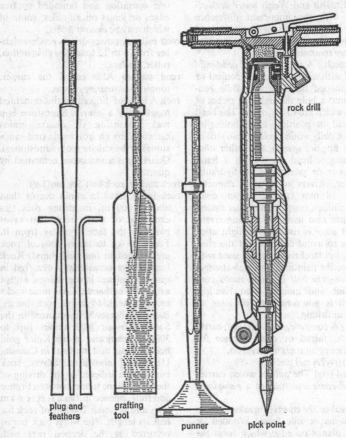

plug and feathers   grafting tool   punner   pick point

Rock drill (sectioned) and some tools for use in it

compacted so that there is no chance of movement.

rock flour [s.m.] US term for *silt*-sized crushed rock.

rock mechanics [r.m.] The science of the rocks and stones in the ground, their fabric, strengths, stresses, strains, friction, elasticity, equilibrium, creep, ductility, flow under pressure, and the use of these properties in tunnelling and mining generally, often helped by laboratory testing. It includes the study of blasting, *rock bursts*, *rock noise*, *bumps*, rock breaking and the stability of rock slopes. Rock mechanics makes use of many testing methods and instruments that are used also in *soil mechanics*, as well as the evidence of boreholes and *geophysical* surveys, *well logging*, etc.

rock noise [r.m.] *Rock bursts* are often preceded by differences in the minor noises that are given out by rocks. Listening instruments have therefore been devised to record them.

Rockwell hardness test [mech.] A *hardness* testing method in which the depth of penetration of a conical diamond point (for hard metal) or of a steel ball (for softer metal) is measured. Like the *diamond-pyramid* method it is suitable for testing *case-hardened* material. *See* **Brinell hardness test, scleroscope hardness test.**

rod [sur.] *See* **staff.**

rodding (1) Unblocking drains with *drain rods*. *See* **inspection chamber.**

(2) In USA the *punning* of concrete. *See also* (B).

rod float [hyd.] or **velocity rod** A wooden rod weighted at its lower end, designed to float in a vertical position with most of its length submerged so as to average the velocity in the stream throughout its submerged depth. *See* **float.**

rod man [sur.] American term for a *staff man.*

rolled asphalt A wearing course or base consisting of hard *asphalt* and *coarse aggregate* laid hot and rolled until it is nearly free of voids.

rolled-steel joist or **r.s.j.** An I-beam made of one piece of steel passed through a *hot-rolling* mill. *Compare* **cold rolling.**

rolled-steel section Any hot-rolled-steel section, including *rolled-steel joists*, *channels*, *angle sections*, bulb angles, zeds, rails, and so on. This is usually the cheapest steel, since the rolling process is continuous. *Compare* **tubular sections.**

roller A heavy vehicle, usually self-propelled but sometimes towed, the main tools for the *compaction* of earth fill or roads. The two types are very different. *Road rollers* are never towed, earth rollers often are. Earth is compacted with *pneumatic-tyred rollers*, *sheepsfoot rollers* or *vibrating rollers.*

roller bearings [mech.] Hard steel cylinders in bearings which have low friction. Compared with the best plain bearings their *rolling resistance* is at most one half and usually about one quarter. The advantages of roller bearings are outstanding where locomotives have replaced rope haulages. Small changes in resistance make a very large difference to the number of trams which a loco can pull, but even large changes in resistance do not alter the number which a rope can pull.

roller bit [min.] In *rotary drilling* for oil-wells and in other deep holes (down to 5 km) a drilling bit with several toothed rollers which are rotated by the turning of the drill rods. They are used for hard rock, since in spite of their complicated shape they last longer. This fact may be decisive even if they drill more slowly because the withdrawal of the drill pipe, changing of the bit, and sending the bit back into the hole may stop drilling for 5 to 10 hours. Roller bits are rented from the makers in USA, since most oil companies are not equipped for refacing them with *hard facing*. *See* **turbo-drill.**

roller gate [hyd.] A hollow cylindrical *crest gate* for dam spillways. It is

227

carried on large toothed wheels at each side which mesh with steeply sloping racks up which the gate travels as it is being opened. *See* sector gate.

rolling lift bridge [stru.] A bridge of which the lifting part has at its shore end a segment bearing on a flat (rolling) surface.

rolling load [stru.] A *moving load*.

rolling resistance [mech.] That part of the tractive resistance which is caused by friction between track and wheels. It is most of the tractive resistance on level track. For old colliery tubs it may reach 50 kg per ton. With mine cars on *roller bearings* on good track the resistance may be as low as 2 kg per ton.

rolling-up curtain weir A *frame weir* in which the frame remains upright. The barrier consists of horizontal planks which increase in thickness with their depth below water. They are connected by chains and drawn up to open the weir.

rollway [hyd.] The overflow portion of a dam; an overflow spillway (ASCE MEP 11).

roof bolt, rock anchor, rock bolt [r.m.] A device for holding up the roof that originated in mines. Holes about 2 m long are drilled into the roof and a bolt, slightly longer, with a thread on the outer end is pushed into the bottom of the hole. It is held firmly either by an end wedge driven into the split end of the bolt or by an expanding cone or by a rapid-hardening synthetic resin or by other grout. Rock bolts are now also used for holding up railway cuttings and other excavations. By ordinary beam theory, if a roof bolt only doubles the thickness of rock spanning over an opening, the roof strength is multiplied by eight.

root The part of a dam which merges into the ground where the dam joins the hillside.

rooter A towed *scarifier*.

Rootes blower [mech.] A *rotary blower* consisting of a pair of hourglass-shaped members which interlock and rotate together. It gives a higher pressure than the average fan of (0·07 to 0·2 bar) 0·7 to 2 m water gauge and delivers fairly large volumes, so it is suitable for forcing ventilating air through long pipelines.

rope [mech.] Steel-wire rope is generally used for most hoisting or haulage purposes, *fibre rope* being more flexible but less strong. For the steel of which ropes are made, *see* prestressed concrete. Ropes are described in the following way. A 25 mm 6/19 rope is of 25 mm dia. with 6 *strands* each of 19 wires. *See* lay.

rope diameter [mech.] The diameter of a steel-wire rope is the greatest diameter obtainable across the strands. *Fibre ropes* are usually described by their circumference, not by their diameter.

rope fastenings [mech.] The best fastening between a steel-wire rope and its socket is the white metal capping used for man-winding shafts in Britain. Where this method of capping rope is inconvenient, ropes are usually doubled back on themselves round a steel *thimble* and fixed with *bulldog grips*.

ropeway *See* aerial ropeway.

Rossi-Forel scale [stru.] This scale for the intensities of earthquakes, evolved by Rossi and Forel, grades earthquakes from 1 (very slight) to 10 (catastrophic). In a grade 8 earthquake, large cracks appear even in ordinary houses and they may be damaged beyond repair.

rotary blower [mech.] An air compressor suitable for pressures up to 0·7 bar above atmospheric, often a *Rootes blower*.

rotary drilling [min.] (1) A method of drilling deep holes for oil, gas, etc., from 15 to about 100 cm dia. Lengths of heavy hollow drill pipe screwed together pass down the hole and carry a cutting bit at their tip. (*See* fishtail/roller bit.) *Drilling fluid* is pumped down the pipe, passes round the cutting edge of the bit, cools it, and brings up the broken rock. The first crude rotary drill was invented and used by the Baker brothers, drilling contractors in Dakota, 1882. It required much development and was first effectively used at Spindletop, Texas, in 1901. Rotary drills are always used for holes deeper than 1800 m, often for shallower holes, and they have drilled down to 4·5 km. (*See* **cable drill.**) Cores can be obtained by fitting *corers* instead of ordinary drilling bits. *See* **turbo-drill, reverse-rotary drilling.**

(2) Drilling a hole for blasting by a rotating (usually electrically driven) auger-shaped drill steel. The detachable bit usually has a *hard facing* on the cutting edge. In such hard rocks as granite, rotary drills cannot compete with *hammer drills.*

rotary excavator (1) A machine used for excavating the circular, 3·66 m dia. tunnels of the London *tube railways* in conjunction with the *Greathead shield.* It can maintain a consistent advance of 50 m per week. *See* **Hallinger shield.**

(2) **bucket-wheel excavator** or **wheel excavator** A machine with a vertical digging wheel, on a horizontal axle, which carries large buckets on its rim. These machines, used for quarrying, particularly in German brown coal mines, are perhaps the world's biggest excavators, weigh over 5000 tons, and are able to move over 5000 tons of earth or coal per hour. They are carried on crawler trucks.

rotary meter A *current meter.*

rotary pump, rotodynamic pump [mech.] Many types exist, but the *centrifugal pump* is the best known in civil engineering.

rotary screen [mech.] or **trommel** The commonest screen for sizing gravel, or broken stone. It is a rectangular plate bent round to a cylindrical shape, with holes punched in it of suitable size. If the holes are of two different sizes, the larger holes are at the lower end, and the screen thus classifies into three sizes: oversize, intermediate, and undersize.

rotary snowplough A snowplough with a rotating blade to shoot the snow off the road.

rotational slide [s.m.] or **cylindrical slide** A failure of a clay slope which involves slipping of the earth on a curved surface. Much research was done on this sort of failure in Sweden after several hundred metres of Gothenburg harbour slid into the sea in 1916. The Swedish *circular arc* method was then evolved by Petterson and developed by Fellenius (1927).

rotation recorder An instrument which measures the very slight rotation of the support of a bridge during loading. *See* **spread recorder.**

rotative drilling [min.] *See* **rotary drilling** (2).

roughness [hyd.] A value which enters into every formula for flow in pipes or channels and expresses the friction or resistance to flow due to the surface texture of the channel or pipe.

round [min.] In tunnelling or shaft raising or sinking, a set of holes drilled for charging and firing together, generally involving breaking the rock for a *pull* of 1·2 to 2 m. It includes *cut/lifter/relief/rib holes.*

round-headed buttress dam A mass-concrete dam built of parallel buttresses which are thickened at the water end until they touch each other. The appearance is like the *multiple-arch dam.* The spillway may be a curved slab which passes over, joins, and stiffens the downstream ends of the buttresses. This dam may be of mass concrete except for the spillway slab and is considerably cheaper than the multiple-arch dam but slightly heavier.

Royal Commission standard [sewage] The standard set by the Royal Commission on Sewage Disposal (1898–1915) was that sewage effluents should not contain more than 30 milligrams of suspended solids per litre, nor have a *BOD* above 20 mg/litre – the so-called '30:20 standard'. Even after this fairly high standard is reached the effluent must be diluted by eight times its own volume of receiving water with a *BOD* below 2 mg/litre. Such standards are not everywhere easy to meet.

r.s.j. A *rolled-steel joist*.

rubber-lined pipe [min.] Steel or iron pipe, used for transporting *hydraulic filling*, wears very quickly and some mines have therefore installed pipe with 6 mm thick rubber lining. This lasts more than 7 years compared with the 2 weeks' life of unlined pipe.

rubber-tyred rollers *Pneumatic-tyred rollers*.

rubble concrete Masonry consisting of large stones set in joints of 15 cm of concrete and faced with ashlar. Used in massive work such as dams.

rubble drain or **blind/spall/stone drain** A trench filled with stones selected so that they allow water to flow through it. *See* **drain**.

rubble-mound breakwater [hyd.] or **mound breakwater** One of the two main types of *breakwater*. It is built of stones up to 5 tons in weight (occasionally 10 tons) dumped on top of each other at slopes which are nearly flat between tide marks (12 to 1) and about 1¼ horizontal to 1 vertical at depths greater than 5 m below low water. Rubble under water is now sometimes stabilized by grouting with fluid bitumen and sand injected at 200°C. Rubble is sometimes used as a foundation for *blockwork*.

ruling gradient [rly] The *limiting gradient*.

rumble strip or **serrated strip** or **jiggle bars** On a highway, a slightly raised strip of asphalt, plastic, etc., across the lane of traffic that is approaching a hazard. The strip is 10 to 15 cm wide and 1 to 3 cm high. Some 10 to 20 are placed together at a spacing sufficient to warn the driver of the approaching hazard.

rummel Scots term for a *soakaway*.

runner [mech.] The rotating part of a *water wheel* or *turbine*.

runners Vertical timber sheet piles 5 cm or more thick driven in by hand ahead of the digging at the edge of an excavation. They may be pointed with an iron shoe at one side of the timber so that as each pile is driven in it is forced tightly against its neighbour.

running ground [min.] Very wet or very dry sand or silt which flows like a liquid. It is usually dealt with by *forepoling* or close timbering or by other special methods of support or by *artificial cementing* of the ground or by *wellpoints* or similar drainage methods which strengthen the soil.

run-off The amount of water from rain, snow, etc., which flows from a catchment area past a given point over a certain period. It is the rainfall less *infiltration* and *evaporation*. In a stream it can be increased by springs of *groundwater* or reduced by loss to the ground. *See* **influent stream**.

run-off coefficient The *impermeability factor*.

S

sacrificial anodes The anodes used in *cathodic protection*.

sacrificial protection The property possessed by coatings of zinc, cadmium, aluminium, and so on to protect an iron surface, although the coating may not cover the whole surface. The zinc, cadmium, or aluminium is dissolved first (sacrificially) by the water, like the anode in *cathodic protection*.

saddle A steel block over the tower of a *suspension bridge* or aerial ropeway which acts as a bearing surface for the rope passing over it. *See also* (B).

safe-load indicator [mech.] *See* radius-and-safe-load indicator.

safety belt [min.] A harness or belt worn by a man to prevent him dropping more than 0·6 m while working. A remote anchorage belt is sometimes used by quarrymen. Since this belt allows a drop of 1·8 m it is provided with a shock absorber.

safety factor *See* factor of safety.

safety fuse [min.] or blasting fuse A train of black powder enclosed in a waterproof braided textile, used for firing *detonators* in small-scale work in quarries or metal mines. It burns at 0·6 m per minute ±10%. For underwater work, special fuse must be used.

safety rail *See* check rail.

safety valve [mech.] A valve fitted by law to all boilers. It opens at a pressure slightly above that at which the boiler works. It thus releases the excess of steam and reduces the pressure. The noise of escaping steam also draws attention to the fact that the boiler pressure is too high.

sag bar [stru.] An *anti-sag* bar.

sag correction [sur.] or catenary correction A *tape correction* to the apparent length of a level base line due to the sag in the tape. The measured length is longer than the straight length

between supports by $\dfrac{w^2 l}{24 t^2}$ metres where w is the weight of the hanging length of the tape in kg, l is the apparent length between supports in metres, and t the tension of the tape in kilograms.

sagging moment [stru.] A bending moment which causes a beam to sink in the middle. Usually described as a positive moment. *See* hogging moment.

sag pipe [hyd.] A water pipe for carrying an irrigation canal under a road or other obstacle. It is also called, very often but inaccurately, an inverted siphon.

St Nazaire Bridge [stru.] *See* cable-stayed bridge.

saltation The bouncing movement of sand grains carried by wind or water, usually hitting the bed at a flat angle, between 10° and 16° to the horizontal. The result of many impacts in the same direction is to cause the sand bed to creep forward. A fast grain will shift one on the bed which is six times its diameter, that is, 200 times its own mass.

sample [min.] A small amount taken from a rock exposure or mass of broken mineral or other material which is analysed for its content of valuable mineral. *See* random sample, representative sample.

sampler (1) [min.] or mechanical sampler or sample splitter A device for reducing the volume of a crushed sample to a *representative sample* which can be handled in the laboratory, for example a *riffle sampler*. It may also be a device for taking samples at fixed time intervals from a stream of solid or liquid.

(2) [s.m.] *See* soil sampler.

(3) [hyd.] An instrument for examining the bed or water on it in hydro-

231

graphic surveying. It may be a *bottom sampler*, a *sand catcher*, etc.

sampling spoon [s.m.] *See* soil sampler.

sand [s.m.] Granular material (composed mainly of quartz) of 2 to 0·06 mm in size. It has no *cohesion* when dry or saturated but has apparent cohesion when damp. *See* classification of soils.

sand blast [mech.] A compressed-air jet which throws sand or flint on to a surface to be smoothed or cleaned or etched for decoration (glass). Shot or steel grit are often used because they are less dangerous to the lungs than *silica* dust. *See* shot blasting.

sand catcher [hyd.] or sand-grain meter A hydrographic instrument through which the water flows and deposits sand. The instrument is then brought up to the surface and the sand quantity measured.

sand drain [s.m.] *See* vertical sand drain.

sand fill [min.] or sand filling *See* hydraulic fill, etc.

sand filter (1) A filter for domestic water, through which the water flows downwards. It consists of the following layers from the bottom upwards: 15 cm of coarse stone, 25 cm of coarse gravel, 90 cm of sand becoming finer towards the top, where it should be clean quartz grains of 0·3 to 0·4 mm nearly uniform size. The filter is covered with water, which flows slowly through. The upper surface becomes clogged with bacteria but is replaced periodically.

(2) A filter working on the same principle as above but with coarser sand for purifying *sewage* effluent.

sand-grain meter *See* sand catcher.

Sandö Bridge [stru.] Until the completion of the *Parramatta Bridge*, this was the largest reinforced-concrete arch bridge built, having a clear span of 264 m. The concrete in the 200 mm test cubes had an average crushing strength of 38 N/mm^2 at only 7 days. It spans the Angerman river, north Sweden.

sandpaper surface A road surface from which sharp pieces of aggregate protrude not more than 5 mm.

sand piles A means of deep *compaction* of a silty soil by dropping into it a heavy weight such as a pile-driver ram. The ram makes a hole in the ground into which sand is poured. The ram then drives the sand farther in and the process is repeated as required. If carried out with damp concrete the process makes a *driven cast-in-place pile*. *See* dynamic consolidation, Vibroflot.

sand pump or bailer or shell pump or sludger A long tube, open at the top, fitted with a *check valve* at the bottom. It is lowered into a borehole drilled with a *cable drill* or similar rig to extract mud, cuttings or water.

sand pump dredger A *suction dredger*.

sandstone [s.m.] A sedimentary rock formed mainly of *quartz* grains of *sand* size cemented with calcite or iron compounds, usually both, since pure calcite and pure sand are both white or colourless and white sandstone is rare. *See* matrix, quartzite.

sand trap [hyd.] An enlargement in a conduit where the stream velocity is designed to drop so that any sand which it carries can settle and be drawn off at a low level.

sandwich construction *See* (B).

sandwick [s.m.] A type of *vertical sand drain*.

saturated air Air containing the greatest amount of water vapour possible at the given temperature. It is therefore at a *relative humidity* of 100%.

saturation line [s.m.] The *water table*.

saucer [hyd.] A flat *camel* used for floating a ship past a shallow place.

saw files [mech.] Files with an extremely fine *cut*, and therefore a large number of teeth per centimetre.

scabbing The loss of patches of surface dressing from a road. *Compare* fretting.

scabbling or scappling Stone flakes laid in a 23 cm thick bed under stone *pitching* in a *revetment*.

scale (1) [d.o., air sur.] The ratio between the dimensions of a plan or a map and those of the object represented. The scale of an air photo is the focal length of the camera divided by the height of the aircraft at the instant the photo was taken. *See* **scale drawing**.

(2) [d.o.] A piece of boxwood, metal, ivory, or plastic 15 or 30 cm long, graduated in accordance with precise ratios, proportionally to metres or feet. *See* **Armstrong/fully-divided/open-divided scale**.

(3) Black iron oxide enveloping iron or steel which has been forged or otherwise *hot worked*. It should be removed before paint or primer can be put on.

scale drawing [d.o.] A mechanical drawing which shows an object with all its parts in the same proportion of their true size. Each dimension on the drawing is the same fraction of the true dimension of the object. This fraction is the *scale*.

scaling (1) [d.o.] Measuring dimensions on a drawing with a scale.

(2) [min.] Immediately after blasting, as soon as the air is clear but before the miners return to the face, the charge hand or foreman goes in alone and with a bar about 2 m long knocks down loose rock from the roof and sides so that the men can safely work there.

scappling *Scabbling*.

scarifier, ripper or **rooter** An implement which may be self-propelled or towed behind a tractor, with downward projecting tines for breaking a road surface 0·6 m deep or less.

scissors crossover or **scissors junction** [rly] A junction between two parallel tracks, shaped like a pair of scissors. It is possible to go from one track to the other when travelling in either direction, and in this it differs from the simple crossover, in which the passage from one track to the other can be made only along one junction track.

scleroscope hardness test [mech.] The estimation of the *hardness* of a metal by measuring the rebound from it of a standard diamond-tipped hammer.

scotch block [rly] A wedge or block temporarily fixed to a running rail to scotch a wheel of rolling stock, that is to block the rail.

Scotch derrick [mech.] *See* **derrick**.

scour or **erosion** Removal of the sea bed or of a river bed or banks by waves or flowing water.

scouring sluice [hyd.] or **scour pipe** or **washout valve** An opening in the lower part of a dam through which accumulated sand, gravel, or other rubbish can be occasionally expelled. Unfortunately, scour pipes are usually ineffective, and therefore some reservoirs silt up quickly. Boulder Dam reservoir (USA) is expected to have a useful life of only 100 years before it fills with silt.

scour protection Protection of earth or other submerged material by steel-sheet piling, *revetments*, *rip-rap*, a brushwood *mattress*, or a combination of such methods.

scow A *dumb barge*.

scraper A *bowl scraper* or *scraper excavator*, or *scraper loader*.

scraper bucket The excavating part of a *scraper* or *scraper loader*.

scraper excavator A *multi-bucket excavator*.

scraper loader [min.] or **slusher** (USA) or **scraper** A loader for underground or surface consisting of a *double-drum haulage* engine, a hoe-shaped or box-shaped scraper bucket dragged by the ropes, a *return sheave* and a ramp up which the rope pulls the bucket with its load of material. The ramp often contains the engine and is mounted on wheels over the mine track. Mine cars run in under it and are quickly loaded.

screed (1) or **screed board** or **screed rail** or **tamper** A wood or metal templet with which a concrete surface is finished. It is a joist set on edge, held by one man at each end and slightly longer than the width of the bay being concreted. Each end rests on forms or screeds which are set to the correct level for the slab surface. The screed rail may be cambered but is usually straight. *See also* (*B*).

(2) A layer of mortar 2 to 7 cm thick, laid to finish a floor surface or as a bed for floor tiles, often called, more grandly, *jointless flooring* (*B*).

screen (1) A sheet of wire mesh or punched steel plate on which granular material is sieved to separate it into various sizes (to classify it).

(2) In the treatment of sewage or *raw water*, a device that strains out some of the solids from a mixture of solids and water. It can be made of parallel, wedge-shaped wires or bars or round wire or wire mesh or steel plate with holes punched through it as in the *trommel*. At its most refined it is a *micro-strainer*. In a sewage works the use of a *comminutor* eliminates the need for handling the solids. At reservoir intakes, screens are usually racks of massive bars. They should be installed parallel to flow lines, not perpendicular to them. Although this is expensive in screen area, it is less likely to result in blockage or over-topping of the screens or their collapse. At sewage works, screens are part of *preliminary treatment*. Coarse screens may be used to remove large solids from the crude sewage, so as to protect from damage the pumps at the works inlet. They are followed by fine screens to strain out smaller solids before the grit removal tanks. They are often cleaned by a rake mechanism. Screens are designed for a water speed through them of 1·2 to 1·4 m/sec. at maximum flow.

screen analysis [s.m.] or **sieve analysis** The *mechanical analysis* of soils or ores by screens without *wet analysis*. It therefore lacks detailed information on the *clay* size particles.

screened material [s.m.] Material which has passed over or through a screen. *See* **oversize**.

screening The use of a *screen*.

screenings A reject from screening, either *oversize* or undersize.

screw [mech.] or **set screw** A metal rod enlarged at one end to a head, with a *screw thread* (*B*) cut or forged on the full length of the shank, up to the head. On a *bolt* the screw does not run the full length of the shank.

screw conveyor [mech.] A *helical conveyor*.

screw pile A spiral blade fixed on a shaft screwed into the ground by winch or capstan. 'Solid' screw piles have a steel shaft 10 to 20 cm dia. fixed to a steel or cast-iron screw of 1 to 1·7 m dia. Cast-iron cylinder screw piles have a hollow shaft about 1·2 m dia. Concrete screw 'jetty cylinders' 0·45 to 1 m dia. (with 10-cm thick walls) are not strong enough to be screwed since concrete is weak in shear. The spiral shoe is therefore screwed down by a steel shaft (mandrel) within the cylinder. The mandrel is withdrawn when the screw has reached bottom. The cylinders may or may not be filled with concrete, but can in any case be driven to very great depths and carry large loads. They are suitable for use in soft silts or clays.

screws *Caisson disease*.

screw shackle [stru.] or **tension sleeve** or **turn buckle** A long cylindrical nut threaded internally with a right-hand thread at one end and a left-hand thread at the other. It connects two rods in a diagonal brace and can be used for putting a small prestress on it. When the nut is tightened it draws the ends of the brace together.

screw spike [rly] *Coach screws* (*B*) used as rail fastenings (USA).

SCUBA (Self-Contained Underwater Breathing Apparatus) or **aqualung** A SCUBA diver carries his air cylinders on his back and is much more mobile than a man *diving* in standard diving dress, but he can stay under water only for so long as his cylinders allow him. Since he suffers the full pressure of the water on his body his depth also is severely limited. Nevertheless a good SCUBA diver can make several dives a day of 10 to 20 minutes each to 40 metres, and he can work for 2 hours at 13 m. Below 5 m depth SCUBA divers should not work alone but in teams of two or three. The US Geological Survey uses teams of three, one of whom carries the writing tablet, the others the *clinometer* or other instruments. Rubber 'wet suits' should be worn in cold water to keep the men warm.

scumboard [hyd.] A board which dips below the surface of a fluid to prevent scum flowing out.

seal In manhole covers, the airtight joint between cover and frame. *See* double-seal manhole cover, *also* (*B*).

sealant or sealing compound (1) A fluid of plastic consistency laid over a joint surface or the outside of a *joint filler* to exclude water. Hot bitumen, rubber strip, plastic strip, hessian caulking, synthetic resins are used, but a more recent and sophisticated sort are the building *mastics* (*B*) of which the best are perhaps the two-part sealants made of *polysulphide*.

(2) A durable coating of plastics such as epoxy resin or polyurethane, painted on the face of *form lining* or timber *formwork* to enable it to be re-used many times.

(3) or liquid-membrane curing compound A coating (e.g., for roads, *bituminous emulsion*) over a damp, recently cast concrete surface, which prevents loss of water, and thus ensures proper *curing* of the concrete.

(4) A treatment for a set concrete floor, which strengthens the concrete surface or binds the aggregate, ensuring that it does not *dust*. Sodium silicate solution has been successfully used for many years.

(5) *See* sealing compound (*B*).

sea-level correction [sur.] A *tape correction*. It is a deduction from the measured length of a base line above sea level to bring it to its value at sea level. If R is the earth's radius at sea level, *h* the height above sea level and *l* the base length, the deduction is $\frac{h}{R} \times l$. R = 6378 km at the equator, 6357 km at the poles.

sealing coat Bitumen, road tar, or an emulsion of either, applied as a thin film to a road surface.

sealing drop shafts to rock [min.] When the cutting edge of a *drop shaft* has reached hard ground, a watertight joint must be made between it and the rock, since this is often the point of maximum water pressure. If the bedrock is a stiff clay, the cutting edge can seal itself automatically by pushing itself into the clay by its own weight, but this would be unusually lucky. Generally the bottom of the shaft must be filled with concrete. This plug of concrete must then be drilled through and injected with cement grout to seal the fissures in the rock. When all the fissures are sealed the concrete plug must be excavated by drilling and blasting.

sealing pneumatic shafts to rock [min.] Since men have access to bedrock in the working chamber of the *pneumatic* shaft or *caisson*, a special technique is used which cannot be used with the open *drop shaft*. The shaft is first excavated 0·9 m into the bedrock and 0·3 m outside the shaft all round. During the excavation the shaft lining is held up on posts 0·9 m long. The rock outside the shaft is then lined with a smooth concrete wall just larger than the shaft. When the wall is completed, a ring of 12 cm of oakum is placed round the perimeter of the shaft. The men leave the chamber after a light explosive charge is placed at each post to drive it into the centre of the shaft. All the shots are fired simultaneously and the lining drops on to the oakum making a watertight joint with the rock. The rock can then be grouted and the fissures sealed before the shaft is deepened.

seam welding [mech.] *Resistance seam welding*.

seating A surface which carries a large load.

seat of settlement [s.m.] That soil thickness below a loaded foundation within which 75 % of the *settlement* occurs.

secant modulus of elasticity [stru.] For materials like concrete or prestressing wire which have a variable *modulus of elasticity* (E), the value of E used must be either the slope of the tangent to the stress-strain curve (as for elastic materials with a straight-line curve like *mild steel* up to the *yield point*) or that of the secant. The secant is the line joining the origin of the curve to (for example) the 0·1% *proof stress* point on the curve. For materials within their elastic range the secant and tangent coincide.

secondary beam [stru.] A beam carried by other beams, not carried by columns or walls. *Compare* **main beam.**

secondary sedimentation [sewage] Any sedimentation that follows *secondary treatment*. (All secondary treatment is preceded by a sedimentation, the primary sedimentation.) Sedimentation tanks are provided to remove the solids (humus) from the *effluent* from *trickling filters* (humus tanks), as well as after the *activated sludge process*.

secondary treatment [sewage] or **biological treatment** or **aerobic treatment** Apart from *sewage farms* which are obsolescent in cold climates like the UK, there are two main biological treatments (*trickling filters* and *activated sludge* processes) for the *effluent* from sedimentation (primary treatment). Both of them bring air (oxygen) into the water, enabling micro-organisms that need air to feed on the sewage and multiply. So long as the effluent is aerated it remains fresh and does not putrefy.

second cut [mech.] A grade of *file* tooth. *See* **cut.**

second-foot [hyd.] A unit of flow, one *cusec.*

second moment of area The technically correct term for *moment of inertia* of a section.

second-order or **secondary triangulation** [sur.] or **trilateration** A *triangulation* or *trilateration* with sides about 10 to 20 km long. *See* **first order, third order.**

section (1) [d.o.] A mechanical drawing of an object as if cut, at a position chosen to show certain details. It may be a *cross-section* or a longitudinal section.

(2) [stru.] The shape of a *rolled-steel section*, extruded light alloy member, etc.

sectional elevation [d.o.] A section of an object which shows, apart from the material cut in the section, various parts in *elevation*, which can be seen by looking beyond the sectioned part.

sectional tank A water tank built of pressed-steel pieces, usually 1·2 m square with external flanges, drilled for bolting outside the tank. The greatest depth usual is 5 m, at which depth frequent tie bars within the tank are needed. These tanks are very quickly erected and need little skilled labour. They have also been made of cast-iron pieces, 0·6, 0·9 or 1·2 m square, to 3·6 m greatest depth.

section leader [stru.] or **checker** or **leading draughtsman** A *structural designer* in charge of a small group of draughtsmen or *designer* draughtsmen. A section leader is usually also the checker but the details of organization are very variable.

section modulus [stru.] *See* **modulus of section.**

section properties [stru.] The area of a structural section, its moment of inertia, modulus of section; in fact all those geometrical properties which affect the strength of a member in bending.

sector gate [hyd.] or **sector regulator** A *roller gate* in which the roller is a sector of a circle instead of a cylinder. Some types fit into a pit below sill level when open, but the usual arrangement is for the gate to be raised when open.

sediment (1) Any material which settles

in a liquid, hence specially the material which is carried and dropped by a river, often called *silt*. Even in the worst floods a river or stream cannot carry more than 1% of its own weight in *bed load* and sediment.

(2) [s.m.] A soil or rock that has been formed by laying down in water, often also described as *stratified*.

sedimentation (1) [s.m.] Settlement, the sinking of soil or mineral grains to the bottom of the water which contains them. Large particles settle much faster than small particles of the same shape and density. The principle, scientifically stated in *Stokes's law*, is made use of in *classifiers*, *elutriators*, *cyclones*, coal washers, *wet analysis*, and so on. *See* flocculation.

(2) [sewage] *Primary treatment*.

seepage [hyd., s.m.] Groundwater flow, *infiltration*, leakage, etc.

seepage force [s.m.] *See* capillary pressure.

seepage line [hyd.] A *flow line*.

seepage loss A loss of water through the bank of a canal which is expressed as millimetres loss in depth per 24 hours, or as cubic metres lost per square metre of bank and bed (wetted perimeter). For the best clay the loss is 0·25 cu. m and increases with the permeability of the soil up to 5 cu. m per square metre per 24 hours for gravels. *Compare* absorption loss.

segmental sluice gate [hyd.] A *radial gate*.

segregation Because large stones drop farther in the same conditions than small ones, concrete can segregate when poured down a chute, dropped from a height, or punned too much or too little. Segregation is a separation of the concrete into over-sanded and under-sanded masses. It greatly weakens the concrete, and causes *honeycombing*, but can be prevented by correct grading, careful *placing* or punning or *vibration* or use of a *trémie*.

seiche [hyd.] The *wind surge* noticed in Lake Geneva.

seismic design [stru.] *See* lateral force.

seismic prospecting *Geophysical* methods of ground investigation that usually do not rely on cores from boreholes, although a short borehole is drilled sometimes for placing a small explosive charge in the ground. They are especially useful for investigating layered rocks like clays or coal seams. *Geophones*, placed at measured distances from the source of shocks or vibrations (shot hole), record the time of arrival of waves or their reflections and enable velocities to be calculated. Sound velocities vary from 150 m/sec. in earth to 2200 m/sec. in chalk or 8000 m/sec. in uniform, hard olivine rock. Where the information is required from soils that are less than about 15 m deep, a sledge hammer may be used instead of explosives, reducing disturbance to people nearby. Rocks through which seismic waves pass at a higher speed than 2000 m/sec. are generally too strong to be broken by a *ripper*.

seismograph [min.] An instrument at the ground surface which records the electrical effects transmitted to it by a *seismometer* and thus shows the times and amplitudes of earth shocks.

seismology The study of *earthquakes*.

seismometer Either a *geophone*, used in *seismic prospecting*, or a device for detecting earthquake shocks. An early seismometer made in Japan about A.D. 136 consisted of balls dropping from a dragon's mouth into a frog's to show the direction of the shock.

self-anchored suspension bridge [stru.] A suspension bridge with no anchorages because the cables are attached to the ends of the *stiffening girders* beyond the towers. Though this is a true bridge structure, it was used in Mantua, Italy, in 1964, for roofing a paper factory 250×30 m in plan, with the roof 19 m above ground. Like many other structures of its Roman designer, Pier Luigi Nervi, the building, overshadowed by its 50 m high towers, is spectacular, and probably expensive, but it is also practical, having few interior columns and being infinitely extensible sideways.

self-cleansing gradient [hyd.] A *gradient* at which the flow in a pipe of a certain diameter can carry out any solids which ordinarily come into it. The gradient should be neither too steep nor too sluggish. Designers now ordinarily aim at a flow velocity of 76 cm/sec. once daily in a circular sewer running full. In a 150 mm dia. sewer this is achieved at a slope of 1 in 174. As the sewer diameter increases, the necessary gradient diminishes, so that a 300 mm dia. sewer needs only 1 in 410 and a 600 mm dia. sewer only 1 in 965. The steepest allowable gradient for a 150 mm dia. sewer is 1 in 10, preferably 1 in 27.

self-docking dock [hyd.] A *floating dock* built in sections each of which can be docked (lifted up) on the others and repaired as need be. *See* **dock.**

self-reading staff [sur.] A *levelling staff* so graduated that the observer looking through the telescope of the level can read the elevation at which his line of sight cuts the staff. Nearly all staffs in building work are of this type. *See* **Sopwith staff, target rod.**

self-stressing cement *Expanding cement.*

semi-skilled man A workman such as a *rigger* or builder's labourer, who has learnt his work by helping others and has a degree of skill rather less than that of a *skilled man* or a *tradesman* (*B*). He has risen from labourer in his trade and may become a skilled man.

semi-submersible A floating vessel, much of which is deep below the waterline, to give it stability in high wind, designed for drilling oil or gas wells. Some of these vessels carry eight navigation engines and screws, two at each corner, controlled by a computer to hold the vessel exactly central over the drill hole. If it moves far off centre the drill tube can snap. In spite of its name, this vessel is intended not to sink, unlike the *submersible.* Another type, the Wimpey Sealab, is a 6000-ton ship with a vertical hole through the middle where the drilling rods pass. It was in use in 1973 in 55 m of water off the Northumberland coast, drilling 180 m into the sea bed, seeking coal seams for the National Coal Board. This ship has six 40-ton winches to hold it in position, connected to anchors on the sea bed during drilling.

sensible horizon [sur.] or **apparent/visible horizon** The seen *horizon.*

sensitive clay [s.m.] The most sensitive clays are subject to *liquefaction* in *flow slides. See* **sensitivity ratio.**

sensitiveness or **sensitivity** [sur.] The responsiveness of an instrument to slight alterations in the quantity which it measures. The sensitiveness of a level or theodolite *bubble* is expressed in seconds of arc per millimetre of bubble movement.

sensitivity ratio [s.m.] A measure of how much *remoulding* may affect a clay. It is the ratio of the unconfined compressive strength in the undisturbed state to that in the remoulded state. Since clays are plastic, an exact failure point is not always found in the strength tests, and for greater accuracy the strengths at equal strains may be measured. For British alluvial clays the sensitivity ratio is from 2 to 5. For sensitive clays it is much higher.

separate system [sewage] A drainage system in which rainwater and sewage are carried in separate *sewers. See* **combined system, partially separate system.**

separator A *distance piece.*

serrated strip A *rumble strip.*

service reservoir, distribution reservoir, clear-water reservoir A *reservoir* that is designed to be large enough to store at night the excess of day-time demand over night-time demand and to deliver it to consumers by day. It may receive its water by pumping or by *gravity main,* as convenient.

service road A small road parallel to a main road. It is used by traffic stopping at houses and shops so as to avoid obstruction to through traffic.

set (1) [hyd.] The direction of flow of water.

(2) [mech.] A bend in a piece of metal. *See* **cold sett, permanent set.**

(3) The penetration of a driven *pile* for each blow of the *drop hammer.*

set screw [mech.] *See* **screw.**

set square [d.o.] (**triangle** in USA) A triangular piece of wood or transparent plastic material used for mechanical drawing. It is always made with one right angle but the other angles may be 60° and 30°, or both 45°, or adjustable.

sett (1) or **pitcher** A small rectangular block of hard stone, such as granite or quartzite, used for paving a road which carries heavy traffic. It measures 15 cm deep by 7 to 10 cm by 15 to 23 cm.

(2) A *follower* used in pile driving.

(3) A blacksmith's hammer-shaped cutting chisel, either a *cold sett* or a hot sett.

setting The boards (*runners* or *sheeting* or *poling boards*) held in place by a pair of timber *frames* supporting an excavation. One setting consists of all the boards held by a pair of frames.

setting out Putting pegs in the ground to mark out an excavation, marking concrete to locate walls, or preparing dimensioned rods for carpentry or joinery. Large-scale setting out is done by a civil engineer, small-scale work by a foreman of a trade.

setting up *See* **upsetting, set-up.**

settlement [stru.] Downward movement of a structure such as a railway bridge, dam, or building, due to compression or movement of the soil below it. It need not be harmful unless different parts settle by different amounts (*differential settlement*). *See* **inherent/interference settlement, gross loading intensity, pore-water pressure, seat of settlement, subsidence.**

settlement crater [stru.] It has been observed that uniformly loaded soils settle in such a way that a previously level surface becomes basin-shaped over the loaded area, particularly if settlement is due to compression of a clay. This crater of settlement is the main cause of *differential settlement* of buildings.

settlement joint A joint that allows part of a building, for example, to settle relatively to the neighbouring part in the event of mining or other subsidence.

settling basin [hyd.] One sort of *sand trap.*

settling velocity *See* **terminal velocity.**

set-up [sur.] A location at which a surveying instrument, particularly a *theodolite*, is stationed. Since several minutes are needed for centring an instrument over the station point, levelling it, and adjusting it, surveyors take great care that their set-ups are not disturbed. *See* **temporary adjustment, three-tripod traversing, upsetting.**

Severn Bridge A road bridge over the river Severn in the west of England; a suspension bridge of 988 m span, designed by Freeman, Fox & Partners for the consulting engineers Mott, Hay & Anderson, and completed in 1966. The aerodynamic design of the *stiffening girder* saves so much steel that this bridge has been copied in the *Humber* and *Bosporus* bridges.

sewage Water-borne waste – the water of a community after it has been used. In the UK it flows down the property owner's *house drain* into the *sewer* of the *water authority.* Ordinarily it is equal in volume to the water consumption of the community, but in old sewers this *dry weather flow* is increased by the amount of the inward leakage – infiltration. In hot countries it may be reduced by outward leakage – exfiltration.

sewage disposal The disposal of (*a*) *effluent* and (*b*) *sludge.* Effluent which forms over 99% of sewage can, by *sewage treatment*, reach a condition approaching *Royal Commission standard* in a modern works, and then passes to a river or other receiving

239

water. Sludge is more difficult to dispose of because it starts at about 95% water, de-watering is difficult, and disposal on farms may be dangerous if there are poisonous metals from industry in the sludge. Much sludge from the UK is tipped at sea. In the USA this is shortly to be forbidden and in Europe it may soon contravene international agreement (Oslo Convention).

sewage farm A farm where sewage *effluent* manures and irrigates the soil. Sandy soil is much more suitable than clay for a sewage farm since sand is porous and filters the effluent as it passes through. Few sewage farms remain in the UK but where the climate is warmer and land is less expensive, it is a suitable disposal method.

sewage gas, sludge gas The gas from *digestion* tanks. Two-thirds methane (CH_4) and one third carbon dioxide (CO_2) with small amounts of other gases, it has been effectively used on sewage treatment plants both for power generation in gas engines and for heating the digesters from which it originates. If there is much hydrogen sulphide gas (H_2S) this must be removed before the gas is used because it is extremely corrosive.

sewage treatment Separation of the 0·1% pollutants from the 99·9% water in sewage. It can include four treatments – *preliminary, primary, secondary* and *tertiary treatments*, sometimes a fifth, *advanced treatment*.

sewer A pipe or underground *open channel* for carrying water or *sewage*. A sewer is usually the property of a *water authority* in the UK, a *drain* of an individual. Every sewer is fed by drains or by other sewers. *See* **combined/partially-separate/separate system.**

sewerage The *water authority's* network of *sewers*; the means by which *sewage* is removed.

sewer pill A skeleton-framed wooden ball of nearly the diameter of the sewer which it floats down. As it passes it cleans the sewer walls. *See* **go-devil.**

sexagesimal measure, sexagesimal graduation [sur.] Division of a circle into 360 degrees, each degree having 60 minutes, and each minute having 60 seconds, formerly universal in Britain. *Compare* **centesimal.**

sextant [sur.] or **nautical sextant** A hand-held instrument for measuring angles up to about 120° in any plane, and used at sea for measuring the altitude of a heavenly body such as the sun. Its main parts are two mirrors, that is, one fixed *horizon glass*, and one *index glass* which is silvered all over and connected to an arm with a vernier moving along a scale of degrees. The objects between which the angle is required are brought to coincide in the index mirror and horizon glass, and the sextant reading is then noted. The nautical sextant is accurate to about 30 seconds of arc, much more precise than the smaller *box sextant*.

shackle (1) A *wrought-iron* or *manganese-steel* chain or pinned coupling connected between wagons forming a train. The strength of a shackle in tons may be taken as $0.5\, d^2$ where d is the pin dia. in centimetres (BS 3032, 3551).

(2) A lifting ring on a crane hook or over a *kibble*. The parts of a *lewis* (B) are joined by a ring called a shackle.

(3) *See* **screw shackle.**

shaft Generally any slender or tapering object; a ventilating pipe; the part of a chimney which projects above the roof; the handle of a tool; and specifically:

(1) [min.] A vertical or sloping passage from the surface to the workings, used for ventilation or travelling or hoisting, or all three.

(2) [mech.] A cylindrical metal rod which rotates on its centre line and transmits power by its rotation.

shaft plumbing [min.] The operation of transferring one or two points at the surface of a vertical shaft to positions below them at the foot of the shaft. This can be done by a specially fitted theodolite, but the operation is called plumbing because, for shallow shafts, it is easily done with wire and plumb bob. A theodolite which is set up at the foot of the shaft is used for sighting the lower ends of the wires. A series of readings is taken on the wires as they sway backwards and forwards. Usually each bob is submerged in a bucket of water or thick oil to damp its movements. Accurate work is essential, since the orientation of the underground workings depends on these two points only 3 m or so apart. *See* **instrumental shaft plumbing, Weisbach triangle.**

shaft-plumbing wire [min.] Iron, steel, copper, brass, or phosphor-bronze wire, not usually thinner than 0·8 mm. Copper or iron wire are ductile enough to unkink themselves without breaking and are suitable for shallow shafts. Steel wire as used for *prestressed concrete* is much stronger, but rusts more easily and with phosphor-bronze is more used for deep shafts.

shaft sinking [min.] Excavating a shaft downwards. This is the usual method of excavating a shaft – raising is only rarely practicable for important shafts.

shaking test [s.m.] A rapid way of determining whether a sample of fine-grained soil is a *clay* or a *silt*. Coarse particles larger than 0·5 mm must first be screened out. The wet *remoulded* sample is held in the palm of the hand and tested in the following way. The surface of the soil is smoothed with a knife and the soil is shaken by tapping the hand. The soil then begins to glisten with the water, which is pushed out of it as the grains slip past each other into a denser position due to the shaking. The soil pat is then squeezed, causing it to expand (in a direction perpendicular to the squeeze) like a dense sand during shearing (*see* **critical voids ratio of sands**). The result of the squeezing is that the water disappears from the surface, re-enters the soil and the sheen vanishes. Clays show none of these changes. Very fine, clean sands react most quickly.

This property of a silt is called *dilatancy.*

shale [s.m.] A laminated clay or silt which has been compressed by the weight of the rocks over it. Unlike slate it splits along its bedding planes. Shales vary in hardness from slaty rock to hard clay.

shallow foundation [stru.] A *pad foundation, strip footing, short bored piles,* etc. *Compare* **deep foundation.**

shallow manhole An *inspection chamber* of the same cross-section all the way up.

shallow well A shaft sunk to pump surface water only. *See* **deep well.**

shaping Forming an earth or road surface to the correct contour, usually with *graders* or *dozers.*

shear [stru.] or **shear force** The load acting across a beam near its support. For a uniformly distributed load or for any other symmetrical load, the maximum shear is equal to half the total load on a simply supported beam, or to the total load on a cantilever beam.

shear centre or **centre of stiffness** [stru.] A point such that, when the plane of applied horizontal load passes through it, the structure will deflect in the direction of the applied load without twisting. It may be inside or outside the plan area of the structure.

shearing [stru.] Failure of materials under *shear.* It can be seen in the action of a pair of shears or scissors.

shearlegs or **shears** or **shear legs** A pair of poles lashed together at the top with a pulley hung from the lashing, used for lifting heavy loads. *See* **derrick** (2).

shear modulus [stru.] The *modulus of rigidity* (G). It is equal to the shear stress divided by the shear strain. *See* **Poisson's ratio.**

shears (1) *Shearlegs.*

(2) [mech.] A machine for cutting steel plates or sections.

shear slide [s.m.] A *landslip* in which a mass of earth slides as a block away from the material below it.

shear strain [stru.] The angular displacement of a member due to a force across it (shear force). It is measured in radians.

shear strength The stress at which a material fails in shear. It is the same in all directions for steel, very different in different directions for wood, and is usually measured on the glued face for glues. *See also* **cohesive soil, shear tests.**

shear stress [stru.] The shear force per unit of cross-sectional area, expressed in kilonewtons/m^2 or lb per sq. in. like other stresses. *See* **cube test.**

shear tests [s.m.] The shear strength of soil samples is often measured in the laboratory by the *box shear test* or by the *triaxial compression test*. However, since the behaviour of soils in place often differs greatly from their laboratory behaviour, the *vane test* has been developed for testing the shear strength of a soil at the foot of a borehole.

shear wall A *core wall* (2).

sheathing (1) *See* **boarding** (*B*).

(2) A sheet-metal covering over underwater timber to protect it against *marine borers*.

(3) *Sheeting*.

sheave [mech.] A grooved pulley wheel, particularly the pulleys over which steel-wire *ropes* pass in mine hoists or haulages.

sheepsfoot roller. A towed roller for *compaction* of clay soils, with one or more drums which can be water ballasted. The drums have a number of steel bars about 10 cm long, welded radially to their surfaces. A typical sheepsfoot roller has a 1·1 m dia. drum, a loaded weight from 9000 to 22,000 kg per m width of drum, and footprint pressures from 0·5 to 2 N/mm^2. Much heavier rollers have been built for use after the typical sheepsfoot roller; they have footprint pressures up to 7 N/mm^2. *See* **tamping roller.**

sheeters Light steel vertical poling boards for protecting trench sides, driven down by a pneumatic tool before the trench is excavated.

sheeting or **sheathing** Rough horizontal or vertical boards held against the sides of trenches by *struts*, *walings*, or *soldiers*, or a combination of them.

sheet pavement Road surfacing like asphalt or concrete, which is very much smoother for traffic than stone *block pavement*.

sheet piles Closely set piles of timber, *reinforced* or *prestressed concrete*, or steel driven vertically into the ground to keep earth or water out of an excavation. *Bored piles* are often successfully incorporated with the concrete of a basement retaining wall. *See* **barge bed, clutch, diaphragm wall, steel sheet piling.**

sheet-pile wall or **sheet piling** A wall of *sheet piles*, which may be a *cantilever wall* or anchored back at one or two levels to a *dead man* as a *tied retaining wall*.

sheet steel *See* **steel sheet.**

shelf angle [stru.] A mild-steel *angle section* riveted or welded to the web of an I-beam or channel section to support the formwork or the hollow tiles of a concrete slab.

shelf retaining wall A reinforced-concrete retaining wall with a *relieving platform* built on to its upper part.

shell (1) [stru.] or **thin shell** A thin, curved plate-like structure which can be an extremely elegant roof. Shells are usually designed by specialists, since the mathematics is advanced. Dischinger in Germany built the earliest shells, the first large shell being the Düsseldorf Planetarium 1926. Most shells are of concrete, in which 76 mm thickness for 30 m span is regarded as normal, but many timber shells have been built. Some steel shells exist, however, to which concrete is applied as an insulation (foamed slag or vermiculite concrete or plaster). *See* **Leipzig market halls, membrane theory.**

(2) A *sand pump*.

shell-and-auger boring An old percussion drilling method, still used for drilling holes in *site investigation*. Hand rigs can bore to 20 cm dia. 24 m deep, and to 0·6 m dia. but shorter depths. The auger is used for boring in clays, the *sand pump* for sands, particularly below the water table. A rope can be used for the shell but sectional boring rods must be used for turning the auger. Small boulders are broken up by a chisel bit on the rods. A *shear legs* or light three-pole *derrick* carries the weight of tools and rods. Holes more than 100 m deep have been drilled by three men with a three-pole derrick but a *truck-mounted drilling rig* is now more commonly used for deep holes if they can be reached by a lorry.

Shell-perm process [s.m.] Injection of bitumen emulsion into a permeable soil to reduce the flow of water into an excavation. The emulsion contains a coagulator to make it solidify in the ground. This effectively closes the pores but does not strengthen the ground.

shell pump A *sand pump* for bailing out boreholes.

shell roof [stru.] *See* shell.

shield A steel hood which protects men driving a circular tunnel through soft ground. The *Greathead shield* is used for driving the tunnels of the London *tube railways* which are lined with cast-iron pieces built up in *rings* 508 mm wide. This shield is therefore fitted with jacks all round its edge which push on the cast-iron lining and advance the shield about 508 mm into fresh ground. A complete new ring of lining can then be built up from the segments brought into the tunnel. Tunnels are driven like this for many hundred metres with only 10 mm of error in the lining at any point. *See* **Hallinger shield, rotary excavator, silt displacement**.

shielded-arc welding *Arc welding* in which the weld is protected from the atmosphere by argon, helium or other gas liberated from the coating on the *electrode* or from a gas cylinder through a hose.

shielded metal-arc (SMA) or **stick welding** US terms for *manual metal-arc welding*.

shift [sur.] The radial displacement from the circular shape needed to make from a circular curve, a spiral (transition) curve.

shim [mech.] or **pack** A thin steel plate inserted between two surfaces to fill a gap. A shim is thinner than a pack.

shin [mech.] (1) A replaceable edge of a *mouldboard*.

(2) A railway *fishplate*.

shingle beach A beach of stones that are more or less of the same size, enabling the beach to be self-draining. The large holes between the stones allow the water to pass, so the beach is steeper than a sand beach.

ship caisson [hyd.] or **sliding caisson** A tall, floating box which is used for closing the entrance to a lock, dry dock, or wet dock. It fits on to grooves in the walls and sides of the entrance when this is closed and into a recess (camber) in the dock wall when the entrance is open. Caissons have been made of riveted or welded steel and of reinforced concrete. *See* **step**.

shoe A *pile shoe*. Also a *cutting curb*. *See also* (*B*).

shop weld [mech.] A weld made at the workshop. As with riveting, shop welding is often cheaper and stronger than site welding, but some joints must be made at the site if the pieces transported are to be of easily manageable size.

shore protection [hyd.] Prevention of scour by *breakwaters*, *graded filters*, *groynes*, and every sort of *revetment*.

short bored piles [stru.] On a clay soil, piles about 25 cm dia. or even less, and 2 m long, which carry light foundation loads such as those of a house to below that part of a clay that cracks in summer.

short column [stru.] A column which is so short that if overloaded it will fail not by *crippling* but by crushing. For columns of this sort the *slenderness ratio* does not need to be calculated except as a check that it is less than is allowed for a short column. *See* lateral support.

short ton or net ton The American ton of 2000 lb. *Compare* long ton.

shot blasting [mech.] Cleaning a steel surface by projecting steel shot on to it with centrifugal steel impellers or a compressed-air blast. It is a preparation for painting or *metal coating* (*B*). *See* sand blast, wheelabrating.

Shotcrete *Gunite* (USA).

shot firing *See* blasting.

shovel (1) A hand tool for moving coal, stone, concrete, etc., or for mixing concrete, plaster, or mortar.

(2) A mechanical *excavator*.

shrinkage (1) The shrinkage of concrete during hardening can amount to 0·0004 of its length at one year or half this value at two months. Cement mortar shrinks by a similar amount. The numerical value of the shrinkage is important for prestressed concrete because it partly determines the *losses of prestress*. According to BSCP 110:1972, concrete prestressed at 3 to 5 days after casting and kept wet (at 90% relative humidity) shrinks only 100×10^{-6} (0·0001) compared with 300×10^{-6} for concrete kept at the normal 70% relative humidity. When the prestressing takes place at a later age, the shrinkage is much smaller. For example, with 7 to 14 days' age at prestress these values fall to 70 and 200×10^{-6}. Half the shrinkage takes place in the first month after stressing and three-quarters of it in the first six months. *See* moisture movement.

(2) [s.m.] The shrinkage of earth banks after construction. Since earth fill measured before excavation may occupy a smaller space when finally compacted in the embankment (but a larger space after excavation and before compaction) there is considerable confusion about the meaning of this term. The usual comparison is between the volume of material in the compacted bank and that of the excavation from which it came. Ameri-

can railway construction figures show 10% initial shrinkage and 15% after complete settlement. An exception is dry clay from deep pits which swells on contact with air. *See* bulking.

shrinkage joint *See* contraction joint.

shrinkage limit [s.m.] The maximum water content for a given soil at which a reduction in water content decreases the volume of the sample. It describes the limit between the solid and the plastic states of a clay, and is usually distinguished by a colour change, the clay becoming much paler at water contents below the shrinkage limit. *See* consistency limits.

shuttering That part of *formwork* which either is in contact with the concrete or has the *form lining* attached to it.

side board A board used for timbering the sides of a heading, usually held by *side trees*.

side-entrance manhole A *deep manhole* in which the access shaft is built not over but to the side of the *inspection chamber*. A passage leads to the inspection chamber from the foot of the shaft, or the inspection chamber merges with the shaft.

side forms *Road forms*.

side-jacking test [s.m.] A load test on a soil formation in a trial pit made by jacking apart two vertical bearing plates on opposite faces of the pit, a method developed from the plate bearing test.

sidelong ground A hillside slope along which the ground must be cut to expose the formation for a road or other structure. Cuts on slopes often interfere with the stability of the soil uphill and may cause landslips.

side pond [hyd.] A storage pond beside a lock chamber which reduces considerably the water loss in lockage.

side rail *See* check rail.

sidesway [stru.] Slight sideways movement of a *frame* in its own plane caused by wind or other horizontal forces or unsymmetrical loading.

sidetracking In *directional drilling*, the drilling of a branch hole at any point.

side tree Posts 7 to 15 cm thick holding the *head trees* and *side boards* in a heading.

sidewalk American term for the *footway* of a road.

siding machine A machine which cuts back the edge of a grass verge to a required line.

sieve analysis [s.m.] *Screen analysis*.

sight distance The *visibility distance*.

sight rail [sur.] A horizontal board set at a certain height above a required level, for example 1·8 m above the invert level of a drain. With a *boning rod* 1·8 m long and two sight rails it is possible to check the levels set out for the drain in the trench for the full distance between the rails and for a short distance beyond them.

sight rule [sur.] An *alidade*.

silent pile-drivers *Hydraulic pile-drivers* and *vibrating pile-drivers*.

silica SiO₂. Silicon dioxide which occurs as crystalline quartz and non-crystalline chalcedony, agate, flint, sardonyx, and many other varieties. The greater part of *sand*, *sandstone*, and *quartzite* is silica. Although some of its varieties are semi-precious gems, silica is the commonest known solid material. *See* extender (*B*).

silica brick *Refractory* brick which contains over 90% silica and being bonded with lime will stand temperatures from 1650° to 1750°C before it softens.

silicate injection *See* **Joosten process**.

silicon carbide or **carbon silicide** SiC. An important constituent of the abrasive *Carborundum*.

sill (1) A timber laid across the foot of a trench or heading under the *side trees*. A *liner* nailed to the sill keeps the side trees apart.

(2) [hyd.] The horizontal overflow line of a measuring notch or dam spillway or other weir structure. *See also* **lock sill**.

silo A tall, often cylindrical, reinforced-concrete tower (occasionally of steel or timber) used for storing grain, cement, or similar materials. The smaller silos are sometimes built of precast segments which are reinforced by spiral wires tightly wrapped round the outside and protected by a cement mortar or *gunite* cover. Tall silos may be built with *sliding forms*.

silt (1) [s.m.] Granular material finer than sand but coarser than *clay*, that is from 0·002 to 0·06 mm (*see* classification of soils). It feels gritty between the fingers but the grains are difficult to see. It can be distinguished from clay by the *shaking test* or by rolling it into a thread. A thread of silt crumbles on drying, a clay thread does not. *Rock flour* and *loess* are materials of silt size. *See* **shaking test**.

(2) [hyd.] *See* **sediment, silting**.

silt box A loose iron box at the bottom of a gulley for collecting grit. It is pulled out and emptied occasionally.

silt displacement A method of using a *shield* for tunnel driving in nearly fluid silts in USA. As the shield is driven forward the silt is forced into the tunnel through two rectangular openings, like toothpaste from a tube. The miners cut it with wires and load it out.

silt ejector A *hydraulic ejector*.

silt grade material [s.m.] Material of *silt* size.

siltation [hyd.] *Silting*.

silting [hyd.] The deposition of *sediment* in a river or on the sea bed. Silt is removed by dredging or by inserting groynes when it obstructs navigation or the flow of the river. Most harbours have to be dredged.

similarity, dimensional similarity *See* **dimensional analysis**.

simple beam [stru.] or **simply-supported beam** A beam subject to *simple bending*.

simple bending [stru.] The bending of a beam which is freely supported and has no *fixed end*.

simple curve [sur.] An arc of a circle joining two straights with no *transition*.

simple engine [mech.] Usually a reciprocating engine from which the steam or compressed air is passed to the atmosphere after expanding in one cylinder only.

simple framework [stru.] A *perfect frame*.

simply-supported beam *See* **simple beam**.

Simpson's rule [d.o.] A rule for estimating the area of an irregular figure. The figure is first divided into an even number n of parallel strips of width d. The lengths of the boundary ordinates (lines separating the strips) are measured. There will then be $n+1$ boundary ordinates, of lengths h_0, h_1, h_2, and so on to h_{n-2}, h_{n-1}, and h_n. The area of the figure is

$$\frac{d}{3}[h_0+h_n+2(h_2+h_4+\ldots h_{n-2})$$
$$+4(h_1+h_3+\ldots h_{n-1})].$$

Compare **prismoidal formula, trapezoidal rule**.

single-acting [mech.] A description of *reciprocating pumps* or compressed air or steam engines in which only one side of the piston works and every second stroke of an engine is a power stroke. Every second stroke of such a pump delivers fluid. A single-acting pile hammer drops its weight under gravity alone. *Compare* **double-acting**.

single-cut file [mech.] A file with *cuts* (4) in one direction only, used for filing soft material.

single-pass soil stabilizer [s.m.] A powerful machine with four rapidly rotating toothed milling wheels in contact with the soil. These rotors pulverize the soil to a measured depth, mix it with a liquid binder (water, bitumen, etc.) and intermingle the soil with cement or other solid binder which has been spread ahead of the machine. The original soil stabilizers (1944) were single-rotor, multiple-pass machines, but the multiple-rotor, single-pass stabilizers cover the ground more quickly. After the soil has thus been treated and has had liquid added to bring it to its *optimum moisture content*, the road has to be graded, shaped, rolled with sheepsfoot rollers, wobble-wheel rollers, and steel rollers, and finally given a wearing surface.

Per centimetre of depth, soil cement costs about half as much as reinforced concrete, and it is economical as a base in almost any large road programme, provided that the soil type is right.

single-sized aggregate For concretes, an aggregate of a size between two adjacent sieves in the series listed under *fineness modulus*. Thus aggregates from 38 mm to 19 mm or from 19 to 9·5 mm are single-sized. But roadstones may need much closer sizing, so this definition may not be accepted for them and is in any case too wide. *Macadam* may be from 19 to 13 mm and this would be a half-size material.

single sling A *sling* with an iron or steel ring at one end and a hook at the other end. *See* **two-leg sling**.

single-stage compressor [mech.] A machine which compresses air to its full pressure in one cylinder (or one stage of a centrifugal compressor). These are little used for pressures above 4 bars and only for small capacities, since compression in stages is more economical of power.

single-stage pump [mech.] A centrifugal pump with one *impeller*. It could be built to lift water 180 m, but generally a lift of 30 m per stage is normal. For 180 m, therefore, a six-stage pump would ordinarily be used.

sinker drill [min.] A large hand-held *rock drill* used for shaft sinking and other down holes. It may weigh 30 kg or more.

sinking bucket [min.] A *kibble*.

sinking pump [min.] A pump built for keeping a shaft dry during sinking. It may be driven by electricity, compressed air, or steam, but is always robust, to withstand falling stones, and built so that its height is about ten times its greatest width. In this way it occupies very little space in the crowded shaft bottom. It is often a *submersible pump* and may be a *borehole pump* with a protective frame round it.

sintered carbides [mech.] A term sometimes preferred for *cemented carbides*. *See* sintering.

sintered clay *Expanded clay* aggregate (*B*). *See* lightweight aggregate.

sintered fly-ash A *lightweight aggregate* made by pelletizing and then sintering *fly-ash*. It became regularly available in Britain about 1962.

sintering Heating a powder until it begins to melt. This gives it some mechanical strength while maintaining its porosity and is used in the manufacture of *lightweight aggregates* such as Aglite, Leca or Lytag. Cemented carbides are made by sintering hard carbides and metal powders of various melting points with cobalt, which has a low melting point and fuses them together.

sinuous flow [hyd.] *Turbulent flow*.

siphon [hyd.] (1) A closed pipe, part of which rises above the *hydraulic gradient* of the pipe, but not more than the head due to the atmospheric pressure (maximum 10 m). Water may thus be forced through it by atmospheric pressure.

(2) *See* sag pipe.

siphon spillway [hyd.] A dam spillway which is built as a siphon passing over the crest of the dam. The water must rise to the crest of the siphon before the siphon primes itself and begins to flow, but the siphon will go on flowing until the water falls below its inlet (which is below the crest). There can thus be a difference of more than 1 m between the two levels at which flow starts automatically and stops automatically.

site Land which is used or is to be used for construction. In USA often called a lot.

site exploration or **site investigation** The examination of the surface and subsoil at a site to obtain the information needed for the design of the foundations and therefore of the remainder of the structure. The most expensive part of this work is the sinking of boreholes or test pits, shafts, or headings under the structure to a depth below the foundation equal to 1·5 times the width of the building unless *bedrock* is encountered above this level. Normal practice in Britain is to require the boring to have a 15 cm dia. casing so that *undisturbed samples* of 10 cm dia. can be taken without difficulty. The cost of exploration for a large project (several million £) may amount to 0·5% of the cost of the project, but for a small scheme even 5% may be too little. This work is almost always done by a specialist firm.

site weld A weld made at the site, unlike a *shop weld*.

size analysis, size distribution, size grading *See* grading curve.

skeleton (1) [sur.] A network of accurate survey lines obtained by *triangulation*. From these lines the details of the countryside can be plotted by *plane tabling*, *stadia work*, or similarly rapid but relatively inaccurate methods.

(2) [stru.] A building frame of steel or concrete.

sketch *See* drawing.

skew bridge A bridge which is oblique to and therefore longer than the gap.

skids Lengths of round or rough timber, steel rail, or pipe placed under a heavy object when it is being moved, to prevent it sinking into the earth.

skilled man A leading hand in a modern trade which has expanded too quickly for the apprenticeship system to become general (general *riggers*, *bar benders*, *rivet testers*, *steel erectors*). They are generally not called tradesmen though they may have more skill and adaptability than many tradesmen. Most of them work to drawings. Since there is no apprenticeship system, most skilled men have risen from labourer.

skimmer equipment or **skimmer** A digging bucket mounted to slide along an *excavator* jib. The jib is held horizontally and the skimmer takes a slice of soil as it moves away from the machine. Skimmers do not dig below the level of the crawler tracks.

skimming (1) Removing the irregularities of the surface of the soil.

(2) [hyd.] Diverting surface water by a shallow overflow to obtain the cleanest water.

skin friction (1) The resistance of the ground around a pile or caisson to its movement. Usually proportional to the area of contact, it increases with the depth of penetration. *See* **negative skin friction, bentonite mud.**

(2) That part of the resistance to flow that is caused by *roughness* rather than by eddying.

skip A hoisting bucket or *kibble* used in excavation or shaft sinking, or a carrier on an aerial ropeway.

slab (1) The thin part of a reinforced-concrete floor between beams or supporting walls.

(2) Any large, thin area of concrete such as a wall, a road, or a roof. *See* also (*B*).

slab-and-beam floor *See* **beam and slab floor.**

slab track Rail track in which *sleepers* are eliminated because the rail clips or other fixings are cast into the concrete used instead of *ballast*. The continuous concrete foundation is slow to build because the concrete must harden, but the periodical maintenance needed for ballasted track is unnecessary. The support given by the concrete is so good that railway engineers argue that lighter rails could be used on it. Because of the slowness of construction, slab track is now being prefabricated.

slack-line cableway or slack-line cableway excavator A *cableway* with one low and one high tower between which a track rope with adjustable tension is suspended. A digging bucket hangs on carrier wheels from the track rope and is controlled by a haulage rope from a winch at the lower tower. Spans vary from 90 to 300 m and digging can go as deep as 24 m below water level. The towers can run on rails or be dismantled, moved, and re-erected periodically to work over the whole site. Its range is far beyond that of any mobile machine such as a *dragline*, particularly in river beds.

slack-water navigation [hyd.] or still-water navigation A *navigation* with no current or a very slight current. This is made possible in rivers by keeping up the water level with *weirs* which separate it into *reaches* joined (or separated) by *locks*. The water is thus made deeper and the current is slower than before the weir was built.

slag The waste glass-like product from a metallurgical furnace, which flows off above the metal. The slags most used in building and civil engineering in Britain are *blast-furnace slags* (*B*).

slag cements Cements made by grinding blast-furnace slag and mixing it with lime or *Portland cement* or dehydrated *gypsum* (*B*). Slag is also used in making *expanding cement* and *supersulphated cement*. *See* **Trief process.**

sledge hammer or sledge A heavy two-handed double-faced hammer used for breaking stone and for timbering.

sleeper (1) [rly] (In USA a rail tie) A steel or pressure-creosoted wooden or *prestressed concrete* beam passing under the rails of the permanent way and holding them at the correct *gauge*. Wooden sleepers usually measure 2·6 m × 13 cm × 25 cm. Precast prestressed-concrete sleepers weigh about $3\frac{1}{2}$ times as much as wood sleepers but have a longer life.

(2) A *foot block*.

(3) The horizontal leg of a Scotch *derrick*.

sleeve [stru.] A metal pipe, slightly larger in bore than a reinforcing bar, in which the bar can be inserted, for butting against its continuation bar. The bars can be wedged or bonded in with synthetic resin mortar. Sleeves enable more steel to be inserted into a small concrete section than would be possible with overlapping bars. Resin mortars, however, have low fire resistance. *See also below and* (*B*).

sleeve grouting [s.m.] The use of *packers*, *tube à manchette*, etc.

slender beam A beam which would tend if overloaded to fail by buckling in the compression flange. For concrete it applies to beams which are longer than 20 times their width. The compressive stress in such a beam must be reduced in proportion to its *slenderness ratio*. The greatest slenderness ratio allowed for concrete beams is 60. For timber and steel the allowable slenderness ratios are higher because the tensile strengths are also higher.

slenderness ratio [stru.] The effective height of a column divided by its *radius of gyration,* the value $\dfrac{l}{k}$ in the formula for the *Euler crippling stress.* This is simplified for concrete, in which columns are usually rectangular and calculations are therefore based on the effective height divided by the least width. If this exceeds 15 the allowable stress is considerably reduced until, at 45, the allowable stress is 0. For steel a slenderness ratio of 200 is often allowed, and for timber about 150. For brickwork, stone, or mass-concrete walls, no greater ratio of effective height to breadth than 24 is allowed, and usually 18 is the maximum. At ratio 1 for masonry the stress *reduction factor* is 1 and at ratio 18 it is 0·30, at 24 it is 0·20.

slewing [mech.] Rotation of a crane jib. It may be simultaneous with *derricking*.

sliced blockwork *Blockwork* for breakwater construction built in sloping, nearly vertical courses so that the placing of the submerged blocks is much easier than in *coursed blockwork*. Each block being lowered by the crane must rest on two of its neighbours and slides naturally into position.

slickensided clay [s.m.] A description of *stiff-fissured* clay.

slickensides Polished, grooved surfaces on the faces of cracks in rocks, formed by movement along them. They are usually seen in fault planes. The scratches show the direction of movement but do not necessarily show

which side has been upthrown and which downthrown.

slide [s.m.] *See* landslip.

slide rail [mech.] A steel or cast-iron mounting for a belt-driven machine which enables it to be moved as the belt stretches, so as to tighten the belt. Generally the electric motor is bolted to the slide rails and it is the motor which is adjusted.

sliding caisson [hyd.] A *ship caisson*.

sliding forms or **continuously moving forms** *Formwork* for building a reinforced-concrete silo or lift shaft or other wall of smooth outline and concrete cross-section, which is raised either continuously or at short intervals at about 15 cm per hour (faster in hot weather, slower in cold weather). This rapid way of casting walls has the advantage that when pouring is continuous no construction joints exist, but excellent site organization and supplies are needed, as well as a high capital outlay on jacks, the formwork, the crane and the working platform for the men that is raised with the formwork. Other more ambiguous terms used to describe this system are: *climbing forms, moving forms*, and *slip-forms*. The system can also be used for building a horizontal structure, e.g. tunnel lining with *travelling forms*.

sliding gate [hyd.] A *crest gate* which has a high frictional resistance to opening and can therefore be used only in small sizes. For this reason the *roller gate* has been developed.

sliding joint In concrete work a gap in the steel and the concrete, fitted with sliding surfaces to ease relative movement in the joint plane. *See* movement joints.

sliding-panel weir [hyd.] A *frame weir* with wooden panels which slide between grooved uprights.

sliding-wedge method [s.m.] The *wedge theory* for determining graphically or by calculation the passive or *active earth pressure* on a *retaining wall*. When the properties of the soil are known from laboratory tests on undisturbed samples this method is preferable, particularly for clays, to the use of *Rankine's theory*.

sling A length of rope or chain for hanging an object from a crane hook. A steel wire rope with a loop at one end is a special type of sling called a *bond*. Slings may be single, two-leg, three-leg, or four-leg, with *reeving* or non-reeving end links. The latest rope slings are braided, not twisted, or may be of synthetic fibre.

slip (1) [s.m.] A small *landslip*.

(2) or **slipway** A concrete or stone slab which slopes down to the water's edge. It supports a vessel being built or repaired. *See* **cradle, traversing slipway.**

slip circle [s.m.] The assumed *circular arc* of failure of a clay bank.

slip dock A dock with a sloping bottom and a gate to keep out water.

slip factor The *coefficient of friction* between a *high-strength friction-grip bolt*, or group of bolts, and the steel members which are gripped. The slip load is found by testing assemblies and the slip factor deduced from the tests. From it can be calculated the safe working load at 70% of the slip load.

slip-form (1) *Sliding forms.*

(2) A narrow section of *formwork* in slab or wall shuttering that can easily be removed, and is designed to be struck first, thus making it easy to strike the remaining larger panels. It may also be called a wrecking piece or wrecking strip.

(3) A loose temporary vertical plate in a wall mould to separate the expensive *face mix* (*B*) from the cheaper backing mix during casting – withdrawn as soon as the mould is full.

slip-form paver A machine that, working on a prepared base, builds concrete roads under electro-hydraulic control of line and level, pulling its road forms with it. The concrete must be stiff or the edges collapse as the forms slide off them. The machine can lay

thousands of metres of road in a day but like the *Barber-Greene* machine is usually limited by supply of material. *See* **concrete spreader.**

slip joint [stru.] A *contraction joint* between two sections of wall, which allows one to move relatively to the other and can sometimes be kept waterproof. It usually consists of a vertical tongue at one side fitting into a groove at the other side.

slip plane [s.m.] A hazardous sloping surface such as a clay bed or fault plane, along which a *landslip* may be likely.

slip ramp, slip road, or **ramp** A road connecting a *motorway* to a road at another level.

slip scraper [min.] A scraper used for placer mining or for moving stocks of material above ground. It consists of a hoist with two ropes, one fitted to each side of the scraper bucket, and two return sheaves which may be on movable poles held by guy ropes.

slip surface [s.m.] The surface of failure of an earth bank. *See* **slip circle, sliding-wedge method.**

slipway *See* **slip.**

slope (1) or **gradient** The inclination of a surface expressed as one unit of rise or fall for so many horizontal units.

(2) [min.] In British collieries a *drift* (4).

slope correction [sur.] A deduction from a measured sloping length to bring it to the corresponding horizontal length. For slopes which rise a height h in a tapered length l, the following approximation is within 1 mm for a rise or fall of 10 m per 100 m slope and the error is very much less for slighter slopes. The correction is $\frac{h^2}{2l}$, and for this slope works out at 0·500 instead of 0·5013, which is more exact. *See* **tape corrections.**

slope gauge [hyd.] A depth indicator consisting of a staff laid at a slope and graduated correspondingly to give a more precise reading than a vertical rod.

slope staking [sur.] The marking of the ground surface by pegs or stakes at points where earthworks in cut or fill meet it.

slow bend test *See* **longitudinal bend test.**

slow test [s.m.] A *drained shear test.*

slough (1) Of an earth slope, to slide or break off.

(2) A secondary river channel in which the flow is sluggish (USA).

sludge [sewage] Solids settled out from sewage, ordinarily well above 99% water and very difficult to *de-water* below 80% water. It is nevertheless well worth extracting from sewage because it contains about 50% of the pollutants in it.

sludge disposal [sewage] Sludge is disposed of by burning or by dumping at sea or on farm land. The last is not safe for sludges from industrial areas, which may contain poisonous metals. London, Glasgow and other UK cities dump their sludges at sea. In the USA this will shortly be forbidden.

sludge gas *Sewage gas.*

sludger (1) A *sand pump.*

(2) A tool for scraping materials out of a hole drilled in rock before inserting the explosive.

(3) A pump of any sort for *sludge.*

slug [mech.] A relatively small quantity of fluid in a pipeline which does not mix with the main fluid in the pipe. For instance the *slurry* of *oil-well cement* for cementing an oil-well *casing* is driven through the gap at the foot of the casing and up between the casing and the rock outside it by the pressure from the drilling fluid pumped down the drill rods. The cement slurry is a slug sandwiched between two masses of drilling fluid.

sluice [hyd.] (1) A gate to hold back water. Small ones slide vertically, large ones are of many different types.

(2) A channel for taking a rapidly flowing stream of water.

slump test A test for the stiffness of wet concrete. A conical mould is filled with concrete, well rammed, and then carefully inverted and emptied over a flat plate. The amount by which the concrete cone drops below the top of the mould is measured and is called the slump. This test is only valuable when the same aggregates are used all the time and in the same proportions. It then gives a rough idea of the water content of the mix. However, it has been much used in the past and is still used. *See* **compacting factor test, flow-table test, V.-B. consistometer.**

slurry Any fluid mixture of fine solids and water, particularly one which contains cement.

slurry trench, slurry excavation The use of a bentonite slurry (or other *thixotropic* mud) to hold up the walls of a trench during excavation by grab or other mechanical means. A *diaphragm wall* is one use of the slurry trench.

slusher *See* **scraper loader.**

slush ice *Frazil ice.*

smithing [mech.] The *forging* of iron or steel when hot.

smith welding [mech.] *Forge welding.*

smooth [mech.] A description of the *cut* of a file.

smoothing iron A hot iron tool for smoothing asphalt and sealing joints in it.

SN curve *See* **stress-number curve.**

snatch block A block or sheave with an eye through which it can be fixed by lashing to a scaffolding or pole. It is possible to put a rope over the groove on the wheel without threading the end through. For this purpose one of the side straps of the wheel is hinged. It can be lifted, the rope passing under it and over the pulley, and the strap then refixed. It is much used by *riggers.*

snow course A course marked on the area drained by a stream, along which *snow samples* are taken to estimate snow depth and density for the spring melting.

snow density The water content of snow expressed as the ratio of the depths of snow before melting and as water.

snow load [stru.] A live load for which a flat roof in temperate or cold climates may be designed. In the south of England it is taken as 75 kg/m².

snow plough A machine for moving snow off a road or railway. A blade snow plough is towed by a tractor or lorry. A rotary snow plough has a rotating blade.

snow sample A core of snow taken by a sampling pipe on a *snow course*, from which the *snow density* can be measured and compared with previous years.

snow sampler A set of light jointed tubes for taking *snow samples* and a spring balance which reads directly the depth of water corresponding to a given weight of snow.

soakaway (In USA a **dry well,** in Scotland a **rummel**) A pit which may be either empty or filled with large stones and is lined (if at all) with stones or bricks laid without mortar. Surface water is drained into it to soak away into the ground.

soffit *See* **crown,** *also* (*B*).

soft clay [s.m.] A soft *clay* is one which can easily be moulded in the hand and dug with a spade.

soft-suspension theory [stru.] The theory that foundations carrying vibrating machinery would automatically not be *resonant* if the foundation were large enough has been proved false. Foundations must be designed for a ground pressure and area which are not dangerous for the frequency of the machine which they carry.

soil (1) [s.m.] In the engineering sense, soil is *gravels, sands, silts, clays, peats* and all other loose materials including topsoil, down to bedrock. In agriculture only the *A-, B-,* and *C-horizons* are soil.

(2) *Sewage* as opposed to surface water or waste water.

soil analysis [s.m.] *See* **mechanical analysis.**

soil auger [s.m.] *See* **shell-and-auger boring, auger.**

soil-cement [s.m.] *Soil stabilization* by the use of cement.

soil consolidation [s.m.] *See* **artificial cementing,** *also* **consolidation.**

soiling *See* **resoiling.**

soil mechanics The investigation of the composition of soils, their *classification, consolidation,* strength, the flow of water through them, and the *active* and *passive earth pressures* in them. The science was christened under this name at the first International Conference of Soil Mechanics and Foundation Engineering at Cambridge, Massachusetts, in 1936. *Ground engineering* includes much of soil mechanics. The instruments and methods include many that are the same as in *rock mechanics. See also* **critical voids ratio of sands, frictional soil, soil stabilization.**

soil mixer [s.m.] A machine used for pulverizing soil in *soil stabilization.* The term includes *plant mixers* as well as travel mixers.

soil profile A vertical section showing the succession of *soils* at a site.

soil sample [s.m.] Any specimen of soil, for example an *undisturbed sample.*

soil sampler [s.m.] or **clay sampler** or **sampling spoon** A tube which is driven into the ground with the object of obtaining an *undisturbed sample.* They are used mainly for clays, since the technique of getting undisturbed samples of clean sands is very much more complicated and difficult. *See* **core catcher, Raymond standard test.**

soil shredder [s.m.] A machine used in *soil stabilization* consisting of two half drums which just do not touch, rotate in opposite directions, and break up soil.

soil solidification *Soil stabilization.*

soil stabilization [s.m.] or **soil solidification** Any artificial method of strengthening a soil to reduce its shrinkage and ensure that it will not move. Common methods are mixing the soil with cement or waste oil or imported soil, also *compaction* or merely covering with a *primer.* It is a cheap method of making roads which carry little traffic, and is therefore used in Africa and America where populations and traffic are less dense than in Europe. Soil stabilization was developed in the southern states of the USA from 1935 onwards, and that country now has over 100 million sq. m of soil-cement pavement. Other common binders are lime (specially for clays), lime fly-ash, and bitumens. *See* bulk spreader, processing, single-pass soil stabilizer, soil mechanics, soil mixer, soil shredder, spotting, wet-sand process.

soil survey [s.m.] A thorough examination of the soils at a site, recorded in a report on their strengths, etc. *See* soil mechanics.

soldier In trench timbering, an upright which is held in place by struts to the soldier on the other side. On their outer face the soldiers hold the horizontal sheeting against the earth. In this timbering, walings are not used. (*Compare* puncheon.) Hence any heavy upright timber.

soldier beam A steel *rolled section* driven into the ground to carry the force from a horizontal sheeted earth bank (USA).

solenoid [elec.] A very common device consisting of a coil of wire wound round a cylinder. A current passes through the coil and gives the coil an electro-magnetic polarity. This is intensified by placing soft iron strips in the cylinder. The current in the coil magnetizes the soft iron very strongly, making an *electromagnet* which has many uses, particularly in *protective equipment* such as circuit breakers.

solid map A *geological map* showing no *drift* but only those formations below the drift, that is the solid, usually called bedrock by engineers.

solid web [stru.] A web of a beam consisting of a plate or other rolled section but not a *lattice*. A box girder is usually regarded as a solid web girder.

soling Large stones. *See* pitching.

solution injection [s.m.] *See* artificial cementing, injection.

sonde A long tube used in *well logging*, containing *geophysical* equipment; it is lowered into a hole and has an electrical cable connecting it to the surface, that provides a record of the rock properties as the sonde passes through each rock.

sonic pile-driver US term for a vibrating pile-driver.

Sopwith staff [sur.] A self-reading telescopic *levelling staff* divided into three sections which are set one above the other when the staff is fully extended to 14 ft. It is graduated in feet, and tenths and hundredths of a foot, the thickness of the horizontal lines being 0·01 ft, alternately black and white. Telescopic staffs exist, with metric graduations.

sorted sand [s.m.] Civil engineers and geologists disagree fundamentally about the meaning of the terms 'well' or 'badly sorted' or '*graded sand*'.

sounding (1) [sur.] Determining the depth of the ocean or river bed by an echo-sounder or sounding line. Sounding with a measuring staff is possible but not for depths above 5 m.

(2) [s.m.] Driving a steel rod into the soil to measure the depth of bedrock. *See* penetration tests.

sounding lead [sur.] The *hand lead* on a *sounding line*.

sounding line [sur.] A *lead line*.

southing [sur.] A distance measured southwards from an east–west axis. *See* latitude.

space frame, space structure [stru.] *Plane frames*, including *trusses*, repeat themselves at regular intervals and need to be held or stiffened against wind loads by bracing or walls. Space frames on the other hand are three-dimensional and so may be stable against wind by themselves. But their main advantage from the architect's viewpoint is that they span large gaps with few or no intervening columns. They usually cover such large spans that it is impossible for them to compete in cost with plane frames and their much smaller spans. Space structures include domes, *barrel vaults*, *double-layer grids*, *folded-plate roofs*, *lamella domes*, suspended cable structures, tent structures and many others. Shells, being very specialized, are usually not considered as space structures.

space grid, space deck [stru.] A flat, *double-layer grid*.

space lattice [stru.] A *space frame* which is built of *lattice* girders, or any other open framework.

spad [sur.] American term for a *spud*, a surveyor's nail.

spader *See* grafting tool.

spall *See* pitching, *also* (*B*).

spall drain *See* rubble drain.

span [stru.] The distance between the supports of a bridge, truss, arch, girder, floor, beam, etc. *See* clear span, effective span.

spandrel wall A wall carried on the extrados of an arch, filling the space below the *deck*. *See* spandrel (*B*).

special steel [mech.] *Alloy steel*.

special structural concrete According to BSCP 110:1972, special concretes are those that contain *admixtures*, *lightweight aggregates*, extra-dense aggregates or *cements* other than *Portland*, *blast-furnace*, *low-heat*, or *sulphate-resisting*, or that involve any special surface finish or structural requirement.

specific adhesion The chemical bond between glued or cemented substances as opposed to the *mechanical bond*. Strong specific adhesion can exist between two quite smooth surfaces, mechanical bond cannot.

specification A detailed description prepared by a consulting engineer or architect to tell the contractor everything about the workmanship which cannot be shown on the drawings.

specific gravity *See* relative density.

specific retention [hyd.] The moisture content by weight held in a soil against gravity by capillary attraction, after being saturated and allowed to drain for a week. It is only about 5% in uniform sand such as dune sand but in a clay may be thrice this amount. Consequently rain will pass more easily through the dune sand than through the clay, and the groundwater beneath it will be recharged more quickly.

specific speed [mech.] (1) The specific speed of a centrifugal pump of known performance is:

$$\frac{3 \cdot 65 \times \text{rpm} \times \sqrt{\text{m}^3/\text{min.}}}{\text{head at maximum efficiency}}$$
$$(\text{metres})^{0 \cdot 75}.$$

The specific speed describes the performance of a certain design of impeller and is fixed for any given design. It is the speed in rpm at which a geometrically similar impeller of suitable diameter would turn to deliver $1 \text{ m}^3/\text{min.}$ at 1 m head.

(2) The specific speed of a water turbine of known performance is:

$$\frac{\text{rpm} \times \sqrt{\text{bhp}}}{\text{ft (m) head}^{1 \cdot 25}}.$$

The specific speed, like that for a pump, indicates the design of the *runner*. It is that speed at which a geometrically similar runner of suitable diameter would turn to develop 1 brake horsepower under 1 ft (m) head. The conversion factor from UK hp and feet to metric hp and metres is: metric specific speed $= 4 \cdot 446 \times$ UK specific speed.

For heads above 450 m only the Pelton wheel is suitable; between 450 and 60 m there is a choice between Francis and Pelton turbines. Other choices exist for the lowest heads. Pelton wheels have specific speeds from 10 to 20 rpm, Francis turbines from 20 to 120 rpm, Kaplan turbines from 120 to 150 rpm.

specific surface The ratio of the exposed area of a powder to its weight or volume, usually expressed in sq. cm per gram. It is a measure of the fineness of a powder and is used for describing cements. The greater the fineness of a cement the more quickly will it harden. *See* fineness modulus.

specific yield [hyd.] The specific yield of an aquifer is the amount of water it yields when it drains by gravity. The value can occasionally reach 45% but a good gravel yields 25% and a clay rarely more than 3%. High porosity is essential for a high specific yield but does not guarantee it. Clays are as porous as the best aquifers but their yield is minute.

spelter [mech.] Zinc of less than 99·6% purity used for galvanizing. In USA *hard solder* (*B*) is also called brazing spelter.

spider line or spider web *See* cross hair.

spike *See* screw spike, track spike.

spile (1) A wood pile.

(2) [min.] or spill A sharp-edged thick board: a *forepole*.

spiling *Forepoling*.

spillway [hyd.] or wasteway or waste weir An overflow channel, particularly one over a dam.

spillway gate *See* crest gate.

spiral curve [sur.] or spiral In joining a circular arc to a straight on a road or railway, a spiral provides a *transition* which is often used. It is a curve whose radius gradually increases from the point where it joins the circular curve to the point where it becomes straight. It is more used in railways than in roads.

splice [stru.] A joint, often between members of the same cross-section, so as to extend their length, for example stanchions, concrete piles, reinforcing bars. Stanchions can be extended by bolted *fishplates* (like rails) or by welding; piles by welding or lapping their reinforcement and filling in new concrete made of *rapid hardening cement*. Reinforcement can also by spliced by mechanical clamps.

splice bar or splice piece A *fishplate*.

split bubble [sur.] A *prismatic coincidence bubble*.

spoil *See* waste.

spontaneous liquefaction [s.m.] *See* liquefaction.

spool A cast-iron *distance piece* between timbers.

spot level [sur.] The elevation of a point.

spotting [s.m.] In *soil stabilization*, laying bags of stabilizer in position on the ground to be stabilized, at regular intervals.

spot welding Usually *resistance spot welding*, but *MIG* and *TIG* spot welding also exist.

spout-delivery pump [mech.] A pump like the contractor's *diaphragm pump* which delivers water no higher than itself. *Compare* force pump.

Sprague and Henwood core barrel [min.] An American *core barrel* mounted inside a diamond drilling bit on ball bearings. It can take rock cores down to 25 mm dia., but is generally not used for taking undisturbed samples of *soils*, since the movement of the core barrel disturbs the core.

spray bar The pipe with jets which spray binder on to a road from a *pressure tank*.

sprayed concrete *See* gunite.

sprayer A *tank sprayer*.

spray lance The pipe of a *hand sprayer* carrying the jets for spreading the binder on to the road.

spread or rate of spread The area covered by a given quantity of material such as chippings or road binder. *See* spreading rate (*B*).

spreader (1) A machine which travels on railway track and spreads dumped material with its 4·5 m wide blades.

(2) *See* concrete spreader.

(3) A strut in tunnel or trench timbering.

spreader beam or yoke A stiff beam hanging from a crane hook, and with ropes or chains hanging from different points along it. It is used for lifting a long reinforced-concrete pile or a large glass sheet or any other long fragile object to prevent breakage during lifting.

spread footing A *footing* which is wide, and therefore usually of reinforced concrete.

spreading box An appliance which

receives road materials and spreads them in a uniform layer without compacting them.

spread recorder In bridge testing, an instrument which measures the outward spread of an *abutment* during loading. *Compare* **rotation recorder.**

springing [min.] Enlarging a blasting hole by *chambering*.

spring points [rly] *Points* which are held closed by springs, except when they are *trailing points*, and the flanges of the train wheels open them.

spring washer [mech.] A *washer* which consists of a steel ring cut through and bent to a slow helical curve. It prevents a nut from unscrewing and may be used instead of a *lock nut*.

spud (1) [sur.] (or **spad** in USA) A nail used by mine surveyors for hanging a plumb bob as a mark for a survey station, generally with a hole or notch in it for the plumb bob string.

(2) or **anchoring spud** A steel post on a *dredger* which may be lowered by a toothed rack or by ropes until it is fixed in the bottom to serve as an anchorage. Two are often provided, one fore and one aft.

spudding In pile driving, raising and dropping the pile so as to enlarge the hole and reduce driving friction. Sometimes a weight (spud) of larger diameter than the pile is used instead of the pile, since this extremely severe treatment may damage the pile (USA).

spur [hyd.] or **spur dyke** (or **wing dam** in USA) A *groyne* built out from a bank of a river, having a head so armoured that it cannot be removed by scour. It diverts the flow from a scoured part and may encourage silting elsewhere.

square-mile foot [hyd.] A volume of water 1 ft deep over 1 sq. mile.

square thread [mech.] A robust screw thread used for transmitting a thrust, but, unlike the *buttress screw thread*, capable of transmitting it in both directions.

squibbing *See* **chambering.**

squirrel-cage motor [elec.] A robust alternating-current motor used for many purposes. The rotor consists of a number of stout, parallel copper or aluminium bars on the perimeter, joined to end rings of the same metal. It has the advantage that there need be no electrical connection between the rotor and the outside of the motor. It can therefore without difficulty be given a flameproof enclosure.

stability (1) [stru.] The resistance of a structure to sliding, overturning, or collapsing. A structure can be tested (on paper) for stability by verifying that it tends to return to its original state after being disturbed.

(2) The stability of an emulsion is its tendency to remain an emulsion and to resist *breakdown*.

(3) *See* **dimensional stability** (*B*).

stabilized soil [s.m.] *See* **soil stabilization.**

stabilizer [s.m.] Any material added to a soil in *soil stabilization*. It may be a chemical which absorbs water or a waterproofer like bitumen or a cement or a resin. Resins are required in smaller quantities than other stabilizers, only 2 to 5 kg per sq. m per 15 cm thickness being needed.

stadia hairs [sur.] Two horizontal lines in the *reticule* of a *theodolite* telescope, symmetrically above and below the line of sight. They are set at a distance apart such that they subtend a particular known angle at the eye, usually equal to 0·01 radian. This means that any *intercept* of L m on a remote staff proves that the staff is at a distance of 100 L m plus or minus the *additive constant*. In this case 100 is the multiplying constant.

stadia rod [sur.] A special levelling staff with bold graduations for stadia work.

stadia work [sur.] or **tacheometric surveying** or **tacheometry** The use of the *stadia hairs* and a levelling staff for determining the distances of visible points. It is an extremely quick way of mapping, particularly when used with the *plane table*. An accuracy of 1 in 500 is obtainable, which is often more accurate than the plotting of the results. The only complication arises with inclined sights, for which a correction must be applied. The rod is held vertical (with the help of a spirit level or plumb bob) and will therefore not be perpendicular to the line of sight of the telescope except when rod and telescope are on the same level. For all ordinary purposes the true horizontal distance is $\cos^2 d$ times the apparent horizontal distance, $100 \times$ staff *intercept + additive constant*, where d is the angle above or below the horizontal. The use of a horizontal staff and an *optical wedge*, though slower, can be much more accurate than the vertical staff method. *See also* **anallatic telescope, Stanley compensating diaphragm.**

staff [sur.] (or **rod** in USA) A rod of wood or light alloy with easily read graduations painted on it, used in levelling or *stadia work*. *See* **Sopwith staff,** *also* BS 4484.

staff gauge [hyd.] A graduated scale on a rod or metal plate or the masonry of a pier on which the level of the water may be read.

staff man [sur.] (In USA **rod man**) A man who carries a *levelling staff* for a surveyor in *stadia* or levelling work.

stage [hyd.] The water level measured from any chosen reference line; in USA, **gage height.**

staging A working platform on to which men shovel earth in pit sinking. It may be so called because the shovelling is done in stages, each staging being about 1·2 m above the next below.

stalk [stru.] (1) or **stem** The vertical part of a reinforced-concrete *retaining wall*.
(2) The central outstanding part of a tee-section. *Compare* **table.**

stanchion or **stauncheon,** etc. A vertical steel *strut*. Cast-iron stanchions were used until about 1870 before cheap steel was available, but steel is now preferred because it is less brittle. A concrete strut is usually called a column.

standard (1) [sur.] A U-shaped metal casting fixed on the upper plate of a

theodolite, carrying the telescope trunnions.
(2) *See* **standardization.**

standard deviation [stat.] The square root of the average of the squares of the deviations of all the observations. It measures the dispersion or spread of the observations and is the square root of the *variance*. *See* **coefficient of variation, probable error.**

standard diving gear or **standard diving dress** or **hard hat diving gear** or **helmet diving gear** The old type of diving dress with lead-soled boots and weights and a heavy tinned copper helmet. It protects the *diver* from the cold and from dirty water, but in other circumstances *SCUBA* is often preferred. In standard diving dress the diver can receive his air supply for breathing by a hose from the surface.

standard error [stat.] The *standard deviation* of many samples of the mean. It shows the amount of inconsistency between the sample and the consignment mean.

standard gauge [rly] A width of 1·435 m between inner faces of the rails of a track, slightly increased on sharp curves and reduced to about 1·432 m on continuously welded straight track. It is universally used in Britain and the European continent for passenger railways. Only in Russia is there a *broad gauge*. *Narrow gauge* also exists.

standardization (1) Agreement between producer and consumer under the authority (in Britain) of the *British Standards Institution* on certain tests, dimensions, tolerances, and qualities of a product for its purposes. When agreement is reached it is published as a *British Standard*.
(2) [sur.] *See* **standardization correction.**

standardization correction [sur.] A *tape correction* for a tape which is not of the right length when pulled to the correct tension at the *standardization temperature*. It is an added or subtracted correction of so much per 100 m.

standardization length *See* **comparator base.**

standardization temperature [sur.] The temperature at which a tape is compared with a standard tape of known length.

standard pile A *guide pile*.

standard section A *rolled-steel section*, or a light alloy *extruded* section.

standard specification *See* **standardization.**

Standard Wire Gauge *See* (*B*).

standing derrick *See* **derrick** (1).

standing pier A bridge pier with spans each side of it, as opposed to an abutment pier.

standing-water level [s.m.] The level at which the ground water finally stands in a hole or pit which is left open for some days. All the pores of the ground are filled with water below this level but above it any water in the pores is held there against gravity by *capillary* attraction and the larger pores may not be filled. *See* **water table.**

stand pipe [hyd.] A pipe rising vertically from a soil mass or water main under pressure. It may be closed at the top by a valve for drawing off water, or it may be open-topped and rise to a height above the hydraulic gradient to show the water pressure in the pipe or soil. If connected to an open tank at the top it forms a *surge pipe*. The open top ensures that the pressure near the foot of the stand pipe cannot be higher than that due to the head of water at the open top, and high pressures due to *water hammer* are thus released.

stank (1) A small timber *cofferdam* made watertight with clay.

(2) To make watertight; to seal off.

Stanley compensating diaphragm [sur.] A *compensating diaphragm* designed specially for *stadia work*.

starling Piles (usually timber) driven into the river bed upstream of a bridge pier (and downstream in tidal water) to protect it from floating rubbish, ice, and so on.

starter [elec.] or **motor starter** *Protective equipment* which ensures that a motor shall not receive too high a current when starting up. It may be automatic or hand operated.

starter bar or **starter** A bar projecting through a *construction joint* so as to knit the adjoining masses of concrete effectively together. A starter bar should be embedded each side of the joint by a length which is usually at least 45 times the bar diameter.

starter frame A *kicker*.

statically-determinate frame [stru.] or **isostatic frame** or **perfect frame** A frame in which the bending moments and reactions can be determined by the laws of statics alone.

statically-indeterminate frame [stru.] or **hyperstatic frame** or **redundant frame** A frame in which the bending moments and reactions cannot be calculated from the equations of statics because the frame has more members or more fixity than a *perfect frame*. In such a frame additional equations must be introduced to determine the forces in each member. Often these equations make use of *strain energy* or *deflection*.

static head [hyd.] The difference in level between two points, such as between the reservoir level and the tailwater level of a water turbine.

static load The amount of weight placed on a structure without any increase for *impact*.

static moment [stru.] The static moment of a section about an axis YY is also called its first moment of area about the axis. It is the sum of the products obtained by multiplying each element of area a by its distance x from YY. This can be expressed thus: first moment = the sum of $(x \times a)$ or $\Sigma(xa)$. *See* **centroid, moment of inertia.**

static penetration test [s.m.] Soil tests in which the testing device is pushed into the soil with a measurable force, as opposed to *dynamic penetration tests* in which the testing device is driven in by blows from a standard hammer. *Plate bearing tests*, the *penetrometer*, and the *cone penetration test* are examples, possibly also the *vane test* and the *Proctor plasticity needle*.

statics [stru.] The study of forces and bodies at rest, a branch of mechanics which is the basis of structural engineering.

static suction lift *See* **suction head.**

station [sur.] A point at which an angle is measured in *traversing*, *triangulation* or *trilateration*, or any other reference point in surveying. Permanent stations above ground are marked by an indentation on a metal plate set in stone or concrete. Below ground they are set in *spuds* or wooden plugs in holes drilled in the roof.

stationary dredger A *bucket-ladder dredger* which is not self-propelled and discharges its dredged material into a hopper barge or a pipeline. Mining dredges are also in the same sense not self-propelled, but this is never mentioned since it is taken for granted.

statistical uniformity [stat.] A term used to describe variation, in quality characteristics of materials or manufactured articles, which is stable and determinate in the sense that statistical methods of analysis and prediction may be employed to define relationships between samples, consignments, and batches. The *level of control* is a measure of the statistically uniform variation of a product.

statistics The study of *populations* and their variations from the *mean*. This includes the study of measurements and their errors (*see* **probable error**) which is much used in surveying. It is also used for estimating the strength (or mineral content) of a batch of several hundred tons of concrete (or ore) from a few samples, the probable error of the estimate, and the significance of the variations.

stauncheon *See* **stanchion.**

staunching piece [hyd.] or **staunching bead** In concrete dams a vertical gap left between successive bays of concrete. This gap is not concreted until most of the *shrinkage* in adjoining bays has taken place. It is shaped like a concrete column and may be reinforced. *See* **stank.**

staunching rod [hyd.] A strong rubber rod in contact with a *crest gate* which is compressed between the gate and the structure to form a watertight joint.

stay [mech.] (1) A tie bar or diagonal brace to prevent movement.

(2) A *guy* rope.

stay pile A pile driven or cast in the ground as an anchorage for a *land tie* holding back a *sheet-pile* wall, etc.

steady flow [hyd.] *Streamline flow.*

steam boiler *See* **boiler.**

steam curing Maturing of precast concrete members in a steam oven to accelerate the chemical action of *curing*. After two hours in a steam oven, highly stressed members of a precast, prestressed concrete bridge have been stripped from their moulds. There are two methods of steam curing cement products, the low-pressure method and the high-pressure or *autoclaving* method. The latter is the better but naturally the more expensive since the curing is done within a pressure vessel which is about 2·5 m dia. 30 m long, and has to withstand 10 atmospheres of steam pressure.

steam engine [mech.] A piston-driven engine, a *prime mover* worked by the force of the steam on the piston. It is a typical *reciprocating* engine. *Compare* **steam turbine.**

steam roller A road roller driven by a *steam engine*. These are now obsolete in Britain although they are much simpler mechanically than the more economical *Diesel engines* which are replacing them.

steam shovel or **steam navvy** The original design of *excavator*, driven by its own *steam engine*, usually coal-fired. Electrical or *internal-combustion engine* drive is now usual.

steam turbine [mech.] A machine with vaned wheels which are driven round by the force of high-pressure steam blown on to the vanes. It is useful for power generation and large stationary

259

engines generally, since it is much more efficient than the *steam engine*.

steel (1) [mech.] or **carbon steel** An alloy of iron and carbon with less than 1% of all other components. *Dead-mild steel* may have 0·1% or less, *high carbon steel* up to 1½% carbon. The hardness of high-carbon steel is increased and its ductility lowered by heating and *quenching*. *Compare* **alloy steel.**

(2) [min.] A *drill steel*. Its end is either threaded to take a *detachable bit* or forged with a bit by the mine smith.

steel band [sur.] A *band chain*.

steel bender or **steel fixer** *See* **bar bender.**

steel erector or **constructional fitter and erector** or **iron fighter** A *skilled man*, one of a team of two who climb on to a *steel frame* and fix each end of a steel beam as it is lowered to them by a crane. *See* guy **derrick** (*illustration*).

steel frame A load-carrying building skeleton formed mainly of *rolled-steel sections* meeting each other at right angles. Nowadays in cities most of the site connections are made by bolts. Riveted connections are no longer made, because of advances in *welding* techniques and the noise of riveting. The brick infilling of a steel building frame was in the past considered to contribute nothing to the strength of the frame, but research has shown that it is an important load-carrier.

steel-grit blasting [mech.] A form of *shot blasting*.

steel ring [min.] A *ring* of pressed steel 10 mm thick, used in USA for lining a tunnel or circular section. Shaft rings are usually of cast iron and known as *tubbing*.

steel sheet In Britain, steel thinner than 5 mm, plate being 5 mm or thicker, but on the continent of Europe, 3 mm is the limit between sheet and plate.

steel sheet piling Sheet piling of interlocking rolled-steel sections driven vertically into the ground along the edge of a guide waling before excavation is begun. When the sheet piling is completed the excavation can be begun in safety. It keeps out flowing ground and often also water, but requires heavy strutting against either of these, unless its penetration depth below the lowest dig level is relied upon to support it. In this case the penetration depth is about equal to (or more than) the length of piling above dig level; also a very strong piling section must be used. Strutting or tying back saves steel, and is therefore used where possible.

steel tape [sur.] *See* **tape.**

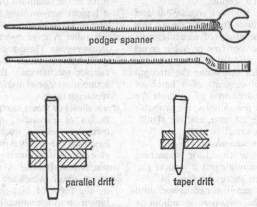

podger spanner

parallel drift   taper drift

Steel erector's tools

steel-wheeled roller Usually a *tamping roller*. Rollers of this type are popular for *compaction* of controlled tips in the UK, operated by waste disposal authorities. They can compact refuse to a density of about 1 tonne per cu. m, starting at 200 kg per cu. m.

steel-wire rope [mech.] *See* rope.

steening or **steining**, etc. The lining of a well or *soakaway* with stones or bricks laid usually dry, sometimes with mortar.

Stellite [mech.] *Hard-facing* alloy of cobalt, chromium, and tungsten with a little carbon, manganese, silicon, and iron. It is very much harder than steel, and is applied by welding to the wearing parts of drilling tools such as *fishtail bits* or dredger bucket teeth. *Compare* cemented carbides.

stem *See* stalk.

step To step a lock gate is to place it in a vertical position. *Ship caissons* are often too large to travel by any method except towing by sea. They therefore arrive at the port of use in a horizontal position in which they are stable. The process of stepping is slow and difficult. The term may be derived from the stepping of a mast – placing it in a vertical position on the strengthening timber or step over the keel.

step iron or **foot iron** A galvanized, heavy, *malleable-cast-iron* staple built into the walls of a brick or concrete *inspection chamber* at about 0·3 m vertical spacing to enable men to climb in and out.

stepped foundation A *benched foundation*.

stereometric map [sur.] A map showing valleys and hills which can be fully visualized by merely looking at the map.

stereoplotter [air sur.] A *plotting instrument*.

stereoscope [air sur.] A hand instrument for looking at a stereoscopic pair of photos, which enables hills and valleys to be clearly visualized.

stereoscopic pair [air sur.] Two air photographs, overlapping and taken on the same survey of *vertical photographs*, which provide stereoscopic vision when seen through a plotting machine or *stereoscope*. One pair can be oriented with three levelled points and two points of known coordinates, but this is the minimum *ground control*.

stereoscopic or **three-dimensional vision** The ordinary vision of human beings, in which depth or distance are seen and can be estimated. A *plotting instrument* enables *vertical photographs* to be seen stereoscopically.

Stevenson's formula A formula for the height of waves, developed by gales travelling over F sea miles of water, the *fetch*. It states that the height in metres is equal to $0·46 \sqrt{F}$. It applies only to unobstructed deep water, since even submerged sandbanks can cause the waves to break. Its values are too high for fetches of 300 sea miles or more. One sea mile $= 1852$ m.

stick welding US term for *manual metal-arc welding*.

stiff clay [s.m.] *See* clay.

stiffened suspension bridge A *suspension bridge* with *stiffening girders*.

stiffener [stru.] or **web stiffener** A small member, such as an angle, welded to a slender beam or column *web* to prevent buckling of the web. These are often placed under concentrated loads. *See* joggle.

stiffening girder A *girder* built into a *suspension bridge* to distribute the loads uniformly among the *suspenders* and thus to reduce the local deflections under concentrated loads. A suspension bridge does not need stiffening if the maximum deflection is less than one three-hundredth of the span. *See* self-anchored suspension bridge, Severn Bridge.

stiff-fissured clay [s.m.] or **slickensided clay** *Clay* which is stiff at depth when kept dry but is filled with a network of cracks through which water can pass easily. The London clay, like others of this type, is subject to slips in hilly areas. *See* artificial cementing.

stiff frame [stru.] A *redundant frame*. A

261

frame described as just stiff is a *perfect frame*.

stiff-leg derrick [mech.] An American term for the Scotch *derrick*.

stiffness [stru.] (1) Of a material, the stiffness is its resistance in GN/m^2, etc., to deflection, more often called its *modulus of elasticity* or E value.

(2) Of a structural member such as a beam or column, its resistance to bending or buckling. It is proportional to the E of the material, to the *I* of the section, and to the reciprocal of its span. For beams of the same material the stiffness is thus proportional to

$$\frac{I}{l}$$

stilling pool [hyd.] or **water cushion** An enlargement and deepening of the river at the foot of a dam spillway to lower the speed of flow and reduce scour.

stilling well [hyd.] or **gauge well** A chamber which communicates with the main body of the water by a small inlet. It may contain a *recording gauge*.

still-water navigation [hyd.] A *slack-water navigation*.

stimulation [hyd.] Artificially increasing the output from a well by methods such as applying acid to an *aquifer* containing limestone or dolomite, or fracturing it with explosives or with high-pressure water or by combinations of these methods.

stinger A pontoon attachment to the rear of a *lay barge*, which reduces the stress on the pipe as it leaves the barge, by helping to bed the pipe gently into a catenary. In 120 m deep water, the catenary will be about 370 m long, with 46 m of stinger at the forward end.

stirrup A *binder* (3).

stock rail [rly] The fixed outer rail at a *turnout*, against which the point is held. *See* **points.**

Stokes's law [s.m.] or **Stokes's formula** (1850) An expression for the settling velocity of spherical particles in fluid. It is utilized for determining the effective diameters of those parts of a

soil sample which cannot conveniently be sieved, being smaller than 0·07 mm. The *terminal velocity* in water is $\frac{(S-S_w)\,gd^2}{30\,n}$ cm per minute, where

S, S_w = relative densities of particle and water

g = acceleration of gravity (981 cm per second each second)

d = particle diameter, millimetres

n = viscosity of water gm per cm per sec.

See **elutriator, vel.**

stone *See* **coarse aggregate.**

stone-block paving *Sett* paving in which the stones are accurately cut to a rectangular shape to reduce the joint thickness to the minimum.

stone drain A *rubble drain*.

stop end A *stunt end*.

stop log [hyd.] or **stop plank** or **flashboard** A baulk, plank, precast concrete beam, or steel joist which fits between vertical grooves in walls or piers to close up a spillway or other water channel. The baulks are laid horizontally on top of each other to form a *cofferdam. Compare* **needle weir.**

stop valve [mech.] A valve used for turning on or shutting off completely a supply of fluid. *See* **discharge/gate valve.**

storm pavement A gently sloping bank to a *breakwater*.

storm sewer or **stormwater sewer** A sewer which normally carries no flow but after heavy rain carries *stormwater* overflow directly to a river.

stormwater (1) Water discharged from a *catchment area* after heavy rain.

(2) In *combined* or *partially-separate* drainage systems, a stated excess of the drainage water above the dry-weather flow at which the sewage is allowed to overflow into a river after passing through *stormwater tanks*. Usually the total flow must be three times the average dry-weather flow before the sewage overflows to the river.

stormwater overflow or **storm overflow** or **separation weir** [sewage] In a *combined* or *partially separate* sewerage system, a weir within a *sewer*, which allows excess water in it to overflow after heavy rain, discharging it into a *storm sewer*.

stormwater tanks Tanks in which solid material from *stormwater* settles, enabling the *effluent* to go for treatment in the *sewage* works nearby as capacity becomes available.

straight-run bitumen A bitumen obtained as residue after distilling a suitable petroleum.

strain [stru.] A change in length caused usually by a force applied to a piece, the change being expressed as a ratio, the increase or decrease divided by the original length. *Elastic strain* is wholly recoverable, but *permanent set* is not. The instantaneous strain of good concrete loaded to 14 N/mm² can be 0·06% or more, and this increases with time because of *creep*. So great is the creep that the final strain of similar concrete stressed only to 3·5 N/mm² is also 0·06% after a year of creep. The strain of steel stressed to 100 N/mm² is also about 0·06% and so is that due to a free thermal expansion (or contraction) of 50°C.

strain ageing [stru.] Increase of strength and hardness with time after cold working or other overstressing. It is seen in steel and iron, but also occurs in *light alloys*.

strain energy [stru.] (1) The energy stored in an elastic body under load.

(2) A method of structural analysis based on the amount of work (energy) stored in a loaded frame. It is a method of wide application, but many simultaneous equations must be solved. *See* **resilience**.

strain gauge [stru.] A sensitive instrument for measuring small deflections in machines or structures. From these deflections the strains can be calculated. *Acoustic* and *electrical strain gauges* are well known, but mechanical and optical strain gauges also exist.

strain hardening [stru.] *Hardening* due to cold working.

strake [mech.] A metal lug or cleat fixed to a pneumatic-tyred wheel or conveyor belt to improve its grip.

strand (1) [mech.] A number of wires grouped together by twisting. With other strands, usually laid helically round an oil-filled hemp core, it makes a rope. Most ropes contain 6 strands round a hemp core and most strands are built of 6 wires round 1 central wire of the same diameter, so that the pattern of 6 round 1 goes from the strand to the rope. Other strands contain 19 wires (12 round 6 round 1) or 37 wires (18 round 12 round 6 round 1). *See* **lay, locked-coil rope, rope.**

(2) Compared with the strand in a hoisting or haulage rope, strand for *prestressed concrete* has the same structure except that its core is invariably of steel. As in ropes, the commonest strand has 7 wires. Compared with wire *tendons*, strand allows more force to be put into a given concrete section, and *die-formed strand* is a further improvement. *See* BS 3617, 4757.

stranded caisson A *box caisson.*

Stran-steel American *cold-rolled* steel sections fixed together in pairs by spot welding to provide a nailing slot between them.

strap [mech.] A metal plate or thin bar used for fixing butt-jointed timbers or other members. The *fishplate* is developed from it.

stratified flow [hyd.] *See* **density current.**

stratified soils [s.m., hyd.] Soils or rocks that have been laid down by deposition from the water of rivers, lakes or seas. Because they have pronounced horizontal layering (stratification) their permeability is usually greater in this direction than vertically.

stratigraphy The study of soils or rocks, their properties and geological time sequence. Such information is useful to engineers who have to make excavations or find *groundwater*.

streamline flow [hyd.] or **laminar/steady/viscous flow** Fluid flow in which the movement is continuous and usually parallel, the movement at each point being constant. The head loss due to friction is only proportional to the first power of the velocity. The upper limit of speed of streamline flow is Reynolds's *critical velocity*. *See also* **turbulent flow.**

street A ribbon of land used for a public *highway* in a town. In USA the term is often reserved for east–west highways. *Compare* **avenue, boulevard, freeway, parkway.**

street refuge *See* **refuge.**

strength [stru.] (1) The strength of a material is measured by its greatest safe working stress. This is equal to the *yield point* or the *ultimate strength* or the *proof stress* divided by an appropriate *factor of safety*. *See* **modulus of elasticity.**

(2) The strength of a structural part is its ability to resist the loads which fall on it.

strength of materials The calculation of stresses due to tension, compression, shear force, bending, torsion, and any of these stresses combined, including the study of failures of materials and of deflections. This is an important subject for structural engineers and is an essential preliminary to the study of *structural design*. *See* **theory of structures.**

stress [mech.] The force on a member divided by the area which carries the force, formerly expressed in psi, now in N/mm^2, etc. *See* **compression, effective pressure, fatigue, principal stress, shear, tension.**

stress analysis [stru.] The determination of the stresses in the different parts of a loaded structure. *See* **photo-elasticity.**

stress circle [stru.] *Mohr's circle.*

stress concentration [stru.] Sudden changes of cross-section in a structural member such as notches, holes, or screw threads cause stress concentrations which can be detected by *photoelastic* analysis. Such sudden changes of section are called stress raisers, and can be avoided by curving the surface of the bar at each change of section. The change of shape is thus made gradual instead of rapid, and the stress also changes gradually, avoiding *notch effect*.

stressed-skin construction [stru.] or **geodetic construction** Terms borrowed from the aircraft industry, in which *sandwich construction* (*B*) of frames or fuselages is usual. As the name suggests, the surface material is structural and not, like slate, a mere weather-resisting cladding. It has been used by the makers of plywood houses, in which the plywood wall cladding is glued to the load-bearing members. *Shells* are special examples of it.

stress-number curve [mech.] or **S-N curve** A curve obtained in *fatigue testing*. It shows the range of stress in a material plotted against the number of cycles to failure.

stress raiser *See* **stress concentration.**

stress relieving [mech.] Heating steel to a temperature below the *critical point*, followed by slow cooling to relieve internal stress. *Compare* **normalizing.**

stress-strain curve A curve, showing the result of a (usually tensile) test on a metal test piece, in which the *strains* are plotted against *stresses*. The stresses are calculated as the load divided by the original area of the piece, in spite of its *contraction in area* above the *yield point*. *Compare* **load-extension curve.**

stretcher A *liner*.

striding level [sur.] A sensitive *level tube* used for cross-levelling a *theodolite* telescope. It is fitted at each end with a leg projecting downwards from the tube. These legs stand on the telescope trunnions.

strike [min.] The horizontal line in the plane of a fault or a sedimentary rock, at right angles to the hade or *dip*.

striker [mech.] A helper to a *blacksmith* or *angle-iron smith*.

striking (1) Removing *formwork* or other temporary supports from a structure.

(2) *See* struck capacity.

stringer [stru.] or stringer beam A long horizontal member which ties together the heads of trestles in wooden trestle bridges or provides support under a *rail*, parallel to it, in a steel railway bridge.

strip (1) To strike *formwork*.

(2) [air sur.] *See* vertical photograph, also (*B*).

strip footing or strip foundation A foundation for a wall or for a close succession of piers. It is ribbon-shaped, projects slightly each side of the wall, and may be of brickwork, timber (if permanently submerged), mass concrete, or reinforced concrete.

stripping (1) Clearing a site of turf, brushwood, topsoil, or the first layer of soil.

(2) *Striking* formwork.

(3) Loss of binder or aggregate from a road surface. *See* ravelling, scabbing, also (*B*).

struck capacity The capacity of a bucket, mine car, *kibble*, skip, or other container, calculated as if it were full of water, so that all material above the edges is imagined to be struck off with a straight edge. The rated capacity of an *excavator* bucket is its struck capacity.

structural analysis The early part of a *structural design*, which consists of determining what forces are carried by all the parts of a structure and what proportions the forces bear to the loads on it.

structural design [d.o.] The proportioning of members to carry loads in a structure in the most economical way. A structural design is carried out in two main parts, the first being a rough estimate of the loads with the *structural analysis*. When the structural analysis is checked and found satisfactory the loads are more accurately estimated. The second half of the design consists of the proportioning of the members according to the calculations of the first half, together with the adjustment of the original calculations to any final altered sizes

of parts. This is the main work of a *structural engineer*, since most conventional building types have been sufficiently analysed and need no further analysis in the drawing office. *See* theory of structures.

structural designer [d.o.] One who makes *structural designs*. He is an experienced draughtsman and usually though not necessarily a qualified structural engineer.

structural designer-draughtsman [d.o.] A designer who draws his own designs and generally has no draughtsman working for him.

structural draughtsman [d.o.] One who makes structural drawings, that is drawings of those parts which carry load in buildings and structures, usually in metal or concrete but sometimes in brickwork or masonry. He may be, but does not need to be, a qualified structural engineer. His main tools are a ruling pen, some scales, and a set-square.

structural engineer A person who in Britain is professionally qualified by being a member or associate member of the Institution of Structural Engineers. His main work is *structural design*.

structural engineering technician *See* technician engineer.

structural steelwork *Rolled-steel joists* or built-up members fabricated as building frames, by riveting, welding, or bolting, or all three.

structure (1) The load-bearing part of a building.

(2) Anything built by man, from a hydraulic fill dam built of earth or a *pyramid* (*B*) of stone to a hydroelectric power station or an earth satellite. A structure is not necessarily roofed, a building is.

strut [stru.] A *long column*, usually of wood or metal, not necessarily vertical.

Stub's iron wire gauge *See* Birmingham wire gauge.

stud [mech.] A threaded rod; a *bolt* with no head. *See* stud gun (*B*), stud welding (*B*).

stuffing box [mech.] A recess, filled with packing, fitting tightly round a piston rod to prevent leakage of steam from an engine or water from a pump.

stumper A *tree-cutter*.

stunt end or **form stop** or **stop end** or **day joint** Vertical shuttering placed across a wall, slab, or trench to form a *construction joint* which ends the day's concreting.

sub-base A bed of material laid under a road base on the natural ground to strengthen it, to improve the drainage, or for some other purpose.

subcritical flow [hyd.] In an *open channel*, flow is said to be slow or tranquil or subcritical when the *Froude number* is less than 1. *See* **hydraulic jump.**

sub-grade (1) The natural ground below a road.

(2) The *formation*.

sub-irrigation Irrigation by raising the water level near the roots of plants.

submerged-arc welding An *automatic welding* method in which a bare or covered consumable wire *electrode* travels along the weld under a mound of flux. The lower part of the flux melts and protects the weld.

submerged float [hyd.] (1) A *rod float*.

(2) A *subsurface float*.

submerged tunnel *See* **immersed tube.**

submerged weir [hyd.] A *drowned weir*.

submersible A submarine to carry one or more men, designed for work in deep water where divers cannot work. It may have a mechanical hand (manipulator), television cameras or geophysical survey equipment for examining a pipeline or the sea bed. A 2800-ton Vickers submersible surveyed 21 km of sea-bed pipeline in 13 days in 1972. It was claimed it could work at 420 m depth.

submersible pump [mech.] A centrifugal pump which may be driven by compressed air or electricity and can be wholly submerged in water. *See* **borehole/deep-well/sinking pump, filter well.**

subsidence or **settlement** Downward movement of the ground surface for any reason:

(1) [min.] Filling of a mined area reduces surface settlement to such an extent that, with the best hydraulic filling, only 5 % of the seam thickness is noticed as *settlement* at the surface. The surface movement extends to about 35° outside the vertical from the edge of the mined area, but the worst damage is caused at about 14° from it.

(2) [hyd.] Surface settlement caused by over-pumping of *aquifers* has been known to exceed 3 m over large areas of California and Mexico, often reaching 4·8 m. It results from collapse of the aquifer structure and destroys much of its storage capacity permanently. If a building is founded on piles below the subsiding soil it may remain isolated above ground while any stairs leading down from it slowly collapse. In Mexico City such problems are so serious that pumping within the inner city is prohibited. *See also* **settlement.**

subsoil (1) [s.m.] The weathered *soil* immediately below the topsoil.

(2) The ground below *formation level* also called the subgrade or foundation.

subsoil drain A *field drain* laid just below the ground surface and covered with stones. If it connects to a foul drain the water must pass through a trap first. To protect a road foundation from *frost heave*, subsoil drains are sometimes laid about 1·5 m down so that capillary water stays at least 0·3 m below the foundation.

substructure That part of any structure which is below ground, in particular the foundations and piers of a bridge. The substructure of a suspension bridge can include its towers which are 150 m high.

subsurface erosion [s.m.] *Piping.*

subsurface float [hyd.] An underwater *float* tied by a line to a surface float which indicates its movement.

subsurface flow [hyd.] *See* **density current.**

subtense bar [sur.] A bar of accurately

known length (usually 2 m), held horizontally on a tripod at a point whose distance is required. The surveyor notes the readings of the horizontal circle of his theodolite at each end of the bar and, by subtraction, deduces the angle it subtends. From this angle the distance from theodolite to bar can be calculated, or read from tables. It is slower but much more accurate than *stadia work* with a vertical staff. An accuracy of 1 in 7000 has been claimed.

subway (1) In UK an underground footway.

(2) In USA an underground railway.

suction-cutter dredger [hyd.] A *suction dredger* provided with a rotating *clay cutter* at the end of the suction pipe. It can dig stiff clay or gravel. *See* draghead dredger.

suction dredger [hyd.] A *dredger* without digging buckets, which digs by powerful suction pumps. The mud-and-water mixture is either pumped away along a *floating pipeline* to land which is being reclaimed, or it is dumped in a hopper barge, the clear water being allowed to overflow until the mud in the barge is thick enough to be removed. This dredger is often used for providing the fill for *hydraulic-fill dams*.

suction head or static suction lift The height to which a pump can lift water on its suction side, measured from the free water level in the sump. Theoretically this is about 10 m (1 atmosphere) at freezing point, 0°C, and diminishes to 0 at boiling point, 100°C. In practice, good pumps at ordinary temperatures should not be so fixed that they have to suck more than 4 to 6 m. Centrifugal pumps lift less than reciprocating pumps.

suction pad, vacuum pad In *vacuum lifting*, a device which clings by vacuum to the piece being lifted. It connects and disconnects quickly, so for concrete is faster than lifting by crane hook, and spreads the load better.

suction valve [mech.] A *check valve* on a suction pipe near its entry to the *sump*.

sudden drawdown [hyd.] Rapid drop in water level such as is caused by tidal variations. It produces a critical condition in the design of a dam or quay wall or any earth slope, since the support given by the water is removed at a time when the soil is saturated.

sudden outburst, gas outburst [r.m.] An explosion, usually of coal at a coal face, caused or at least accompanied by the release of a large volume of methane, sometimes with other gases, often with fatal results for the men at the face. Outbursts of methane have also occurred in salt mines and potash mines. Unlike *rock bursts*, sudden outbursts can occur in shallow mines, and in Britain occur in certain anthracite mines, very much shallower than those where rock bursts happen.

sue load [hyd.] The heavy and increasing load on a *slipway*, transferred from the front wheels of the *cradle* as a ship is drawn out of the water.

sulphate-bearing soils [s.m.] If groundwater contains more than 0·1% of SO_3 or if a clay contains more than 0·5% of SO_3, *high-alumina cement* should be used for all concrete in the ground. *Portland pozzolana cement* may sometimes give enough protection at lower cost. No precautions need be taken with foundation concrete in water which contains less than 0·02% SO_3 or clay which contains less than 0·1% SO_3. *See also* sulphate-resisting cement.

sulphate-resisting cement A *cement* that is generally available in the UK. It resembles *ordinary Portland cement* but is less easily attacked by sulphates in the soil. It generates slightly less heat than *ordinary* but more than *low-heat cement*. It is sometimes used as a substitute for low-heat cement, which is not usually available in the UK. *See* BS 4027, *and* supersulphated cement.

summary of reinforcement A *cutting list*.

summit canal A canal crossing a summit,

which therefore needs to have water pumped to it.

sump A pit in which water collects before being baled or pumped out. The pump suction dips into a sump.

sumpers [min.] British term for *cut holes*, especially in shaft sinking.

supercritical flow [hyd.] In an *open channel*, flow is said to be fast or rapid or supercritical when the *Froude number* is more than 1. *See* **hydraulic jump.**

superelevation or **cant** or **banking** A tilt given to a road or a pair of rails at a bend to counteract the effect of centrifugal force. For locomotive-drawn trains and for roads, the outside of the curve is higher than the inside. For rope-drawn trains the slope is reversed, the inner rail being higher.

superficial [d.o.] Relating to a surface or an area.

superficial compaction [s.m.] The *compaction* of soils by the *frog rammer*, hand punning, vibration, *pneumatic-tyred rollers*, *sheepsfoot rollers*, or similar methods in layers usually not exceeding 15 cm. *Compare* **sand piles, vibro-flotation.**

superimposed load [stru.] A *live load* which is imposed by building regulations on the design of floors, etc. For example in Britain 195 kg/m² for floors of dwellings.

superintendent American title for a contractor's *agent* or a *resident engineer* or resident architect.

superload [stru.] *Live load* or *superimposed load.*

superposition [stru.] The principle of superposition is a principle which simplifies structural calculations, and can be used for solving the forces in *redundant frames*. Briefly it means that the stresses in a member due to one system of loading can be added to the stresses in it due to another system of loading. The redundant frame is split up first into two or more *perfect frames* having some members in common. The forces in the perfect frames are determined by statics and those which

occur in the same member are added algebraically, the algebraic sum being the total force in the member. The method is exact for symmetrical loading and only slightly inaccurate for unsymmetrical loading.

superstructure [stru.] The visible part of a structure; that part above the *substructure.*

supersulphated cement or **metallurgical cement** A *cement* made mainly from blast-furnace slag, which resists attack by sulphates even more than *sulphate-resisting cement*. It resists weak acids provided that the water/cement ratio of the concrete is 0·45 or less. *See* BS 4248.

support The removal of coal or ore under a railway, canal, or reservoir constitutes removal of support and may be a cause for legal action.

support moment [stru.] *Hogging moment.*

suppressed weir [hyd.] A *measuring weir* whose sides are flush with the sides of the channel. It has therefore no *end contractions*, and is thus the contrary of a *contracted weir*. The contractions may be suppressed at one or both sides or at the bottom or at all three positions.

surcharge Any load above the earth which is level with the top of a *retaining wall*. Surcharges may be temporary (live) loads such as lorries, locomotives, cranes, or stacked goods; or permanent (dead) loads such as earth sloping up from the top of the wall or a building above the top of the wall. A surcharge increases very considerably the *active earth pressure* on the wall. This increase can be removed completely by a *relieving platform*. *See* **barge bed, retaining wall.**

surcharged wall A retaining wall carrying a surcharge, such as an embankment, above its top.

surface-active agent A *surfactant.*

surface detention [hyd.] The thin sheet of water that covers the ground during rain. When this water reaches a stream it becomes *run-off.*

surface dressing A wearing surface consisting of a layer of chippings or gravel on a thin layer of fresh road tar or bitumen.

surface float [hyd.] A *float* on the surface of water.

surface tension The property of a fluid surface to behave as if it were covered with a tight skin (the meniscus), so that a needle or fine powder can be made to float on cold water (for example) without being wetted. The wetting power of water can be increased and its surface tension and *capillarity* reduced by mixing soap or other *surfactants* with it.

surface-tension depressant [min.] A *surfactant*.

surface water The *run-off* from unpaved or paved land or buildings, as opposed to *soil* or waste water.

surface-water drain Any pipe for rainwater in the ground. It is usually of at least 10 cm dia.

surfacing The top layer of a road, e.g. *asphalt*.

surfactant A substance which emulsifies, disperses, dissolves, or penetrates other substances, or makes them froth, in fact a *depressant* of *surface tension*.

surge (1) [stru.] A horizontal force applied to a high level of a building usually by a crane accelerating or braking. Crane surge is applied at crane rail level. It cannot exceed 0·25 of the greatest weight at each wheel, since this is the highest coefficient of friction between crane wheel and rail. *See* **wracking forces.**

(2) [hyd.] A sudden increase in pressure in a pipeline caused by a valve closing at its lower end. *See* **surge pipe, water hammer.**

surge pipe [hyd.] An open-topped *stand pipe* for releasing surge pressures when water does not need to be saved. The water spills over the top. *See* **surge tank.**

surge tank [hyd.] An open tank connected to the top of a *surge pipe* to avoid loss of water during pressure *surges*. A surge tank is usually connected to

the pressure pipes leading water to the turbines at a water-power station.

survey (1) A map or drawing showing, for a *topographical survey*, the layout of the ground; for a *geophysical survey*, the variations in gravity, resistivity, magnetic intensity, radioactivity, temperature; or, for a *geological map*, the outcropping strata. *See* **soil survey, solid map, traverse.**

(2) To make a survey.

surveying The measuring of the earth's surface so as to draw a true map of it. Surveying is either small-scale, *plane surveying*, or large-scale, *geodetic surveying*. *See also* **borehole surveying.**

surveying errors *See* **error, tape corrections.**

surveyor A vague term which may mean a member of several very different professions which fall into two groups, first mining or *land surveyors*, secondly *quantity* (*B*) or *building surveyors* (*B*). The Royal Institution of Chartered Surveyors includes all types of surveyor in its membership.

surveyor's draughtsman [d.o.] One who prepares maps or drawings for a *land* or mining *surveyor*. He needs no diploma but may be a qualified surveyor. (*Quantity surveyors* (*B*) rarely prepare drawings.)

surveyor's transit *See* **engineer's transit.**

suspended-frame weir A *frame weir* in which during floods the frames are hung above water level from a bridge.

suspended span The middle, short, freely supported span of, e.g. a *cantilever bridge*.

suspended structure or construction [stru.] Suspended structures, apart from the suspension bridge, are relatively new and of two main types. The first includes tents, canopies or awnings of textile, often of impressive appearance, difficult or impossible to calculate but splendid for exhibition purposes, and initiated by the German architect, Otto Frei. Any tent has masts under pure compression, with ropes and tent material under pure tension. The other type of suspended structure is a modern multi-storey block. The columns around the edges of the building are replaced by vertical tie bars or cables that are much more slender and so do not obstruct vision. The main floor loads are carried up by the tie bars to beams cantilevered at roof level from one or more central piers or *cores*. Because of the overhanging beams at roof level this type has been called an umbrella structure. *Air houses (B)* are pure *tension structures*, and are 'suspended' in another way.

suspender A vertical hanger in a *suspension bridge*, by which the road is carried on the cables.

suspension bridge A road bridge hung from a pair of *steel* cables, each carried by two towers, one at each bank. The cables are anchored into the rock or to a large mass of masonry behind the towers. The weight of the road is carried by vertical rods (suspenders) which are spaced at uniform intervals between road and cables at each side. *See* **Akashi Kaikyo Bridge, Severn Bridge, stiffening girder, Verrazano Narrows Bridge** *and illustration below*.

suspension cable A steel-wire rope carrying a suspension bridge. Two are needed for each bridge. They are often spun on the site.

suspension-cable anchor A mass of masonry in soft ground, or a fixing deep into rock, on the land side of a suspension bridge tower, to hold the ends of the suspension cables.

sustained yield or **safe yield** [hyd.] The highest annual rate of withdrawal from an *aquifer* or basin, which does not have undesirable results such as damage to the aquifer, or *encroachment* of nearby sea water. Normally the safe yield does not exceed the average annual *recharge*.

swamp shooting *See* peat blasting.

swash height [hyd.] The height to which the water from waves reaches on a beach. For a shingle beach it is often taken as 1·7 times the height of deep-water waves.

sway [stru.] Sideways movement of a frame, particularly *sidesway*.

sway rod [stru.] or **sway brace** A diagonal brace to resist wind or other horizontal forces on a building.

Swedish cylindrical surface [s.m.] *See* **rotational slide.**

swelling pressure [s.m.] The pressure exerted by a contained clay when it absorbs water. It can amount to considerably more than the pressure of the overlying soil.

swelling soils, expansive soils [stru.] Clay

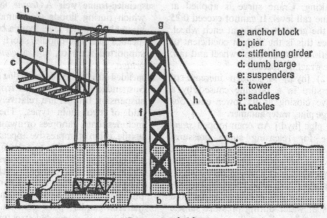

a: anchor block
b: pier
c: stiffening girder
d: dumb barge
e: suspenders
f: tower
g: saddles
h: cables

Suspension bridge

soils swell when they take in water and shrink when they dry out. Trouble from foundations that swell is unusual in northern Europe where the soil is almost always wet. The opposite trouble, of foundations settling in summer because of the shrinkage of clays, is, however, quite common in cold countries. In arid or semi-arid climates all over the world swelling clay raises cellar floors and forces cellar walls inwards. One solution is to use deeper foundations. Another is to ensure that foundations are not wetted by rainwater from the house roof, by surrounding the house with cast concrete slabs to direct the water away from the house.

SWG [mech.] *Standard Wire Gauge* (*B*).

swing bridge or **pivot bridge** or **turn bridge** [stru.] A *movable bridge* that swings on a vertical pivot at its centre, to allow vessels to pass.

swinger A pointed bar about 0·9 m long, used for moving *runners* in trench timbering.

swing-jib crane [mech.] A crane with one horizontal leg (instead of two like the Scotch *derrick*) on which is the counterweight. It swings through 360° on a pivot with its counterweight and is thus much more mobile. Like the Scotch derrick it can travel on tracks or be stationary. *See* **Titan crane, tower crane.**

switch (1) [rly] *Points.*
(2) [elec.] An appliance which opens or closes an electric circuit.

switch blades [rly] *Points.*

switchgear [elec.] Plant, including switches or *circuit breakers*, for controlling or protecting a power circuit.

Sydney Harbour Bridge A steel, two-hinged trussed arch bridge of 509 m clear span, erected by temporarily cantilevering the ends from each shore until they met in the middle. It was built in 1932. *Compare* **Kill Van Kull Bridge.**

systematic errors [sur.] or **cumulative errors** Those *errors* which are either always positive or always negative, as opposed to *compensating errors*.

table [stru.] The flat part of a tee-section from which the *stalk* rises.

tacheometer [sur.] A telescope, usually in a theodolite, used for measuring distance by its *stadia hairs*.

tacheometric surveying or **tacheometry** *See* **stadia work.**

tack coat A thin coat of bitumen or road tar or emulsion laid on a road to improve the adhesion of a course above it.

tack rivet A rivet which does not carry load, but is put in for convenience of construction or to comply with regulations.

tack weld A temporary weld that holds steel parts together during fabrication.

Tacoma Narrows Bridge A *suspension bridge* of 853 m central span and 335 m end spans which collapsed in November 1940 a few months after its completion. It failed during a stiff breeze which caused a fluttering movement of oscillation and twisting (*aerodynamic instability*), but was rebuilt in 1950 to withstand winds of 200 kph. *See* **vortex shedding.**

tail bay, tail gate, tail race, tailwater [hyd.] A downstream bay, lock gate, channel, etc.

tail rope [min.] A haulage rope which passes round a *return sheave*, as opposed to a direct (or main) rope.

Tainter gate [hyd.] A *radial gate*, named after Burnham Tainter.

tally [sur.] A distinctive plastics (formerly brass) label, marking every metre on a surveyor's 20 m chain. The tallies at 5, 10 and 15 m are numbered and red, the others are yellow, of different shape and not numbered (BS 4484).

tamp To *pun.*

tamper A *screed board*, sometimes with a mechanical *vibrator* on it.

tamping roller or **steel-wheeled roller** A tractor for *compaction* of soils, having two or more large steel wheels with tapered steel projections. Although resembling the *sheepsfoot roller* (apart from the shape of the projections) it travels faster and is more suitable for soils without clay.

tandem roller A road roller having rolls of about the same diameter behind each other on the same track. Ordinarily there are two rolls but *see* **three-axle tandem roller.**

tangent distance The distance from an *intersection point* to a *tangent point* in the setting out of a road or railway curve.

tangent point A point on a curve at which it joins a tangent or changes its curvature (in the setting out of roads or railways).

tangent screw [sur.] A fine-adjustment screw which moves the line of sight a short distance. One is usually fitted on both the horizontal and vertical circles of a *theodolite*.

tank sprayer A *pressure tank* on wheels.

tape [sur.] A ribbon of steel, *invar*, or fibreglass coated with pvc, etc., graduated usually in metres and millimetres and coiled in a steel or leather case when not in use. Used by surveyors, engineers, and builders, the most accurate tapes are of invar, but the steel tape is accurate enough for nearly all purposes in engineering. *See* **band chain, tape corrections.**

tape corrections [sur.] The following corrections are applied as a matter of course to all lengths measured accurately by steel or invar tape: *slope, temperature, sag, standardization, gravity,* and *sea-level corrections.* Standard tension for steel or invar tapes is usually 5 kg at 20°C.

tapered-flange beam A *rolled-steel joist* with the inner surfaces of its flanges tapered, usually at 98° to the web.

tapered washer A *bevelled washer.*

taper file [mech.] A triangular *file* with fine teeth for sharpening saws.

tare The weight of an empty lorry, wagon, or other container.

tar emulsion *See* **bituminous emulsion.**

target or **traverse target** [sur.] An object centred over a traverse point or *trigonometrical station*, which can be easily and accurately sighted by a *theodolite*. The special targets in use in *three-tripod traversing* often have their own built-in bubble tube and *optical plummet*, enabling the theodolite to use the same *set-up*.

target rod [sur.] or **target staff** A *levelling staff* with a sliding target which is raised or lowered by the *staff man* until the instrument man signals to him that it is on his line of sight. The staff man then reads and notes the staff reading. *Compare* **self-reading staff.**

tarmacadam or **coated macadam** A road material consisting of stone coated with tar or a tar-bitumen mixture. It has very little fine aggregate and a high proportion of voids.

tarmacadam plant A plant for making *tarmacadam.*

tar paving Tarmacadam surfacing laid in one or two courses for very light traffic or playgrounds.

technician engineer A person with practical engineering ability but with lower academic qualifications than a *chartered engineer*. Chartered engineers need a university degree, technician engineers need to reach only Higher National Certificate level. Civil engineering technicians, like civil engineers, are expected to have some knowledge of about 20 engineering subjects and to specialize in one or two of them, e.g. drawing office work, soil testing, concrete technology, planning and programming of a contract, roadbuilding, hydrometry, site organization and control, etc. They have at least five years' experience of civil engineering work in the office and outside, and can belong to the Society of Civil Engineering Technicians, which is in the Institution of Civil Engineers' building in London and was founded in 1968. Similar arrangements apply for structural engineering technicians, but they are of course expected to specialize in structures. Some 30 engineering institutions in all belong to the Council of Engineering Institutions (founded 1965) or to its Engineers Registration Board, with a view to the registration of their technician engineers or chartered engineers.

tee-beam (1) or **tee-iron** or **tee-section** A *rolled-steel section* shaped like a T, composed of a *stalk* and a *table*.

(2) Part of a reinforced-concrete floor in which the beam projects below the slab. In *hollow-tile floors* the stalk cannot be seen, since the soffit of the hollow tile coincides with the soffit of the tee-beam.

tee-iron or **tee-section** A *tee-beam.*

tee-square [d.o.] A device consisting of two pieces of wood joined to form a tee, that enables parallel lines to be drawn on a *drawing board.*

telecontrolled power station [elec.] A hydroelectric power station, for example in the Alps, which is not manned but wholly controlled by radio. *See* **remote control.**

telemeter [sur.] A fitting to a theodolite telescope, which contains an *optical wedge.*

telemetry [hyd.] Remote transmission of data from flow meters, etc. It enables water measurement stations to be unmanned and can be applied to other measurements.

telfer *See* **telpher.**

teller [sur.] A *tally.*

telltale [stru.] A piece of thin glass or other indicator, cemented firmly across a crack in a structure that is settling, to indicate by its cracking whether the crack continues to widen. The date is marked on it.

Tellurometer [sur.] In 1973 Tellurometer Ltd were making six different types of Tellurometer for *electronic distance measurement*. Originally with two identical instruments, one at each station, a 'master' and a 'remote' instrument, both measured the length at the same time. The latest instrument weighs only 2·5 kg. It can be set up over a *theodolite* and there is no remote instrument, the master transmitting infra-red rays which, at the remote station, are reflected by a prism.

telpher or **telfer,** sometimes called a **monorail** An electric hoist hanging from a wheeled cab rolling on a single overhead rail, occasionally from a rope. It is used in factories, hung from roof girders indoors, and over dams during their construction. When out of doors an overhead gantry must be built to carry the rail. The difference between *aerial ropeways* and rope-borne telphers is that telphers are driven by a motor or engine in the cab, ropeways are pulled by a rope driven by a stationary engine. Telphers are usually electrically driven.

temper [mech.] (1) To temper steel which has been hardened by *quenching* is to reheat it to a temperature below the *critical* and then to cool it rapidly. The *hardness* of the steel is thus reduced (tempered) to an amount which varies with the temperature from which it is cooled. The higher the tempering temperature, the softer is the steel. *See* **hardening.**

(2) To toughen non-ferrous metal by *annealing* and sometimes rolling.

(3) The state of hardness of metal. Thus a metal at low temper is relatively soft and *ductile*. A metal at high temper is hard and brittle.

temperature correction [sur.] The temperature correction of a steel tape used at a temperature different from its *standardization temperature* is equal to 0·000011 m per metre of measured length, L metres, per degree C of difference. This amount, in millimetres, $0·011 \times L \times T°C$, must be deducted if the temperature is below the standardization temperature, added if it is above the standardization temperature. *See* **invar, tape corrections.**

temperature gradient A change in temperature per unit length. In building, the temperature gradient through an outside wall is carefully studied before the position for the *vapour barrier* (B) is decided.

temperature steel [stru.] Reinforcement which is inserted in a slab or other concrete member to prevent cracks due to *shrinkage* or *temperature stresses* from becoming too large. It generally amounts to a minimum of about 0·1% of the cross-section in any direction, the requirement for a slab, which is two-dimensional, being therefore about 0·2% altogether. If, as usual, more steel than this is inserted to take bending or other stress, this requirement is disregarded.

temperature stress [stru.] A stress due to temperature rise or drop. If the expansion due to temperature rise or the contraction due to temperature drop is restrained, the member concerned is stressed in compression during rising temperature or tension during falling temperature. *See* **strain.**

tempering [mech.] *See* **temper.**

temporary adjustment [sur.] An *adjustment* to a surveying instrument made at each *set-up*, such as levelling or centring. *Compare* **permanent adjustment.**

tenacity [mech.] *Tensile strength.*

tendon [stru.] A *prestressing* bar, *cable*, rope, *strand* or wire.

tensile force [stru.] *See* **tension.**

tensile strength [mech.] A loose but convenient term often used as an abbreviation for *ultimate tensile stress*. It is much higher than the greatest safe *stress*. *See* **tension, working stress.**

tensile test [mech.] A test in which a piece of standard shape, made of metal, mortar, concrete, wood, etc., is pulled in a testing machine until it breaks. Often the load is recorded for every measured extension so that a graph called the *load-extension curve* of the test can be drawn. *See* **beam test, necking.**

tension [stru.] A pulling force or *stress*. Metals and wood take tension well, but masonry, including concrete, is generally not allowed to take any tension except in the dispersal of concentrated loads. In this case bricks with good adhesion (not pressed bricks), and *frogs* (*B*) and joints filled solid may be allowed a tension of 0·1 N/mm². Unreinforced concrete in foundations is sometimes allowed 0·3 to 0·7 N/mm² tension. *See* **proof stress, ultimate tensile strength, yield point.**

tension carriage [mech.] A frame carrying a pulley round which an endless belt or rope passes to be tensioned. The frame can move, e.g. for tensioning the traction rope of an *aerial ropeway*.

tension correction [sur.] The *tape correction* to be applied to a tape used at a tension which is not that at which it was standardized. If the difference in tensions is p, l the measured length, a the cross-sectional area of the tape and E its *modulus of elasticity* the correction is $\dfrac{l \times p}{a \times E}$. This must be added to l when the standardization pull is lower, and subtracted from l when the standardization pull is higher than that at which l is measured.

tension flange [stru.] The side of a beam which is in tension, usually the lower side, particularly in the middle of a beam on two supports. It is the upper side of a cantilever beam.

tension pile [stru.] An *anchor pile*.

tension sleeve [stru.] A *screw shackle*.

tension structure [stru.] The only structures that completely eliminate stresses other than tension in their building material are pressurized *air houses* (*B*), often called air domes, balloon structures, Fabridams, inflatables, inner tubes, pneumatics or radomes. All of them contain a fluid, usually air at a pressure slightly above atmospheric. (Fabridams contain water.) All stresses are tensile and are carried on the 'balloon skin'. Ordinary structures with more than the usual amount of tension are often called *suspended structures*.

tensor or **hydraulic tensor** or **hydrostressor** Equipment used in laying *continuously welded track*, that pulls a rail at about 70 tons maximum pull, so as to bring it (in cold weather in the UK) to the length that it would have at about 21° to 27°C. The pull needed to lengthen a rail weighing 54 kg/metre is about 1·6 tonnes per degree C.

terminal (1) The shore end of an undersea pipeline.

(2) A telephone and teleprinter connected to a computer, which enable the telephone subscriber to buy time on the computer without having to suffer the even higher expense of buying or hiring one.

terminal velocity [s.m.] or **free-falling velocity** or **settling velocity.** The maximum velocity which a body can attain when falling freely in a fluid (usually air or water). It can be determined for spherical particles by *Stokes's law*.

terotechnology [mech.] The design, installation, commissioning, operation, maintenance and replacement of machinery, plant or equipment. *See* BS 3811:1974 'Glossary of maintenance terms in terotechnology'.

terracing *See* **contour ploughing.**

tertiary treatment [sewage] or **polishing** After *secondary treatment*, processes of treatment of *sewage* effluent that improve its quality, sometimes to better than the *Royal Commission standard*. It can include long-term settlement in lagoons (oxidation ponds), irrigation over grass, and filtration either through fine wire mesh (microstraining) or through a *sand filter* of some type.

Terzaghi [s.m.] The founder of modern *soil mechanics*. *See* **consolidation, graded filter.**

test cube A 15 cm or 10 cm cube of concrete used in Britain as a sample of the concrete strength. It is crushed usually at 7- or 28-days' age. It is kept in damp sand for the whole of this period except the first day, during which it is in the mould. Ordinarily a 7-day cube has two-thirds of the strength of a 28-day cube. *See* cylinder test.

testing machine [mech.] A machine used for loading test pieces or structural members to determine their deformations at given loads and their breaking strengths. The commonest machines are for tension, compression, *impact*, and *fatigue*.

test piece [mech.] A piece of mortar moulded to shape or a piece of metal or wood turned (or cast) or cut to shape, for testing in a testing machine.

test pit Term used in USA for *trial pit*.

tetrahedron A solid figure having four faces only. Steel-framed skeleton tetrahedra were used to break the force of the water in the Rhône, during the construction of the famous dam at Génissiat, France, 1945. *See* tetrapod.

tetrapod An equiangular figure of the same general type as a tripod, with a fourth leg rising from the intersection of the other three. Since it has four legs, one leg is always vertical when the other three are on a flat base and

it is extremely stable. In *breakwaters* (Casablanca) large reinforced-concrete tetrapods of about 15 tons weight were (1950) piled up to break the force of the waves and reduce their scour. *See* tetrahedron.

theodolite [sur.] or **transit** A surveyor's instrument for measuring horizontal (and usually vertical) angles. It consists of a telescope rotating on a horizontal axis, called the trunnion axis, carried on a forked *standard* fixed to the circular upper *plate*. The lower plate is carried on the *tribrach*, which has usually three levelling screws and a centring device between them for bringing the theodolite plumb over a station. The theodolite was invented in the sixteenth century by an Englishman, Leonard Digges. In 1785 a telescopic theodolite for the first time linked the English to the French triangulation. It had no vertical circle, but its horizontal circle of 3 feet diameter enabled angles to be measured to an accuracy of one second of arc. The first transit instrument was built early in the nineteenth century. *See* optical plummet, three-tripod traversing.

theory of structures The study of

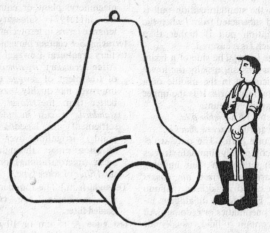

Concrete tetrapod weighing 15 tons

structures and their stability and strength. It does not properly include *strength of materials*, but in this book 'stru.' covers these subjects and *structural design*.

thermal boring *Thermic boring*.

thermel [elec.] Any instrument which includes a *thermocouple*.

thermic boring or **thermal boring** A method of boring holes into concrete by the high temperature of a burning steel tube (lance) packed with steel wool through which an oxy-acetylene or similar gas mixture is passed to ignite the end of the lance. After ignition, oxygen alone is fed, to keep it burning. If concrete is heavily reinforced it can be cut more easily than if it is unreinforced, since the reinforcement burns in the oxygen jet. *See* **jet drilling.**

thermit or **thermite** A mixture of aluminium powder and iron oxide used in the *alumino-thermic* welding of steel rails and other steel parts. A temperature above the melting point of steel is generated, so that the parts to be welded must be enclosed in a mould of clay or other *refractory* material. A generally trouble-free electrical and mechanical bond is thus formed. *See* **ignition powder.**

thermocouple [elec.] Two wires of different metals soldered or welded together at one end, connected to an appropriate circuit at their other ends. If the pairs of metals are suitably chosen and the temperature of the joined ends is different from the other ends a current will flow. Many *pyrometers* use this effect. *See* **thermel.**

thermo-osmosis [hyd.] Water and water vapour move, other things being equal, in the direction of heat flow, i.e. towards cooler ground because this is also the direction of increasing surface tension. Thermo-osmosis is important in cool or icy regions because it can cause accumulations of ice underground. *Compare* **electro-osmosis.**

thimble [mech.] A pear-shaped ring formed of steel sheet built into the end of a *fibre* or steel rope by splicing or doubling the rope on itself to form a convenient loop. Often used with *bulldog grips*. *See* **reeving thimble.**

thin section [min.] A slice of rock cut to about 0·02 mm thickness by grinding and polishing, for examination under the *petrographic microscope*. The rock is fixed to a glass slide by Canada balsam or other glue.

thin shell [stru.] *See* **shell.**

thin surfacing A *bituminous carpet*.

third-order or **tertiary triangulation** or **trilateration** [sur.] A *triangulation* or *trilateration* with sides from 1 to 10 km long. *See* **second-order.**

thixotropy A property first intentionally developed with oilwell *drilling fluids* in the USA early this century. They were made of *bentonite* slurry so that they would hold the chippings from the drilling bit which would otherwise lock the drill pipe and prevent drilling. When a thixotropic fluid is allowed to stand it gels and holds even large rock chips. Such fluids are used in *slurry trenches*, etc.

three-axle tandem roller A *tandem roller* with three rolls in sequence covering the same ground.

three-dimensional vision *See* **stereoscopic vision.**

three-hinged arch or **three-pinned arch** An arch which is hinged at each support and at the crown. It has the advantage that each half can sink relatively to the other without damaging the arch. For this reason it is often used where *differential settlement* is likely. It is statically determinate.

three-legged derrick *See* **derrick (4).**

three-leg sling A *sling* made of three chains or ropes with a hook at the end of each. The chains are hung from one *thimble* or ring.

three-point problem [sur.] (1) The problem in *plane-tabling* of locating the *set-up* on the plan when only three points on the plan can be seen from the set-up.

(2) Determining the dip and strike

of a seam or vein or fault when only the elevation and position of three points on it are known. (These are obtained by cores from boreholes, usually with a core barrel which is not *oriented*.)

three-tripod traversing [sur.] *Traversing* with a *theodolite* that can be detached from its *tribrach* without disturbing the tribrach centring. Three similar tripods are in use and each carries in turn the theodolite, the *target*, and sometimes a *subtense bar* or a staff for distance measurement. As soon as the observer has finished his readings at one point, he unclamps the theodolite from the tripod and fixes the sighting target on to it. He then moves on to the *foresight* station and clamps on the theodolite while his assistant brings up the rear tripod (his previous *backsight*) and sets it up at the next foresight station. Much of the labour of set-ups is thus avoided. The tripods may each have their own *optical plummet* and centring head. *See* **electronic distance measurement.**

throat [mech.] The least thickness of a *weld*. The strength of the weld is calculated on the throat thickness.

through bridge A bridge in which the lower *chord* carries the road or railway. *Compare* **deck bridge.**

thrust [stru.] (1) A horizontal force; particularly the horizontal force exerted by retained earth.

(2) An inclined force such as that from a *raking shore* (*B*), or the total force in an arch.

thrust bearing *See* **end thrust.**

thrust borer *See* **pipe pushing.**

tidal dock A dock which has no gates. The water inside is therefore always at the level of the water outside it.

tidal lag [s.m.] The delay between high tide (or low tide) in an estuary and the highest (or lowest) resulting level of the neighbouring groundwater.

tide gauge or **tide predictor** An instrument with which the tides in any known set of channels can be predicted.

tie (1) [stru.] A member carrying tension.

(2) [rly] or **rail tie** An American term for railway *sleeper*.

tied retaining wall [stru.] A *retaining wall* anchored to a *dead man*; the contrary of a *cantilever wall*.

tie line [sur.] A line which joins opposite corners of a four-sided figure and thus enables its sides and angles to be checked by *triangulation*.

tie rod [stru.] A *tie*, generally a steel rod, often threaded.

TIG welding or **tungsten-electrode inert-gas shielded-arc welding** (in USA **gas-tungsten arc, GTA welding**) Welding of most commercial metals with a non-consumable tungsten electrode and a shield of argon or other gas provided through a hose, either pure or mixed with others. The shielding gas and the filler rod are varied to suit the metal being welded. For *automatic welding* the torch is usually water cooled. Manual welding is also possible.

tight-fitting bolt *See* **turned bolt.**

till [min.] or **tillite** Mainly American terms for *boulder clay*.

tilt [air sur.] The angle between the vertical and the optical axis of a camera. It is rarely more than 3° and can in practice be kept within 1°, which is usually satisfactory in *vertical photographs*.

tilting gate [hyd.] A *crest gate* for dam spillways, so designed that the water pressure opens it at a certain level. It closes automatically when the water level has dropped to normal.

tilting level [sur.] A *level* with a *bubble* fitted on the telescope so that the axis of rotation does not need to be vertical. The telescope must, however, be levelled at each sight.

tilting mixer A *concrete mixer* which discharges its contents by tilting the rotating drum. It is a common small *batch mixer*, standardized in Britain at sizes from 200 litres upwards.

timbering The support of the ground in excavations whether with wood, steel, concrete, or light-alloy units, but usually with wood.

time and motion study *See* **motion study.**

timekeeper A clerk who calculates men's wages from their hours worked, or from their tonnage or other output.

timing [air sur.] The time interval between successive exposures of an air camera determines the distance between them, the *air base*, which varies with the aircraft speed and height. The interval is calculated to give about 60% lap between successive *vertical photographs* so that all points are generally photographed twice and some three times. The size of photograph, focal length of camera, speed, and altitude of aeroplane, all enter into the timing calculation. *See* **photogrammetry.**

tine (1) A prong of a harrow or rake.

(2) An excavating point or tooth in the mouth of a *dragline* bucket, *excavator* bucket, *grab*, *scraper loader*, etc.

tip grade American term for the *toe line* of piles.

tipping lorry A lorry which can discharge its contents backwards, or occasionally sideways.

tipping wagon or **jubilee wagon** A small wagon on narrow-gauge track, pivoted for side- or end-tipping.

Titan crane A *crane*, usually of at least 50 tons capacity, which differs from the *Goliath crane* in that the portal frame carries a *swing-jib crane*, which can command a considerable distance outside the portal legs. It is used for building *blockwork* piers and for ship construction. *See illustration below.*

TNT [min.] *Trinitrotoluene*, a powerful *explosive*.

to-and-fro ropeway A *jig back*.

toe (1) The part of the base of a dam or *retaining wall* which is on its free side, away from the retained material. *See* **heel.**

(2) [min.] The toe of a blasting hole is the inmost end of it, where the explosive is placed. *See* **burden,** *also* (*B*).

toe filter [s.m.] A *graded filter* on the free side of an earth dam at its lower end, designed to protect it against *piping*.

toe level A *toe line*.

toe line (In USA **tip grade**) or **toe level** The level to which the feet of piles are driven.

toggle mechanism [mech.] A mechanism used for applying heavy pressure from a small available force, used in the *jaw breaker* and many other applications.

ton A unit of weight. In Britain the ton

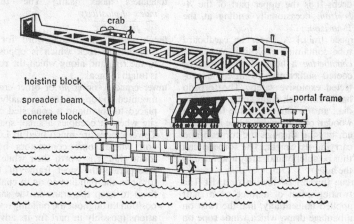

Titan crane setting 30-ton blocks in breakwater of coursed blockwork

is now usually 1000 kg, the metric tonne, but was formerly 2240 lb (the long ton). In USA more usually 2000 lb (the short ton). The long ton is equivalent to 1016 kg, that is 1·016 tonne. *See* **hundredweight.**

tool *See* (*B*).

top frame or **ground frame** A *frame* in timbering, set at or just below ground level to guide the first *setting* of *runners*.

topographical surveying [sur.] The work of the *land surveyor*, that is measuring or mapping land.

topographical surveyor *See* **land surveyor.**

topping (1) The concrete laid over the blocks in a *hollow-tile floor*. It forms the compression flange of the *tee beams* which it makes with the ribs, and is usually about 5 cm thick.

(2) A layer of mortar, preferably not less than 5 cm thick, laid over a concrete floor to provide a smooth surface on which the floor finish can be laid.

(3) A road surface, a *wearing course*.

topsoil [s.m.] The layer of the soil which by its humus content supports vegetation. It is usually the top 15 cm of the soil in Britain, but in wet tropical climates may be one metre or more deep. It is the upper part of the *A-horizon*, occasionally ending at the *B-horizon*.

torpedo [min.] A paper or cardboard tube containing explosive, used after *chambering* a hole which cannot be cooled sufficiently to insert unprotected explosive safely. The torpedo has 1 cm thick walls, may be 12 cm dia., and is plugged at the foot by a wooden plug to which a line is attached, passing through the torpedo and carrying its weight. The torpedo can thus be quickly and safely lowered into the hole.

torque [mech.] or **torsion** or **twist** The twisting effect of a force on a shaft applied tangentially, like the twist on a haulage drum which winds rope on to its circumference.

torque wrench *See* **impact spanner.**

Torshear bolt A development (1960) of the *high-strength friction-grip bolt*, which makes correct tensioning of the bolt certain, and inspection easy. The bolt thread is longer than usual, and the extension to the thread is separated from the main part of the thread by a groove cut round it to a precisely controlled depth. A special compressed-air-driven *impact spanner* grips the extension to the thread and rotates it, simultaneously holding the nut against rotation. (Access is thus only needed on one side, and one man can always tighten any bolt alone.) When the torque applied by the tool exceeds the strength at the groove, the bolt shears, and the tension is correct.

torsion *Torque*.

tortuous flow *Turbulent flow*.

total pressure [s.m.] The pressure on a horizontal plane in a mass of soil due to the weight of the material above it plus any applied loads. *See* **effective pressure.**

toughness [mech.] The resistance of a material to repeated bending and twisting, measured by the amount of work in kilojoules needed to break it in an *impact test*. Toughness implies tensile strength and ductility.

toughness index [s.m.] The ratio $\dfrac{index\ of\ plasticity}{flow\ index}$.

tough way Quarrymen's word for a direction in rock which is opposite to the *rift*, and along which the rock is tough to break.

tower crane A *swing jib* or other crane mounted on top of a tower, usually so placed to command a congested city site where it occupies a small space. Tower cranes are much used in London where some contractors have found that it is worth their while to incorporate the steel frame of the tower in the building so as to enable them to keep the crane in the same position throughout the building operations (possibly in part for its advertisement value). Occasionally the feet of the tower are placed on wheels which travel on rails.

tower gantry *See* **derrick tower gantry.**

towers [stru.] The world's highest tower is probably the Metro Centre communications tower in Toronto, Canada, 625 metres high to the top of its antenna. The 75-cm-thick concrete, main core wall is 7 m across the inside and contains some prestressing cables 425 m long, stressed by the Swiss company Losinger Systems.

township [sur.] In USA the 36 sq. miles enclosed between adjacent range lines (which run north–south 6 miles apart) and adjacent township lines (which run east–west 6 miles apart).

tracer [d.o.] A semi-skilled person in a drawing office who makes *tracings*.

tracing [d.o.] (1) To place transparent paper or cloth over a drawing and copy it line for line and word for word.

(2) A copy of a drawing made in this way.

tracing cloth [d.o.] *See* **tracing linen.**

tracing linen/paper [d.o.] Transparent linen or paper for making drawings or tracings from which *contact prints* can be taken. *See* **drawing paper.**

track [rly] The rails, sleepers and ballasted formation, which carry a train or crane, or the single rail of a *telpher* or monorail.

track cable A steel-wire rope, often *locked-coil rope*, on which the wheels of the carriers of a *cableway* or *aerial ropeway* travel. In a *monocable ropeway* the track cable is also the traction rope.

tracking Lines of wear in a road surface, caused by vehicles following in each other's tracks.

track-laying tractor [mech.] A *tractor* which travels entirely on crawler tracks. *Compare* **half-track/wheeled tractor.**

track spike [rly] (1) A square-section, heavy steel nail driven into a wooden sleeper to fix a flat-bottomed rail.

(2) A 16 mm dia. rod 15 cm long with a head and a blunt point, driven into a hardwood *treenail* bored for it

and already inserted into a hole in a concrete or wooden sleeper. They are also used in Britain for fixing cast-iron chairs or plates to sleepers. *See* **rail fastenings.**

track stringer A timber about 10×25 cm laid under each rail instead of using *sleepers* where the ground is soft. *See* **stringer.**

traction rope The haulage rope of an *aerial ropeway* or cableway, as opposed to its *track cable*.

tractive force [rly] The amount of pull available at the drawbar of a tractor, locomotive, etc. It is equal to the locomotive weight $\times$ the coefficient of friction on level track. The coefficient of friction is a maximum of 0·25 on sanded rails, usually much less. Therefore the maximum pull is $0.25 \times$ the weight of the locomotive. On upgrades the tractive force is reduced by the loco weight $\times$ the gradient, on downgrades the tractive force is increased by the same amount.

tractive resistance [rly] or **coefficient of traction** The frictional resistance to motion per ton hauled. At starting it is 2 to 3 times the running resistance. Running resistances on level track vary from 1·8 kg per ton with roller bearings on clean smooth track to 23 kg per ton with plain open bearings on bad track. It is made up of rolling resistance between rails and wheels, bearing friction, air resistance, and additional resistance due to curves and slopes. It is the ratio of the *tractive force* to the weight of the train.

tractor [mech.] A self-propelled vehicle which may be *track-laying*, *half-track* or *wheeled*, generally used for towing a *bowl scraper*, *rooter*, *grader*, or *plough*; but often used as a mount for a *dozer*, winch, or other implement. Normal tractor horsepowers vary from 25 to 115, *drawbar pulls* from 2700 to 1200 kg in first gear (2·5 kph), to 700 to 4500 kg in fifth gear (5 to 8 kph). These speeds are for tracked vehicles. Wheeled vehicles are much faster. A tractor fitted with a *power take-off* can be used, when properly loaded with sidebooms and counterweights, as a crane, dragline, or pile driver.

tractor shovel A *loading shovel* which may be mounted either on crawler tracks or on road wheels. Since it cannot slew, it is tipped by reversing away from the heap of material and moving towards the discharge point. It is suitable for confined spaces and is made with a maximum lift of about 3 m.

tradesman or **craftsman** *See* (*B*).

traffic engineering The US Institute of Traffic Engineers' 'Transportation and Traffic Engineering Handbook' (1976) of over 1000 pages includes more than 20 chapters by specialists on their subjects, excluding the structural design of highways. Included are: traffic statistics; the characteristics of vehicles, of humans, of traffic, of urban travel and of mass transportation; also road markings, traffic signs and traffic signals; traffic speed and flow theory and supervision; highway capacity, the use of computers, the planning (modelling) of future transport in the city and in the region; geometric design of the highway; parking for cars and bikes; loading, unloading; environmental considerations. The term *transportation engineering* has come into use only since 1965 and reflects the traffic engineer's unceasing problem, increasing as car ownership increases. He is pushed to provide more roads for those who work in cities, yet city dwellers protest that he is destroying their environment. He must therefore encourage all forms of transport which might reduce the number of automobiles on the road, bikes, railways, boats, pipelines, etc.

trailer dredger, trailing dredger A *draghead dredger*.

trailing cable [elec.] A flexible, rubber-insulated conductor or set of conductors in the same insulation, which provides power for a *conveyor, crane, dragline, loader, telpher,* or similar machine.

trailing points [rly] *Points* which are approached by a train in such a direction that it first meets their pivot (or heel).

training wall [hyd.] A wall built to contain a river.

training works [hyd.] Any structure designed to influence the flow, scouring or silting capacity of a river. *See* **dyke, groyne, levée, spur.**

trammel [d.o.] A board containing two grooves which intersect at right angles. In these grooves the two ends of a beam compass can slide and describe ellipses.

Trammel drain A perforated *field drain* laid in a trench in the usual way except that a porous, synthetic sheet material is wrapped round it, leading water to the drain from a 'filter slot' in the trench, containing sand. First installed in 1975 it is said to be highly effective.

tramway *See* **aerial/twin-cable ropeway.**

Träneberg Bridge A reinforced-concrete arch bridge near Stockholm with a clear span of 181 m. The arches are rectangular, hollow box-girders with about 0·75% total steel. *See* **Parramatta Bridge.**

transducer A device that converts one form of energy into another form, usually electrical into mechanical or the reverse, e.g. a telephone earpiece or mouthpiece, or a microphone or pick-up or a strain gauge. They can be transmitters or receivers (detectors) or both (transceivers).

transfer [stru.] For prestressed concrete, transfer is the moment when the concrete is stressed and some of the load is transferred from the steel to the concrete.

transformer [elec.] A device for converting one voltage of alternating current to another voltage. The ease with which power can be transformed (stepped up or down) in this way is the main reason for the supremacy of alternating current over direct current in situations where power is consumed far from the generator.

transient Something such as a sound, or voltage surge or water pressure wave, that occurs for a moment only. They are usually sudden increases in pressure and are important in hydraulics as well as in the design of electrical networks, since they can rise to high values that may cause destruction in pipes or open channels or harbours.

transit [sur.] (1) or **transit instrument** A *theodolite* which can *change face*. *See* **engineer's transit**.

(2) To *change face* of a theodolite telescope.

(3) The *culmination* of a star.

transition curve or **easement curve** A curve which eases the change between a straight and a circular curve. It is often a spiral.

transition length [rly] The length of a *transition curve*.

transit man [sur.] In USA an instrument man who is working at a transit instrument.

transit mixer A *truck mixer*.

transmission length [stru.] The *grip length* of a *prestressing* tendon in concrete.

transpiration [hyd.] Discharge of water from plants into the air as vapour. It increases with increasing wind, sunshine and temperature, and varies from plant to plant, but between the soil moisture contents of *specific retention* and *wilting coefficient* the amount is more or less constant for each plant of a given size and species. Transpiration reduces the daytime flow of springs in the summer but barely affects it at all in winter when the leaves have fallen.

transportation engineering The study of the movement of goods or people by any type of vehicle or pipeline, rail, boat, bus, car, etc. – a recent development of *traffic engineering*.

transporter bridge A bridge consisting of a *lattice* girder spanning between two towers at each side of a gap. It carries vehicles across the gap in a container which is slung at road level by ropes under a crane *crab* on the girder. *See below.*

transporter crane or **cantilever crane** A long *lattice* girder carried on two lattice towers which may be fixed or travel on rails at right angles to the girder. A *crab* travels along the girder and a grab or hoist hangs from the crab. It can thus be used for excavating or stock-piling material, or for loading or unloading ships or trains. When called a cantilever crane, usually at least one end of the girder overhangs its tower. *See* **cableway transporter, materials handling**.

transverse loading [stru.] *Beam* loading.

trapezoidal rule [d.o.] An estimate of the area of an irregular figure divided into n strips of equal width d, each strip being a trapezium. If the length of the first strip is l_1, that of the last l_n, and the sum of the intermediate strips is Σl, the area is equal to $\frac{d}{2}(l_1+2\Sigma l+l_n)$. *Simpson's rule* is more exact.

trap points [rly] Points placed in running rails to prevent incorrect switching of a train.

trash rack [hyd.] US term for parallel bars or a *screen* across a stream to catch floating rubbish, always provided at the intake to a turbine and for *raw water*.

trass (1) A volcanic ash from the Eifel mountains near Coblenz, resembling *pozzolana*.

(2) Burnt-clay clinker which is used as a water-resistant cement when ground. *See* **Portland pozzolana cement**.

traveller (1) [mech.] A pair of beams (or a single beam) carrying the moving hoist (*crab*) of an *overhead travelling crane*. They are mounted on wheels at each end and run on the crane rails.

(2) The central *boning rod* which is moved along the ground to check the ground levels between two *sight rails*.

travelling forms Usually large, built-up *formwork* for casting walls or the linings of tunnels or culverts, built on a carriage on rollers or wheels, enabling the forms to be moved without dismantling them. Movement may be intermittent or continuous. If continuous, the system can be regarded as a *sliding form* and in fact some authorities do not distinguish between the two. To avoid confusion it might be better to regard travelling forms as moving horizontally and sliding forms as moving vertically.

travelling ganger A *walking ganger*.

travelling gantry A gantry which is built on wheels to travel on rails and is provided with a hoist and *crab*.

travelling screen [hyd.] (1) A canvas diaphragm in a frame which fits closely across the section of a uniform channel and travels with the water. It is a *float* which gives a measure of the average velocity.

(2) A movable *trash rack*.

travel-mixer [s.m.] A self-propelled *soil mixer* which takes in soil at its front end from a *windrow*, and discharges it after mixing it to the *optimum moisture content* with *stabilizer*. See **mix-in-place, pulverizing mixer, single-pass soil stabilizer.**

traverse [sur.] A *survey* consisting of several connected lines of known length which meet each other at measured angles or *bearings*. See **closed/compass/open traverse.**

traverse tables [d.o.] Tables of the differences of *latitude* and departure for different angles. They are generally more used by navigators as a quick check on their position than by surveyors.

traversing [sur.] See **progression, traverse.**

traversing bridge or **retractable bridge** [stru.] A *movable bridge* that retreats from the waterway to allow a ship to pass.

traversing slipway A slipway for ships which are less than about 500 tons weight, on which the ship after being hauled up the slipway can be moved sideways (traversed) to another berth for repair, leaving the *slip* free.

traxcavator A *loading shovel* or *tractor shovel*.

treamie See **trémie.**

tree cutter or **stumper** or **treedozer** A horizontal toothed blade placed ahead of the mouldboard of a bulldozer, or a tractor equipped with this blade.

treenail or **trenail** A hardwood or synthetic plug or collar drilled to take a *chair* screw in British railways. The treenail is driven into a hole in the sleeper after the chair is placed over it so that a projection of the treenail from the sleeper passes through the chair. The screw driven in then holds both chair and sleeper tightly. See also (*B*).

trémie (also **tremmie** in USA) A sheet-metal hopper with a pipe leading out of the bottom of it, used for placing concrete under water. The foot of the pipe is so arranged as to be always below the level of the concrete, with the top of the concrete in the pipe above water level. In this way the concrete in the pipe is always under a higher pressure than the water outside it and is unlikely to be diluted by water. Placing by a trémie prevents *segregation* of the concrete, and closely resembles the placing of the grout in *Colcrete*. If a large area has to be concreted, this must be done by several trémies simultaneously, about 2·5 m apart, carried on staging or barges. Flow out of the trémie is reduced by lowering the hopper and increased by raising it. The concrete should rise uniformly at about 0·4 m per hour. The rate of concreting must be related to the size of the panel so that no panel takes more than four hours. This ensures that the first concrete to pass through does not stiffen before the panel is completely concreted. The concrete level is checked by sounding with a pole. At the start of concreting the trémie pipe is full of water and this must be expelled by a suitable plug placed in the hopper to separate the water from the concrete. If nothing else is available a ball made from old cement bags will do. The weight of the concrete pushes it through the pipe and mixing of water with concrete is prevented. But if the pipe outlet is lifted above the concrete, it will again fill with water and the process of expulsion of water will have to be repeated. If a concrete pump can reach the same distance as the trémie, it may be able to replace the trémie completely. Quite apart from the underwater concreting, a trémie is useful to prevent *segregation* where there is a large drop between the point where the concrete is discharged and that where it is placed. *See* **diaphragm wall.**

trenail *See* **treenail.**

trench A narrow, long excavation with timbered or bare sides, vertical or battered.

trench box Equipment that provides quick support in a trench and is dropped into place with a crane. It consists of two parallel steel-faced sheets held apart by struts, which may be adjustable. One type, made of composite steel joists and glassfibre with steel cladding, weighs 2 tons but measures 2.44×2.88 m. The boxes may be stacked on top of each other in a deep trench, but must be removed while the excavator is deepening the trench.

trench compactor A *frog rammer.*

trench drain A *French drain.*

trench excavator or **ditcher** or **trencher** or **trenching machine** A self-propelled machine, usually on *crawler tracks*, specialized for digging trenches. It is operated either by a *bucket-ladder excavator* or by a chain of buckets on a wheel. A trencher can dig neat, clean-sided trenches very rapidly from 18 cm wide $\times$ 1 m deep to 1.5 m wide $\times$ 4.3 m deep. A normal digging speed gives 0.3 m of travel per minute.

trench hoe A *backacter.*

trenching machine *See* **trench excavator.**

trepan A large tool dropped on a string of boring rods down a shaft excavated

in rock under water. It is dropped about 0.3 m at each stroke and turned slightly at the same time. It weighs from 2 to 30 tons and is from 2.4 to 5.5 m dia. It is used in the *forced drop shaft, Honigmann,* and *Kind Chaudron* methods of shaft sinking.

trestle A timber, reinforced-concrete, or steel structure, generally a *bent* connected to similar parallel bents each side. It usually supports a temporary or permanent bridge or an *aerial ropeway.* Some of the members are often continuations of *raking piles* driven into the ground below to carry the weight of the structure.

trestle bridge A bridge resting on trestle *bents* which are of timber in a temporary structure, of steel or reinforced concrete in a permanent structure. It is often used over a foundation of low bearing capacity since this sort of structure can be very light in weight.

trial pit or **trial hole** (In USA **test pit**) A pit dug to determine the type of ground, or to prospect for mineral.

triangle [d.o.] American term for *set square.*

triangle of error [sur.] The triangle formed in the graphical solution of the *three-point problem* in plane tabling, when the three lines drawn from the three points do not meet owing to inaccuracies.

triangular notch [hyd.] or **triangular weir** or **vee notch** A *measuring weir* of V-shape used for measuring small discharges. A useful mnemonic formula for discharge over a $90°$ notch is in British units: Q cusecs = $2.5h^{2.5}$, h being the depth of the water at the apex in feet.

triangulation (1) [sur.] The measurement of a large area of land by covering it with a network of triangles of which all the angles are accurately known. One side of a triangle (the *base line*) is also measured with great accuracy, and from it the lengths of all the other sides of the triangles are calculated by trigonometry. *See* **trilateration.**

(2) [stru.] Designing a *truss* so that

every shape enclosed by its members is triangular, no quadrilateral without a diagonal being allowed. If the joints are assumed hinged, the truss is a *perfect frame*.

triaxial compression test [s.m.] or **confined compression test** A test of a soil sample contained in a rubber bag surrounded by liquid under pressure. A load is applied by a piston to one end of the rubber bag and the deformations, loads, and pressures are recorded. *Undrained tests* are rapid, but *drained shear tests* (often called slow tests) require much more time and are correspondingly more expensive. *Compare* **unconfined compression test, vacuum method of testing sands.**

tribrach [sur.] The frame under a *theodolite* which carries the three *foot screws* below it.

trickling filter or **bacteria bed** or **biological filter** or **contact bed** or **continuous filter** or **percolating filter** [sewage] A bed of filter medium such as rock, clinker, blast-furnace slag or specially made plastics units, which exposes *sewage* effluent to the air and thus to the action of micro-organisms that oxidize it. In types with a *dosing tank* the flow is intermittent. It is not a filter in the sense of a *graded filter* or a *sand filter*.

Trief process A method of making *Portland blast-furnace cement* by grinding the slag wet at the site and there mixing it with the cement.

trigonometrical station [sur.] or **trig station** A survey station used for large-scale *triangulation*.

trigonometrical survey A survey based on a *triangulation*.

trilateration [sur.] Measurement of all the sides of a network of triangles, usually by *electronic length-measuring instruments*, a method of establishing accurate survey points that has superseded *triangulation*, at least for large-scale work. *First order trilaterations* have longer sides than second or third order ones.

trimmers [min.] *See* **rib holes.**

trimming (1) The final tidying up of an earthwork surface.

(2) Framing round or otherwise strengthening an opening through a floor, roof, or wall, whether of timber or other material. *See* (*B*).

trinitrotoluene or **TNT** A high explosive which produces considerable quantities of carbon monoxide, but it can be used for dry holes in civil engineering, in large quarry blasts in headings, or in *chambering*. *See* **detonating fuse.**

trip coil [elec.] A *solenoid*-operated device for opening a *circuit breaker* or other *protective equipment*.

tripod [sur.] A three-legged support (with telescopic legs if used underground) for a surveying instrument.

trommel A *rotary screen*.

troughing or **trough sections** *Rolled-steel sections* shaped like a broad U and riveted or welded together in *bridge decks* or other heavy floors with the U alternately upwards and downwards. Troughing is often covered with a concrete slab for which it acts as the permanent formwork.

trough sections *See* **troughing.**

truck mixer, transit mixer A large concrete mixer permanently built on to a lorry, to carry *ready-mixed concrete* from the *batching plant* to the point of use. It is possible on some types to withhold some of the water until the site is reached. The smallest truck mixer carries 3 cu. m of concrete.

truck-mounted crane A *mobile crane*.

truck-mounted drilling rig or **earth borer** A mechanical *auger* mounted on a lorry. It can drill holes for *bored piles* or small shafts 0·76 m dia. to 6 m depth in 10 minutes, and sometimes of larger diameter. This is many times faster than *shell-and-auger boring* by two or three men with a three-pole derrick.

true bearing [sur.] The horizontal angle between any survey line and the true north. *See* **bearing.**

true meridian [sur.] The geographical north–south plane, not the magnetic meridian.

true section [d.o.] A cross-section drawn with the same vertical and horizontal scales.

true-to-scale print [d.o.] A *contact print* made with black ink lines on tracing or opaque paper or cloth. It is generally a print of the best quality but may need more than the few minutes required for *blueprints* or dyelines.

trunk sewer, trunk main A large *sewer* or *main*.

trunnion axis [sur.] The horizontal axis of rotation of a *theodolite* telescope.

truss [stru.] A frame, generally nowadays of steel (but also sometimes of timber, concrete, or *light alloy*), to carry a roof or bridge, built up wholly from members in tension and compression. It is generally a *perfect frame* or nearly so and may be *pin jointed*. There is usually some fixity at the joints which is not taken into consideration in the calculations but adds to the stiffness of the frame. *See* (*B*).

trussed arch [stru.] A steel arch built of rolled-steel sections like the *Sydney Harbour* or *Kill Van Kull bridges*.

trussed beam [stru.] A timber or other beam stiffened to reduce its deflection by a steel tie-rod (camber rod), which is held at a short distance from the beam by struts.

tsunami [hyd.] A seismically generated wave of great destructive force, known in the north Pacific around Japan.

tubbing [min.] A cast-iron lining for circular tunnels or shafts, built up from segments of a circle, flanged and drilled for bolting together. One set of segments (360°) is called a *ring*.

tube (1) [stru.] A steel or light-alloy pipe used in welded construction to form lightweight trusses. *See* **tubular sections**.

(2) A concrete pipe of any diameter with joints within its thickness.

(3) *See below*.

tube à manchette [s.m.] A perforated tube, with rubber sleeves (manchettes) covering the holes, inserted into a borehole to be grouted. When the grout pressure in the pipe increases the sleeves expand and release the *grout*. The hole in the ground is about 10 cm dia. and the tube à manchette is rather smaller, about 8 cm. The first grout injected is of plastic consistency. A second tube, of 2 cm dia., is then introduced for the fluid grout injection. This tube has *packers* each side (above and below) of the chosen grout outlet, which by their position select the release hole in the tube à manchette. In passing through the sleeve the grout breaks through the plastic grout and into the surrounding ground. The plastic grout prevents vertical leakages and the exact point of injection can be chosen, leading to high economy in grouting materials and time of grouting.

tube railway An underground electric railway running in a cylindrical tunnel, excavated by mining, not *cut-and-cover* methods. In London each tunnel of 3·66 m dia. is occupied by one track. The tunnels are driven in pairs using the *Greathead shield*, and are lined with cast-iron *rings*.

tubular sections or **hollow sections** Steel tubes, rectangular, square, or circular, which are strictly speaking not *rolled-steel sections* though they are manufactured hot and, for design purposes, are treated by the structural designer in the same way. The smallest sizes, up to about 125×50 mm, are made by the welding together of two plates bent to a channel shape. Larger sizes than this are made as seamless tubes, a process rather more laborious and expensive than rolling. These sections are obtainable in Britain up to 460 mm outside dia. and 19 mm wall thickness, or 250×250 mm or 304×203 to 12 mm wall thickness. Such massive sections can be extremely useful as struts or beams. They are easily painted to protect them from rust, and the inner surfaces do not rust at all if the ends are sealed. Light alloy sections of these shapes are generally referred to as *extruded sections*.

tucking board A narrow horizontal board in a *tucking frame*, the thickness of the *poling boards*, placed on edge horizontally over the top of one *setting*, behind the waling to ensure that the upper setting of poling boards is held by the *waling*.

tucking frame or **middling frame** or **poling frame** A *frame* in timbering, in which *walings* support *poling boards* at their top and bottom ends.

tungsten carbide [mech.] A very hard material which may be brazed with an oxy-acetylene flame in a cobalt *matrix* on to the cutting edge of a *core barrel*, *fishtail bit*, or other boring tool. *See* cemented carbides.

tunnel An underground passage, open to daylight at both ends. If open at only one end it is a *drift* or *adit*. The London underground railways are probably the world's largest underground network and include tunnels 30 km long; but one of the world's longest tunnels in 1973, completed in that year, was the Orange-Fish tunnel, South Africa. Of 5·35 m finished diameter, with a concrete lining 23 cm thick, it is 82 km long. It irrigates the semi-arid Great Fish River valley in the eastern Cape Province, with water from the Orange River.

tunnelling speed Tunnelling in London clay with the Price *rotary excavator* a steady advance of 213 m per month was kept up in a 3·66 m dia. shield-driven tunnel. In tunnels where blasting is required, a 1956 hydroelectric contract in Scotland achieved a record of 244 m per week. In USA several mole excavators have exceeded 500 metres per week.

tunnel lining The covering over the rock or soil of a tunnel to prevent it falling in or to reduce the friction of the fluid which will pass through it. The commonest linings are timber (temporary), concrete cast-in-place, *gunited* mortar, cast-iron *rings*, precast concrete segments developed from them, and the oldest type, brickwork or masonry. In USA recently *steel ring* segments have been used.

tunnel vault *See* barrel vault.

tup A *drop hammer*.

turbidity current [hyd.] *See* density current.

turbine [mech.] A rotating *prime mover* driven by water, gas, or high-pressure steam, often used for driving an electric generator. *See* steam/water turbine.

turbo-drill [min.] An oil-well drilling machine designed by the Russians to overcome some of the difficulties of *rotary drilling* at depths below 3 km. All types operate as turbines driven by *drilling flluid* pumped down from the surface at high pressure. By the 1970s however they were developing in a quite opposite direction from this. Turbines of small diameter were being used for short *directional* holes at the surface, and in hard rock where the support of drilling fluid was not needed, they were air driven. The Dyna-drill is made 4·5 cm dia., to drill a hole of 7·6 or 9 cm dia.

turbulence [hyd.] A state of flow in which the liquid is distuıbed by eddies. *See below*.

turbulent flow [hyd.] or **eddy/sinuous/tortuous flow** Flow at a speed above the *critical velocity* of Reynolds. Flow in this state is the opposite of *streamline flow* and is unsteady and eddying.

turfing The covering of an earth surface with growing grass cut from another site. It can also be a *revetment* to slopes which are usually covered by water, made by laying turves on the slope according to a technique like *sliced blockwork*.

turn bridge [stru.] A *swing bridge*.

turn buckle [stru.] A *screw shackle*.

turned bolt or **tight-fitting bolt** or **bright bolt** A bolt used in steel-to-steel connections, turned on a lathe to reduce it to a truly circular shape of exact dimension. The thread (and the nut) are of the same nominal dia., *d*, as for a *black bolt* but the unthreaded part (barrel or shank) is appreciably larger ($d+1\cdot5$ mm). The hole dia. as for a black bolt is $d+1\cdot6$ mm and the shank clearance is therefore only 0·1 mm. The shank is therefore a tight fit in the hole and for this reason these bolts are allowed to carry 20% more load than a black bolt or rivet. Because of the exorbitant labour expense in reaming each hole to exact size, they are obsolete and have been replaced by *high-strength friction-grip bolts*.

turning point [sur.] A *change point*, or *station*.

turnout (1) [rly] A junction between one track and another leading off it including the *points* and any accessories.

(2) [hyd.] A junction from an irrigation canal to a subsidiary canal taking water from it. It may be a wooden box for a small turnout or a glazed stoneware or concrete channel for larger ones.

turntable [rly] A round platform pivoted at its centre. Locomotives are run on to it and sent off in the reverse direction or on to another line as required.

twin-cable ropeway or **tramway** An *aerial ropeway* with carriers running on parallel track cables in opposite directions, both rows of carriers being pulled by the same *traction rope*. The track cables are two heavy, stationary, often *locked-coil ropes*, anchored at one end and tensioned by weights at the other, usually carried on opposite sides of the same towers.

twist *See* torque.

two-hinged arch or **two-pinned arch** A *rigid frame* which may be arch-shaped or rectangular but is hinged at both supports.

two-leg sling A *sling* made of two chains or ropes hanging from one *thimble* or link, and each having one hook at its lower end.

two-part sealant *See* polysulphide sealant.

two-pinned arch A *two-hinged arch*.

two-stage compression [mech.] Air compression in two stages, usual for pressures above 4 bars or horsepowers above 100. Two-stage compression with an *intercooler* is usual when compressing air for rock drilling. *Compare* four-stage compression.

two-way grid [stru.] A *space frame*, a *grid* (3). *See* double-layer grid.

U

ultimate bearing capacity of a pile The ultimate bearing capacity of a pile, according to BSCP 2004:1972, is the load that causes it to settle one tenth of its diameter, unless some other definition be found from the load/settlement curve. This is sometimes determined by the CRP (constant rate of penetration) test, conveniently by jacking down from a beam connected to two anchor piles. The pile, if in clay, is jacked down at 0·75 mm per minute, or if in sand or gravel at double this rate. The maximum force on the graph (before it begins to decrease) is the ultimate bearing capacity. If no maximum is reached, the force at a penetration equal to one tenth of the pile diameter can be taken as its ultimate bearing capacity. Another value for the ultimate bearing capacity can be found from *Hiley's formula*. For a single pile, a factor of safety of 2 or 3 should be applied to the ultimate bearing capacity, to give the safe load.

ultimate bearing pressure The pressure at which a foundation sinks without increase of load. In *plate bearing tests* the ultimate bearing pressure is taken as that pressure all over the plate at which the settlement amounts to one fifth of the plate width.

ultimate compressive strength [stru.] The stress at which a material crushes, the usual way of defining the strength of a brick, stone, or concrete.

ultimate strength [stru.] or **breaking strength** The highest stress (of any sort) which a material can withstand before breaking.

ultimate tensile strength/stress [stru.] The load at which a specimen breaks, divided by its original area (before breaking). It is usually called the ultimate strength, or tensile strength. *See* **Brinell hardness test.**

ultra-filtration The use of ultra-fine filters to strain out particles smaller than 10 microns, sometimes as small as 0·002 micron. To prevent the upstream side of the filter from being blocked with material that cannot pass, it is constantly washed by the incoming stream, so that the main downstream water contains slightly more solids than upstream. What passes through the filter is almost pure water, with most of the dissolved salts removed. The method can therefore be used for *de-salination*.

ultra-high-early-strength cement A *cement* of composition similar to *ordinary Portland cement*, but much more finely ground even than *rapid-hardening cement*, so that very high early strength can be obtained without additives. It is not always available in UK.

ultrasonic flow meter [hyd.] Equipment for measuring the flow in a river or stream, which, unlike *measuring weirs*, can be used in a navigable channel. There are two transmitter-receivers, on different banks, one appreciably downstream of the other, and located at about 0·6 of the depth from the surface, at the level of the average flow rate. Electronic circuitry determines the frequency of the pulses received, those downstream being at a lower frequency than those in the upstream receiver. From the difference in the frequencies the flow rate can be determined, since the ultrasonic pulse velocity is known. This use of the *Doppler shift* has been practised also in an analogous method, the laser Doppler anemometer for measuring air flow.

ultrasonic pulse attenuation *Non-destructive* measurement of the viscous rather than the elastic properties of concrete. Strong concretes have high pulse velocity and low pulse attenuation (damping) properties.

ultrasonic testing Two methods of non-destructive testing (ultrasonic pulse velocity and *ultrasonic pulse attenuation*) are used for determining the strength of concrete and other materials. In the velocity method a pulse of longitudinal vibrations, transmitted by an electro-acoustical *transducer* held on to the concrete, is received by a second transducer or probe, and its speed through the concrete is electronically measured. Ultrasonic frequencies are used so as to obtain a pulse with a sharp onset and to generate maximum energy in the direction of the pulse. The velocity increases as the concrete quality improves. This method is often used in conjunction with the *rebound hammer*. It can also be used to determine the presence of defects. The relation between strength and velocity is very complex, and varies with the cement and aggregate content and type, the maturity and the curing of the concrete. Sound can be heard at frequencies up to about 20,000 cycles/sec. but it becomes inaudible at higher (ultrasonic) frequencies. Testing frequencies for concrete are between 20,000 and 150,000 cycles/sec. and for other materials may be up to 20 million cycles/sec.

unconfined compression test [s.m.] A crushing test on a soil sample which is carried out without lateral restraint. (*See* **triaxial compression test**.) Half the unconfined compressive strength of a clay is generally equal to its *cohesion* or shear strength. The test can be carried out on a clay sample 76 mm long, 38 mm dia. at the borehole with portable apparatus. It is of little use for clean sands or gravels, but extremely useful for cohesive soils.

unconfined water *Groundwater* that is overlain by air-filled, therefore unsaturated ground, unlike *confined water*.

underflow (1) [hyd.] Movement of water

in the soil, under ice, or under a structure.

(2) [s.m.] The oversize material of a *classifier*.

underground railway A railway laid wholly or mostly below street level. *See* **cut-and-cover, tube railway.**

underpin To provide new, deeper support under a wall or column without removing the superstructure, so as to allow the load on the building to be increased, or to allow the ground inside or outside it to be lowered, or to prevent settlement of the foundation. It is the construction of foundations for a building which exists. *See* **pretesting, dry pack.**

underplanting A contract on which the machinery is overloaded is said to be underplanted. Similarly, one where the machinery has not enough work to do is overplanted.

under-reaming The widening out of the foot of a *bored pile* or of a foundation pier such as the *Gow caisson* to increase its area or to give an anchorage against lifting by wind or in *permafrost* regions. *See* **reamer.**

undersize [s.m.] *See* **classifier.**

undisturbed sample [s.m.] A sample of cohesive soil from a borehole or trial pit which has been *remoulded* so little that it can be used for laboratory measurements of its strength without serious errors. Generally a *soil sampler* is driven into the ground, turned through 360° to shear the core at the foot of the tube, extracted from the borehole with the sample within it, filled with paraffin wax, covered with screw caps, and sent to the laboratory for testing. Cores may also be tested at the site with the *unconfined compression* apparatus.

undrained shear test [s.m.] A *quick test* or *consolidated quick test*.

unequal angle An *angle section* in which the two legs are of unequal length. *Compare* **equal angle.**

uniformity coefficient [s.m.] *See* **coefficient of uniformity.**

uniform sand [s.m.] A sand, most of

whose particles are of uniform size. It has a steep *grading curve*, that is it is not a *graded sand*.

unit hydrograph, unit graph [hyd.] A method of deducing storm flows that has superseded the *Lloyd-Davies* or 'rational' formula with its unjustified assumptions that rainfall is of constant intensity in both time and space and that the catchment area has uniform *permeability* also in time and space. The unit graph shows, for a particular basin, the time-varying flows from 1 inch (25 mm) of rainfall over it. The time bases of floods from storms of equal duration are the same, therefore the unit graph can be deduced from another of the same duration but different rainfall on the basin. Unit graphs are useful for forecasting peak flows. If possible, one should be obtained for each duration of storm.

unit stress [mech.] Expression used in USA for *stress*.

unit weight The weight of unit volume of material, its *density*.

universal beam [stru.] A standard shape of *rsj*, many of which, formerly, were known as broad-flanged beams. They are also used as stanchions.

universal motor [elec.] A motor which is usually of less than 1 horsepower and can work on alternating or direct current.

unstable A description of a structure which lacks *stability*.

unstable frame [stru.] A frame which contains too few members or too little fixity to be a *perfect frame*.

upending test *See* dump test.

uplift (1) [hyd.] An upward force on earth due to water leaking into a dam or from any point where water is under high pressure. Uplift pressure of water may cause fine sands to become *quicksands*. Uplift of this sort can be prevented by draining the water or sealing the leaks. *See* flow net.

(2) [stru.] Lifting of a structure caused by (1) or by *frost heave* or, on the windward side, by wind force, or in a dry climate by *swelling soil*. *See* under-reaming.

upper transit [sur.] The upper *culmination* of a star or the sun.

upsetting [mech.] or **setting up** Increasing the diameter of a red-hot steel bar by striking it on the end. This is sometimes done for that part of a bar which is threaded, to ensure that the threaded part stands above the rest of the bar and that the thread does not weaken it. It is not usual for short bars but may save an appreciable amount of steel in long tie-rods. Hot steel *rivets* are upset in the hole which they fill when they are struck on the head by hammer blows.

V

vacuum concrete Concrete poured into formwork fitted with a *vacuum mat*. The vacuum mat sucks out surplus air and water from the concrete and produces a dense, well-shrunk concrete from which the forms can be removed for walls and other vertical faces in 30 minutes after the beginning of processing. The concrete reaches its normal 28-day strength in 10 days and has a 25 % higher crushing strength although it can be placed in a really workable, sometimes sloppy condition. Savings in cement and formwork can thus be appreciable.

vacuum lifting The raising by crane hook and sling of concrete slabs cast on the ground, through a suction attachment to the sling. The suction attachment works like a *vacuum mat* and therefore has a lift equal to about 100 kN (10 tons) for each sq. metre in contact with the slab.

vacuum mat A stiff flat metal screen faced by a linen filtering fabric, the back of which can be kept under a partial vacuum by a vacuum pump connected to it through a hose. It is used in making *vacuum concrete*. The linen filter makes a flat smooth surface and can be replaced by a patterned material when the surface to be processed requires it. A 7-hp motor is required for keeping up the vacuum of a 3·66 m square panel of vacuum mat. *See also* **vacuum lifting**.

vacuum method [s.m.] *See* **groundwater lowering**.

vacuum method of testing sands [s.m.] A method of *triaxial* testing of a sand sample by maintaining a partial vacuum in the rubber tube containing the sample. The outside of the tube is under atmospheric pressure. The resultant pressure on the tube is thus equal to the difference between the two pressures.

vacuum pad A *suction pad*.

vacuum pump [mech.] or **air pump** A pump which extracts steam or air from a space so as to maintain it at a pressure below atmospheric. The vacuum is usually measured in millimetres of mercury below atmospheric, the maximum being about 740 mm. Such pumps are needed for all the vacuum processes listed above and for the condensers of steam turbines.

vadose water [s.m.] (1) Underground water above the standing water level.
(2) American term for what is called in Britain *held water*.

vadose zone or **zone of aeration** The ground above the *water table*. In deserts it may be 500 m thick.

valve [mech.] A device to open or close a flow completely (stop valve) or to regulate a flow (discharge valve).

valve tower [hyd.] A tower built up from the bed of a reservoir. From it the control valves of the pipes which draw off water at different levels are operated. It may be of cast iron, stone, or concrete.

vanadium [mech.] The hardest known metal. It is used for making very strong alloy steels with chromium or manganese. These alloy steels contain from 0·2 to 1 % of vanadium.

vane test [s.m.] A four-bladed vane is inserted into a soil at the foot of a *borehole*. It is rotated by a rod at the surface with a measured force until the soil shears. This *in-situ soil test* gives shear strengths that have been found to give consistent results down to 30 m depth except in *stiff-fissured clays*.

vapour pressure or **vapour tension** The saturated vapour pressure of a liquid is the pressure at any given temperature exerted by the vapour above the liquid. When the vapour is not in contact with its liquid the vapour pressure is usually less than the saturated vapour pressure unless condensation is occurring (dew is falling). The saturated vapour pressure increases as the temperature rises. *See* **saturated air.**

vapour tension *Vapour pressure.*

variance [stat.] The square of the *standard deviation*. It is the average of the squares of the deviations of all the observations.

variation [sur.] *See* **magnetic variation.**

V.-B. consistometer test A British standard alternative to the *compacting factor* test for the *workability* of concrete, as well as its *slump.* A non-corroding metal cylinder, 20 cm high, of 24 cm bore, contains a strong conical mould 20 cm dia. at the foot and 10 cm at the top, 30 cm high, which is filled with concrete. The mould is lifted and the concrete subsides into the 24 cm dia. cylinder. A transparent, slightly weighted disc is lowered gently on to the concrete and the *slump* is measured. A vibrator is switched on until the whole lower surface of the disc is seen to be covered with cement grout. Measured by stopwatch, this time is considered to be that of full compaction. It is therefore a measure of the concrete workability, described in 'V.-B. seconds' (BS 1881:1970).

V-cut *See* **wedge cut.**

vee notch [hyd.] *See* **triangular notch.**

vel A unit of size, abbreviated from 'velocity in an air elutriator'. The vel is a measure of the size of an air-transported particle. Thus a particle of x vel in size has a maximum free-falling velocity in air of x cm/sec. With 20 cm/sec. free-falling velocity, (particles 20 vel in size) coal particles are below 76 microns (0·076 mm).

velocities in pipes [mech.] Normal allowable velocities in pipes for different fluids are as follows in m per second. Air 9 to 15, compressed air 7 to 12, steam 50 to 75, water 1·5 to 3.

velocity head [hyd.] or **kinetic head** The energy per unit weight of water due to its velocity (v). It is equal to $\dfrac{v^2}{2g}$ kg-m per kg where v is in m per second and g is 9·81 m per second each second. The numerical result in kg-m per kg, if written in metres, is also equal to the vertical distance the fluid must fall freely under gravity to reach its velocity v.

velocity of approach [hyd.] The mean velocity in the channel of a *measuring weir* at the point where the depth over the weir is measured.

velocity of retreat [hyd.] The mean velocity immediately downstream from the *measuring weir.*

velocity ratio [mech.] The distance through which the force applied to a *machine* moves, divided by the distance moved by the load. *See* **mechanical advantage.**

vena contracta [hyd.] The narrowest point in the cross-section of a *nappe* or jet beyond the plane of the weir or hole from which it issues. The stream lines converge towards this point and diverge away from it. At this point they are therefore parallel.

Venturi flume [hyd.] A *control* flume consisting of a short contraction followed by an expansion to normal width. The difference in level of the surface of the water gives a measure of the flow. *See* **Parshall measuring flume.**

Venturi meter [hyd.] or **Venturi tube** A *flow meter* for closed pipes in which there is a constriction (throat) followed by an expansion to normal width. The pressure is measured at the throat where the pressure is reduced and upstream where the width is normal, small pipes leading to gauges from these points. The quantity flowing is related to the pressure difference between these points. This meter can be made into a *water meter.*

Venturi tube *See* **Venturi meter.**

verge or **margin** The unpaved ground beside a road at or near road level, often of rough grass, but forming part of the legal highway. *See also* (*B*).

Verrazano Narrows Bridge A *suspension bridge* New York City, with 6 lanes and 2 decks. Its main span of 1298 m was the largest in the world, when it was opened on 21 November 1964. *See* **Akashi-Kaikyo Bridge, Humber Bridge.**

vertex *See* **crown.**

vertical alignment *See* **longitudinal profile.**

vertical circle [sur.] The metal or glass ring graduated in degrees and fractions of a degree, which shows the angle of slope of the telescope on a *theodolite*.

vertical control [sur.] Connecting a survey with *bench marks* that are well within the accuracy required for the survey.

vertical curve Between two lengths of a road or railway which are at different slopes, a curve is inserted. It is concave upwards at the foot of a hill or convex upwards at the summit. It provides a gradual change from one slope to the other.

vertical interval *See* **contour interval.**

vertical photograph [air sur.] A photograph of the ground taken from the air with a camera pointing vertically down. This is the usual photograph from which *mosaics* are built up. Generally the photographs are taken with the pilot travelling along a strip at a *timing* calculated to give 60% lap between each photograph and its neighbours in the same strip. Neighbouring strips also overlap but only by 30%. *Compare* **oblique photograph,** *see* **plotting instrument, collimation mark.**

vertical sand drain [s.m.] A boring through a clay or silty soil, filled with sand or gravel to enable the soil to drain more easily. Its special purpose is to accelerate the *consolidation* of a loaded cohesive soil. Owing to the low *permeability* of clays, their consolidation is slow since it depends only on the removal of water. Sand drains accelerate the drainage of a clay loaded by an earth dam or other heavy weight if their spacing is appre-

ciably less than the thickness of the clay. They do not need to reach a permeable soil below the clay, but it is preferable that they should do. Sandwicks, developed by Cementation Ground Engineering Ltd, ensure continuity of the sand plug and consequently of the drainage and enable the drainage holes to be small without risk. They are tubes woven from polypropylene, which is permeable to air and water, able to hold sand without loss or breakage, and filled with selected sand before insertion into the hole.

viaduct A road or railway bridge over a valley. Like an *aqueduct* it consists of a series of spans carried on piers at short intervals. The ancient Pont du Gard in the South of France combines aqueduct and viaduct, although the aqueduct is not now used.

vial [sur.] A *level tube* or a circular bubble.

vibrated concrete *Concrete* compacted by vibration from an *internal* or external *vibrator*. It requires very much less water for effective placing than does concrete compacted by punning, therefore it is much stronger. The *formwork*, however, must also be stronger when the concrete is to be vibrated. Concrete in *hollow-tile floors* is not vibrated.

vibrating pile-driver (In USA **sonic pile-driver.**) A *pile-driver* which originated in USSR and was used on a large scale at the Gorki hydroelectric scheme in 1949, probably for the first time. One type of vibrator has two powerful electric motors rotating in opposite directions, mounted on top of the pile to be driven, which may be a sheet pile or a bearing pile. In appropriate soil they are both silent and rapid, because of the acceleration, about 12 times gravity, imparted by the vibrator. The principle of vibration is also used in *pipe-pushing*, and in extracting piles or pipe.

vibrating plate A unit handled by one man, which is suitable for *compaction* of soil in a confined space. The vibration of the horizontal plate, some 1 by 1·5 m or larger, fluidizes the soil beneath, enabling the operator to push the plate in any direction.

vibrating roller A self-propelled or towed *roller* with a mechanically vibrated roll. *See* **compaction.**

vibration of foundations [stru.] Heavy or powerful machines permanently installed in a building should have foundations designed to be of such mass and shape that the machine frequency is $1\frac{1}{2}$ to 2 times the natural frequency of the combined system of foundation and machine. In any ground a smaller difference than this is undesirable, but in sand or gravel it is dangerous and may lead to rapid compaction of the subsoil and settlement of the machine foundation. *See* **resonance.**

vibrator A tool which vibrates at a speed from 3000 to 10,000 rpm and is inserted into wet concrete or applied to the formwork to compact the concrete. Concrete vibrators are of six types. For precast work, (1) platform vibrators, small vibrators carried by one or two men moving up and down a pile or lamp post; (2) table vibrators, which may vibrate vertically for heavy work or with rotary movement for light pieces. For concretes cast in place, (3) *internal vibrators* are the best known type, (4) *external vibrators* are used more in the factory than on the site because of the extra strength required for the formwork. For road slabs (5) a hand screed 3·7 m long requires one vibrator, for greater lengths two vibrators are fixed on the screed. For very large capacities (6) *concrete-vibrating machines* are used. (7) [s.m.] Vibrators are also used for the compaction of loose soils; *see below, and* **vibrating plate.**

Vibroflot or **vibroflotation** or **vibro-replacement** A *geotechnical* process for compacting clean sands or gravels. A vibrating cylinder 38 cm dia., 2 m long with water or air jets at both ends is lowered into the ground by a crane. Its vibrations and the lower water jet allow it to sink easily and to compact the surrounding soil. The upper jets enable it to be withdrawn easily. The compaction obtained can be seen at the surface by the size of the crater produced; it may be 2·4 m dia. The process works best with clean sand but soft silt or clay can also be compacted. The crater is filled with clean gravel or coarse sand to the original level and re-vibrated until a strong, thick column of gravel is formed to the required depth for use as a foundation. *Sand piles* treat the same sort of soil but by impact rather than vibration.

Vicat needle An apparatus for measuring the setting time of a cement by the pressure of a special needle against the cement surface.

Vickers hardness test [mech.] A hardness test used for testing very thin hard *cases* by the *diamond pyramid*, or for softer materials with a hard steel ball. The indentations are measured by a low-power microscope.

Vierendeel girder [stru.] or **open-frame girder** A *Pratt truss* without the diagonal members and with rigid joints between top and bottom chords and the verticals. Many welded steel or reinforced-concrete trusses have been built in this way in Belgium and they are named after Prof. Vierendeel of that country. They are convenient to use when diagonal members would be obstructive, as for instance in stiffening a *buoyant raft* between basement level and ground or first floor.

Vignoles rail [rly] A *flat-bottomed rail.*

virtual slope [hyd.] The *hydraulic gradient.* It shows the loss in pressure per unit length due to friction.

viscometer or **viscosimeter** An instrument for measuring viscosity, which estimates the gel strength of a *drilling fluid* by measuring the viscosity during flow and after it has been standing for some minutes. *See* **thixotropy.**

viscosity [hyd.] The resistance of a fluid

to flow. It is equal to the tangential force per unit of area required to maintain unit relative velocity between two parallel planes at unit spacing.

viscous flow [hyd.] Another description of *streamline flow*.

visibility distance or **sight distance** The distance for which an object is visible to an observer, both at the same height above the road, sometimes specified as 1·5 m.

visible horizon *See* **sensible horizon**.

voided slab or **cored slab** [stru.] A slab resembling a *hollow-tile floor*, in which the hollow clay blocks are replaced by blocks of foamed polystyrene or other *void formers*.

void former A block of expanded polystyrene or other synthetic foam or a cardboard or sheet metal box which is placed in the tension area at the bottom of a concrete slab in the same way as the hollow tiles in a *hollow-tile floor*. Being buoyant they must be firmly held down to prevent them floating, e.g. by nailing to the deck shutter.

voids [s.m.] Spaces between separate grains of sand, gravel, or soil, occupied by air or water or both.

voids ratio [s.m.] The ratio of the volume of voids to the volume of the solids in a sample of soil or aggregate. For clays the voids ratio may need to be defined at a stated pressure, since

clay contracts with rise in pressure. *See* **critical voids ratio of sands, porosity, relative density.**

volumetric efficiency [mech.] The volume of water which leaves a pump cylinder for each piston stroke, divided by the volume swept by the piston (piston area × stroke).

volute [mech.] A spiral casing to a fan or a centrifugal pump, so shaped as to reduce gradually the speed of water or air leaving the *impeller*, transforming it into pressure without shock.

vortex shedding [stru.] A wind blowing on a chimney or suspension bridge or other exposed structure will produce, in certain conditions, vortices (eddies) on alternate sides of it. If the frequency of this vortex shedding approaches the natural frequency of vibration of the structure, the alternating buffeting will cause it to suffer dangerously large vibrations. The *Tacoma Narrows Bridge* had the additional disadvantage that its period of oscillation in twisting was close to its period in bending.

voussoir arch An arrangement of wedge-shaped blocks set to form an arched bridge. After about 1910 this method was completely displaced by concrete or steel bridges, which were both cheaper and lighter in weight, until 1964, when the *Parramatta Bridge* was completed.

W

waffle floor [stru.] A concrete floor slab with deep, square recesses in the soffit. The recesses lighten the slab by removing concrete which adds no strength. It spans in two directions and is suitable for large spans.

wagon drill A *rock drill* mounted vertically on a three- or four-wheeled wagon with steel or rubber tyres. It is used for drilling large or small dia. holes in quarrying and can drill 12 m deep or more.

wagon retarder [rly] *See* **retarder** (2).

wagon vault *See* **barrel vault**.

wake [hyd.] Recurring eddies downstream of an obstacle.

waling (In USA **wale**) A horizontal beam usually of wood or steel or reinforced concrete, which supports *poling boards*, runners or *sheet piles* or the earth next to an excavation, and is held in place by horizontal struts (called *braces* in USA).

walking dragline A *dragline* of very large capacity, which is built with moving feet instead of with *crawler tracks*. While working it is seated on discs of about 6 m dia. on which the ground pressure is about 0·035 MN/m² instead of the 0·17 MN/m² which would be needed under tracks. These machines cannot be used as shovels.

walking ganger A travelling *ganger*, one who supervises the work of several gangs and is thus not a working ganger.

wall friction Friction between the back of a retaining wall and the retained soil. It generally improves the stability of the wall.

Warren girder [stru.] A triangulated truss consisting of sloping members between horizontal top and bottom members and without verticals. *Compare* **Pratt truss**.

wash boring Sinking a *casing* or *drive pipe* to bedrock by a jet of water within it.

It is used for casing off loose ground before *diamond drilling* starts in the solid, but not for getting reliable soil samples.

washer [mech.] A steel ring placed under a bolt head or nut to distribute the pressure, particularly when the bolt passes through timber. The washer prevents the timber crushing. *See* **bevelled washer**.

washland [hyd.] Land enclosed between a river and a flood embankment which may be 1 or 2 km away and 40 km long. The washland both holds the water and allows it to flow.

washout valve [hyd.] A *scouring sluice*.

waste or **spoil** The excess of excavation over fill – building or mining rubbish.

wasteway [hyd.] or **waste weir** A *spillway*.

water authority In 1974, the ten newly created water authorities of England and Wales took over from local authorities their responsibilities for *water supply*, *sewerage*, *sewage treatment* and land drainage followed in Scotland by the *river purification boards* in 1975.

waterbar A jointing strip made of galvanized steel, lead, copper, rubber, bituminous material, plastics (PVC), or other material, inserted into plastic concrete or mortar so as to exclude water after the concrete has hardened. The waterbar may cross an expansion joint and be cast into the pieces both sides of the joint, but this would not be done with rigid waterbars, only with rubbery ones.

water-bearing ground Ground below the *standing-water level*.

waterbound macadam A road surface of gravel or broken stone made by watering clay or sand or *hoggin* into the gaps between stones.

water/cement ratio The weight of water divided by the weight of cement in a *concrete* or mortar. The lower the water/cement ratio, the stronger is the concrete. *See* **Abrams' law.**

water content [s.m.] *See* **moisture content.** (For timber *see* (*B.*))

water cushion [hyd.] A *stilling pool.*

water cycle The *hydrological cycle.*

water-filled structure [stru.] A steel frame containing water in its hollow columns, and sometimes also in the beams, to prevent them weakening in case of fire and so to eliminate the need for clumsy-looking but fire-protective cover outside the steel. One spectacular example is the United States Steel Corporation building in Pittsburgh, containing nearly 2000 tons of water in its columns. Similar buildings exist in France and Britain.

water gauge [min.] A vertical U-tube containing water, used for measuring the pressure difference caused by the mine fan or between the two sides of an air door. 60 cm of water gauge is equal to about 67 millibars pressure.

water hammer [hyd.] Any sudden very high pressure in a pipe caused by stopping the flow too rapidly. *Surge tanks*, *stand pipes*, or relief valves are provided on large pressure-pipes to relieve them of this pressure which might burst them. The *hydraulic ram* works by water hammer.

water-jet driving *Jetting.*

water lowering *Groundwater lowering.*

water meter [hyd.] An instrument which indicates the quantity of water which has flowed through a pipe. It is an integrating *flow meter.*

water of capillarity [s.m.] Water above the *standing-water level*, but in close contact with it.

water pollution control *Sewage treatment.*

waterproofing *Tanking* (*B*), applying a *damp-proof course* (*B*) or *cavity tanking*, etc.

waterproof membrane [s.m.] *See* **flexible membrane, tanking** (*B*).

water reducer A *plasticizer.*

water-repellent or **hydrophobic cement** *Ordinary Portland cement* with stear-

rates mixed in, often used in screeds and renderings. It is occasionally used also when a cement is needed that has to keep longer than usual in the bag without becoming lumpy. Water-repellent white cement keeps white longer than other cements used in concrete or mortar.

water requirement [hyd.] The amount of water from all sources required by a crop for its growth and maturity.

watershed [hyd.] (1) or **water parting** (in USA a **divide**) The summit and dividing line between two *catchment areas*, from which water flows away in two directions.

(2) In USA the term watershed may mean a catchment area.

water supply [hyd.] The *impounding*, treatment, pumping and piping of drinking water for customers by a public authority. In Britain *water authorities* have existed only since 1974, but several private water companies happily co-exist with them. The Water Act of 1973 reorganized the water supply and sewage disposal industries of England and Wales, as well as flood control and drainage of land generally. *See* **waterworks.**

water table [s.m.] or **saturation line** The surface, which may be undulating, of the *standing-water level. Compare* **perched water table.** It is important in *earth dams* that the saturation line does not reach the surface of the dam. For this reason a *graded filter* is often provided at the toe of the dam. The water table is the boundary between the zone of saturation below it and the zone of aeration above it. *See* **groundwater lowering.**

water test The *hydraulic test* for drains.

water treatment [hyd.] *Waterworks* processes that make water drinkable, including water softening to make it suitable for washing or for use in steam boilers. Iron also needs to be removed since it colours the water.

water-tube boiler [mech.] A steam boiler in which the water and steam pass through tubes in the furnace. It is very much larger and more efficient than the *fire-tube boiler*.

water turbine [mech.] A wheel turned by the force of water, a development from the *water wheel* which was generally not of high power nor very efficient. Turbines now made attain 500,000 hp. The main types used are the *Pelton wheel* for high heads, and the *Francis turbine* for low to medium heads, modified in USA as the *Kaplan turbine*. The main difference between the Pelton wheel (impulse turbine) and the Francis type (reaction turbine) is in the very high speed of the Pelton jet. The Pelton jet gives its energy to the wheel and the wheel is not wholly surrounded by water but partly by air. *Reaction turbines* are not acted upon by a jet but by relatively slowly moving water at high pressure which completely surrounds the wheel and forces it round. *See* **specific speed.**

water wheel A wheel turned by the force of flowing water. It was the successor to the *treadmill* (*B*) and some water wheels were shaped like it. The term is now reserved for overshot and undershot wheels but it could logically be used for the much more powerful and efficient modern *water turbines*.

waterworks A site at which *raw water* is treated and sent out as a *water supply*. Treatment usually includes *screening*, *coagulation*, *flocculation*, *clarification*, *filtration* and *disinfection*, in that order. Although waterworks are now an essential part of life in the UK, it should be remembered that as their output increases, so does the volume of sewage. Therefore if sewage treatment plants do not increase their throughput more rapidly than waterworks, the amount of sewage pollution is bound to increase.

wattle work *Hurdle work*.

wave pressure The pressures on breakwaters due to waves may amount to 300 kN/m² in exposed places and only 100 kN/m² in such relatively sheltered places as the Great Lakes of North America.

wearing course or **carpet** or **road surface** or **topping** The top, visible layer of a road.

weather-resistant or **weathering steels** [stru.] Several low-alloy steels mentioned in BS 4360 'Weldable Structural Steels,' have various percentages of chromium (0·3 to 1·25%) manganese (0·6 to 1·5%), and copper (0·25 to 0·4%). Perhaps the best-known type is Cor-Ten in UK and USA. These steels rust very much more slowly than ordinary steels, but faster than *stainless steel* (*B*).

web [stru.] The vertical plate joining the flanges of a *rolled-steel* or extruded *light-alloy* joist or of a *built-up* girder or timber beam.

web stiffener [stru.] *See* **stiffener.**

wedge *See* **plug and feathers.**

wedge cut [min.] or **V-cut** or **centre cut** A layout for the *cut holes* in tunnelling or shaft sinking so that they slope towards each other like the faces of a wedge and nearly meet.

wedge theory [s.m.] Coulomb's analysis of the force tending to overturn a retaining wall (1776). He based it on the weight of the wedge of earth which would slide forward if the wall failed.

wedge-wire screen A screen made of wedge-shaped parallel wires with their wide edges uppermost. This sort of screen rarely clogs and is used for dewatering sands or grits over openings from 4 to 0·1 mm and with or without vibration.

weephole A hole to allow water to escape from behind a retaining wall and thus to reduce the pressure behind it. The water leaking through may make unsightly stains on the wall. Sometimes, therefore, weepholes are replaced by a *field drain* of ample capacity, carefully laid in coarse stone behind the wall, at the level where the weepholes would have been, to drain the water out to the end of the wall.

weigh batcher A *batching plant* for concrete in which all the ingredients of a mix are measured by weight (except water).

weighted average [stat.] An average obtained from a series of values after each value has received an appropriate 'weight'. The weight of each value is a factor by which it is multiplied, corresponding to its trustworthiness and importance. After the values have been multiplied by their weights they are added together, and then divided by the sum of the weights (not, as usual, by the sum of the values). The result is an average which takes account of the opinions of the observer about his values, and should be more reliable than a simple average.

weighted filter *See* **loaded filter.**

weighting (1) [stat.] Applying weights to observations to obtain a weighted value as for *degree days* (*B*), *weighted averages*, etc.

(2) Loading a *pneumatic caisson* with cast iron, water, or other *kentledge* to prevent it floating and make it sink.

weir [hyd.] A wall built across the full width of a stream, with a horizontal crest over which the water flows. It is built either to hold up the water, to help boats to pass through a lock, or to reduce floods, or as a *measuring weir*.

weir head [hyd.] The depth of water in a *measuring weir* measured from the weir crest or the bottom of the notch to the water surface upstream of the weir. It does not include the *velocity of approach*.

Weisbach triangle [sur.] A *set-up* at the foot of a vertical shaft during *shaft plumbing* from which both of the plumb wires can be sighted, thus forming a triangle with an angle at the *theodolite* of up to half a degree. More accurate observations of the wires can be taken in this way than with the theodolite in line with the wires. The Weisbach set-up is used for orienting the underground workings.

weld [mech.] A joint between pieces of metal or plastics at faces which have been melted or made plastic by heat or pressure or both. *Filler rods* may be used. *See* **welding**, etc.

weldability [mech.] A property of *electrode* and parent metal combined, estimated by the power to make good welds by as many processes as possible, and tested by the *longitudinal bead test*. Its opposite is *hardenability*.

welded frame [stru.] A *bent* consisting (at its simplest) of two legs and a beam joined by welding. It is architecturally attractive, saves steel, and sometimes may be cheaper than a frame of trusses and stanchions.

welding [mech.] Joining two surfaces by fusion or pressure or both, heating them by electric arc, electric *resistance welding*, or flame. Most methods of welding structural steel are *arc-welding* methods. *See also* **automatic welding, butt weld, carbon-arc/fusion/metal-arc/ plastic welding, thermit.** *Also* BS 499, Glossary of terms for welding and cutting of metals.

welding thermit [mech.] *See* **thermit.**

well [hyd.] (1) A shaft or borehole sunk in the ground to obtain water, oil, etc.

(2) An *absorbing well*.

(3) A *well foundation*.

well borer or **well sinker** A *skilled man* or tradesman who sinks a *shallow well* with pick and shovel, sometimes doing no timbering until he gets to the bottom. He then steens the well with bricks laid dry (or with mortar) for the full height. The work is dangerous, but sinkers make their own estimates, do their own sinking, and often work only in their own district where they understand the ground.

well-conditioned triangle [sur.] A triangle which is nearly equilateral. An error in the measurement of an angle makes the smallest error of distance in such a triangle.

well curbing or **pit boards** American term for sheeting to keep earth out of a pit.

well drain An *absorbing well*.

well foundation A foundation excavated like the *Gow* or *Chicago caissons* by sinking a pit of small diameter.

well hole A large vertical borehole, about 15 cm dia., used in quarries when blasting a heavy *burden*.

Wellington formula The *Engineering News formula* for driven piles.

well logging, borehole logging *Geophysical* techniques, originally developed in exploring for oil, which determine in uncased boreholes the rock properties and whether they contain oil, gas, or water, fresh or saline. A *sonde* is lowered to determine the rock *resistivity*, porosity and electrical properties, but other surveys include *calliper*, fluid-resistivity, fluid-velocity, hole direction and temperature investigations. Most sondes provide a graph along part or all of the depth of the hole. *See also* **borehole logging.**

wellpoint A 50 mm dia. tube, sunk usually by *jetting* into a water-bearing soil, fitted with a close-mesh screen at the foot and connected through a *header* pipe to a suction pump at the top. Usually a number of wellpoints are connected to one header. They are sunk outside an excavation to reduce the pumping required within it and to increase the strength of the ground by the flow of water towards the wellpoints, away from the excavation. An excavation in sand cannot become quick if effectively wellpointed. Filters are created around the feet of the wellpoints by mixing coarse sand with the jetting water as the wellpoint approaches its formation level at the end of the jetting. The sand must be coarser than that in the formation. The water flow is also reduced, enabling the coarse sand to settle around the pipe and form a filter around the tube screen. *See* **groundwater lowering.**

well sinker *See* **well borer.**

westing [sur.] A *coordinate* measured westwards from an *origin*; a westward *departure*.

wet analysis [s.m.] The *mechanical analysis* of soil particles smaller than 0·06 mm (the smallest convenient standard sieve). It is done by mixing the sample in a measured volume of water and checking its density after various periods with a sensitive *hydrometer*. Several days may be needed for a test. Even with a *centrifuge* to give the particles a settlement force of many hundreds of times gravity, the test is slow. *See* **dispersing agent, Stokes's law.**

wet cube strength Since the wet strength of any concrete is well below its dry strength, it is important in cube tests to specify whether the cube is tested wet or dry, and if wet, exactly how wet. For the sake of uniformity and fairness, many BS specify water saturation, with the surface water wiped off, but this is not always fair, particularly to aerated concretes, which have a low wet strength.

wet dock A *dock* in which the water is kept at high-tide level by dock gates which are opened only at high tide. A lock is usually provided to enable vessels to pass in or out at all states of the tide.

wet drilling [min.] Drilling in hard rock, with water injected down a hole in the centre of the drill to keep the dust down and reduce the danger of dust disease to the men drilling.

wet galvanizing [mech.] A coating of zinc laid on to steel by passing it through a bath of molten zinc on which floats a layer of flux. Before dipping, the steel is passed through pickling tanks. *See* **galvanize.**

wet mix Concrete with too much water. *See* **Abrams' law.**

wet-sand process [s.m.] A *soil stabilization* process for sand. Special road oil (SRO, a creosote with cut-back bitumen and a wetting agent) and hydrated lime are mixed with the sand in the proportions of about 6% SRO and 2% lime.

wetted perimeter [hyd.] The length of surface in contact with water in a channel, measured round its curves. *See* **hydraulic mean depth.**

wet welding Underwater welding. It is not easy, and British Oxygen believe that a welder needs six months' training to become proficient; but in 1973 they believed it was possible, at least at depths down to 40 m.

wet well [mech.] The sump of a pumping station. *Compare* **dry well.**

wharf A *berth* parallel to the waterfront. It may be of solid or open construction. In solid construction the wharf holds back all the earth behind it like a retaining wall. In open construction no earth is retained, the wharf is carried on piles of timber, steel, or precast concrete driven into the bed. Open wharves can be used only for vessels of shallow draught.

Whatman paper [d.o.] A coarse-grained thick paper, hand-made from linen rags. It can be colour-washed without cockling.

wheelabrating [mech.] *Shot blasting* with steel grit or shot thrown from a fast-spinning wheel.

wheeled tractor A rubber-tyred *tractor* which travels on 2, 3, or 4 large wheels like those of *dumpers*. The two-wheeled type is usually permanently hitched to a *bowl scraper*. These machines travel much faster than crawler tractors, at about 25 kph over rough ground. By this high speed they can greatly increase the economic haul distance of bowl scrapers, but since they have a low *drawbar pull* they need help during digging and the filling of the bowl from a *pusher tractor* behind the scraper. An innovation which eliminates pusher tractors is the twin-power scraper, in which a second engine drives the scraper wheels. Wheeled tractors are sometimes used as *loading shovels*.

wheel excavator [min.] *See* **rotary excavator** (2).

wheel gauge [rly] The distance from outside one wheel flange to outside the other. It is 13 to 19 mm less than the *gauge* of straight track.

wheel scraper A *bowl scraper.*

whip *See* **bond** (2).

Whipple-Murphy truss A bridge truss like the *Pratt truss*, but rather more complicated.

Whirley crane A large revolving crane used in USA, mounted on wheels, rollers, skids, or a gantry.

whiskers Tiny single crystals of much greater length than diameter (about 1 to 10 microns dia.) which have been proved to be at least 20, sometimes 50 times stronger than steel. The materials so far made as whiskers include alumina, Al_2O_3; carbon (graphite); and silicon carbide (Carborundum). They might be developed to become as useful a reinforcement for concrete as glassfibres have been. Glassfibres are strong for the same reason that whiskers are strong – their very small diameter reduces the possibilities for flaws.

white cement *Portland cement* made from clays and limes with no iron in them, and if burnt with coal, from coal with no pyrite (FeS_2) to discolour it.

white metal [mech.] or **anti-friction metal** A tin-based alloy, more than half tin, containing also lead, copper, and antimony. It is used for lining bearings, capping ropes, and making small castings.

Whitney stress diagram [stru.] The diagram of stress distribution in a reinforced-concrete beam according to the ultimate load theory (*plastic design*).

whole-circle bearing [sur.] A *bearing* which defines a direction by its horizontal angle measured clockwise from true north.

whole-tide cofferdam A *full-tide cofferdam.*

wicket A small gate or door forming part of a larger one, hence a sluice in a lock gate.

wicket dam [hyd.] A movable barrier made of *wickets* or shutters revolving about a central axis (ASCE MEP 11).

wide-gauge railway A *broad-gauge* railway.

wiep (pl. **wiepen**) A continuous *fascine* or cable made of willow or hazel which forms the frame members of a Dutch *mattress.*

303

wilting coefficient [hyd.] The water content of a soil, below which plants wilt and die even in damp air. It varies from 0·9% in coarse sand to 16% in clay.

winch [mech.] A hand-operated winding drum or a small engine-driven haulage or hoist.

wind beam [stru.] or **windbrace** A beam inserted into a structure solely to resist *wind force*.

wind force [stru.] or **wind load** The force on a structure due to *wind pressure* multiplied by the area of the structure at right angles to the pressure.

windmill A wheel turned by the wind to generate power, pump water, or grind corn, etc. *See* **prime mover.**

wind portal [stru.] A portal designed to resist *wind force.*

wind pressure [stru.] The pressure in kN/m² of wall or roof area due to wind. It increases with the wind velocity roughly according to the formula stated under *Beaufort scale.* On sloping roofs a suction on the lee side occurs which may be nearly as much as the pressure on the windward side. *See also* **Duchemin's formula.**

windrow [s.m.] A ridge of soil consisting of the spill from a *grader. See* **blading back, travel-mixer.**

wind shear or **wind surge** [hyd.] The effect of wind in raising the water level on a lee shore. In 1953 wind raised the sea level by 2·7 m in East Anglia and 3 m in the Netherlands. Wind-induced oscillations of water level occur in enclosed waters such as Windermere, Loch Ness, Lough Neagh and the Baltic Sea – in Lake Geneva as 'seiche'. In the Baltic the period of oscillation is about 15 hours, in the lakes from 20 to 45 minutes according to the size and *fetch.*

windshield [stru.] Usually a tubular concrete wall that protects the flues within it from wind forces. The tallest in the UK in 1973 was at Drax power station, 259 m high. The second tallest, at Grain power station, tapers from 40 m outside dia. at the base to 24 m dia. at the top, 244 m above ground. The wall thickness at ground level is 1·5 m and it is only 380 mm thick for the top 100 m. There are five circular brick flues inside the windshield, each of 7 m dia.

wind tunnel A usually conical or cylindrical structure through which air is blown at measured speeds to test its effect on models of suspension bridges, towers, and other shapes which may be affected by wind.

windy Scots term for pneumatic. Thus a windy drill is a *rock drill.*

wing dam [hyd.] A *spur.*

wing wall or **abutment wall** A wall at the abutment of a bridge which extends beyond the bridge to retain the earth behind the *abutment.*

winter gritter *See* **gritter.**

wire drawing (1) [mech.] *Cold drawing.*

(2) [hyd.] The pressure drop in a flowing fluid as it passes through a small opening, for example in a *Venturi meter.*

wire gauge [mech.] *See* (*B*).

wire lath American term for *expanded-metal* lathing.

wire-line core barrel A *core barrel* contained within the drill pipe of a diamond drill, which can be withdrawn by steel rope, and is suitable for vertical or steeply sloping holes. It avoids the delay of pulling out the drilling pipes when a core is being withdrawn and so allows fast coring progress.

wire-mesh reinforcement Chicken-wire, *expanded-metal*, or welded intersecting fabric of light rods, used for reinforcing concrete or mortar.

wire-rope [mech.] Steel-wire rope. *See* **lay, rope, strand.**

wobble-wheel roller A *pneumatic-tyred roller* with wheels which are suspended freely on springs to follow the irregularities of the road, used in *soil stabilization.*

wood-block paving Softwood blocks used as a road surface by laying them with the grain vertical on a smooth concrete base in hot tar which glues them to the concrete. It was much used in British cities before 1940, but the cost of wood blocks has now made it uneconomical. *See also* (*B*).

wood-stave pipe Pipes built of wood boards tied together with steel straps. They have only a short life when they are alternately wet and dry but if continuously wet they last longer. They are sometimes used in USA for water supply and for transporting hydraulic filling.

work [mech.] The product of a force and the distance through which it moves, thus the work done in raising 5 kg through 2 m (or 2 kg through 5 m) is 10 kg-m. It is to be distinguished from *energy* and from power which is a rate of doing work. Energy can, however, be expressed in the same units as work, and often is. *See* conversion factors, **efficiency, horsepower.**

workability The ease with which a concrete can be placed. Wet concretes are workable but weak. Workability can be measured by the *slump test*, the *compacting factor test*, and by the *V.-B. consistometer test* (BS 1881). *See also* **Abrams' law, consistence, plasticizer.**

work-hardening [mech.] or **strain hardening** *See* **hardening.**

working chamber The chamber at the foot of a *pneumatic caisson* in which the men stand on the ground and work in *compressed air* at excavation or construction. It is connected to the outside world by a *man-lock*, sometimes also by a *materials lock* or *hydraulic ejector*.

working drawing [d.o.] A *detail*.

working shaft A shaft sunk to excavate a sewer or other tunnel and filled in after the sewer is built.

working stress [stru.] The *stress* which is considered to be a safe maximum in ordinary conditions. For mild steel the working stress is about half the *yield point*. For grade A softwood and ordinary concrete it is about 7 MN/m^2 in bending compression. The most economical structural designs are now done by working to a *load factor* rather than to a working stress.

worm conveyor [mech.] A *helical conveyor*.

wracking forces [stru.] Horizontal forces in the plane of a *bent*, for instance wind or crane *surge*, which tend to distort a rectangular shape into a parallelogram.

wrought aluminium alloy [stru.] *Light alloy* which has been cold-rolled, forged, pressed, drawn, or *extruded*, and is therefore not described as 'cast'.

wrought iron [mech.] Very malleable, fibrous pure iron, with such a low carbon content (less than *dead-mild steel*) that it cannot be *hardened* by quenching. It is soft, does not rust so easily as steel but is more expensive, and therefore has been replaced by dead-mild steel or manganese steel even for such uses as small domestic water pipe or chain-making.

X

Xylonite [stru.] A *thermoplastic* (B)
material like celluloid used for making
models in *photo-elastic analysis*.

Y

yard [sur.] A unit of length, 36 in. or 3 ft or 914·4 millimetres long.

yard trap A *gulley trap*.

yield (1) [mech.] The permanent deformation (*permanent set*) which a metal piece takes when it is stressed beyond the elastic limit. A piece which yields is in lay terms bent or stretched or *buckled*.

(2) A slight horizontal and slighter vertical movement of a loaded retaining wall. This movement allows the earth thrust to fall to the value known as the *active earth pressure*. *See also* **volume yield** (*B*).

yield point [mech.] or **yield stress** The stress at which noticeable, suddenly increased deformation occurs under slowly increasing load. This occurs for mild steel at a stress slightly above the *elastic limit*. For *light alloys*, and cold-drawn or high-tensile steels, many of which do not have such a pronounced yield point as mild steel, the 0·1 or 0·2% *proof stress* is taken as the yield point for estimating safe stresses.

yoke (1) A *spreader beam*.

(2) Stiff steel angle-sections on timbers bolted in a horizontal frame round the *formwork* for a rectangular column. The formwork is wedged tightly to the yoke during the casting of the concrete.

Young's modulus [mech.] *The modulus of elasticity* of a material.

Z

Z Abbreviation for *modulus* of *section*.

zee American spelling of Z, pronounced zed in Britain.

zeolite Many types of mineral used in *base exchange* water softening, including some synthetic ones.

zirconia [min.] ZiO_2 zirconium oxide, a *refractory* which can be used at very high temperatures.

zone of aeration [hyd.] The ground above the *water table*.

zone of saturation [s.m.] The ground below the *water table*.

zoned construction for dams Where there is not enough clay or where conditions are unsuitable in an earthen dam to place large volumes of clay, zoned construction makes good use of local materials. The clay *cut-off wall* has *graded filter* zones each side of it, transition zones beyond these and rock fill outside.

FOR THE BEST IN PAPERBACKS, LOOK FOR THE

In every corner of the world, on every subject under the sun, Penguin represents quality and variety – the very best in publishing today.

For complete information about books available from Penguin – including Pelicans, Puffins, Peregrines and Penguin Classics – and how to order them, write to us at the appropriate address below. Please note that for copyright reasons the selection of books varies from country to country.

In the United Kingdom: For a complete list of books available from Penguin in the U.K., please write to *Dept E.P., Penguin Books Ltd, Harmondsworth, Middlesex, UB7 0DA*

In the United States: For a complete list of books available from Penguin in the U.S., please write to *Dept BA, Penguin, 299 Murray Hill Parkway, East Rutherford, New Jersey 07073*

In Canada: For a complete list of books available from Penguin in Canada, please write to *Penguin Books Canada Ltd, 2801 John Street, Markham, Ontario L3R 1B4*

In Australia: For a complete list of books available from Penguin in Australia, please write to the *Marketing Department, Penguin Books Australia Ltd, P.O. Box 257, Ringwood, Victoria 3134*

In New Zealand: For a complete list of books available from Penguin in New Zealand, please write to the *Marketing Department, Penguin Books (NZ) Ltd, Private Bag, Takapuna, Auckland 9*

In India: For a complete list of books available from Penguin, please write to *Penguin Overseas Ltd, 706 Eros Apartments, 56 Nehru Place, New Delhi, 110019*

In Holland: For a complete list of books available from Penguin in Holland, please write to *Penguin Books Nederland B.V., Postbus 195, NL–1380AD Weesp, Netherlands*

In Germany: For a complete list of books available from Penguin, please write to *Penguin Books Ltd, Friedrichstrasse 10 – 12, D–6000 Frankfurt Main 1, Federal Republic of Germany*

In Spain: For a complete list of books available from Penguin in Spain, please write to *Longman Penguin España, Calle San Nicolas 15, E–28013 Madrid, Spain*

FOR THE BEST IN PAPERBACKS, LOOK FOR THE

PENGUIN REFERENCE BOOKS

The Penguin English Dictionary

Over 1,000 pages long and with over 68,000 definitions, this cheap, compact and totally up-to-date book is ideal for today's needs. It includes many technical and colloquial terms, guides to pronunciation and common abbreviations.

The Penguin Reference Dictionary

The ideal comprehensive guide to written and spoken English the world over, with detailed etymologies and a wide selection of colloquial and idiomatic usage. There are over 100,000 entries and thousands of examples of how words are actually used – all clear, precise and up-to-date.

The Penguin English Thesaurus

This unique volume will increase anyone's command of the English language and build up your word power. Fully cross-referenced, it includes synonyms of every kind (formal or colloquial, idiomatic and figurative) for almost 900 headings. It is a must for writers and utterly fascinating for any English speaker.

The Penguin Dictionary of Quotations

A treasure-trove of over 12,000 new gems and old favourites, from Aesop and Matthew Arnold to Xenophon and Zola.

FOR THE BEST IN PAPERBACKS, LOOK FOR THE 🐧

PENGUIN REFERENCE BOOKS

The Penguin Guide to the Law

This acclaimed reference book is designed for everyday use, and forms the most comprehensive handbook ever published on the law as it affects the individual.

The Penguin Medical Encyclopedia

Covers the body and mind in sickness and in health, including drugs, surgery, history, institutions, medical vocabulary and many other aspects. 'Highly commendable' – *Journal of the Institute of Health Education*

The Penguin French Dictionary

This invaluable French-English, English-French dictionary includes both the literary and dated vocabulary needed by students, and the up-to-date slang and specialized vocabulary (scientific, legal, sporting, etc) needed in everyday life. As a passport to the French language, it is second to none.

A Dictionary of Literary Terms

Defines over 2,000 literary terms (including lesser known, foreign language and technical terms) explained with illustrations from literature past and present.

The Penguin Map of Europe

Covers all land eastwards to the Urals, southwards to North Africa and up to Syria, Iraq and Iran. Scale – 1:5,500,000, 4-colour artwork. Features main roads, railways, oil and gas pipelines, plus extra information including national flags, currencies and populations.

The Penguin Dictionary of Troublesome Words

A witty, straightforward guide to the pitfalls and hotly disputed issues in standard written English, illustrated with examples and including a glossary of grammatical terms and an appendix on punctuation.

FOR THE BEST IN PAPERBACKS, LOOK FOR THE

PENGUIN DICTIONARIES

Dictionaries of all these – and more – in Penguin